COUNSELING METHODS AND TECHNIQUES

An Eclectic Approach

Mark E. Young
Stetson University

Merrill, an imprint of Macmillan Publishing Company
New York

Maxwell Macmillan Canada
Toronto

Maxwell Macmillan International
New York   Oxford   Singapore   Sydney

Cover photo by David Muench
Editor: Linda A. Sullivan
Production Editor: Constantina Geldis
Cover Designer: Thomas Mack
Production Buyer: Pamela D. Bennett

This book was set in New Baskerville by TCSystems Inc. and was printed and bound by R. R. Donnelley & Sons Company. The cover was printed by New England Book Components.

Macmillan Publishing Company
866 Third Avenue
New York, NY 10022

Macmillan Publishing Company is part of the Maxwell Communication Group of Companies.

Maxwell Macmillan Canada, Inc.
1200 Eglington Avenue East, Suite 200
Don Mills, Ontario M3C 3N1

Library of Congress Cataloging-in-Publication Data

Young, Mark E.
    Counseling methods and techniques : an eclectic approach / Mark E. Young.
        p.   cm.
    Includes bibliographical references and index.
    ISBN 0-675-21321-5
    1. Counseling.   I. Title.
BF637.C6Y58 1992
158′.3—dc20   91-21524
                                                                         CIP

Printing: 1 2 3 4 5 6 7 8 9   Year: 2 3 4 5

All photos by Trudy Embry

To my parents, E. O. and Helen West Young—
All that I am or ever hope to be, I owe to them

PREFACE

The major aim of this book is to teach counseling methods and techniques using an eclectic framework. In these pages, more than 15 major counseling methods from a variety of theoretical approaches are explained. Although there are literally thousands of specific techniques of counseling and psychotherapy, the techniques discussed in this text are those most commonly used and that seemed to me to form a set of basic methods on which to build.

Chapter 1 gives some necessary background on the history and current status of eclecticism as a theoretical position in counseling and psychotherapy. The remaining chapters revolve around the concept that the process of counseling has five sequential steps. In the first step, building the client/counselor **relationship** is the major focus of counselor activity. Chapter 2 provides an overview and a review of relationship enhancement techniques and listening skills.

As the client/counselor relationship continues to develop, a number of other relationship issues and problems surface. One of these issues involves dealing with the emotional response of the client and the counselor to each other, called transference and countertransference. A related challenge is that of dealing with clients who are culturally different or who are members of special populations. The perceived competency and effectiveness of the counselor with these clients is often hampered by misunderstandings and miscommunications. The problems and challenges of transference, countertransference, and special populations are discussed in Chapter 3.

Gathering information and assessment is the second step in the counseling process. Testing, observation, and other informal assessment measures help the counselor become aware of factors affecting problems faced by the client. These issues are addressed in Chapter 4. Once a problem has been jointly defined and background data have been collected, the client and counselor move on to the third step of the counseling process, **treatment planning and goal setting** (Chapter 5).

The fourth step of the counseling process is called **implementing therapeutic methods** (Chapters 6 through 10). This step forms the basic thrust of the book.

The techniques of counseling and psychotherapy are presented in these chapters and are grouped around one of six curative factors, or underlying therapeutic principles, that seem to form the basis for modern psychotherapeutic effectiveness. These factors are the *Relationship* between client and counselor (Chapters 2, 3, and 11), *Enhancing efficacy and self-worth* (Chapter 6), *Practicing new behaviors* (Chapter 7), *Lowering or raising emotional arousal* (Chapter 8), *Activating expectations and motivation* (Chapter 9), and *New learning experiences* (Chapter 10). A mnemonic device, REPLAN, is used to jointly identify curative factors and to cue the therapist in thinking about the best avenues of therapy. The system of treatment planning outlined in Chapter 5 uses these factors as its base. In order to learn the techniques in this book, it is not necessary to adopt this REPLAN system. There are several valid ways of systematically applying an eclectic framework and incorporating the learnings of this book, including some other prominent eclectic models presented here alongside the REPLAN system.

There are 15 major counseling methods in the book in addition to the review of basic listening skills. Each technique is explained using an identical six-part format. First, an *overview* of the method briefly describes the theoretical underpinnings and the client problems that have benefited from its administration. Next, the *method* is broken down into a series of simple steps so that it can be conceptualized and practiced more easily. After that, the *problems and precautions* associated with the technique are discussed. *Variations* on the method are then explained as they might relate to other contexts, including group and marriage and family settings. Next, a *case example* is drawn showing how the technique might be integrated into a treatment plan. An additional feature of this text is the *feedback checklist*, which is a boxed summary of the steps in each method. The checklist is designed to provide feedback for students when practicing the technique in class or in taped supervision sessions.

The fifth and final step in a counseling relationship is **evaluation** (Chapter 11). Evaluation is a time when counseling goals are reevaluated and the efficacy of counseling methods is assessed. Either a decision is made to terminate counseling or the contract between client and counselor is *replanned*, meaning that the five-part process recycles, beginning with the client restating his or her current concerns. The counselor may employ new assessment methods and once again contract with the client to achieve specific counseling goals, or together they may end the relationship or decide upon a referral. By establishing evaluation as a part of the treatment plan, the counselor can avoid losing valuable time pursuing goals that the client may have abandoned and can simultaneously engage the client by involving him or her as an active partner in the therapeutic process. Chapter 11 also deals with documenting progress in therapy and with problems associated with termination of the counseling relationship.

SOME IDEAS ABOUT TEACHING COUNSELING TECHNIQUES

The organization of this book is based on the pedagogical assumption that the most effective way for students to learn is to initially gain some theoretical knowledge from reading and from lecture/discussion. Second, students benefit from descriptions of techniques that clearly outline the sequential steps of the method. Third, students learn more quickly through vicarious learning activities, such as classroom role plays, teacher demonstrations, and reading case examples in the book. Finally, students need the opportunity to practice and receive feedback on their performance. The best learning situation is for students to read the material in the book, to attend a lecture that deals with the theoretical orientation and assumptions of a technique in depth, and to see the technique demonstrated by videotape or through role-playing with an instructor. Students should then have the opportunity to practice and receive feedback on the techniques in the presence of their instructors and peers. Reading this book alone without practice and supervision by a skilled practitioner is not recommended as an effective way of learning psychotherapy.

SOME NOTES ON TERMINOLOGY

Since this book will be used by a variety of mental health professionals, I have used the words *therapist* and *counselor* and *psychotherapy* and *counseling* as interchangeable terms. These terms may actually be thought of as poles on a continuum, with *counseling* being more "here and now" and more associated with ordinary developmental problems. *Psychotherapy* is usually described as dealing with more severe disorders in a more emotionally intense fashion and often for a longer period of time. Although there are reasons for being more choosy about my words here, many of the techniques presented can be used at both ends of the continuum and there seemed to be no reason to differentiate between them in this context. I have used the term *client* rather than *patient* as it does not smack so much of a medical model suggesting a "sick" individual.

ACKNOWLEDGMENTS

Any writer, and especially an eclectic therapist, owes a debt to many different individuals. I wish to acknowledge those people who have personally shaped my thinking, who taught me skills, and who served as my mentors and whose ideas have comingled with mine: Darshan Singh, Rajinder Singh, J. Melvin Witmer, James Pinnell, Thomas Sweeney, Harry DeWire, John Nolte, James Faulconer, Helen Rucker, Ken Holroyd, Ellene Milié Summers, Jesse Carlock, and Judith Smith Wright. In addition, these individuals taught me through their writings: Jerome Frank, Ernst Beier, J. L. Moreno, Carl Rogers, Alfred Adler, Sigmund Freud, Raymond Corsini, B. F. Skinner, Albert Ellis, Jay Haley, Eric Berne, and Claude Steiner.

I appreciate the helpful comments of those who reviewed various drafts of the manuscript: Richard M. Ashbrook, Capital University; A. Michael Dougherty, Western Carolina University; Robert E. Doyle, St. John's University; Robert L. Frank, University of Northern Iowa; Martin Gerstein, Virginia Tech University;

Samuel T. Gladding, Wake Forest University; Janet C. Heddesheimer, George Washington University; Nancy L. Murdock, University of Missouri–Kansas City; Michael M. Omizo, University of Hawaii at Manoa; and Holly A. Stadler, University of Missouri–Kansas City.

I also thank Linda Sullivan, my editor at Merrill, an imprint of Macmillan Publishing, and the administration and faculty of Stetson University for their support. I am indebted to Judy O'Neill, as well as students Kristi Myers-Sutter, Rebecca Herrero, Karen Spicer, Pat Crowe, and Paul Granello, who gave me useful feedback on my writing and taught me through their learning. Finally, I must recognize my most demanding critic and staunchest supporter, my wife, Jora DeFalco Young, and my children, Angela and Joseph, for their encouragement and love.

BRIEF CONTENTS

CONTENTS

CHAPTER THREE

Transference, Countertransference, and Relationships with Special Populations: Challenges in Developing the Client/ Counselor Bond   **55**

CHAPTER FOUR

Assessment   **83**

CHAPTER SEVEN

Practicing New Behaviors   **173**

CHAPTER EIGHT

Lowering and Raising Emotional Arousal   **199**

FEEDBACK CHECKLISTS

CHAPTER ONE

Eclecticism: Foundation and Future

KEY CONCEPTS

▼ *Counselors need theories to focus and direct their efforts.*

▼ *Research suggests that theoretical orthodoxy is waning and that no one theoretical orientation has been found to produce superior results.*

▼ *Eclectic theory is becoming more accepted as a way of organizing therapeutic interventions.*

▼ *Eclecticism has been a recurring theme in the history of counseling and psychotherapy.*

▼ *Several new eclectic models are now in widespread use, including Lazarus's multimodal therapy.*

▼ *This book proposes a problem-focused eclectic system called REPLAN, which is based on the work of Jerome Frank and his notion of common curative factors.*

INTRODUCTION

At some point in every therapist's academic training, a great thirst for practical methods develops, and we want to throw down our purely theoretical books in disgust. This urge often occurs when our favorite theoretical system appears to become inadequate with clients who are so different in their personalities and problems that one theory does not seem to fit all. To make matters worse, when we go to the writings of the seminal thinkers in psychotherapy, such as Freud, Rogers, and Adler, we often find only passing references to the actual means or techniques that they used to produce change. For instance, words such as free association are mentioned but never seem to be adequately explained. Simultaneously, we hear of exciting new techniques used by other therapists, and the hunt begins to collect as many techniques as we can.

When I reached this stage in my own training, I replaced books on personality and counseling theories with technique-oriented "cookbooks" that I thought would be useful in the real world of counseling. Unfortunately, I ran into the inevitable problem about which my teachers had warned me: the knowledge that I gained from my "cookbooks" had become more a grab bag of procedures rather than an understandable system. I might apply several different techniques in a counseling session, but I was not confident about my reasons for doing so. I did not have a system to tell me *which* technique to use or *when* to use it.

There are two central conclusions I have drawn as a result of my dilemma and subsequent experience. First, counselors need both a theoretical system and clear directions on how to perform a wide variety of techniques. Let us consider each part of this statement separately.

Counselors need a theory to serve as a guide for assessment and treatment planning. As Kurt Lewin said, "There is nothing more practical than a good theory." A theory tells us what to observe and record. Also, the power of a technique will be diffused if it is applied in isolation—if the technique is not part of an integrated treatment plan. There must be something that ties the various methods together in the mind of the client as well as the therapist and moves them together in the same direction. In my opinion, theory must also be an "open system" that can incorporate useful techniques from other systems and new discoveries in medicine and other disciplines.

Most counselors also need to learn a variety of techniques simply because, as generalists, we cannot control the types of clients we end up treating. For example, even clients who have very specific problems, such as substance abuse, may also have marital conflicts that might be best handled by the same therapist. I believe that one can become familiar with a number of therapeutic methods and learn to flexibly apply them without subscribing to the originating theory. The counselor must, however, understand the theory that spawned the method or risk combining methods that are antagonistic.

The second major tenet is that treatment should be tailored to the client. This is quite different from an approach that views the therapeutic alliance as a means to win the client over to the therapist's position and sees all failures as resistance on the part of the client. Tailoring the treatment to the client has been called "riding the horse in the direction it is going." This metaphor implies that since each person is unique, psychotherapy should be formulated to meet the unique needs of the individual. It suggests a collaboration and a respect for the client's viewpoints.

These conclusions mean that a text about counseling methods must not emphasize only theories nor should it have a "cookbook" approach; rather, it should present a systematic eclectic model, one in which a theory or system guides the selection of counseling techniques. In the analogy of Norcross (1986), one method of making a quilt is to sew together the scraps of material that are nearest to you. Another way is to start with a pattern and find the materials that you need. This latter method is what I have tried to do here. The REPLAN system, which you will discover in these pages, is a skeletal framework designed to allow the clinician to utilize a variety of compatible methods and techniques to achieve the goals of unique people, our clients.

Before accepting this brief rationale for eclecticism the reader should know that eclecticism is a cutting edge issue. It is controversial, yet vital. It is also a subject with a fairly long history in the literature of psychotherapy. In this chapter, we will take on the task of defining eclecticism and will give a brief history of the approach. After that, some emerging eclectic models will be discussed and a new one—the REPLAN system, based on the concept of six curative factors underlying all theoretical approaches—will be presented.

A common therapeutic factor or mega-factor is one that has been identified as the underlying curative force behind a number of techniques. For example, the use of unconditional positive regard and listening behaviors tends to build the therapeutic alliance. Some of these mega-factors were identified by Yalom in his research into group therapy (1985). He distilled 12 curative factors that operate in group therapy from client reports.

This book is constructed around research that has identified six major curative factors in psychotherapy and counseling (Frank, 1981). The majority of counseling methods now in use could be described as primarily associated with one of these six curative factors. Organizing methods in this way helps to achieve some understanding of how therapists can use different means to achieve similar ends. In the training method developed in this book, treatment goals arrived at by the counselor and the client play the primary role in determining the selection of counseling methods. The counselor identifies the basic curative factor or factors that will be the initial focus of treatment and selects treatment approaches associated with that factor or factors; however, for breadth, other eclectic methods are also presented in this book, including multimodal therapy and Linda Seligman's DO A CLIENT MAP. The methods in this book can obviously be adapted to other forms of eclectic practice.

PHASES OF THE COUNSELING PROCESS

Figure 1.1 shows the stages of the counseling process. This process, as it relates to the organization of this book, is described in the preface. The basis for structuring the counseling interview in this five-part manner is derived from the work of such counseling and human relations theorists as Allen Ivey and Robert Carkhuff and from the clinical process model of Dimond (cf., Dimond & Havens, 1975). These individuals see the counseling process as a series of steps that counselors seem to use regardless of theoretical persuasion (cf., Dimond, Havens & Jones 1978; Ivey & Mathews, 1986).

The arrows show the typical progression of counseling from assessment to treatment planning to implementing methods to evaluation. At the heart of the process is the counseling relationship, which provides the "core conditions," or supports, for the other stages. The relationship is the glue that holds the process together. At times, the relationship itself becomes a problem that must be assessed and treated. For example, transference and countertransference issues may arise. At other times, the relationship itself becomes a curative factor, healing the wounds from older relationships. It also provides the trust and safety needed to undergo some of the more demanding therapeutic measures. Finally, in the evaluation phase, the therapeutic relationship is put on hold, ends, or changes dramatically. In short, relationship-building and relationship exploration issues are a constant in psychotherapy; they appear in the beginning, the middle, and the end of counseling. This is why they occupy a central position in charts and diagrams depicted throughout this text.

FIGURE 1.1
Stages of the counseling relationship.

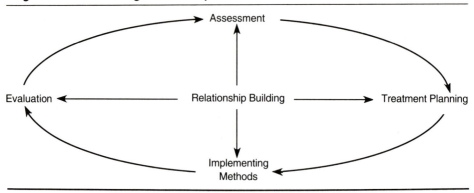

THEORETICAL ISSUES

Should Counselors Have a Theory?

Arnold Lazarus (1981) asserted that it is not necessary for a therapist to have a theory. From this point of view, fussing about theories is "much ado about nothing." It has often been pointed out (cf., Lambert, 1986; Lichtenberg, 1985; London, 1972; Smith and Glass, 1977) that theoretical viewpoint is overemphasized since all therapists tend to do the same things, get similar results, and use techniques that are not associated with the theory that they espouse. Garfield (1980) has found that even when therapists are committed to a particular theory, they do not choose it based on scientific evidence but for a variety of personal reasons. If this is true, why must counselors have a theory at all?

Frank (1971) argues, though, that psychotherapists need theories. Theories are important because they give the counselor a sense of meaning, confidence, and direction. It is hard to imagine a truly atheoretical position that does not build upon some sort of guiding system to organize incoming data from the client or to develop a treatment plan. Human beings are theory-making creatures. This may be especially true in a field like psychotherapy that is young and filled with uncertainty. Given the advantages of theory-based counseling, the real question becomes, "What kind of theory should I have?"

At a recent workshop, a participant asked Jay Haley about the underlying psychopathology behind a client's behavior since, according to psychodynamic theory, these background problems should be solved before changing the client's behavior. Haley said, "That does not seem like a very good theory to have for this client" (Haley, 1989). His words shocked and amused the audience, but his point was an important one. A theory is something the therapist must choose, and it must be of help to the client as well. A theory, like a pair of glasses, is something one must be able to put on and off; otherwise, the glasses may become blinders.

Theory should be in the service of the client: it is a good servant but a poor master. Let me try to illustrate this point further.

Theoretical Focus and Direction

A theory provides both focus and direction. A theory provides focus by allowing the therapist to simplify the client's problems. It explains the client's problems as "irrational beliefs," "learned helplessness," "unresolved oedipal issues," etc. By simplifying, the therapist can direct energies towards specific areas that are believed to be central to the client's problems. Theories help the therapist survive an overload of information. Theories help organize incoming data. Unfortunately, because of the special glasses that we put on, we tend to see things that support our theories and ignore things that do not.

Take, for example, the analytically oriented therapist who is trained to find the "psychopathology of everyday life." This therapist has learned to search for signs and symptoms that support a diagnosis. This is where the "law of the instrument" rears its head. This law states that we tend to see what we are looking for. For example, if you are considering the purchase of a new kind of car, you suddenly notice that the road seems to be filled with them. Similarly, the diagnostician who is in love with a particular diagnosis, such as co-dependency or passive-aggressive personality, will find many hidden cases. There is an Indian saying: "The pickpocket in the crowd sees only pockets." When one's attention is directed, especially through hours of training, some things come into sharp focus and other things remain blurred.

Besides providing focus, theory also gives direction and confidence, confidence that undoubtedly reassures the client. The therapist with a theory begins immediately working with the client in a planned and coherent manner. Unfortunately, some theories are so rigidly prescribed that the direction of treatment is the same for all clients, and the therapist becomes disillusioned when the theory does not appear to be applicable. The therapist soon finds that the best-laid plans cannot account for the unique situations presented by unique clients.

The point of this discussion is that it is important to have both focus and direction. Focusing on one problem at a time gives the client confidence as that area begins to improve. But the focus must not be so exclusive that the client's individuality is obscured. Just like an ecological balance in nature, it is likely that a person's problems in one area are intimately connected with other areas of his or her life. Marital problems almost inevitably affect work performance, which may affect work relationships, and so on. In the same way, therapy must have a treatment plan, or direction, but it must not be followed slavishly. The definition of a useful theory is one that provides both enough structure to give confidence and direction to therapist and client and a reasonable flexibility that allows input from the client and a recognition that, throughout therapy, additional problems may be added and existing goals may be modified.

WHAT IS ECLECTICISM?

Definitions

The broadest definition of eclecticism is that it is a theory that selects what is best from among many theoretical stances. What is best means what works. This definition highlights a common ingredient of eclectic counselors; they are pragmatic. As Paul (1967) stated, the task of the eclectic therapist is to ascertain "what treatment, by whom, is most effective for this individual with that specific problem (or set of problems), and under which set of circumstances" (p. 111).

A more negative definition says that an eclectic therapist is one who does not adhere to a single viewpoint. It emphasizes that the eclectic counselor may be disillusioned or has taken the nihilistic position that no theories are true or useful. Beyond this dichotomy are a number of other positions. We will visit these later in the chapter.

Research in Eclectic Preferences

Several studies have shown eclecticism to be the most common theoretical orientation of therapists (Garfield and Kurtz, 1977; Jayartne, 1982; Norcross and Prochaska, 1982; Smith, 1982). These researchers reported that the preference for eclecticism among the clinicians questioned was between 32% and 54%.

A recent study surveyed 100 mental health counselors and 100 counselor educators (Young & Feiler, 1989) and found that 75% of the respondents (69% return rate) did not hold to one particular theoretical viewpoint. This study used several different questions to test the winds of change in counseling theory. It asked participants to rate the theories they currently favor and to predict what the most influential theories would be five years from now. Table 1.1 compares the results of these two questions.

The table shows that three possible theories of the future are eclecticism, family systems, and cognitive-behavioral. All three share some common features. They do not represent a narrow theoretical viewpoint, and practitioners use a variety of methods and techniques. As a field, it appears that counseling is moving away from schools towards broader integrating approaches and eclecticism.

Criticisms of the Eclectic Approach

Although the definition of eclecticism as a hybrid of the best of all other systems seems attractive, many have challenged it as undisciplined and likely to breed confusion. For example, Eysenck (1970) described eclecticism as a "mish-mash of theories, a hugger-mugger of procedures, a gallimaufry of therapies, and a charivaria of activities having no proper rationale and incapable of being tested or evaluated" (p. 140). Eysenck's criticism is valid if the eclectic therapist has no coherent rationale for the approach. The second criticism, that eclecticism is incapable of being tested or evaluated, is valid only if eclectic therapy cannot be

TABLE 1.1

Theoretical orientations of counselors and counselor educators and predicted theoretical trend in the field five years from now.

Theoretical Orientation	Current	Predicted Trend in 5 Years
Eclectic	32	26
Person-centered	22	7
Family systems	10	23
Cognitive-behavioral	6	16
Reality therapy	6	2
Psychoanalytic	5	2
Psychoeducational	3	4
Behavior modification	3	4
Multimodal	3	5
Adlerian	2	1
Gestalt	2	1
Rational emotive	2	2
Ericksonian hypnosis	2	3
Existential	1	0.1
Other	3	4

Note: Data in percentages based on $n = 125$.

Source: From *Trends in Counseling: A National Survey* by M. E. Young and F. Feiler (p. 5), 1989.

shown to be as effective as therapy by more orthodox methods. At this juncture, the evidence does not suggest that any theoretical school is better than any other (Smith & Glass, 1977).

Recently, the merits of eclecticism have been undergoing a vigorous debate (Blocher, 1989; Ginter, 1988, 1989; Hershenson, Power & Seligman, 1989; Kelly, 1989; Nance & Myers, 1991; Simon, 1989, 1991). One argument against eclecticism (especially in the training of counselors) (Patterson, 1986) is, that unless a counselor knows the philosophy and assumptions of a theory, he or she is analogous to a technician who can fix what is broken but does not know why. If one does not understand the causes of human behavior, one will not know how to operate in new and different situations (McBride & Martin, 1990). Interestingly, counselor educators, who would presumably be well versed in theory, report themselves as eclectic more than any other category of counseling professionals (Hollis & Wantz, 1983; Young & Feiler, 1989).

This criticism, that it is important to know why, can be answered in several ways. First is the assertion that modern psychotherapy, since the death of Freud, is only about 50 years old and is far from any consensus about the causes of human problems. Any suggestion that we know much about the whys of human behavior seems somewhat grandiose. This criticism may also be based on the mechanistic premise that a client's problems have identifiable causes or that the way to solve these problems is to track down original causes. This medical model was criticized years ago by behaviorists who found that disorder could be treated without understanding the cause. Gordon Allport also countered this argument with the discovery of "functional autonomy." He recognized that once a disorder develops, it begins to have a life of its own. Once a behavior is established, it may be essentially independent of the motives and drives that instigated it. If the argument were that eclectics do not have a single, rich, and wide-ranging vision about personality, motivation, and philosophy of life, this criticism would have to be accepted.

Second, this argument supposes that being fully versed in a particular theory makes one very flexible in dealing with new situations. On the contrary, we find that unimodal therapists seem to respond to every client with the same approach and the same techniques (Lazarus, 1981). The unimodal approach ignores the evidence that certain techniques may be better for different clients and for different disorders.

Research Supporting Eclectic Practice

Lambert (1986) reviewed psychotherapy outcome research with respect to eclectic psychotherapy and came to four basic conclusions:

1. A substantial number of patients improve without formal psychological intervention.
2. Psychological treatments are, in general, beneficial.
3. A variety of factors common across therapies account for a substantial amount of improvement found in psychotherapy patients. (Of the so-called common curative factors, Lambert identifies three: support, learning and action factors.)
4. Specific techniques can be selected on the basis of their peculiar effectiveness. (There is some evidence for the use of particular techniques for particular problems.)

Some of the implications of Lambert's conclusions are that an eclectic approach should be just as effective as any other noneclectic intervention and more effective than no treatment. Second, an eclectic theory with a sound rationale and credibility among clients should be able to restore morale and capitalize on expectancy or placebo effects. Third, for maximum effectiveness, eclectic therapies should focus on common factors as well as the development of specific techniques. Fourth, in those cases where specific treatments are found to be effective for specific problems, eclectic therapists are in a better position to capitalize on the method since they should have developed a way of integrating them into a flexible treatment approach.

Figure 1.2 is derived from a review of psychotherapy outcome research by Lambert (1986). It shows the percent of improvement as a result of various factors.

History of Eclecticism

There are now between 100 and 460 systems of counseling and psychotherapy (Corsini, 1981; Herink, 1980; Parloff, 1979). These smaller streams are, for the

FIGURE 1.2

Percent of improvement in psychotherapy clients as a function of therapeutic factors.

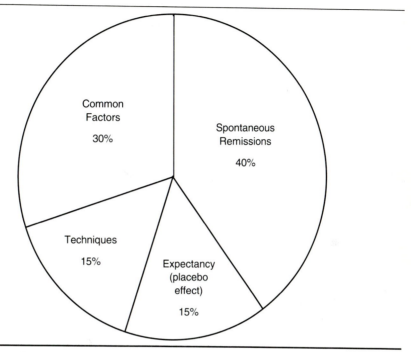

Source: From Implications of Psychotherapy Outcome Research for Eclectic Psychotherapy (p. 437) by M. J. Lambert in *Handbook of Eclectic Psychotherapy* edited by J. C. Norcross, 1986, New York: Brunner/Mazel, Inc, Copyright 1986 by Brunner/Mazel, Inc. Reprinted by permission.

most part, branches of the three great rivers of thought: the psychoanalytic, the behavioral, and the humanistic viewpoint. Others such as nondirective psychoanalysis and cognitive-behavioral therapy represent a confluence of two or more approaches.

Almost from its inception, psychotherapy has experienced the tension between theoretical orthodoxy with its rigid training requirements and its coherent point of view and the flexibility and creativity of integrative or eclectic approaches. The disintegration of psychoanalysis as the single most influential paradigm was due, to a great extent, to the defection of its practitioners who could not ignore effective behavioral techniques. In tracing the history of eclecticism, it is necessary to go back nearly 60 years to that time when psychoanalysis was losing its grip. For the sake of brevity, let us consider six pivotal events, or milestones, that mark the development of eclecticism.

The first event occurred in 1932 when French, the highly influential psychiatrist, delivered an address before the American Psychiatric Association. In his address, French described the common elements between Pavlovian conditioning and psychoanalysis. Specifically, he discussed the learning principles that might lie behind certain defense mechanisms. This address was delivered near the peak of American involvement in psychoanalysis, and discussing it in the same breath with learning principles was near to heresy.

A second important event was the publication of the classic book by Dollard and Miller (1950), *Personality and Psychotherapy*. The major influence of the book was to awaken psychodynamic thinkers to the learning principles behind a number of their own concepts, such as anxiety and displacement. It is likely that this book influenced the development of cognitive-behavioral thinking by showing that many internal events were worthy of study. The book also describes the use of modeling and other behavioral techniques that, the authors concluded, already existed in the tenets of psychoanalysis.

The third milestone was the publication in 1950 of Thorne's *Principles of Personality Counseling*. Thorne, a psychiatrist by training, knew that medicine was not plagued by opposing schools of thought. He believed that this was because the basic principles of anatomy and physiology were known and that these principles guided the practice of medicine. He believed that if basic principles of mental functioning were known there would be no confusion about how to direct treatment. While the book was highly influential in furthering the cause of eclecticism by directing thinking towards a more empirical approach, confusion about basic principles did not wane but actually grew more heated in the 1960s.

In art, politics, and music, the 1960s was a time of revolution. In psychotherapy, the orthodoxy of psychoanalysis was being challenged and was replaced by an adherence to smaller schools of psychotherapy. Among these were behavior therapy, Gestalt therapy, rational emotive therapy, client-centered therapy, transactional analysis, and encounter. Many of these therapies offered certification and training programs. Debates were held between Carl Rogers and B. F. Skinner. Fierce loyalties were at least partially directed at the charismatic leaders of these schools. From the perspective of the 1990s, this was a necessary stage in the development of psychotherapy and counseling because the shattering of the psychodynamic paradigm left many without a theoretical home. The decade was fertile ground for the development of innovative methods that were quickly shared among the practitioners of various schools. Ironically, the popularity of the various schools ultimately led to their downfall. Instead of remaining intensely loyal, practitioners found that there were a number of effective tools at their disposal. By the 1970s these schools were waning in popularity. A survey of psychologists confirms that loyalties to particular schools are now dead (Smith, 1982).

The work of Arnold Lazarus (1967, 1976, 1981) must be considered the fourth monumental contribution to the development of integrative approaches to counseling. At first, Lazarus was identified as a behavior therapist, but by 1967, he had introduced the term *technical eclecticism* to describe his practice. Lazarus believed he could employ a variety of techniques from other disciplines without agreeing to the underlying principles of the theory from which they were derived. For example, Lazarus commonly used role-playing techniques, which had originated in psychodrama and Gestalt therapy. But he used the method to provide for behavioral rehearsal rather than the cathartic effect for which it was theoretically intended. Lazarus continued to expand his ideas and was soon calling his methods "broad spectrum behavior therapy." By 1976, he had developed multimodal therapy, which is described later. Lazarus continues to be named by his peers as one of the most influential of all psychologists (Smith, 1982).

The last event we will discuss is one that is even now changing the face of the profession. General systems theory is the basis for a new movement in counseling and therapy: the family systems approach. In a nutshell, a system is defined as a dynamic organization of multiple parts that interact (von Bertalanffy, 1968). An organism (like a person) is a system that exists within larger systems (family, community, etc.). In Rogerian terms, we use the term *person* to indicate that an individual is a unique entity or system, not just a collection of organs. In family systems terms, an individual is usually seen as a moving part of a family system. Like gears in a clock, each family member's behavior affects the functioning of every other member and the adjustment of the family as a whole.

In addition, many family systems advocates believe that a large portion of a person's behavior is the result of the past influence of original family members. This also means that family systems theorists may first try to treat the entire family and even the extended family rather than simply focusing on one individual. Some adherents refuse to treat individuals separately, feeling that the tremendous power of the family will quickly nullify gains made by any individual. It could be argued that family systems is technically eclectic since practitioners may agree to a basic set of theoretical propositions but utilize a variety of techniques, including structural, strategic, etc. In fact, the field is so diverse and volatile that new issues like co-dependency and abuse quickly come and go, leaving the family systems arena without central leadership or a set of principles.

Family systems theories have been steadily gaining supporters. The American Association for Marriage and Family Therapy (AAMFT) has rapidly grown in size and influence. Interest among counselors in marriage and family issues is evidenced by the fact that the American Association for Counseling and Development (AACD) has recently gained a new affiliate, the International Association for Marriage and Family Counseling (IAMFC). As Table 1.1 shows, the participants in our survey (Young and Feiler, 1989) expect that family systems will become even more prominent in the next five years.

Types of Eclecticism

By its very nature, eclecticism can never be a narrow school of thought. Still, eclectic theories have been characterized as being of three types: technical, synthetic, and atheoretical (Norcross, 1986).

Technical Eclecticism

The technical eclectic still utilizes one organizing theory but may use a number of techniques that originated in other schools of thought. The clinician chooses techniques that conform to the organizing theory and uses compatible methods in the service of the theory. For example, a behavior therapist might use the Rogerian method of reflecting feelings in order to achieve rapport and enlist the help of the client before behavioral techniques are effectively employed. Lazarus's multimodal therapy with its behavioral underpinnings is an example of technical eclecticism.

Synthetic Eclecticism

Synthetic eclecticism denotes those efforts to amalgamate and integrate two or more theoretical positions. Early examples include Dollard and Miller's (1950) attempt to reconcile behaviorism and psychoanalytic thought. Garfield and Kurtz (1977) found 32 different combinations of preferred theories in their study of over 140 clinicians. The three most common combinations were Freudian and learning theory, neo-Freudian and learning theory, and neo-Freudian and Rogerian theory.

Another aspect of the synthetic perspective is the search for common curative factors. Several writers (Frank, 1981; Garfield, 1973; Goldfried, 1980) have advanced the opinion that psychotherapists should examine the fundamental change principles that underlie all effective counseling.

Atheoretical Eclecticism

Atheoretical eclecticism is defined as having no preferred theoretical viewpoint while drawing from many. Norcross and Prochaska (1982) found that less than 10% of the eclectics in their study could be characterized as atheoretical.

ECLECTIC MODELS OF COUNSELING

This section will survey three prominent eclectic models of psychotherapy: multimodal, systematic eclectic psychotherapy, and the transtheoretical approach. For a thorough discussion of these approaches, see Windy Dryden's critique (1986). The last part of this section contains an overview of the REPLAN system, the problem-oriented eclectic model that forms the basis of this book.

Multimodal Therapy

The first approach to consider is the popular and influential multimodal therapy of Arnold A. Lazarus (1973, 1978, 1981). According to Lazarus, a multimodal therapist is one who asks who or what is best for the client. Although this pragmatism reflects the eclectic viewpoint, Lazarus rejects "unsystematic eclecticism" and has sought to build a broad but coherent approach. Lazarus, previously a behavior therapist, was brought to the eclectic camp by both research and his own clinical experience. Systematic follow-up studies were beginning to show high relapse rates for behavior therapy. His experience with clients seemed to tell him that the client's world view and outlook were crucial to lasting behavior change. In other words, he recognized that changes in behavior and in cognition were both important and were synergistic factors. Lazarus first called his approach "broad spectrum behavior therapy." His book, *Behavior Therapy and Beyond* (1971), was one of the first books on cognitive behavior therapy.

Lazarus coined the term *technical eclecticism* to describe the condition of maintaining a single theoretical viewpoint (in this case, behaviorism) while utilizing a variety of techniques from other systems. Multimodal therapy still shows its behavioral roots in its linear approach to causation of problems. It also takes a step beyond by suggesting that therapy is not advanced enough to become enchanted with one set of procedures and that a shotgun approach is often the best way to handle client problems. To this end, he commonly utilizes techniques, such as role playing and imagery work, that originated in the dynamic schools of psychotherapy. To examine the approach more closely, first let us look at the building blocks of the approach, called the BASIC ID.

The *BASIC ID* is both an approach to assessment and a treatment. Each letter of the acronym refers to an aspect of client behavior or thinking that is first assessed and then treated. *B* stands for behaviors; *A* for affect, or emotions; *S* for bodily sensations of pleasure or pain; *I* for mental imagery; *C* for cognitions, or thoughts, values, and assumptions; *I* for interpersonal relationships and behaviors, and *D* represents drug and alcohol and physical health and wellness status and behaviors. In general, interventions are designed for each modality of the BASIC ID and are implemented simultaneously. This is why Lazarus refers to it as a shotgun approach.

The behavioral basis of the multimodal method suggests that all problems have a triggering sequence. In other words, the problem starts in one modality and triggers one or more other modalities. For example, an *environmental event,* such as the loss of a job, might trigger *cognitions,* such as "I am a failure," that in turn trigger the *affect* of depression. This depression then leads to excessive drinking, which is a *behavior.* The triggering sequence concept is flexible enough to account for individual differences. The exact sequence can be discovered through assessment with interventions designed to interrupt the process.

In any case, the multimodal therapist would bring to bear all available methods for interrupting the cycle. Using the example above, the therapist might suggest that the client use cognitive methods to decrease self-defeating cognitions. The counselor might also prescribe pleasurable activities or social contact to decrease the depression and implement behavioral methods for decreasing excessive drinking.

Systematic Eclectic Psychotherapy

Systematic eclectic psychotherapy is Beutler's (1986) model, which is founded on the importance of interpersonal influence or persuasion theory. The process of therapy is one in which the client is persuaded to change attitudes based on exposure to a valued persuader (the therapist).

One factor that enhances persuasion is client/counselor compatibility. This is the degree to which the relationship is solid and safe. Yet there are no generally accepted means of determining compatibility in advance. Although it seems true that similarity on some dimensions may be helpful, other evidence indicates that differences between the two persons may enhance the relationship. It is recommended that therapists bring up background and demographic similarity in the early stages of counseling in order to bond with the client.

Second, the therapist must try to match the expressed needs of the client with therapy techniques since the degree of acceptance that the client has for a particular goal, method, or technique is related to positive therapeutic outcomes. One must consider the client's personality, coping style, and knowledge base. Beutler is concerned that interventions will not be accepted by clients; therefore, knowledge must be gained about their defenses or resistance to certain procedures.

Beutler has identified six areas of persuasive interventions that can be selected after an assessment of the client's defensive style. This provides a match between the client's style and the interventions of the therapist. The six types of interventions are

1. Insight enhancement (e.g., free association)
2. Emotional awareness (e.g., role-playing opposites)
3. Emotional escalation (e.g., confronting)
4. Emotion reducing (e.g., relaxation)
5. Behavioral control (e.g., contingency contracting)
6. Perceptual change (e.g., cognitive restructuring)

Space is not available to adequately describe Beutler's conception of client defensive styles nor other parts of his theory. The interested reader is advised to examine Beutler's (1983) book, *Eclectic Psychotherapy: A Systematic Approach.*

The Transtheoretical Approach

The transtheoretical approach (Prochaska 1984; Prochaska & DiClemente, 1986) is based on a comprehensive study of phases of change and change principles in a variety of theories. These authors identified 10 processes of change in their research, which were obtained in part from clients' reports about how they solved their own problems:

1. *Consciousness raising*—Includes interventions, such as confrontation, and interpretations to make clients aware of problems
2. *Self-liberation*—Includes the notion of improving self-efficacy and means helping the client realize his or her own efforts are crucial in the change process
3. *Social liberation*—Freeing oneself from social expectations
4. *Counterconditioning*—Associating positive outcomes with a situation that was previously associated with a punishment or a painful consequence
5. *Stimulus control*—Manipulating the triggers that bring on negative behaviors, feelings, or thoughts
6. *Self-reevaluation*—Methods that look at the client's values and ready the client for taking action
7. *Environmental reevaluation*—Reassessing environmental demands
8. *Contingency management*—Manipulating rewards and punishments
9. *Dramatic relief*—Vividly experiencing the removal of symptoms
10. *Helping relationships*—Employing the methods of caring, understanding, and commitment to the client's well-being

The second major aspect of the theory is that change occurs in stages based on changes in the consciousness of the problem. *Precontemplation* is the first stage, *contemplation*, the second, and *action and maintenance*, the third. At the precontemplation stage, the client is unaware of problems. Through consciousness-raising techniques, the client moves to contemplation of problems; and in the action and maintenance stage, other change processes are invoked. The 10 processes are used increasingly as one moves through various stages.

A third important aspect of the theory is that change takes place on five distinct but interrelated levels: (1) symptom/situational, (2) maladaptive cognitions, (3) current interpersonal conflicts, (4) family/systems conflicts, and (5) intrapersonal conflicts.

The transtheoretical approach suggests that client and counselor agree upon what level interventions will be focused. In general, the farther one goes through the five levels, the farther away one gets from awareness; therefore, working at the symptom level in the beginning is often helpful in gaining the client's trust and encouraging hope.

REPLAN: A Curative Factors Model for Systematic Eclectic Practice

The eclectic model that is the basis for this book is called the *REPLAN system*. Each letter in the acronym REPLAN refers to a curative factor in psychotherapy. The notion of common factors that make all therapies work is largely due to the lifetime efforts of Jerome Frank (1971, 1981, 1991). Frank (1981) described six common curative factors that he believed all psychotherapies shared. The idea of a common curative factor is related to the findings that all psychotherapies seem to work but no one system can be shown to be superior (cf., Smith & Glass, 1977). Frank then hypothesized that there may be some common elements that are responsible for change that run through all therapies. Frank identified the following factors:

1. The strength of the therapist/client relationship
2. Methods that increase motivation and expectations of help
3. Enhancing a sense of mastery or self-efficacy
4. Providing new learning experiences
5. Arousing emotions
6. Providing opportunities to practice new behaviors

Garske and Lynn (1985) note that Frank's six mechanisms of change exist in varying degrees in different theoretical orientations, and we indicate that it is conceivable that some theories and techniques might contain more of these mechanisms than others. Garske and Lynn conclude that the most beneficial therapeutic orientation is one that is open to other points of view rather than closed in theoretical rigidity. They suggest that a "quiet eclecticism" is taking place in psychotherapists' offices. Therapists are discarding the parts of a theory that do not work and keeping those that do.

Curative Factors in the REPLAN System

As previously acknowledged, the REPLAN system is based on Jerome Frank's concept of six curative factors, which have been modified slightly (Witmer & Young, 1989) and renamed. The acronym REPLAN helps in remembering the key word of each factor and additionally it underscores the need to reevaluate the counseling plan on a regular basis. This REPLAN system forms the basis for treatment planning and progress reports. Each separate curative factor is discussed in its own chapter along with the counseling methods that are most closely associated with it. Although it is true that many counseling strategies employ more than one curative factor, it is surprising how most methods are aimed primarily at one of these common therapeutic constituents. In this way, techniques that are designed to produce similar results can be grouped together in this book. As Lambert (1986) suggested, this approach emphasizes the need for eclectic counselors and therapists to work on common curative factors as well as specific techniques.

Figure 1.3 is a graphic representation of the six curative factors. Note that the client/counselor relationship again holds a central position since it is supposed that the degree to which the other factors are evoked is in some part due to the strength of this alliance.

Each of the curative factors are briefly explained in the sections that follow.

Enhancing the Client/Counselor Relationship.   *Relationship* refers not only to the initial providing of bonding and safety, but also to later aspects of the relationship, such as the resolution of transference issues. The relationship is the hook in the beginning and afterward becomes a laboratory for client self-awareness. Examples of techniques associated with this factor include

- Unconditional positive regard (person-centered)
- Therapist self-disclosure
- Joining with families
- Intimacy-building exercises in groups
- Some hypnotic techniques (Ericksonian)
- Empathy (person-centered)
- Involving oneself with the client (reality therapy)
- Not giving up on the client (reality therapy)
- Resolution of transference (analytic)

Increasing Efficacy and Self-Esteem.   *Efficacy* or *self-efficacy* is the psychological term for an attitude of confidence held by an individual that he or she can successfully perform some task, be it interpersonal or instrumental (Bandura, 1982). *Self-esteem* definitions include efficacy as well as feelings of worth. Worth is the global attitude about the self that one is good or has a right to exist (Witmer, 1985). Lack of self-worth is supposed to be responsible for many self-destructive activities. Not feeling worthy is a common reason for not making changes in one's life. It causes problems in relationships both at work and at home. Enhancing efficacy and self-esteem leads to the client's willingness to achieve therapeutic goals. Examples of techniques associated with this factor include

FIGURE 1.3
Six curative factors in the REPLAN system.

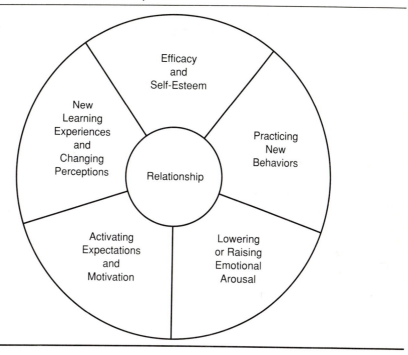

- Self-monitoring (behavioral)
- Countering self-defeating thoughts (cognitive-behavioral)
- Disputing irrational beliefs (cognitive-behavioral)
- Compensatory self-improvement (existential)
- Coping self-statements (cognitive-behavioral)
- Shame attacks (rational emotive therapy)
- Providing feedback to the client

Practicing New Behaviors.   Practicing new behaviors through homework and other methods was pioneered mainly by behaviorists. This curative factor, which is based on learning principles, presupposes that insight and understanding are rarely enough to produce sustained change. The client must also implement learning in as near a naturalistic setting as possible. Practicing new behaviors can take place during a counseling session or while performing homework assignments. Examples of techniques associated with this factor include

- Imaginal rehearsal
- Role playing
- *In-vivo* rehearsal
- Cognitive rehearsal
- Participant modeling
- Hypnotic rehearsal
- Role modeling (reality therapy)

Lowering or Raising Emotional Arousal.   Human performance is affected by too much or too little arousal. Early in the history of psychotherapy, techniques were developed that raised emotions to a high point as a basis for change (abreaction). Cathartic methods bring insights about and awareness of important issues that the client may have buried. Strong confrontation is one method used by drug and alcohol counselors to increase awareness that has been reduced by the processes of denial. Reducing emotional arousal is also curative when an excess of emotion interferes with performance. Examples of techniques associated with this factor include

Arousal Methods

- Amplification (analytic)
- Free association (analytic)
- Body techniques (bioenergetics)
- Emotional production (primal therapy)
- Repetition and exaggeration (Gestalt and psychodrama)
- Hot seat and empty chair (Gestalt)
- Reflection of feelings (person-centered)
- Doubling (psychodrama)

Lowering Emotional Arousal Methods

- Isolation of the client (Morita therapy)
- Relaxation training
- Physical exercise
- Thought stopping
- Meditation

Activating Expectations of Help and Motivation.   This factor includes the therapist's efforts aimed at improving the client's expectations that therapy will be effective and at reminding the client of therapeutic gains. These techniques are designed to reduce the demoralization of the client and aid in maintaining a spirit of hope and optimism. Examples of techniques associated with this factor include

- Encouragement (Adlerian)
- Increasing client perceptions of counselor expertness
- Confrontation of resistance
- Paradoxical methods
- Self-reinforcement/self-control (behavioral)
- Contracting (reality therapy and behavioral)

Providing New Learning Experiences and Changing Perceptions.   Techniques in this area are largely cognitive methods designed to change the client's perceptions about life in general or about specific problems. They can be gradual educational processes or the production of sudden insights. The client may engage in realistic thinking, data gathering, or rethinking past or present problems. Examples of techniques associated with this factor include

- Producing insight through interpretation and confrontation
- Early recollections (Adlerian)
- Dream analysis

- Life-style assessment (Adlerian)
- Spitting in the soup (Adlerian)
- Flooding (behavioral)
- Extinction (behavioral)
- Role training (psychodrama)

Assumptions of the REPLAN System

In general, the REPLAN system is a "prescriptive eclecticism" (Held, 1984). In other words, it focuses on client and counselor goals rather than trying to reconcile various theoretical positions. It is to be expected that counselors will bring their own theoretical orientations into the collaboration with the client. The REPLAN system has five basic assumptions:

1. A structure is needed to organize treatment planning so that the therapist can present a coherent concept to the client and can develop a reasonable and defensible plan.
2. Goals are negotiated between client and counselor. These contracted goals direct the therapy and help client and counselor identify the point at which therapy should end.
3. The therapist should devise the treatment plan based on the client's goals and uses the six curative factors as the basic guide for selecting the general treatment approach.
4. The choice of specific therapeutic techniques should be made on the basis of the client's unique characteristics, especially considering cultural factors and the client's membership in a special population.
5. Each therapy session is organized around the specific agreed-upon goals. While the therapist should be flexible and able to deal with crises as they arise, this system is designed to keep client and counselor on track by making the agenda for each session the same until each goal is achieved or eliminated from the list.

Because it is nearly impossible to set therapy goals early on and expect them to remain the same, the REPLAN system invites client and counselor to evaluate progress towards mutual aims *at each session* and to replan goals when they are reached or become irrelevant.

The REPLAN system can be used productively by three kinds of therapists:

1. Therapists who have a single theoretical orientation but who wish to use some methods derived from other theories
2. Therapists who identify themselves as eclectic and wish to have a systematic way to apply a variety of techniques
3. New therapists who for one reason or another have not aligned themselves with a particular school and want to learn a variety of techniques and to apply them in a systematic way

Counselors and therapists who are closely aligned with a particular school may wish to look at specific techniques in this book and determine how they might be adaptable to the aims of their organizing theory.

CHAPTER SUMMARY AND CONCLUSIONS

Psychotherapy is in a time of "parenthesis," or transition, with traditional schools holding fewer loyal followers. This is partially due to a growing recognition that research has not found any one theory to be superior. Also practitioners, faced with failures when using their chosen school, have come to believe in the efficacy of a wider variety of counseling techniques. At the same time, it has been recognized that theories give therapists focus and direction and increase hope and optimism in clients. The practitioner of tomorrow will need to be able to incorporate the newest findings about effective counseling techniques and, at the same time, be able to communicate coherently to clients and colleagues a rationale for the treatment plan.

In response to the findings of researchers and clinicians, eclectic thinkers have been working since the 1930s to provide an alternative way of accepting a theory, not as a perfect reflection of reality, but as a useful tool. Recent writers, including Lazarus, have proposed models that include techniques from various other schools. The REPLAN model presented in this book uses a problem- and goal-focused method to direct the therapy process. Based partially on the work of Jerome Frank, the REPLAN model, which is more fully developed in later chapters, is a skeletal framework that allows the therapist to apply curative factors to the client's problems. This model recognizes the central importance of one curative factor, the counseling relationship, or therapeutic alliance. This relationship factor is a constant through all phases of psychotherapy. In the next chapter, we will begin to examine the dimensions of this relationship.

FURTHER READINGS

Frank, J. D., & Frank, J. B. (1991). *Persuasion and healing* (3rd ed.). Baltimore, MD: Johns Hopkins University Press. Frank's book is a classic text still used in many graduate programs. Frank was one of the original thinkers to tie social psychological principles of persuasion to psychotherapeutic change. Frank suggests that the therapeutic ritual, techniques, and even the therapy office are in reality tools to be used to influence the client to alter thinking and behavior.

Lazarus, A. A. (1981). *The practice of multimodal therapy.* Hightstown, NJ: McGraw-Hill. Arnold Lazarus is the founder of multimodal therapy. His book cogently puts forth the technical eclectic point of view. Lazarus's viewpoint is generally behavioral, but he integrates everything from imagery to role playing into his therapy. This is a book by a practical yet creative therapist who has developed a simple, workable theory. The case examples in his book reflect his long years of therapeutic experience.

Smith, M. L., & Glass, G. V. (1977). Meta-analysis of psychotherapy outcome studies. *American Psychologist, 32,* 752–760. The Smith and Glass study is often quoted since it supports psychotherapy as more effective than either no treatment or a placebo. The article is of interest to students since it reviews arguments on both sides of the controversy and because of the sophisticated statistical analysis that incorporates the results of other studies.

REFERENCES

Bandura, A. (1982). Self-efficacy mechanism in human agency. *American Psychologist, 37,* 122–147.

Beutler, L. E. (1986). Systematic eclectic psychotherapy. In J. C. Norcross (Ed.), *Handbook of eclectic psychotherapy* (pp. 94–131). New York: Brunner/Mazel.

Beutler, L. E. (1983). *Eclectic psychotherapy: A systematic approach.* New York: Pergamon Press.

Blocher, D. H. (1989). What's in a name: Reactions to Hershenson et al. *Journal of Mental Health Counseling, 11,* 70–76.

Corsini, R. J. (Ed.), (1981). *Handbook of innovative psychotherapies.* New York: Wiley.

Dimond, R. E., & Havens, R. A. (1975). Restructuring psychotherapy: Toward a prescriptive eclecticism. *Professional Psychology, 6,* 193–200.

Dimond, R. E., Havens, R. A., & Jones, A. C. (1978). A conceptual framework for the practice of prescriptive eclecticism in psychotherapy. *American Psychologist, 33,* 239–248.

Dollard, J., & Miller, N. (1950). *Personality and psychotherapy.* New York: McGraw-Hill.

Dryden, W. (1986). Eclectic psychotherapies: A critique of leading approaches. In J. C. Norcross, (Ed.), *Handbook of eclectic psychotherapy* (pp. 353–378). New York: Brunner/Mazel.

Eysenck, H. J. (1970). A mish-mash of theories. *International Journal of Psychiatry, 9,* 140–146.

Frank, J. D. (1971). Psychotherapists need theories. *International Journal of Psychiatry, 9,* 146–149.

Frank J. D. (1981). Therapeutic components shared by all psychotherapies. In J. H. Harvey & M. M. Parks (Eds.), *Psychotherapy research and behavior change* (pp. 175–182). Washington, DC: American Psychological Association.

Frank, J. D., & Frank, J. B. (1991). *Persuasion and healing* (3rd ed.). Baltimore, MD: Johns Hopkins University Press.

Garfield, S. L. (1973). Basic ingredients or common factors in psychotherapy? *Journal of Consulting and Clinical Psychology, 41,* 9–12.

Garfield, S. L. (1980). *Psychotherapy: An eclectic approach.* New York: Wiley.

Garfield, S. L., & Kurtz, R. (1977). A study of eclectic views. *Journal of Consulting and Clinical Psychology, 45,* 78–83.

Garske, J. P., & Lynn, S. J. (1985). Toward a general scheme for psychotherapy: Effectiveness, common factors and integration. In S. J. Lynn and J. P. Garske (Eds.), *Contemporary psychotherapies* (pp. 497–516). Columbus, OH: Merrill.

Ginter, E. J. (1988). Stagnation in eclecticism: The need to recommit to a journey. *Journal of Mental Health Counseling, 10,* 3–8.

Ginter, E. J. (1989). Slayers of monster-watermelons found in the mental health patch. *Journal of Mental Health Counseling, 11,* 77–85.

Goldfried, M. R. (1980). Toward the delineation of therapeutic change principles. *American Psychologist, 35,* 991–999.

Haley, J. (1989, May). *Strategic family therapy.* Symposium conducted at Stetson University, DeLand, FL.

Held, B. S. (1984). Toward a strategic eclecticism: A proposal. *Psychotherapy, 21,* 232–241.

Herink, R. (1980). *The psychotherapy handbook: The A to Z guide to more than 250 different therapies in use today.* New York: New American Library.

Hershenson, D. B., Power, P. W. & Seligman, L. (1989). Mental health counseling theory: Present status and future prospects. *Journal of Mental Health Counseling, 11,* 44–49.

Hollis, J. W., & Wantz, R. A. (1985). *Counselor preparation: 1985–1986.* Muncie, IN: Accelerated Development.

Ivey, A. E., & Mathews, J. W. (1986). A meta-model for structuring the clinical interview. In W. P. Anderson, (Ed.), *Innovative counseling: A handbook of readings* (pp. 77–83). Alexandria, VA: American Association for Counseling and Development.

Jayartne, S. (1982). Characteristics and theoretical orientations of clinical social workers: A national survey. *Journal of Social Services Research, 4,* 17–30.

Kelly, K. R. (1988). Defending eclecticism: The utility of informed choice. *Journal of Mental Health Counseling, 10,* 210–213.

Lambert, M. J., (1986). Implications of psychotherapy outcome research for eclectic psychotherapy. In J. C. Norcross (Ed.), *Handbook of eclectic psychotherapy* (pp. 436–462). New York: Brunner/Mazel.

Lazarus, A. A. (1967). In support of technical eclecticism. *Psychological Reports, 21,* 415–416.

Lazarus, A. A. (1971). *Behavior therapy and beyond.* New York: McGraw-Hill.

Lazarus, A. A. (1973). Multimodal behavior therapy. *Journal of Nervous and Mental Disease, 156,* 404–411.

Lazarus, A. A. (1976). *Multimodal behavior therapy.* New York: Springer.

Lazarus, A. A. (1978). Science and beyond. *The Counseling Psychologist, 7,* 24–25.

Lazarus, A. A. (1981). *The practice of multimodal therapy.* Hightstown, NJ: McGraw-Hill.

Lichtenberg, J. W. (1985). On teaching counseling and personality theories. *Journal of Counseling and Development, 63,* 526–527.

London, P. (1972). The end of ideology in behavior modification. *American Psychologist, 27,* 913–920.

McBride, M. C., & Martin, G. E. (1990). A framework for eclecticism: The importance of theory to mental health counseling. *Journal of Mental Health Counseling, 12,* 495–505.

Nance, D. W., & Myers, P. (1991). Continuing the eclectic journey. *Journal of Mental Health Counseling, 13,* 119–130.

Norcross, J. C. (1986). Eclectic psychotherapy: An introduction and overview. In J. C. Norcross (Ed.), *Handbook of eclectic psychotherapy* (pp. 3–24). New York: Brunner/Mazel.

Norcross, J. C., & Prochaska, J. O. (1982). A national survey of clinical psychologists: Affiliations and orientations. *The Clinical Psychologist, 35,* 1, 4–6.

Parloff, M. B. (1979, February). Shopping for the right therapy. *Saturday Review,* 135–142.

Patterson, C. H. (1986, Summer). Counselor training or counselor education? *Association for Counselor Education and Supervision Newsletter,* pp. 10–12.

Paul, G. L. (1967). Strategy of outcome research in psychotherapy. *Journal of Consulting Psychology, 31,* 109–119.

Prochaska, J. O. (1984). *Systems of psychotherapy: A transtheoretical approach* (2nd ed.). Homewood, IL: Dorsey Press.

Prochaska, J. O., & DiClemente, C. C. (1986). The transtheoretical approach. In J. C. Norcross (Ed.), *Handbook of eclectic psychotherapy* (pp. 163–200). New York: Brunner/Mazel.

Simon, G. M. (1989). An alternative defense of eclecticism: Responding to Kelly and Ginter. *Journal of Mental Health Counseling, 11,* 280–288.

Simon, G. M. (1991). Theoretical eclecticism: A goal we are obliged to pursue. *Journal of Mental Health Counseling, 13,* 112–118.

Smith, D. S. (1982). Trends in counseling and psychotherapy. *American Psychologist, 37,* 802–809.

Smith, M. L., & Glass, G. V. (1977). Meta-analysis of psychotherapy outcome studies. *American Psychologist, 32,* 752–760.

von Bertalanffy, L. (1968). *General system theory* (rev. ed.). New York: Brazillier.

Witmer, J. M. (1985). *Pathways to personal growth.* Muncie, IN: Accelerated Development.

Witmer, J. M. & Young, M. E. (1989, March). *Eclecticism: Fad or new foundation for recasting the counseling profession.* Paper presented at the convention of the American Association for Counseling and Development, Boston, MA.

Yalom, I. (1985). *Theory and practice of group psychotherapy* (3rd ed). New York: Basic Books.

Young, M. E., & Feiler, F. (1989). Trends in counseling: A national survey. Manuscript submitted for publication.

CHAPTER TWO

Establishing the Relationship

Mark E. Young and J. Melvin Witmer

KEY CONCEPTS

▼ *The first stage of the helping relationship is developing a therapeutic alliance with the client. The counselor is most effective when seen as an expert who is trustworthy.*

▼ *The setting where counseling takes place should be free of distractions and provide a welcoming environment for the client.*

▼ *Basic attending and listening skills are the foundations for establishing the relationship.*

▼ *Listening with understanding or responding involves a higher level of skill and includes paraphrasing, reflecting feelings, reflecting meaning, and summarizing.*

INTRODUCTION

This chapter embodies the fundamental skills that are necessary to establish rapport with the client as early as possible in the counseling relationship. Certain fundamental behaviors are associated with the therapeutic alliance, or relationship. In chapter 1, the importance of the relationship was mentioned since relationship issues have an influence on the degree to which the other five curative factors can be evoked. This emphasis is shown graphically in Figure 2.1.

The purpose of this chapter is twofold: first, to highlight the importance of the initial contact with the client and to recognize ways of facilitating a good start; second, to provide a review of foundational relationship skills—attending and following skills. Classroom and homework exercises are included in the text to aid students in the recall of basic counseling principles. These principles are highlighted throughout the chapter and provide the basis for a feedback checklist. This checklist (p. 35) can provide information to the trainee about any areas where improvement is needed. In practice exercises or videotaped role playing, students can receive written feedback on their performance by using the feedback checklists that follow every technique described in this book. Readers completely unfamiliar with the material contained in this chapter should refer to the standard references in this area: Carkhuff (1987), Egan (1990), and Ivey and Authier (1978).

FIGURE 2.1
Curative factors in the REPLAN system.

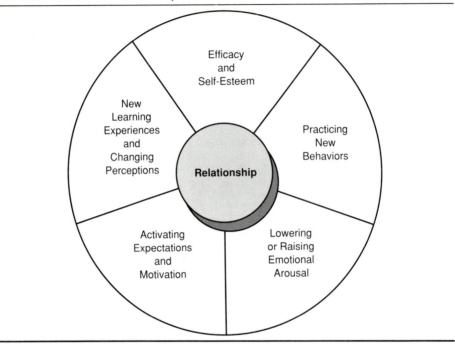

THE THERAPEUTIC RELATIONSHIP

The curative factor most therapists recognize as crucial to success in counseling is the development of a working alliance, or therapeutic relationship (Belkin, 1980; Fiedler, 1950). It is true that clients learn and grow from criticism and they can respect even the most confrontive therapist, but, in general, the aim of the initial interaction is to develop a positive feeling or attraction in the client through the creation of a warm and accepting environment. These conditions have been described by Carl Rogers (1961) as empathy, warmth and caring, genuineness, and positive regard for the client. Second, the goal is to convey that the therapist is a competent person who will provide a safe environment (Strong, 1968). One way of conceiving of these behaviors is that they are forms of persuasion that induce the client to disclose more fully and to form a bond with the therapist (Frank, 1961).

As Table 2.1 suggests, the counseling relationship develops over time and even after initial conditions are established continues to provide a foundation for encouraging change in the client. Phase I is discussed in this chapter. The remaining relationship issues are discussed in later chapters, especially chapter 3, where transference is dealt with, and chapter 11, which focuses on termination.

TABLE 2.1
Phases of the counseling relationship.

Phase	Relationship (Description)	Therapeutic Goals for the Relationship
Phase I Initial contact	- Acquaintances - Testing	1. Saying hello 2. Encouraging self-disclosure 3. Initial transference and resistance issues
Phase II Commitment	- Teacher/student - Negotiating	1. Assessment 2. Treatment planning
Phase III Intimacy	- Conspirators	1. Identification of continuing transference issues 2. Therapist self-disclosure
Phase IV Untying	- Coworkers - Confronting	1. Encouraging client independence 2. Relating "here and now" relationship to treatment goals 3. Resolution of transference
Phase V Termination		1. Saying goodbye 2. Resolving unfinished business

Competence/Credibility

For the relationship to gel, first the therapist must qualify for the job (Yalom, 1985). In other words, it is important for the client to see the counselor as a competent professional. Writers have called this client perception "credibility" (Sue & Zane, 1987) or "expertness" (Barak, Patkin & Dell, 1982; Heppner & Dixon, 1986; Strong, 1968). Clients' expectations of competence are increased by objective evidence of competency: the counselor's office, therapeutic rituals, reputation and even by the certificates and diplomas hanging on the walls (Frank, 1961; Loesch, 1984).

In a review of the literature, Heppner and Dixon (1986) indicate that objective evidence of training as well as certain counselor behaviors and "prestigious cues" affect ratings of counselor expertness by their clients. These behaviors and cues include (1) appearing confident, organized, and interested and (2) nonverbal behaviors associated with attentiveness. Using interpretive statements and psychological jargon was also found to increase ratings of expertness. While these last-mentioned behaviors may seem phoney, they are consistent with Frank's (1961) idea that one of the ways that counselors influence clients is to induct them into a therapeutic ritual and set of procedures. According to Frank, the office setting, the ritual, and therapeutic procedures all help to reassure the client and to combat the demoralization that caused the client to seek help.

Problems in the relationship occur initially when the counselor fails to meet client expectations as a professional. The counselor may be seen as too young or too old. The client may want a male or a female counselor, someone of a preferred ethnic group, or someone from some particular school of thought or training background. The issue of counseling individuals from a special population is explored in a little more depth later. In most cases, client expectations can be explored by the sensitive therapist and can be resolved if the client is able to see the therapist as competent and strengthening. On the other hand, it is often the only alternative to refer resistant clients to another therapist rather than waste valuable time.

The issue of competence has another side. The client may overestimate and idealize the counselor's powers. Some counselors are uncomfortable with the admiration of clients, but it may be difficult and perhaps counterproductive to discourage the client's strong sense of faith in the therapist if it arises. Sheldon Kopp (1978) uses a metaphor to explain this phenomenon. Kopp compares the client to Dorothy in *The Wizard of Oz,* who sees the therapist as a powerful sorcerer (Oz) on the screen. Based on this image of the sorcerer's power, the client goes out and kills the wicked witch. Here, killing the wicked witch refers to the client's efforts to follow therapy plans and make necessary changes. It is only in a later stage that the client is ready *and* able to see the therapist as just a person behind the curtain.

Some therapists find this kind of talk disturbing since it implies that the therapist should try and present a powerful but possibly phoney image. This certainly could have harmful effects for both client and counselor. Counselors are not sorcerers and should not try to feed their egos in the counseling process. On the other hand, it should be recognized that clients very often have these feelings about their therapists and will be influenced by them. A client may have to go through the process of therapy before realizing that the source of strength, just like Dorothy's slippers, is there within themselves all the time. If the client does not abandon his or her magical view of the therapist, the client will not be able to take responsibility for the change process and will instead hope for the wave of the therapist's wand.

Safety and Trust

Before seeking therapy, generally a client must have exhausted both inner resources and social supports. The person may have encountered a major stressor in the past few days or weeks or may have simply become exhausted in trying to deal with an ongoing strain. In addition, the client may be harboring important secrets that he or she does not wish to reveal to the social network. It is an important moment when a client seeks help for problems that may have been troubling him or her for many years. It is vital for the therapist, therefore, to provide a sense of safety so that this opportunity will not be lost.

What can the counselor do to increase feelings of safety in the client? There are no quick solutions to establishing trust. It takes time before the therapist can show evidence that will heighten the client's sense of trust. When trust is established, the client becomes free to self-disclose. Self-disclosure brings about the experiences of intimacy and empathy.

The first steps in developing conditions of safety are obvious. The counselor should demonstrate sincerity, genuineness, and objectivity (Gladding, 1992). At some time in the first session, the counselor should discuss the issue of confidentiality and its limits. Additionally, the counselor can reassure the client that coming to therapy is a sign of health, not illness, and that most concerns the client has about the reaction of employers and others to finding out may be blown out of proportion. One of the most efficient ways of handling client fears is to explain the process and structure of counseling in general. Some therapists use a handout that discusses fees, confidentiality, access to records, and other common concerns.

Experimentally, it has been observed that a concern for confidentiality, attentive nonverbal behaviors, relatively few self-disclosures by the therapist, consistency, and the use of interpretive statements are all associated with greater trust in the therapist (Heppner & Dixon, 1986). While clients may tend to trust therapists who exhibit these kinds of behaviors, it has also been suggested that clients test trustworthiness. Table 2.2 summarizes an article by Fong and Cox (1986) that indicates that the content of certain client behaviors is associated with a deeper process or underlying request or question by the client. These authors recommend that the therapist respond to the underlying process as well as the content and, through self-disclosure and reflection, explore the client's request for reassurance.

In summary, it is important to recognize that counselors influence clients in several important ways. This influence should not be avoided but should be understood and handled responsibly (Senour, 1986). The counselor must be sure that influence is exerted to further therapy goals and to help clients (Strong, 1968). In the next section, some specific suggestions are given for creating a facilitative environment through building a warm and professional atmosphere and through controlling distractions and dealing with early relationship issues, such as time and introducing the client to the process of counseling.

CREATING A FACILITATIVE ENVIRONMENT

Greeting the Client

I have always favored the therapist coming out to the waiting room to greet the client. Sending the client in to the therapist is too much like the formality of a job interview. In the waiting room, the therapist can greet the client or each member of the family, and introductions can be made there or in the privacy of the office if others are waiting.

The counseling office should give the impression of professionalism, not luxury. It should reflect some of the personality of the therapist but not so much as to make the client feel as if he or she is invading the therapist's living room. The

TABLE 2.2
Tests of trust on two levels.

Content: The Client's Test	Process: The Real Question
Information request	Can you understand-accept me?
Telling a secret	Can I be vulnerable with you?
Asking a favor	Are you reliable and honest?
Putting oneself down	Can you accept me?
Inconveniencing the counselor	Do you have consistent limits?
Questioning the counselor's motives	Is your caring real?

Source: From "Trust as an Underlying Dynamic in the Counseling Process: How Clients Test Trust" (p. 31) by M. L. Fong and B. G. Cox in W. P. Anderson (Ed.), *Innovative Counseling: A Handbook of Readings*, 1986, Alexandria, VA: American Association of Counseling and Development.

office should be quiet, comfortable, orderly, and well lit; but fluorescent lighting should be avoided. The impression of informality is helpful especially at the beginning of a counseling relationship. Sigmund Freud called his office a "consulting room." I believe that this is a good impression to present. The office should not be only an outgrowth of the counselor's personality but also a work place.

In terms of furniture, most counselors have a standard set of three chairs. These are set in a triangle, all facing to the center. The extra chair in the session is for a spouse, a friend, or an informant who may accompany the client to the session. If a family session is held, additional chairs are added and arranged in a circle. Generally, it is recommended that the counselor face away from the desk so that there are no obstacles between client and counselor (Pietrofesa, Hoffman & Splete, 1984). Side tables are useful for a clock and the indispensable boxes of facial tissue. Couches are mostly to be avoided. They bring back the feeling of the Freudian era and remind people of a family room's social atmosphere. Couches can also discourage involvement by the client who is able to sit back and become a couch potato.

Distractions

Noise from outside can interfere with the session, disrupting a delicate moment or giving the client the feeling that he or she may be heard by persons outside. The best solution is a solid (not hollow core) door backed with a cork lining or cork bulletin board. Carpeting and acoustic tile also help. A quiet sign and one that says do not disturb should be placed on the outside of the door. In some cases, it may be necessary to purchase a mechanical white noise or ocean sound device that can act as a sound blanket. Position seating to provide the most freedom from glaring lights, noise, and from being overheard.

Other disturbances to be avoided during the counseling session include knocking on the door and phone calls (Benjamin, 1981). Beier (1966), in his classic book on therapeutic communication, *The Silent Language of Psychotherapy*, makes the point that the way in which these distractions are dealt with communicates to the client the importance the counselor places on the counseling appointment. A client once told me that a psychiatrist she consulted ate his lunch during the session. In the same way, the counselor who takes a phone call in the presence of the client is putting the client's needs in second place.

Beier points out that every action of the counselor potentially has therapeutic relevance since we are not sure how actions will be interpreted by the client. The most crucial impression that the therapist must communicate is intense interest in the client's affairs—as if there were nothing else in the world more important or worthwhile.

Some therapists enforce a no-smoking policy in their offices because it can serve as a distraction and as avoidance behavior for clients or because it poses a health risk to the therapist. A few clients may need to take a break in order to smoke. The therapist's rule on smoking can be given in a handout or by way of a small sign.

A final issue concerning distractions is whether the counselor should take notes while the client talks. There are two viewpoints on this question. On the one hand, it is nearly impossible to simultaneously listen, take notes, maintain eye contact, and observe the client. At such times, the client may feel that the therapist is putting more emphasis on the facts of the case than on the relationship, or the client become anxious that personal details are being recorded. On the other hand, some crucial background information is vital to the assessment process. This information can easily be forgotten by the end of the session or, even more likely, by the end of the week when case notes are usually written. Like other counselor behaviors the client may not understand, the counselor can simply explain the procedure (see the discussion under "Previewing and Explaining" later in this chapter). Here is an example of how this might be handled:

Counselor: If you don't mind, I'm going to take some notes on this. I think it is important and I might want to look back on it.

Depending on the client's reaction, the counselor can proceed to take notes or, if it is likely to be disruptive, discontinue. A clipboard is the easiest way to handle note taking, and the counselor should try to return eye contact with the client intermittently. Another simple solution is to wait until the last few minutes of the hour to summarize and jot down missing data with the client's help.

Schmoozing

Schmoozing is a Yiddish word that is the equivalent of our English phrase "shooting the breeze." It refers to discussions between the client and counselor that are merely social and apparently unrelated to the client's problems. Schmoozing has value at some points in therapy: it allows for a truly human encounter between client and therapist. Sometimes the client is curious about the counselor's personal life. Where this curiosity does not endanger the counselor's safety and privacy, schmoozing can help client and counselor develop an egalitarian relationship. Sometimes helpful information about the client's hobbies and special abilities comes to light in this way. Generally, I am against schmoozing and feel that much of the time it serves only the needs of the therapist, keeping things less stressful and passing the time. Schmoozing takes the focus off the major purpose of the session, which is to find solutions for the client's problems.

Dealing with Time

Clients feel annoyed and devalued when they are kept waiting for appointments. It also takes additional time to explain the delay and places the counselor in the position of making excuses, a poor model for personal responsibilty. Of course, there are cases when additional time must be taken to stabilize clients and to make arrangements for their safety before proceeding to the next client, but these are exceptions. In these instances, it is helpful to all parties for the therapist to inform the waiting client that there will be a delay, in the event the client needs to reschedule.

In arranging the office, it is useful to position a clock where it is visible to both parties. Ten minutes or so before the end of the session, the counselor may indicate that time is running out and that a few moments should now be taken to wrap up, plan homework, and reschedule. Counselors who go beyond stated time limitations are communicating that their time is not valuable and that they are not good managers of their own lives.

When the client arrives late, some counselors will extend the session out of sympathy. It could be argued that in this case the counselor is enabling the client to be irresponsible. One approach is to end the session at the usual time, for the usual fee. This response encourages the client to see the counselor's time as valuable. The counselor's policy on this should be in the client handout given at the first session.

Hooking the Client

Therapists often talk about *hooking a client.* This means providing those conditions mentioned earlier: a sense of safety and an aura of competence that can give the client enough hope to return. In a recent talk by the well-known family therapist, Fred Duhl (1987), he took this fishing metaphor to the limit and even dressed up with waders and fishing gear. He gave out a single maxim that summarized his talk: "The ways of the fish are more important than the tools of the fisherman." By this he meant that in order to sustain a therapeutic relationship, the most important job of the therapist is to understand the world of the client.

Understanding the ways of the fish means becoming aware of the client's developmental stage, cultural background, and personal history. It does not matter what tools the therapist has if the client feels misunderstood or put down. Although the metaphor of fishing may not be a good one for a particular client/ counselor relationship, it emphasizes that the counselor must accommodate the client, making the therapy situation attractive and suited to the client's needs.

I once had a client who refused to do behavioral homework assignments because being monitored in this way with charts and graphs made him feel infantile and a little like "a white rat in an experiment." I allowed the client to develop his own procedure for reporting progress and counseling proceeded. Let us take another example. A client with a fundamentalist Christian point of view wishes to see a "Christian counselor." Of course, the therapist must be honest and give appropriate information about his or her religious preference. But first, it is important to understand what the client is really saying. The counselor may be hearing, "I only want a counselor who is 'born again.'" What the client may be saying is, "I want someone who understands my spiritual commitment and who will not dismiss it," or, "I want someone who will help me try to keep my marriage together." If one of these statements is closer to what the client is trying to express, even a wishy-washy Protestant might be able to qualify. There are a number of challenging questions the client might ask before being satisfied that the counseling relationship is going to be safe. Two examples and possible counselor responses follow:

> *Client:* Just how old are you?
>
> *Counselor:* I'm 38. You sound uncertain that someone my age could really understand what you are going through.
>
> *Client:* Do you believe in abortion?
>
> *Counselor:* I'll be glad to answer that. But first, let me find out why this is important to you. Is this something that you are thinking about?

In both cases, the client is given or promised a response, but the client's reason for asking becomes the more important issue in the session.

Previewing and Explaining

During my doctoral internship, I trained medical students in how to talk to their patients. One of the issues the patients continually brought up to the trainers was that new physicians forgot to tell them the reason for a procedure and how it was to be accomplished. For a physician, this means saying, "I am now going to place this instrument in your ear to see if there is any infection." For the psychotherapist, this may mean saying something like, "For most people, therapy means looking at some unpleasant aspects of your life and personality. It is not entirely painless nor is it without risks. In order for me to help you get over your feelings toward your parents, I'd like to know some of the things that have happened that may have contributed to this." The purpose of this dialogue is that, just as in the case of the physician, previewing and explaining the need for a counseling procedure enlists the cooperation of the client. It asks for permission and decreases the feeling of being invaded, which self-disclosure can bring about.

Thus far we have looked at the process of involving the client in the counseling process and of structuring time and the counseling environment. In the next section, we explore skills of listening that cement the relationship between client and counselor.

BASIC ATTENDING AND LISTENING SKILLS

One survey of individuals from a variety of occupations showed that 70% of our waking moments are spent in communication, and of that time, listening occupies 45% (Nichols & Stevens, 1957). Counselors are professional listeners, and although, at first blush, this sounds like the passive act of receiving information, listening is actually an active process that is best accomplished with unwavering attention. *Active listening* means attention to both the verbal and nonverbal messages of the client. It means listening to what is disclosed and what remains below the surface (Reik, 1948). It also means knowing when to be silent. Active listening means communicating one's presence and attention to the client and proving it by reflecting underlying meaning and feelings that lurk below the surface.

In this section, listening skills will be broken into two broad areas: attending skills and following and reflecting skills. *Nonverbal listening* will be called *attending skills*. *Following skills* and *reflecting skills* together make up the category *listening with understanding*, which is sometimes labeled *responding*. After the discussion of each individual skill, some general counseling principles will be stated. Next an exercise for practicing the skill is given and, in some cases, a suggested homework assignment is also provided. The counseling skills named in each counseling principle are listed in Feedback Checklist #1 (p. 35). When practicing the principles in this chapter, through role playing exercises, the checklist can be used to organize feedback from an observer.

Attending to Nonverbal Communication

Attending means listening with one's whole body. It also includes communicating attention to the client. A maxim in listening skills training says that you "can't not communicate." Shutting down communication and hiding communication turn out to be powerful messages to others. Our bodies are not very good liars. Folded arms and drooping facial muscles tend to give us away. But nonverbal messages are also *ambiguous* and, thus, are open to misinterpretation by others. Consequently, it is vital for the counselor to be aware of the client's nonverbal communication and to be sure that he or she [the counselor] is also sending the right messages.

Nonverbal communication affects human interactions, but as noted above, it is often ambiguous. In cases where verbal and nonverbal messages conflict, it is incumbent on the counselor to bring this conflict into the counseling process. Sometimes counselors catch their clients in bodily postures that indicate that the client is hostile or closed. Most often, it is not useful to confront the client's nonverbal communication directly since it often brings about a fracture in the counseling relationship without eliciting much awareness in the client. So, instead, the therapist learns to observe the client's nonverbal communication and to point out discrepancies mainly when they tend to confuse or interfere with communication.

Feedback Checklist #1
Basic Listening and Attending Skills

Instructions: *Following a role-play activity or a taped sequence, the observer should rate the counselor on as many dimensions as possible on the checklist. When improvement is needed, give feedback that is simple, specific, and observable.*

1. To what extent does the counselor use nonverbal communication to provide an atmosphere of warmth and comfort?

Not at All	*A Little*	*Somewhat*	*Moderately*	*A Great Deal*
1	2	3	4	5

Improvement Needed:_____

_____

_____

2. How much does the counselor maintain eye contact with intermittent breaks?

Not at All	*A Little*	*Somewhat*	*Moderately*	*A Great Deal*
1	2	3	4	5

Improvement Needed: _____

_____

_____

3. To what degree is the space between client and counselor comfortable and free of barriers?

Not at All	*A Little*	*Somewhat*	*Moderately*	*A Great Deal*
1	2	3	4	5

Improvement Needed: _____

_____

_____

4. How much does the counselor's posture conform to the ideal of an open, attentive (leaning slightly forward), and relaxed position? (Circle any that are missing or need development.)

Not at All	*A Little*	*Somewhat*	*Moderately*	*A Great Deal*
1	2	3	4	5

Improvement Needed: _____

_____

_____

(continued)

5. To what extent do the counselor's facial expressions reflect attention and empathy?

Not at All	*A Little*	*Somewhat*	*Moderately*	*A Great Deal*
1	2	3	4	5

Improvement Needed: _____

_____

_____

6. How appropriate is the use of touch (if used)?

Not at All	*Barely*	*Somewhat*	*Moderately*	*A Great Deal*
1	2	3	4	5

Improvement Needed: _____

_____

_____

7. To what extent is there adequate use of door openers and minimal encouragers to convey attending and following?

Not at All	*A Little*	*Somewhat*	*Moderately*	*A Great Deal*
1	2	3	4	5

Improvement Needed: _____

_____

_____

8. How much did the counselor rely primarily on open rather than closed questions?

Not at All	*A Little*	*Somewhat*	*Moderately*	*A Great Deal*
1	2	3	4	5

Improvement Needed: _____

_____

_____

9. How much does the counselor employ the appropriate use of silence?

Not at All	*A Little*	*Somewhat*	*Moderately*	*A Great Deal*
1	2	3	4	5

Improvement Needed: _____

_____

_____

(continued)

10. List two or three paraphrases made by the counselor.

A: _____

_____

_____

B: _____

_____

_____

C: _____

_____

_____

In general, how accurate are they?

	Very Inaccurate		Accurate		Very Accurate
1		2	3	4	5

11. List as many as three reflections made by the counselor. Circle the parts of the response that reflect meaning.

Counselor Response A: _____

_____

_____

Counselor Response B: _____

_____

_____

Counselor Response C: _____

_____

_____

Place the letter A, B, and C on the continuum below to indicate the accuracy of each reflecting response.

	Very Inaccurate		Accurate		Very Accurate
1		2	3	4	5

(continued)

12. List one summary made by the counselor. Comment on why it seems to have been used.

Summary: _____

_____

_____

Reason: _____

_____

_____

Counseling Principle 1: Clarify ambiguous nonverbal messages and use this information to understand the client better.

Exercise: View 10–15 minutes of a videotape that shows a client/counselor interaction. During the tape, ask participants to write down any observations concerning client body posture. Afterward, discuss its relationship to the client's concerns. Another possibility is to ask half of the class to observe the client and the other half to be aware of the counselor's posture, movement, etc.

Homework: Record a television show or movie and replay it with the sound off. Try to see if you can guess emotional content by examining the characters' body language.

Eye Contact

Eye-to-eye contact is the first and most important indicator of listening. It conveys confidence and involvement (Ridley & Asbury, 1988). In Western culture, we normally associate lack of eye contact with dishonesty, indifference, or shame. More care needs to be taken when dealing with Asians and others who may be offended by direct eye contact.

Eye contact implies that the client and counselor are sitting at the same level and facing each other squarely. A fixed stare can be disconcerting and should be broken naturally and intermittently.

Counseling Principle 2: Maintain eye contact and face the client directly to show interest but break off the gaze intermittently to maintain client comfort.

Exercise: In this exercise, participants form dyads. One member becomes the client, and the other, the counselor. The client tells the counselor about the day's activities. Meanwhile the counselor listens and avoids eye contact while simultaneously searching through a purse or wallet. The counselor may respond but continues to organize the wallet or purse. Alternately, a scene is set where the client tries to set a new appointment while the counselor shuffles through a stack of papers. Client, counselor, and group give their reactions. The group identifies other behaviors that the counselor might engage in that break eye contact. This exercise sometimes evokes laughter due to the rude behavior on the part of the listener or counselor. It does, however, allow one to feel what it is like to be the recipient of such behavior.

Part two of the exercise involves repeating the conversation, but this time, both client and counselor have their eyes closed and the wallet/purse activity is eliminated. Again, the client, counselor, and group share their reactions.

Physical Distance

Most one-on-one dialogues in this culture take place at a distance of $1\frac{1}{2}$ to 4 feet. Normally about 3 feet is a comfortable space for personal interaction. In general, the smaller the physical distance, the more personal the interaction. Physical barriers such as desks increase distance and add a feeling of formality to the relationship. On the other hand, extremely close quarters can also feel intimidating. Stone and Morden (1976) suggest 5 feet as an optimal distance between client and counselor. In general, the counselor should determine the distance between chairs and allow the client to arrange the chair in a comfortable way.

Counseling Principle 3: Decrease space between client and counselor to increase intimacy, removing physical barriers that make the session too formal.

Exercise: Set up a counseling office for a role-playing situation. Use one chair for the client and another for the counselor. Use a third chair to represent a desk if one is not available. Place the chairs about 10 feet apart and ask two participants to hold a conversation at that distance concerning a minor problem one of them might be having. Ask the group to comment on how the distance affects the conversation. Next, allow the participants to move the chairs to a comfortable distance. Measure the distance with a yardstick or tape measure and see if it matches the guidelines given above. Next move the chairs so close that the participants feel uncomfortable. Measure that distance. If participants from diverse ethnic backgrounds are members of the group, interesting variations can occur. Some people will feel comfortable with an interpersonal distance of 6 inches or less!

Posture

Actions speak louder than words. Posture may be the most often noticed aspect of body language, so it becomes important to have a "posture of involvement." A relaxed alertness communicates, "I am comfortable with myself and I have time to listen to you." A relaxed and attentive posture is one of the fundamental tools for putting the client at ease. Lounging or sprawling in the chair may put the person more at ease, but it may also communicate that the level of the counselor's involvement is minimal. Leaning slightly forward is also suggested at times since it decreases personal distance and conveys caring during moments of peak emotion and attentiveness at other times. It is also suggested that the counselor maintain an open posture—no crossed arms or legs (Egan, 1990). Open postures seem to relax the client and encourage less defensiveness.

Counseling Principle 4: The counselor's posture should reflect attentiveness. This could include leaning slightly forward and maintaining a relaxed, open posture.

Exercise: See Counseling Principle 5.

Gestures and Facial Expressions

Attending behaviors should be the natural expressions of the feelings and thoughts of the therapist. Freudian analysts were formerly trained to avoid reacting to the client's expressions of emotion. Persons trained in the client-centered approach of Carl Rogers, where many of the techniques in this chapter evolved, feel that gestures and facial expressions can be useful tools. Facial expressions that convey the counselor's reactions to the client's joy or sadness, anger or fear, excitement or boredom and can thereby serve as attending responses (Fretz, Corn, Tuemmler & Bellet, 1979; Maurer & Tindall, 1983).

Expressive body movements by the therapist can be distracting to the other person. Fidgeting, playing with a pencil, drumming fingers, frequent shifting of body position, and other such movements can be read by the client as anxiety, impatience, or disinterest. On the other hand, a motionless, statuelike pose is likely to be perceived of as aloof and controlled. The listener who is moderately active in responding to the client's content and affect is more likely to be viewed as friendly, warm, casual, and natural.

Counseling Principle 5: Facial expressions and gestures should be used to show attention and empathy and should not be distracting.

Exercise: Videotape two trainees, one of whom acts as the client and the other, the counselor, for 15 minutes. The individual who runs the camera should spend half of the session focused on the counselor's face and the other half on the counselor's whole body. Even if the counselor is aware of the taping procedure, the exercise is likely to reveal interesting movement and gestures for class discussion.

Touching

While there is much to be said for the healing power of the human touch, certain taboos must be observed (Goodman & Teicher, 1988). Touch can communicate caring and concern especially during moments of grief (Driscoll, Newman & Seals, 1988). Willison and Masson (1986) contend that research supports the appropriate use of touch, which can have a positive impact on clients. Holroyd and Brodsky (1980) recommend touch with socially immature clients to foster communication and bonding and with clients in grief, depression, or in trauma as a way of showing support. They also encourage the use of touch as a greeting or at termination. In addition, touch may be used to emphasize or underline important points (Older, 1982).

Touch can also engender powerful sexual and transference reactions in the client (Alyn, 1988). For a client who has been sexually abused, a good deal of anxiety may be aroused. Perhaps fears about physical contact are overblown in the literature, but many writers have cautioned that it is important to know the client well before initiating touch. Probably the safest client/counselor touching is the handshake or a pat on the shoulder or back. One guideline is to use touch sparingly to communicate encouragement and concern with the knowledge that even slight gestures may evoke sexual feelings in the client. The counselor must be prepared to recognize this reaction in the client and be willing to deal with it when appropriate.

Fisher, Rytting, and Heslin (1976) established three useful guidelines to determine the appropriate use of touch: touch should be appropriate to the situation, should not impose a greater level of intimacy than the client can handle, and should not communicate a negative message (such as a patronizing pat).

It must be recognized here that there is a "pro-hug" school of thought. A hug may be a special gesture at the time of termination, but it seems to be a sort of forced intimacy when used routinely. An embrace may be seen as phoney, and the counselor may actually be seen as less trustworthy (Suiter & Goodyear, 1985).

Counseling Principle 6: Touch should be applied briefly, appropriately, and sparingly to encourage or to communicate concern.

Exercise: Conduct a group discussion on the implications of touching clients. What constitutes sexual touching? Whose needs are being fulfilled? Is it all right for the counselor's emotional needs to be met by hugging a client? In what circumstances would a hug be beneficial or harmful? What about hugging in group therapy?

Homework: Conduct a survey among a few friends or family members. How would they feel about being hugged or touched by their therapist? Try to be objective and prepare a report of their answers.

Listening with Understanding

Following Skills

The primary task of listening is to create an atmosphere free of coercion, manipulation, and game playing. Such an atmosphere facilitates self-disclosure by the client. The first step in creating this climate is to communicate to the client that the counselor is "with them" intellectually and emotionally. Following skills, which can help create coercion-free environments, can be broken down into several specific behaviors. They are door openers, minimal encouragers, open and closed questions, and attentive silence.

Door Openers.   The simple definition of a *door opener* is "a noncoercive invitation to talk" (Bolton, 1979, p. 40). The door opener is initiated by the therapist, but the client determines the depth of the response. More than a passing social response or greeting, the intention of the door opener is to signal availability on the part of the listener. By contrast, evaluative or judgmental responses are *door closers*. A door opener is generally a positive, nonjudgmental response made during the initial phase of a contact. It may include observations of the therapist as in the following counselor statements:

> "I see you are reading a book about Sylvia Plath [observation]. How do you like it?"
> "You look down this morning [observation]. Do you want to talk about it?"
> "What's on your mind?"
> "Tell me about it."
> "Can you say more about that?"

Minimal Encouragers.   *Minimal encouragers* are brief supportive statements that convey attention and understanding. Most of us are most familiar with minimal encouragers in the image of the Freudian analyst behind the couch, stroking his beard and saying "Mm-hmm!"

Like door openers, minimal encouragers are verbal responses that show interest and involvement but still allow the person to determine the primary direction of the conversation. They are different from door openers in that they communicate only that the listener is on track. Such phrases reinforce talking on the part of the client and are often accompanied by an approving nod of the head. Examples of minimal encouragers are

> "I see."
> "Yes."
> "Right."
> "Okay."
> "Hmm."
> "I've got you."
> "I hear you."
> "I'm with you."

Of course these responses are not sufficient to help a client achieve the goals of therapy, but if they are not used frequently enough, the client feels stranded and uncertain. Clients present complex problems and scenes with many players. It is crucial that the counselor convey that the information that the client has painfully revealed has also been received.

Counseling Principle 7: Use door openers and minimal encouragers to recognize the client's message and promote self-disclosure and exploration.

Exercise: Conduct a counseling session in dyads using only minimal encouragers and door openers. First one person has the problem, then the other. Discuss, within your dyad, the results of this experiment. What is the general effect of these techniques? For contrast, try several minutes during which the counselor completely avoids verbal and nonverbal minimal encouragers and door openers.

Open and Closed Questions. Of all following skills, questions are the most easily abused. Research suggests that beginning therapists ask more questions than experienced ones (Ornston, Cichetti, Levine & Freeman, 1968). Excessive questions get in the way of listening, and the answerer usually feels interrogated and evaluated. As we will see later, questions can be used for assessment purposes and as therapeutic tools. In establishing the relationship, though, they can be detrimental.

In a vain search for causes, therapists sometimes ask a lot of why questions. If you ask a 5 year old why he or she stepped in the mud, the inevitable and truthful answer is, "I don't know." It is only when we become adults that we are able to come up with lengthy rationalizations for our behavior. A few decisions that people make, such as buying a car or a house, may have been the result of a rational process. But the best answer to most why questions is usually that "It seemed like a good idea at the time." Certainly this is true even about why people get married or why they make other important life changes. A therapist soon learns to avoid this dead end, which seems to question the client's logic. The counselor begins to ask more open questions, gathering information from the whole of an interview. Egan (1990) among others has mentioned the strong need for clients to tell their stories or fully explain their lives to the counselor. Questions tend to slow down this process and frustrate clients.

There are two types of questions, open and closed. *Closed questions* ask for specific information and usually require a short factual response. *Open questions* allow more freedom of expression. The difference between the two question types is something like the comparison between multiple choice and essay questions used by teachers. Examples of open and closed questions and likely client responses follow.

Closed

Therapist: Are you getting along with your parents these days?

   Client: Yeah. Pretty good.

Open

Therapist: Can you tell me how you and your parents have been dealing with your differences recently?

Client: Well, we haven't been, really. We're not fighting but we're not talking either. Just existing.

Closed

Therapist: Are you married now?

Client: No, divorced.

Open

Therapist: Can you tell me a little about your personal relationships during the past few years?

Client: Well, I've been divorced for six months from my second wife. We were married for over seven years and one day she left me for this guy at work. Since then, I haven't really been up to seeing anyone.

The examples above illustrate that open questions elicit more information than closed questions do while, at the same time, acknowledging the right of the client to refuse. In fact, open questions are often delivered as statements to avoid the feeling of interrogation. Technically, they are still questions since they ask for a response. Examples of some standard open questions include

- Tell me more about it [statement].
- How does this affect you?
- Could you give me more information?
- Let's hear the whole thing [statement].
- Say some more about that [statement].

Counseling Principle 8: Avoid closed questions if possible; rely more on open questions. When it is feasible, turn questions into statements.

Exercise: The training group breaks into triads, each with a counselor, a client, and an observer. It is the counselor's job to conduct the interview and gain relevant background without asking a single question. The counselor may not make a statement that demands a closed answer, such as, "Tell me how old you are." The counselor may say, "Tell me something about yourself." The observer breaks in when the counselor inadvertently slips into questioning or makes closed statements.

Attentive Silence.   In social settings, it is vital to keep a conversation flowing. A deadly silence is a disaster at a party, but therapy does not follow the same rules. Allowing for periods of silence gives the client moments for reflection (Cormier & Cormier, 1991) and the counselor time for processing. Silence is often the most appropriate response to a client's disclosure of loss. Words often seem somehow to deny the validity of a person's grief or are perceived as attempts to sweep feelings under a rug. At these times, the therapist falls back on attentive silence in order to be present without interfering.

Finally, the most powerful use of silence is to nudge the client to disclose. The exercise below illustrates how silence can be a tool to encourage elaboration.

Counseling Principle 9: Use silence to encourage client self-disclosure, to communicate respect, or to allow for reflection.

Exercise: Participants form dyads for this activity. The leader or instructor keeps time and signals the completion of the exercise at the end of two minutes. Both participants maintain eye contact and appropriate posture while remaining completely silent throughout the exercise. At the end of the two-minute period, each dyad discusses their personal reactions with the other members and then with the larger group.

Homework: In conversations with coworkers, family, and friends, instead of immediately responding, build in attentive silence and notice the effect. The purpose of the assignment is to observe the effect of the trainee's silence on the communication of others. Make notes and report findings to the group.

Reflecting Skills

So far we have looked at nonverbal attending and following skills. The third cluster of basic counselor behaviors is called *reflecting skills*. These skills include paraphrasing, reflecting feelings, reflecting meaning, and summarizing. Like attending and following skills, their aim is to communicate understanding but at a deeper level. These reflecting skills from client-centered therapy have been described best by Carkhuff (1987). In general, reflecting means repeating back to the client his or her thoughts and feelings in different words and in a way that communicates real understanding. Reflecting is nonevaluative and nonjudgmental. It goes beyond introductory skills by facilitating a greater depth of understanding and getting at the real meaning the person is trying to express. Reflecting skills are specialized counselor tools, apart from ordinary social conversation. They serve four functions in counseling:

1. They provide a verbal means for communicating empathy.
2. They act as a type of feedback or mirror that enables the person to confirm or deny the impression they are giving.
3. They stimulate further exploration of what the person is experiencing.
4. They are a means for keeping the communication on track by capturing the essence of the client's statements that might be camouflaged.

Paraphrasing

Most of us are familiar with problems in one-way communication. There is a cartoon that pokes fun at the confusion created by an idea that is passed from one department to another that has made the rounds in offices. The cartoon depicts a product—a child's swing—first as it was envisioned by the design department and then at various points in its manufacture until it is actually produced. At each stage it is modified until it is turned into a confusion of ropes and platforms. A more mundane example of the problems with one-way communication is giving directions over the phone. Although the speaker believes that a message was communicated clearly and precisely, there is no assurance that the person on the other end clearly and precisely understood it.

Paraphrasing is the technique of restating the basic message in the listener's own words. It is feedback that focuses primarily upon the content of the message rather than the feelings of the person. It may reflect some feeling, but the emphasis is on the facts, thoughts, or conclusions of the client and does not include analysis by the sender.

Paraphrases are used by the counselor for two basic purposes: First, to clarify confusion on the counselor's part, and second, to repeat some important thought, behavior, or intention embedded in the client's statement, as the following examples show.

Client: I've been taking three medications from three different doctors. Of course, I stopped taking two kinds right away. But that was before the operation and now I am on some pain killers, too. Do you think I should stop drinking with all that medicine?

Counselor Response 1 [paraphrase aimed at decreasing counselor confusion over content]:

OK, let me stop you for a moment. Right now you are taking one medication besides the pain killers and you are drinking alcohol, too?

Counselor Response 2 [paraphrase that focuses on client's thoughts, behavior, or intentions]:

From what I can pick up, you are considering decreasing your intake of prescription medication and your alcohol consumption, too.

Counseling Principle 10: Paraphrase when you do not understand the content or when you want to focus the client on some aspect of the problem.

Reflecting Feelings

Reflecting feelings involves essentially the same technique as paraphrasing. This time, however, the focus is on feelings rather than content—thoughts, ideas, behaviors, and intentions. Reflecting feelings involves expressing in one's own words a description of feelings stated or implied by the client. Feelings can be reflected from verbal or nonverbal responses of the client.

A number of therapeutic events occur when feelings are reflected. For one thing, the client becomes more keenly aware of the emotions surrounding a topic.

For example, the therapist makes a reflection such as, "I can tell that you are terribly angry about that." The client's response may be one of surprise, "Yes! I guess I am." Since a reflection is done in a nonevaluative manner, it communicates understanding of feelings—anger, guilt, and sadness—that the client may not feel it is right to have.

A second important effect is that reflection of feelings brings the client to deeper and deeper levels of self-disclosure. An accurate reflection focuses the client on emotions and teaches the client to become aware of and to report feelings. Even if the reflection is not quite accurate, the client will correct the feeling with one that is more on target.

A third aspect of an accurate reflection is that it has the almost magical power to deepen the relationship between client and counselor. Nothing transmits non-judgmental understanding more completely. This is why this technique, which originated in the client-centered tradition of Carl Rogers, gained such wide usage. It taps the enormous healing properties of the therapeutic, or curative, factor of enhancing the relationship. A beginning counselor who can accurately reflect feelings can provide supportive counseling and understanding without any other tools.

Counseling Principle 11: Use accurate reflections of feelings to improve client emotional awareness, deepen disclosure, and enhance the relationship.

Reflecting Meaning

Once paraphrasing and reflection of feelings are understood and practiced, a third element is introduced, reflection of meaning. *Reflecting meaning* denotes counselor attempts to restate the personal impact of the event the client is describing. This sometimes means employing intuition or hunches (Egan, 1990).

Formula for Reflecting Meaning.   The formula for a good reflective response is "You feel (   ) because (   ) (Carkhuff, 1987). The first blank is filled with a *feeling* or *content plus feeling* and the second blank with the *meaning* it holds for the individual. For example, "You feel very discouraged (feeling) about your proposal being rejected (content) because it represented a great deal of hard work and a cause that has been very important to you (meaning)."

Most beginning therapists reject this formula because it seems too rigid and unnatural. Students are usually instructed to follow the rules for a time before they begin to vary the model to make it more personal. When the counselor learns to make accurate reflections with on-target feelings and meaning, the next step is to learn to make the reflection as brief but as on target as possible. Using the statement above, let's see how the reflection has been reworded and shortened in the following example.

> *Client:* You know how I've been working on this project to start a sheltered workshop? Well, I found out today that the proposal was turned down by the foundation. Oh, well.
>
> *Counselor:* It's discouraging when you've worked so hard.

Counseling Principle 12: A complete reflective response advances hunches or intuitive guesses about the personal meaning of the content and feelings described by the client.

> *Exercise:*   Ask all members of the group to write down a three- or four-line statement that a fictitious client might give as a summary of a presenting problem. It should be written in the first person as follows: "I am having trouble getting my children to mind me. That's not all. I've been very depressed and I'm not going to be able to pay my bills this month. What am I supposed to do?" The trainer or leader reads each one anonymously and the training group takes turns giving a reflection of feeling and meaning using the you feel (   ) because (   ) formula.
>   A good response to the problem above might be "You are feeling overwhelmed because everything is coming apart all at once." The trainer or leader asks for feedback from the group concerning the accuracy of the reflection. Another method is to ask one participant to reflect the feeling and the next participant to rephrase it in more natural terms.

Precautions in Reflecting Feelings and Meaning.   Thomas Gordon's *Parent Effectiveness Training (PET)* (1970) provides an excellent summary of the usual errors in reflecting made by beginning counselors. Some of his suggestions are included in this list of problems and common errors:

1. The first issue is one of *timing.* The essence of timing is not to lag behind in material that the person has finished with nor to push the client by anticipating what they are likely to say.

2. The second issue is one of *depth.* Overshooting is the counselor error when the feeling is described with an adjective that is too strong. Undershooting is when the counselor minimizes the emotional impact. Both errors affect the client's feeling that the counselor understands. Words such as *very, somewhat, slightly,* and the like can be used to vary the intensity of emotions reflected. Even more important is the counselor's feeling vocabulary, which should be expanded. Feelings are like colors and there are a number of subtle shades. The counselor should be familiar with these shadings since a counselor is a "feelings expert."

3. The third issue is *cultural.* Reflections fail when the language is inappropriate because of differences between the client and counselor's cultural history or educational level. Words used must be chosen that are likely to be common to both members rather than a dialect of either.

4. A fourth dimension could be called errors of *analysis.* One possible mistake is to parrot or simply give a reflecting response that is identical to the client's sentence and does not reveal a depth of understanding. At the opposite extreme, overanalysis involves attributing hidden meanings to the client's statements. It is a hunch that is far beyond the client's understanding. For example:

Client: I have been very depressed since my father died.

Counselor [parroting]:
> You've been very depressed.

Counselor [overanalyzing]:
> You miss the presence of a strong male figure.

Summarizing

Summaries are used at all points during a therapy session—beginning, middle, and end. A *reflecting summary* is a counselor statement that brings together main themes and feelings by concisely recapping them. It involves tying together some of the major issues that have evolved up to that point in the session. Of the reflecting skills, it could be considered the broadest brush.

Besides reassuring the client that the therapist has been listening, the summary helps the client make some sense of the tangle of thought and feeling just evoked in the session. The summary also signals the client that the therapist has digested this much and the session can move on. A summary can also be employed to terminate a session with a review of progress, plans, and agreements made.

An effective summary is used at a pause in the session when it appears to the counselor that it may be time to move on to the next step. The next step may be to leave an area of counseling behind, to encourage the client to continue exploring a feeling or theme, or to end the session. The summary provides the impetus for this transition. The summary is especially effective when the counselor

1. focuses the client on major points.
2. includes a summary of content, feelings, and meanings.
3. identifies themes that run through the session.

A theme is a pattern of issues, feelings, or meanings that the client returns to again and again (Carkhuff, 1987).

Examples of some summaries that followed a series of client statements and counselor responses follow.

Counselor [focusing]:
> There seem to be two issues that keep coming up. One of them is the anger towards your sister and the other is your sense that you haven't been able to reach your potential in your career.

Counselor [counselor identifies themes]:
> As you have been talking, I seemed to notice a pattern and I'd like to check it out. You seem to want to end relationships when they begin to lose their initial excitement and romance.

Counselor [ending the session]:
> Let's recap what we have talked about so far. On the one hand, you have accomplished your financial goals but you are far from satisfied with your relationships with friends and family. You have said that this is because you are not very assertive. It sounds as if this is the area we need to discuss in our next session. What do you think?

Counseling Principle 13: Use summaries to signal a transition, focus the session, or identify major themes.

> *Exercise:*   Role-play an office visit of a client in individual counseling. One member of a triad plays the counselor, another the client, and the third uses the Feedback Checklist #1 (located at the end of this chapter) to give the counselor information about the session. The session begins in the waiting room, and the counselor ushers the client into the office. At the end of the 10- to 15-minute session, the counselor should attempt to use a summary as a way of ending this session.

CHAPTER SUMMARY AND CONCLUSIONS

This chapter addressed two important issues associated with the initial phase of the counseling relationship: developing appropriate conditions of trust, safety, and professionalism and learning basic attending and listening skills. A therapist never really moves beyond the need for these basic skills. At any moment, therapeutic movement may require that the counselor revert to these relationship-building skills to support and understand the client. For example, in the next chapter, the task of assessment is examined. Because assessment can be an invasive and even boring procedure for the client, the therapist must use fundamental relationship skills to maintain the client's cooperation. As was stated in the beginning of the chapter, the therapeutic relationship remains the critical curative factor. As the relationship matures, additional skills will be needed to deal with new challenges between client and counselor.

FURTHER READINGS

Carkhuff, R. (1987). *The art of helping VI.* Amherst, MA: Human Resource Development Press. It is said that Robert Carkhuff is the most-cited psychologist. Carkhuff's contribution is that he has systematized the helping process in a learnable form. The importance of learning reflecting skills cannot be overemphasized in counselor training. Carkhuff calls this establishing an "interchangeable base." This book comes with accompanying workbooks and video.

Halstead, R. W., Brooks, D. K., Jr., Goldberg, A., & Fish, L. S. (1990). Counselor and client perceptions of the working alliance. *Journal of Mental Health Counseling, 12,* 208–221. In this research article, the authors compare the strength, importance, and satisfaction of the "working alliance" between pairs of clients and counselors. The literature review and the results may help sensitize counselors to the central importance of the relationship, especially from the client's point of view.

Rogers, C. R. (1961). *On becoming a person.* Boston, MA: Houghton Mifflin. Surprisingly, many contemporary counselors have not read Rogers's book, which is his most personal explanation of the theory of person-centered therapy. Rogers's emphasis on the therapeutic relationship and the explanation of the core conditions for a helping relationship are contained in this work. It lays the foundation for a growth-oriented therapeutic position.

REFERENCES

Alyn, J. H. (1988). The politics of touch in therapy. *Journal of Counseling and Development, 66,* 155–159.

Barak, A., Patkin, J. & Dell, D. M. (1982). Effects of certain client behaviors in perceived expertness and attractiveness. *Journal of Counseling Psychology, 29,* 261–267.

Beier, E. G. (1966). *The silent language of psychotherapy.* Chicago, IL: Aldine.

Belkin, G. S. (1980). *Introduction to counseling* (2nd ed.). New York: W. C. Brown.

Benjamin, A. (1981). *The helping interview* (3rd ed.). Boston, MA: Houghton Mifflin.

Bolton, R. (1979). *People skills: How to assert yourself, listen to others, and resolve conflicts.* Englewood Cliffs, NJ: Prentice-Hall.

Carkhuff, R. (1987). *The art of helping VI.* Amherst, MA: Human Resource Development Press.

Cormier, W. H., & Cormier, L. S. (1991). *Interviewing strategies for helpers* (4th ed.). Monterey, CA: Brooks/Cole.

Driscoll, M. S., Newman, D. L., & Seals, J. M. (1988). The effect of touch on perception of counselors. *Counselor Education and Supervision, 27,* 113–115.

Duhl, F. (1987, May). *A fisherman's guide to interviewing.* Symposium conducted at the meeting of the American Association for Marriage and Family Therapy, Orlando, FL.

Egan, G. (1990). *The skilled helper* (4th ed.). Monterey, CA: Brooks/Cole.

Fiedler, F. E. (1950). The concept of an ideal therapeutic relationship. *Journal of Consulting Psychology, 14,* 339–345.

Fisher, J. D., Rytting, M., & Heslin, R. (1976). Affective and evaluative effects of an interpersonal touch. *Sociometry, 39,* 416–421.

Fong, M. L., & Cox, B. G. (1986). Trust as an underlying dynamic in the counseling process: How clients test trust. In W. P. Anderson (Ed.), *Innovative counseling: A handbook of readings* (pp. 30–33). Alexandria, VA:

American Association for Counseling and Development.

Frank, J. D. (1961). *Persuasion and healing.* Baltimore, MD: Johns Hopkins Press.

Fretz, B. R., Corn, R., Tuemmler, J. M., & Bellet, W. (1979). Counselor non-verbal behaviors and client evaluations. *Journal of Counseling Psychology, 26,* 304–311.

Gladding, S. T. (1992). *Counseling: A comprehensive profession* (2nd ed.). Columbus, OH: Merrill.

Goodman, M., & Teicher, A. (1988). To touch or not to touch. *Psychotherapy: Theory, Research and Practice, 25,* 492–500.

Gordon, T. (1970). *Parent effectiveness training.* New York: Wyden.

Heppner, P. P., & Dixon, D. N. (1986). A review of the interpersonal influence process in counseling. In W. P. Anderson (Ed.), *Innovative counseling: A handbook of readings* (pp. 8–16). Alexandria, VA: American Association for Counseling and Development.

Holroyd, J., & Brodsky, A. (1980). Does touching patients lead to sexual intercourse? *Professional Psychology, 11,* 807–811.

Ivey, A. E., & Authier, J. (1978). *Microcounseling* (2nd ed.). Springfield, IL: Charles C. Thomas.

Kopp, S. (1978). *If you meet the Buddha on the road, kill him!* New York: Bantam Books.

Loesch, L. (1984). Professional credentialing in counseling—1984. *Counseling and Human Development, 17,* 1–11.

Maurer, R. E., & Tindall, J. H. (1983). Effect of postural congruence on client's perception of counselor empathy. *Journal of Counseling Psychology, 30,* 158–163.

Nichols, R. G., & Stevens, L. A. (1957). *Are you listening?* New York: McGraw-Hill.

Older, J. (1982). *Touching is healing.* New York: Stein and Day.

Ornston, P. S., Cichetti, D. V., Levine, J., & Freeman, L. B. (1968). Some parameters of verbal behavior that reliably differentiate novice from experienced therapists. *Journal of Abnormal Psychology, 73,* 240–244.

Pietrofesa, J. J., Hoffman, A., & Splete, H. H. (1984). *Counseling: An introduction.* Boston, MA: Houghton Mifflin.

Reik, T. (1948). *Listening with the third ear.* New York: Pyramid Books.

Ridley, N. C., & Asbury, F. R. (1988). Does counselor body position make a difference? *The School Counselor, 35,* 253–258.

Rogers, C. R. (1961). *On becoming a person.* Boston, MA: Houghton Mifflin.

Senour, M. N. (1986). How counselors influence clients. In W. P. Anderson (Ed.), *Innovative counseling: A handbook of readings.* Alexandria, VA: American Association for Counseling and Development.

Stone, G. L., & Morden, C. J. (1976). Effect of distance on verbal productivity. *Journal of Counseling Psychology, 23,* 486–488.

Strong, S. R. (1968). Counseling: An interpersonal influence process. *Journal of Counseling Psychology, 15,* 215–224.

Sue, S., and Zane, N. (1987). The role of culture and cultural techniques in psychotherapy. *American Psychologist, 42,* 37–45.

Suiter, R. L., & Goodyear, R. K. (1985). Male and female counselor and client perceptions of four levels of counselor touch. *Journal of Counseling Psychology, 32,* 645–648.

Willison, B. G., & Masson, R. L. (1986). The role of touch in therapy: An adjunct to communication. *Journal of Counseling and Development, 64,* 497–500.

Yalom, I. D. (1985). *The theory and practice of group psychotherapy.* New York: Basic Books.

CHAPTER THREE

Transference, Countertransference, and Relationships with Special Populations: Challenges in Developing the Client/ Counselor Bond

KEY CONCEPTS

▼ *Transference reactions are strong feelings of the client that have been carried over from past relationships.*

▼ *Psychoanalysis uses interpretation of transference as a primary tool in correcting problems caused by past relationships.*

▼ *Modern thinkers consider transference to be a cognitive distortion.*

▼ *Transference must be resolved when it interferes with the accomplishment of therapy goals.*

▼ *Resolution of major transference feelings of hostility, dependency, and strong affection involves accepting and normalizing the client's feelings, clarifying and exploring the transference, interpreting the transference, and helping the client find new ways of meeting needs.*

▼ *Countertransference is the name given to the counselor's strong emotional reactions to the client that may encourage the counselor to respond to his or her needs rather than the needs of the client.*

▼ *One challenge to developing an effective client/counselor relationship is trying to develop understanding and to convey acceptance when the client is culturally different from the counselor or comes from some other special population. The counselor must be flexible enough to try to view the problem situation from the client's unique and cultural perspective, if the counseling bond is to be maintained.*

INTRODUCTION

In chapter 2, the basic conditions of trust, safety, and credibility were described. Establishing these conditions is one aspect of the first curative factor in the REPLAN system. Yet, even if these necessary conditions are established early in the counseling relationship, a variety of issues can potentially disrupt or change the therapeutic alliance, diminish trust and safety, and prevent it from reaching a working stage. Chief among these disruptive influences are the issues usually referred to as transference and countertransference and the communication problems that occur between client and counselor because of differences in cultural background or because of membership in a special population. *Transfer-*

ence and *countertransference* are strong feelings between counselor and client that may occur as the result of an increased sense of intimacy following the client's self-disclosure and the therapist's listening with understanding. The primary challenge in dealing with the client who is different from the counselor is developing credibility and empathy with the client in the first place. In this chapter, we will examine the issue of transference reactions first and then take up the issue of special populations.

TRANSFERENCE

Intimacy in the counseling relationship is what sets psychotherapy apart from other helping relationships. During the 1960s the term *encounter* was coined to describe this experience. Intimacy is generally seen as a positive state of agreement and mutual caring. It creates favorable conditions for change (Rogers, 1957) and increases client involvement and compliance with treatment. Intimacy also tends to elicit strong feelings—feelings that may have had their genesis in previous relationships. For this reason, the therapist must be trained and willing to examine the therapeutic relationship itself as a living model of the client's social world.

It is also possible to experience transference reactions immediately on meeting an individual, that is, without the presence of intimacy. Most of us are familiar with automatic feelings of liking or disliking a person on sight. This emotional reaction is most likely due to experiences with a similar person in the past. Many therapists feel that understanding the client's transference reactions to the therapist is vital. On the other hand, many therapeutic relationships never develop into intimate relationships, and serious transference issues do not surface. Some therapists believe it is even possible to achieve therapy goals without a deep personal relationship (cf., Lazarus, 1981), though mutual respect and liking are extremely helpful. Others feel that every therapeutic relationship contains transference and to avoid it is to miss the most crucial aspect of therapy.

In my experience, many clients are able to achieve therapy goals without needing to work through transference issues. For others, it is vital to examine the therapeutic relationship as a first step in setting other relationships straight. Other clients experience such strong feelings toward the therapist that the transference is simply an obstacle that must be overcome in order for therapy to continue. When issues of transference interfere with the attainment of goals, they must be dealt with in an isolated fashion or connected to other relationship problems the client may be experiencing. Table 3.1 again shows the development of the therapeutic relationship described in chapter 2. This chapter will focus primarily on Phases III and IV, during which transference issues fully manifest and are resolved. Coverage will include a look at the most common transference reactions and methods for resolving them. This discussion will be followed by an examination of some problems and precautions of dealing with transference, a relevant case example, a discussion of transference in the group setting, and a note on countertransference. The student is urged to obtain data about his or her performance in this area by using Feedback Checklist #2 (p. 58).

TABLE 3.1
Phases of the counseling relationship.

Phase	Relationship (Description)	Therapeutic Goals for the Relationship
Phase I Initial contact	- Acquaintances - Testing	1. Saying hello 2. Encouraging self-disclosure 3. Initial transference and resistance issues
Phase II Commitment	- Teacher/student - Negotiating	1. Assessment 2. Treatment planning
Phase III Intimacy	- Conspirators	1. Identification of continuing transference issues 2. Therapist self-disclosure
Phase IV Untying	- Coworkers - Confronting	1. Encouraging client independence 2. Relating "here and now" relationship to treatment goals 3. Resolution of transference
Phase V Termination		1. Saying goodbye 2. Resolving unfinished business

Dealing with Transference: Overview and Purpose of the Method

What Is Transference?

As noted earlier, *transference* is a client's carry-over of feelings from past relationships toward a new object—the client/counselor relationship. These feelings can be described as positive, ranging from liking to sexual attraction, or negative, ranging from suspiciousness to hate (Watkins, 1986). Relationship-building activities, such as reflecting feelings and providing conditions of safety, increase feelings of intimacy. Along with this closeness, other feelings and thoughts come to the surface. Gelso and Carter (1985) indicate that all therapists engender a "magnetism or transference pull" in their clients. Negative transference reactions are thought to be an important reason for treatment failures (Basch, 1980) since clients often drop out of therapy rather than face them.

Psychoanalytic Conceptions of Transference

One view of transference is that it is caused by unfinished business from the past. This notion is central to psychoanalysis, which asserts that material comes up from the unconscious because it is unresolved. Freudians believe that resolution of

---

Feedback Checklist #2
Dealing with Transference/Countertransference

Instructions: This feedback checklist is designed to be used by an observer or supervisor to give specific information on the counselor's behavior following a taped session or a role-play experience.

1. To what extent does the counselor adopt a nondefensive, normalizing attitude toward the client's emotional response?

Not at All	*A Little*	*Somewhat*	*Moderately*	*A Great Deal*
1	2	3	4	5

2. How much does the counselor clarify and encourage exploration?

Not at All	*A Little*	*Somewhat*	*Moderately*	*A Great Deal*
1	2	3	4	5

3. Does the counselor interpret by making connections between the therapeutic relationship and other relationships, past or present?

Not at All	*A Little*	*Somewhat*	*Moderately*	*A Great Deal*
1	2	3	4	5

4. Does the counselor help the client find new ways of expressing feelings and meeting needs?

Not at All	*A Little*	*Somewhat*	*Moderately*	*A Great Deal*
1	2	3	4	5

5. To what extent does the counselor show emotional reactions to the client that might interfere with therapy?

Not at All	*A Little*	*Somewhat*	*Moderately*	*A Great Deal*
1	2	3	4	5

Describe:_____

_____

_____

---

transference is the most important aspect of therapy since it allows the client to address emotional issues about parents and siblings. Transference is thought to take the form of either *superego transference* (projecting authority or dependency), *ego transference* (overidentifying with the therapist), *ego ideal transference* (ascribing perfection to the therapist), or *id transference* (projecting desires for nurturance, affection, etc.) (Beukenkamp, 1956).

Traditionally, therapist "neutrality" was stressed in psychoanalytic training because it was important to encourage transference. The analyst became a projection screen for the client and avoided self-disclosure, only providing a voice of reality and interpreting the client's reactions as they related to the past. Interpretation of transference was a key technique for helping the patient correct the past. During interpretation, the analyst explained the connection between current feelings and the patient's history. Neutrality, or objectivity, forced the client to realize that feelings toward the therapist and toward significant others came from inside rather than outside. The way to resolution of transference by this method was to adjust one's life in accordance with insights gained in therapy.

More recent analytical thinkers have questioned the need for neutrality. Wachtel (1977), for example, sees transference more as a projection of the client's unfulfilled current interpersonal needs rather than a simple replaying of primal relationships. He also points out that it is probably an impossible goal to be truly neutral. Whether we like it or not, as therapists, we are part of the play. We are going to evoke positive and negative feelings in clients and they will evoke feelings in us. These feelings cannot be hidden for long, but once exposed, they can become a useful mirror of other relationships in the client's life. As Ralph Waldo Emerson once said, "Use what language you will, you can never say anything but what you are." This does not mean that the therapist has license to respond angrily to a client in order to release emotions. The counselor discusses his or her own reactions only to the extent that they might be useful to the client.

Modern Approaches to Transference

Corey, Corey, and Callanan (1988) indicate that transference is not restricted to psychoanalysis, where it was first identified. Therapists from all theoretical persuasions face transference reactions and develop methods for managing them. One alternative viewpoint that has emerged is to conceptualize transference as a set of cognitive distortions rather than as unresolved conflicts or unfulfilled needs (Sullivan, 1954). These distortions are learned patterns of thinking, not unlike the irrational ideas that have been described by Albert Ellis (1985). Still there is a common notion that binds the modern viewpoint to the psychoanalytic idea. In both conceptualizations, the client is seen as focused on the outside (external causes of behavior) versus the inside (self-direction). This more cognitive viewpoint stresses that the client who has strong positive feelings toward the counselor sees the therapist as the answer to all problems. Conversely, negative transference feelings are primarily due to the client's disappointment in the counselor's inability to meet unrealistic expectations. Watkins (1986) has identified five major transference patterns that fit this notion of cognitive distortion. Table 3.2 is adapted from Watkins and shows these patterns along with the client's attitudes and the counselor's experience of them.

Why Must Transference Be Addressed?

Some writers (cf., Fine 1975, p. 105) insist that the transference of feelings by the client onto the therapist is mainly the result of childhood experiences and one's family of origin. Others (Watkins, 1986) indicate that transference does not need to reach so far back, that it may be based on more recent relationships. For example, it is just as likely that a client may have positive feelings for a therapist because of a physical resemblance to her best friend as it is that the therapist reminds the client of her mother. Regardless of when the historical situation occurred, by definition, the transference reaction is a reliance on old learning that

TABLE 3.2
Major transference patterns.

Client Behaviors/Attitudes	Counselor Experiences
Counselor as Ideal	
Compliments counselor profusely	Feels pride, satisfaction, and all-competent
Imitates counselor	
Wears similar clothing	Experiences tension, anxiety, confusion, anger, and frustration
General idealization	
Counselor as Seer	
Ascribes omniscience and power to the counselor	Experiences "God complex" and self-doubt
Views counselor as expert	Feels incompetent and pressure to be right and live up to client's expectations
Sees self as incompetent	
Seeks answers, solutions, and advice	
Counselor as Nurturer	
Experiences profuse emotion and sense of fragility	Experiences feelings of sorrow, sympathy, depression, despair, and depletion
Cries	Has urge to soothe, coddle, and touch
Feels dependent, helpless, and indecisive	
Desires to be touched and held	
Counselor as Frustrator	
Feels defensive, cautious, guarded, suspicious, and distrustful	Feels uneasy, on edge (walking on eggshells), tense, hostile, and hateful
Experiences "enter-exit" phenomenon	Withdraws and becomes unavailable
Tests counselor	Dislikes and blames client
Counselor as Nonentity	
Shifts topics	Feels overwhelmed, subdued, taken aback, used, useless
Lacks focus	
Is voluble and desultory	Experiences resentment, frustration, and lack of recognition
Meanders aimlessly	
Exhibits thought pressure	Characterizes self as a nonperson

Source: Adapted from "Transference Phenomena in the Counseling Situation" by C. E. Watkins, Jr. (p. 36) in *Innovative Counseling: A Handbook of Readings* edited by W. P. Anderson, 1986, Alexandria, VA: American Association of Counseling and Development.

may not be appropriate in present relationships. It is a defensive reaction and an attempt to maintain the status quo (Paolino, 1981).

Second, the client with strong emotional reactions to a therapist has reduced self-awareness and is focused on the other person. In the case of strong hero worship, for example, the client may be diminishing the self by comparison and thereby may be producing conditions unfavorable to change in therapeutic directions (Singer, 1970).

When Must Transference Be Treated?

Under what conditions should the therapist negotiate resolution of transference as a therapeutic goal? According to Wolberg (1954), transference is to be confronted only when it acts as *resistance*. Resistance can be understood as any conscious or unconscious effort by the client to avoid accomplishing therapy goals or to take on antitherapeutic goals. It is an attempt to return to the pretherapy situation for reasons of safety or habit (Cavanagh, 1982).

Besides conditions of resistance, transference must be dealt with when the negotiated treatment goals directly relate to the client's behavior toward the therapist (Strupp & Binder, 1984). Using the therapeutic relationship as a laboratory, client and counselor can identify and change maladaptive cycles of interpersonal behavior. For example, if a man who has a problem with extramarital affairs begins acting seductively toward his female therapist, this behavior must be discussed since it relates to his original therapy goal—to decrease this behavior. By the same token, it can be argued that mild transferences and attractions should be avoided if they do not interfere or create resistance.

MORE THOUGHTS ON RESISTANCE

The terms *reluctance* and *resistance* often appear in the same context. Reluctance pertains to the client who is unwilling to be involved in counseling in the first place but who is coerced into it by some other person or institution, such as the courts. The issue of accepting and working with reluctant clients is a topic of considerable length. This issue is dealt with more fully in chapter 9, which is devoted to activating client expectations and motivation. In general, though, the initial stages of working with reluctant clients involve testing the client's willingness to become involved in a counseling relationship and finding some areas of agreement, even if the concerns are quite minor. The development of a counseling relationship may then lead to the consideration of more substantive issues. On the other hand, continuing to work on problems that the client rejects may be both fruitless and unethical.

Resistance generally refers to an unwillingness to change after the therapy process has begun (Ritchie, 1986). The resistant client is dealt with in a later chapter as a problem of motivation rather than as an attempt to sabotage oneself or the therapist. Client resistance does surface early in the counseling relationship. Many therapists attempt to get around resistance by firming up the relationship, using testing, free association, art therapy, and other means to access important client issues. Ritchie (1986) identifies three normal manifestations of resistance. They are listed below with some examples and suggestions for dealing with these early aspects of resistance.

Situation 1: The client denies having a problem or assigns the blame for the problem to someone else.

Example: The client abuses alcohol, gets in a car wreck, and breaks both wrists. One of the other individuals in the car is slightly injured.

Counselor Strategy: The counselor generally avoids confronting the client strongly but explores the reasons for the accident, the exact injuries of the individuals, the costs of insurance, inconvenience, etc. The counselor also inquires about similar incidents when the client's drinking caused problems and inquires if things are getting worse or better. In severe cases, confrontation or family interventions may be necessary in order for the client to acknowledge the problem.

Situation 2:   The client acknowledges the problem but does not want to change.

Example: A 20-year-old college student has bleeding gums, hair loss, and dental problems as a result of severe bulimia. She admits that the binging/purging has gotten worse but is resistant to inpatient treatment.

Counselor Strategy: Direct confrontation of the client's problem is indicated. In this case, the client may be referred to a physician, shown evidence of the medical threats of bulimia, and given statistics about the rate of death associated with the disorder. In addition, family and friend support systems may be mobilized to encourage the client to seek treatment.

Situation 3:   The client admits to a problem and wishes to change but does not know how or is afraid to change.

Example: The client is an abused 29-year-old woman, married with two small children. She has recently been seen at the emergency room for two cracked ribs, following an altercation with her husband. She is determined to leave him but is financially destitute and cannot imagine living on her own.

Counselor Strategy: There are two aspects to helping this client. The first part is that the client should be persuaded to take small direct action steps after setting some achievable goals. In this case, for example, the client might be encouraged to go visit the local women's crisis center without necessarily making the commitment to leave her husband. The second step is that the client should begin to personally evaluate her decision to leave her husband in a realistic way and plan for obstacles that will arise. In this process, the client begins to make an informed choice about the decision to change. If the client feels that the counselor has persuaded the change, the client will not take responsibility for the success or failure of the effort.

A NOTE ON COUNTERTRANSFERENCE

This book does not emphasize *countertransference:* the counselor's strong feelings toward the client. It is, for the most part, an ethical and supervision issue rather than a method or technique of therapy. Still, it can seriously disrupt the counseling relationship and is worthy of discussion here.

Countertransference is an issue not fully appreciated by the beginning counselor. When intellectualizing about the counseling relationship, one can hardly imagine the powerful feelings that some clients may elicit. All therapists need ongoing supervision to help monitor the tendency to be too helpful and deal with feelings of sexual attraction as well as anger, fear, and insecurity.

Some therapists try to deal with their feelings by simply disclosing everything to the client. This is a mistake if it is designed to relieve the counselor's discomfort. The counseling relationship is based on a contract that implicitly agrees that the therapist should introduce material only if it is beneficial for the client. Counseling is not a friendship, nor is it always a two-way street. It involves a helper and a helpee. The helper agrees to set his or her own needs aside and do what is best for the client. Table 3.3 describes common counselor emotional reactions, based on information collected by Corey, Corey, and Callanan (1988), but it also includes some ideas of my own. The essence of the table is that countertransference issues are generally emotional reactions to clients, which can lead to certain behaviors on the part of the counselor. Instead of helping the client achieve mutually derived goals, the counselor develops a second (you might say unconscious) agenda that changes the counselor's view of the client as a contractual partner in the therapy process. The counselor has come to see the client as a project, a sexual object, as a friend, or even as a reflection of the self.

Countertransference is as common as transference reactions, and most counselors regularly fall prey to these feelings. I would guess that a great deal of the unethical behavior on the part of therapists is due to these strong emotions, which make us forget our "asocial," contractual role. This is one reason a supervisory relationship is so crucial for every therapist. The supervisor's role is to appeal to the therapist's professional sense and remind the therapist to act in accordance with therapeutic goals.

Of these reactions, probably frustration and anger are the most common. Research by Fremont and Anderson (1986) found that counselors become aggravated when clients (1) show resistance to counseling; (2) impose on the counselor's personal life and time or become too dependent; (3) verbally attack the counselor; (4) draw the counselor into their dynamics, perhaps seeing several counselors and pitting them against each other.

A number of miscellaneous other behaviors that make counselors angry were noted by Fremont and Anderson, some of which relate to the client being perceived as manipulative. We can become angry and feel used if the client attends counseling for some other reason than to accomplish therapeutic ends. The authors identified some anger-producing assumptions—"shoulds" or rules—under which counselors may be operating. Some of these shoulds relate to countertransference:

- The client *should* try to get better.
- The client *should* not become dependent.
- The client *should* appreciate the counselor's effort. Anger by the client is an ungrateful attitude.
- The client *should* not successfully manipulate the counselor.

Although it is certainly all right for counselors to allow themselves to have feelings of annoyance, anger, and disappointment, again, the way to resolve this countertransference is not necessarily to share these feelings with the client. Instead, the counselor should confront the client with manipulative behavior if it

TABLE 3.3
Common patterns of countertransference.

Counselor Emotional Response to Client	Counselor Behavior	Client Seen As
Paternal/maternal nurturing	Overprotective Failure to challenge	Fragile
Fear of client's anger	Reduction of conflict Attempts to please	Agressor
Disgust, disapproval	Rejection	Needy Immoral
Need for reassurance Need for liking Anxiety Insecurity	Socializing Failure to challenge Avoidance of emotionally charged topics	Friend
Feelings of identification	Advice giving Overinvolvement Failure to recognize client's uniqueness	Self
Sexual Romantic	Seductive behavior Inappropriate self-disclosure Reduced focus on presenting problems Inappropriate exploration of sexual topics	Sexual object Romantic partner
Frustration Anger	Extreme confrontation Scolding Criticizing	Product Success

Source: Adapted from *Issues and Ethics in the Helping Professions* (3rd ed., pp. 50–53) by G. Corey, M. S. Corey, and P. Callanan, 1988, Monterey, CA: Brooks/Cole.

seems to be interfering with agreed-upon goals. There are probably times when acknowledging anger toward the client can actually enhance the counseling relationship (Weiner, 1979) (i.e., when such disclosure does not blame the client or damage self-esteem). Clients who are very irritating to others in their lives and have significant interpersonal problems may benefit from this kind of feedback.

In summary, part of the work of a counselor is to constantly monitor one's own feeling states and to judge when self-disclosure is for the benefit of the client or only relieves internal pressure. In general, the counselor's feelings provide an excellent way of gauging the client's effect on other people. Such feedback can be helpful. Another source of anger hinges on counselor expectations for the client that, for the most part, interfere with the counseling relationship. At this point, we will leave the issue of countertransference behind and again focus on methods for helping clients resolve strong feelings brought out by the therapeutic relationship.

METHODS FOR RESOLVING TRANSFERENCE

The resolution of a transference reaction has been called "a corrective emotional experience." It is a way of remediating past relationships by examining the present one. Reflection on and exploration of strong emotions and a reeducational process are the major elements of the method.

The identification and analysis of strong emotions expressed by the client are the keys to dealing with transference. The expression of these feelings sets off corresponding reactions in both client and counselor (Kell & Mueller, 1966). A client's expression of anger, for instance, may make the client feel guilty and the therapist defensive. The three emotional syndromes expressed most often are transference of hostility, dependency, and affection. The steps for dealing with transference are similar for these three major manifestations. They are (1) acceptance of and normalizing the client's feelings, (2) clarifying and exploring these feelings, (3) interpretation, and (4) helping the client find new ways of expressing feelings and meeting needs.

Accepting and normalizing the client's feelings means responding in a non-judgmental and nondefensive way to the client's expression and indicating to the client that such feelings are natural in a counseling relationship. This is an invitation to explore.

Clarifying and exploring maintains the focus on the client by asking the client to express fully his or her reactions and to discuss related issues. At times, it may involve self-disclosure on the part of the therapist to enable the client to understand the effect of his or her behavior.

Interpretation is a technique derived from psychoanalysis in which the therapist reformulates the client's "resistances, defenses and symbols" in terms that the client can understand (Wolberg, 1973, p. 201). This reformulation may involve openly hypothesizing with the client a link between the present experience and earlier experiences. These interpretations can take the form of questions such as, "Do you think these feelings could be similar to the ones you had toward your boyfriend?" They may also be made as statements: "I think your anger is not really directed toward me but toward your wife who encouraged you to come." Statements of this type must be used carefully since they tend to sound "shrinky." The tentative interpretation often has the best chance of encouraging client exploration and acceptance of the interpretation.

Helping the client find new ways of expressing feelings and meeting needs means assisting the client in applying insights that have been learned in the therapeutic relationship. For example, a client's need to be nurtured by the therapist might be best met by finding a group of concerned, nurturing friends. Homework and therapy assignments can help the client work toward this goal.

Hostility as Transference

Step 1: Accepting and Normalizing the Client's Feelings

Hostility is certainly the most difficult transference reaction for most therapists. It tends to evoke anger in the counselor, and a defensive response can be perceived by the client as a weakness, as an admission of guilt, or as a punishment. The client's anger may be triggered by frustration over lack of change or by feelings that the therapist is unfriendly, inept, or destructive. Part of acceptance is to normalize the client's feelings. After having expressed this hostility, the client may be concerned about angering or hurting the therapist or may fear retaliation.

Example

> *Client:* I don't think we're getting anywhere. When are we going to deal with the real issues. I'm sick of coming in here and paying all this money.
>
> *Counselor:* I can tell you're mad. I'm glad you had the courage to be so honest. I can't think of anything that will be of more help to you than dealing with this issue.

Step 2: Clarifying and Exploring

Following an expression of hostility toward the therapist, the client may retreat, fearing punishment, losing control, or hurting the therapist. Exploration of a client's hostile feelings involves continuing to encourage the expression and labeling of feelings while trying to clarify the source of the anger. Reflecting feelings, as discussed earlier in the chapter, is a way to explore and deepen the client's expression.

Example

Client: I don't think this is working, and I am tired of coming in here and being told that it is all my fault.

Counselor Option 1 [clarifying]:
> What made you feel that it was all your fault?

Counselor Option 2 [identifying the source while reflecting feelings]:
> You're frustrated that things are not moving as quickly as you hoped and, to some extent, you feel I am to blame.

Step 3: Interpretation

Generally, interpretations of hostility are difficult for the therapist, who must point out the true source of the client's anger and encourage the client to accept responsibility for his or her own feelings. Below are two examples of such interpretations. The first is rather direct. The second uses the method of reflecting meaning, a method described in an earlier chapter. Reflecting meaning goes beyond what the client says, relating feelings to the client's perception of the world. In these interpretations, an attempt is made to relate the client's hostility toward the therapist to more general feelings about the world outside of the therapy session.

Example 1

> *Client:* You think it's easy for me to give up smoking dope? How would you like to work at that plant, earning minimum wage, not enough money to get an apartment and having to live with your mom. How would you like it?

> *Counselor:* I don't think you are just angry at me. You're discouraged about life in general and I'm the closest target. Does your frustration spill out on other people in your life right now?

Example 2

> *Client:* This is just a job to you. You're just like all the rest. Collect your paycheck.

> *Counselor:* You're angry, not just at me, but because you suspect that no one cares enough to help you.

Step 4: Helping the Client Find New Ways of Expressing Feelings and Meeting Needs

Clients who express anger toward the therapist may require assertiveness training. *Assertiveness training* is an attempt to help people learn to express their feelings while asking specifically for what they want. Clients who exhibit excessive anger or who are indirect or revengeful may be alienating others and thereby engaging in self-defeating patterns. Interpretation has the effect of making clients aware of these patterns, but they still may need assistance either individually or in a structured group in order to learn new and more productive behaviors.

Dependency as Transference

Step 1: Accepting and Normalizing the Client's Feelings

Counselors may find that clients who are helpless and dependent are very depressing and boring, and they may reject them as "complainers." Clients in a crisis, such as divorce or extreme grief, may experience dependency on the therapist for a limited time. Another thing to keep in mind is that dependency may be the result of unmet needs for parenting or nurturance and may be a temporary phenomenon. Dependency is transference when the client sustains the dependent attitude, fails to take independent action, or ascribes accomplishments to the therapist.

Clients may be feeling dependent because they lack confidence in their decisions. For this reason, highly directive therapy may be counterproductive. Expressions of confidence such as "Although I know you are not feeling very secure about your decisions right now, I have a lot of faith in your ability to solve this problem," is one way of accepting the client's feelings and encouraging the client's self-direction.

Step 2: Clarifying and Exploring

One way of heightening and clarifying dependency reactions is to ask the client to focus on the immediate client/counselor relationship.

> *Client:* I can't stand my present job. You know that, we've talked about it before. What should I do?

> *Counselor:* What's going on between the two of us right now?

> *Client:*   What do you mean?
>
> *Counselor:*   I mean that I am aware of several similar conversations we have had that involve you stating a problem in depth, and then I think you expect me to solve that problem.
>
> *Client:*   Well, I need help.
>
> *Counselor:*   I would very much like to help, but I also wonder why you have so little confidence in your own decisions.

Step 3: Interpretation

Interpretation of client dependency must be carefully handled because it may be experienced as a rejection. The following dialogue occurred in an actual taped session between a client and a counselor:

> *Client:*   I had a dream last night that I was waiting outside of your office and everybody was allowed in, including my wife, but I had to stay outside and wait. I have this feeling that you don't have time for me and it's hard to schedule an appointment with you. I think I need to come in every week right now.
>
> *Counselor:*   I think it's almost time to terminate. I think you are becoming too dependent on this relationship.

The client in this case did feel rejected and never returned to counseling. Although this conversation may have had the effect of ending what was to become a dependent relationship, the counselor missed a golden opportunity to make the client aware of these feelings of dependency and of the need for support from a parental figure. Another counselor response might have been: "Your dream and your wish to schedule regular appointments make me think that you want a lot of reassurance right now. At other crucial decision points in your life, have you felt the need for someone to take over some of the responsibility for you?" This response is equally strong, but it uses reflection and paraphrase to interpret the client's response and tends to further exploration.

Step 4: Helping the Client Find New Ways of Expressing Feelings and Meeting Needs

A client's need for succor or nurturance can be met by helping the client develop mutually helpful relationships with others. Another important tool for helping the client involves increasing the client's self-esteem and efficacy. This topic is addressed in depth in a later chapter. A useful preliminary set of responses by the therapist is presented here.

1. Avoid direct advice giving.
2. Actively encourage any attempts toward self-direction.
3. Continue to interpret client's tendencies to give up decision-making power to others.
4. Educate the client on the need for mutually supportive relationships.
5. Involve the client in activities designed to help others.

Example

Client: So that's the story. I've been working there for 13 years. I know my job, and now I have a young guy as a supervisor who thinks he needs to tell me how to do it. How do I handle it?

Counselor: You say you've been working there for 13 years. I would guess you've had a lot of experience dealing with similar kinds of incidents. What have you thought about doing?

Client: Well, I've considered being more assertive and telling him to back off a little, in a nice way.

Counselor [interpretation and encouraging client to meet own needs for approval]: That sounds like pretty good advice. One thing I've noticed is that even though you seem to have good judgment about these things, you appear to want someone's stamp of approval.

Client: I wish I could make a decision without getting everybody's advice first. I make it into such a big deal.

Counselor [goal setting]: That sounds like a therapy goal that we could continue to work on. This problem at work sounds like a good beginning.

Strong Affection: Sexual and Romantic Feelings as Transference

Step 1: Accepting and Normalizing the Client's Feelings

Sexual and romantic feelings toward the counselor are quite common. Such feelings may be the result of transference or attempts to manipulate the therapist. They may also simply be physical attraction. Clients may feel ashamed of these feelings and fail to acknowledge them. The counselor's job is to accept such expressions in a way that minimizes shame and reflects to the client that such experiences are a natural part of therapy.

Step 2: Clarifying and Exploring

Because sexual feelings are often expressed indirectly, the therapist must be willing at times to address hints given by the client directly. One method of exploration is to take a sexual and relationship history, when appropriate. This assessment can lead to hypotheses for interpretation later on. History taking is appropriate when client problems seem to revolve around these issues and when the counselor can remain detached enough not to encourage further sexual transference. Below are two examples of an interchange on this difficult subject. One example demonstrates a bad alternative—"hiding" or avoidance by the therapist; the second shows another way of addressing this issue directly.

Example 1

Client: I wish my husband could be more like you.

Counselor [avoiding]: How long have you been married?

Example 2

> *Client:* I wish my husband could be more like you.
>
> *Counselor [exploring]:* Tell me what you mean.
>
> *Client:* I feel like you and I are really close, and, well, I am really attracted to you. I look forward to coming to these sessions. Do you feel anything like that or am I way off base?
>
> *Counselor [accepting and normalizing]:*
> I am glad you brought this up because I think it's important and it must have been hard for you. As far as I'm concerned, there are no taboo subjects. Sexual attraction sometimes happens in a relationship like ours, and it is something we will have to look at.

Step 3: Interpretation

Interpretation of client sexual feelings must be handled delicately since it is often experienced as unrequited love. Although avoiding the client's sexual feelings is no service to the client, looking closely at these feelings can produce embarassment and feelings of shame. Some common client themes are discussed in the following paragraphs.

The Client's Desire for Affection. The client's desire for affection may be expressed in seemingly innocuous ways, for example, through the giving of gifts.

> *Client:* I brought you this card and some flowers.
>
> *Counselor:* I feel a little uncomfortable. Part of me would like to thank you. But the therapist in me wants to make you aware of what we've talked about before. Isn't this just like the stories you've told me about giving gifts to your friends to get their affection?

Confusion Between Experiences of Intimacy and Sexuality. One of the tasks of early adult maturity is to recognize the fact that one can experience intimacy without sex and sex without intimacy. Clients who have relatively little experience in relationships will confuse the intimacy of a counseling relationship with sexual attraction. Making the client aware of this can be done through taking a relationship history and directly addressing the client's immediate experiences in the counseling situation.

Avoidance of Dealing with "Real Life" Relationships. One aspect of this type of transference is that the counselor is seen as the ideal spouse/romantic partner. The client develops the view that the solution to his or her problems is to abandon some current relationship and seek a partner more like the therapist. If the therapist is able to maintain a truly professional relationship and to focus the client's efforts on "real life" relationships, this attraction is likely to fade.

Example

> *Client:* My girlfriend never does this, just sit down and talk to me.
>
> *Counselor:* When you say this kind of thing, you seem to be saying your girlfriend

should be more like me, like a therapist, listening and supportive all the time. On the one hand, I'm wondering if that is realistic, and on the other, I want to know what you are doing to help create that kind of mutually supportive relationship with her.

Step 4: Helping the Client Find New Ways of Expressing Feelings and Meeting Needs

The clues given in the interpretations above show the major therapeutic direction. The counselor helps the client develop skills in forming or repairing current relationships and forces the client to see that the therapeutic relationship is of rather short duration, not the ideal that the client imagines.

Another direction is for the therapist to help the client see that sexual/romantic feelings are the natural outgrowth of liking and intimacy. Therefore, the client will certainly experience these feelings at other times. Dealing with them in therapy, in a safe environment, will help the client learn to deal with similar situations and feelings without becoming overwhelmed by them.

Problems and Precautions of Transference

Murray (1986) cites the example of a young woman who came to therapy because she felt she was overly dependent on her father. For example, whenever she had car trouble, she turned it over to him. In consequence, she never learned to deal with a service station at all. After a month of therapy, she brought in her insurance policy, which she was having trouble deciphering, and handed it to the therapist who began reading it. After a moment, the therapist laughed and exclaimed, "Look, I'm behaving just like your father!"

This example is a positive interpretation of the transference phenomenon, yet it points the way to avoiding certain pitfalls in dealing with what can be a touchy issue. First, it shows how transference can be interpreted through the use of therapist self-disclosure. The therapist, in the example above, also found a means to avoid shaming the client. The client must feel that sharing feelings and exposing oneself to the therapist will not have negative consequences.

While the therapist must avoid rejecting the client because of transference feelings, sometimes it is in the best interest of the client to be referred to another therapist rather than continuing to focus on transference issues. Referral of a hostile client is made when the counselor believes that another therapist will not evoke such strong animosity or when the counselor feels incapable of maintaining an accepting attitude. If a client's major goal is to learn to deal productively with anger, referral may then be harmful and a waste of time. If dealing with anger is not the major therapeutic issue and the hostility is standing in the way of achieving other goals, the counselor may consider avoiding interpretation of anger, decreasing discussion of the anger, and focusing instead on achieving some small goals to increase the client's confidence in the relationship. Another tactic is to decrease the frequency of the counseling sessions, when appropriate, to diminish the strength of the transference.

A final point is that transference should not necessarily be managed according to the guidelines given here if it is not in the best interests of the client or if it permits the therapist to hide from valid criticism. A client's hostility may, for example, simply be a reaction to other ongoing stresses, not the result of transference. A client may be angry at a therapist for consistently being late for appointments. In both cases, interpreting the client's reaction would not likely be therapeutic. It would be far more productive to help the client reduce stress and to deal authentically with the client than to address transference issues.

CASE EXAMPLE

A client of the author's began the therapeutic relationship with much enthusiasm and high expectations for achieving her goals. She was a 23-year-old only child who felt she could not maintain a serious relationship. After a few weeks, her enthusiasm waned and she expressed disappointment in the therapist. By this time, enough assessment had been done to identify this denouement as being similar to her history of intimate relationships. She began relationships with an idealized picture of her boyfriends and then was quickly disappointed. She came to the counseling session one day indicating that she was angry that I had not been able to give her an earlier session. During her phone call, she had said it was important but not urgent that she see me soon. She admitted that she expected me to know how upset she was and to set up an emergency appointment. When we examined our relationship, the client was able to pick out several times when she left hints and clues about her needs but failed to ask for things directly. I shared my feelings of surprise, being unaware of her real feelings. Naturally, this led to a discussion of how her behavior might have affected other relationships. It was a very significant insight when she realized that she was undermining relationships by her failure to send clear messages about her needs. In her case, this pattern of behavior could be traced back to her upbringing, which did not require that she state her needs and rewarded indirect suggestions. In therapy, she was able to learn some assertiveness skills and practice them in a group setting.

Variations on Transference: Groups

In group settings, Yalom (1985) believes that transference is an omnipresent phenomenon that cannot be avoided but only tackled head on or left to fester. To some extent, all group members have false impressions of the leader based on transference. For example, the leader may initially be granted superhuman qualities by group members. One effect of this kind of transference is that it tends to deemphasize the importance of other group members and their contributions. Even sophisticated group members may abdicate power to the leader, causing the group to evolve into a passive and helpless entity. On the other hand, negative transference, when widespread, can lead to constant challenging of every leader action. Yalom points out that clients may tend to recreate their original family group in this type of therapy setting, complete with challenges to authority and sibling rivalry for the leader's attention.

In a group setting, Yalom feels that transference can be resolved in two basic ways. The first intervention is *consensual validation,* or *reality testing,* in which the therapist asks the member to check out perceptions of the therapist with other individuals in the group. The results of such an intervention may teach the lesson that many of the things we perceive about a person come from within us. As time goes on, clients become more and more expert in the ability to recognize when they ascribe their own issues to others. Simultaneously, group members become more skilled in recognizing the signs of transference in each other (Wolf, 1950). A second way of resolving transference is through increased *therapist transparency* (self-disclosure by the therapist). Although this may actually be harmful in the early stages of the group by lowering expectations and increasing confusion, therapist self-disclosure can quickly shatter illusions of perfection or maliciousness.

RELATIONSHIP ISSUES IN COUNSELING SPECIAL POPULATIONS

What Is the Problem?

There is a growing recognition that our culture is changing. In California, nonwhite students now outnumber whites. By the year 2020, 38% of all U.S. school children will be African American, Hispanic, Asian, and native American (Sue & Sue, 1989). As counselors, we have begun to recognize that our thinking about counseling is changing based on the clients whom we serve. The tools of the past may not work on the culturally different. Counselors now and in the future must be culturally sensitive and culturally aware.

Another important force that brings us to recognize the notion of special populations is the recognition by many that women should have equal rights in our society. Out of the feminist movement has also come a feeling that women have special needs in counseling that require different treatments (Devoe, 1990; Russell, 1986).

In this book, I recommend that the special characteristics of an individual must be taken into account when designing an effective treatment plan. Some counseling techniques will not be acceptable to clients from varying backgrounds. One of the explanations given for the fact that ethnic minorities have under-utilized or failed to benefit from the American mental health delivery system is that we have not developed "culturally responsive forms of treatment" (Sue & Zane, 1987, p. 37). There is significant evidence, however, that culture and special needs affect all aspects of the counseling process, not simply the acceptability of the treatment approach.

Identity with a special population especially affects the relationship between client and counselor. Clients tend to prefer individuals who are similar to them in attitudes, personality, and ethnicity (Atkinson, Poston, Furlong & Mercado, 1989), and counselors also seem to prefer clients who are similar to them. The counselor's ability to be seen as competent and trustworthy may be influenced by gender, race, ethnicity, language, and socioeconomic status. Bonding with the client may be influenced by the counselor's evaluation as to whether the client is cooperative, friendly, and open and whether he or she possesses other culturally defined positive communication behaviors.

Special populations are often stigmatized and deprived of power by the majority cultural group in a society.

What Is a Special Population?

For our purposes, *a special population* is defined as membership in a group that is a minority, is culturally distinct, is stigmatized, is deprived of power, or that has special needs. Special populations include, but are not limited to, ethnic minorities; Viet Nam veterans; the elderly; those from a distinct socioeconomic stratum, such as the homeless; those with serious or chronic illness and pain; prison inmates; gay and lesbian people; children of alcoholics; non-Christians; ex-convicts; and those with physical or mental disabilities (Campbell & Witmer, 1991). This definition is broad. In this way it can include such groups as women who may not be a minority but who are deprived of power and have special counseling needs.

Gaining Knowledge About Special Populations

Counselors may feel overwhelmed when they realize the amount of information that they need to assimilate in order to become socially and culturally fluent. Because it is impossible to do an in-depth study of each special population, some writers despair that counselor training will emphasize the characteristics of special groups at the expense of the counseling basics (Margolis & Rungta, 1986). In contradiction, the opinion that has been expressed in this book—that taking time to see what is special about each client and tailoring the treatment to fit those needs—is considered to be one of counseling's best basics.

A rational approach to an overload of information is to accept that the counselor must be prepared both didactically and attitudinally to deal with special populations, but the counselor must also accept that he or she cannot be prepared for all possible differences. In situations where a client is seen as different, the best counselor position is to become a student again by gaining additional book knowledge and by asking for clients' assistance in becoming more familiar with their backgrounds. Counselor preparation programs should expose the counselor to literature and to practicum and internship experiences where the counselor is involved with different populations. At the minimum, counselors should have studied the culture and history of Asian Americans, African Americans, Hispanic Americans, and native Americans (Sue & Sue, 1989). In addition, the counselor should probably have training in more than one language.

Another approach to this problem has emerged. It has been suggested that counselors should be trained to recognize common features of special populations (Larson, 1982). Campbell and Witmer (1991) have noted nine commonalities that special populations share and that should be investigated by the counselor in understanding and treating the client:

1. All such groups are devalued by society and subtle forms of exclusion and institutional discrimination and oppression exist even in the allocation of health and human services resources.
2. Special populations may be viewed as deviant and abnormal because of their special characteristics.
3. When members of special populations are included, they may be tokens who are not really integrated or influential in the group to which they have been newly accepted.
4. Isolation and limited social support is the result of being a member of a devalued and relatively small group.
5. Members of special populations often have limited financial resources.
6. Discouragement and feelings of helplessness in the face of rejection and failure to accomplish are common.
7. There are limited role models of success in the media and in the client's personal experience.
8. Members of special populations are overobserved. If the client's differences are noticeable, his or her activities are likely to come under more scrutiny because of being highly visible.
9. Members of special populations create subcultures to deal with isolation, rejection, and financial hardships.

The implications of these identified differences for the counselor are as follows:

1. Counselors must educate themselves through specific training.
2. Counselors must sometimes switch to the role of advocate in solving financial and institutional problems.
3. Counselors must be sensitive to nonverbal communication and the use of language that might be offensive to a special group.
4. Counselors must recognize that strategies and techniques useful with the majority population may have to be modified or eliminated.
5. Counselors must become sensitive to differences in emphasis on the role of the family in the client's life.
6. Counselors must recognize that therapy may be unacceptable to some groups and indigenous methods should be explored. An example of this is

that the World Health Organization recommends that Western medical personnel work conjointly with traditional and folk medicine providers.
7. Counselors must recognize the importance of social support and self-help as an important aspect of treatment.

Besides training in specific areas of knowledge about special populations, counselors need to examine their personal and cultural attitudes toward special populations. The counselor must possess or adopt attitudes of empathy (rather than sympathy), tolerance for ambiguity, open-mindedness, and an openness to experience (Corey, Corey & Callanan, 1988). In addition, Sue (1981) asserts that counselors who are skilled in dealing with special populations possess the following attributes:

1. They understand their own value systems and basic assumptions about human behavior and are able to appreciate that the views of others will differ. Counselors may be unaware, for example, how their therapeutic training and views of mental health are based on several strictly Western assumptions. Some of these assumptions are an emphasis on individualism versus duty to family and society, an emphasis on independence and a neglect of client support systems, a focus on changing the individual rather than the system, and a neglect of history and a focus on immediate events (Pedersen, 1987).
2. They understand that special populations have been shaped by social and political forces that may have also been important in shaping their attitudes and values.
3. They understand the world view of the client, are able to share it in some way, and constantly strive to avoid being culturally encapsulated.
4. They are truly eclectic, using skills, methods, and techniques and forming goals that are congruent with the views, values, life-styles, and life experiences of special populations.

Problems with Gaining Knowledge About Special Populations

Until the 1960s, the "myth of sameness" (Smith, 1981) held sway in psychotherapy. This myth affirms that similarity in psychological processes among all people overrides the differences of gender and culture. This attitude has sometimes been called being color-blind. In truth, an individual can be described as part of a particular culture or group, as similar to all human beings, and as unique. When we think of clients only in terms of their membership in a culture or group, we tend to stereotype them. When we see them only as members of the human race, we ignore the special characteristics of their cultural background. When we see them only in their uniqueness, we may fail to help them understand their relationship to humanity and to their cultural heritage.

Because most people do not see the whole person, individuals from special populations often feel misunderstood in their interactions with counselors and with the world at large. For example, Baptiste (1987) has noted that gays who seek counseling are almost always seen as wanting to change their sexual orientation.

This is where a little knowledge about a special population can be a dangerous thing. As Stephen Weinrach (1990) laments, "I am clearly not Jewish enough for some Jews, yet for some gentiles, my just being Jewish is all that matters. In the final analysis, I am a Jew, and I'd have it no other way, even if it kills me" (p. 549). The problem of stereotyping based on cultural membership has stirred some controversy in the field of counselor education and supervision (cf., Lloyd, 1987; Parker, 1987; Pedersen, 1988). One side suggests that counseling is more effective without the generalized knowledge that can easily stereotype members of a cultural group. The other finds this notion to be extreme and promotes the idea that stereotyping is a stage of knowledge that, through time, allows viewpoints to become more sophisticated. Only then can the counselor learn to see the client as both a unique person and as having a cultural identity.

Suggestions for Enhancing the Client/Counselor Relationship with Clients from Special Populations

Credibility

Sue and Zane (1987) identify two important issues that can serve to enhance the client/counselor relationship when dealing with the culturally different client. In many ways these suggestions also apply to individuals from other special populations. *Credibility* is a term that describes the perception of the counselor by the client as competent, expert, and trustworthy. Although knowledge of the client's culture lends credibility to a counselor who is dealing with someone from a different background, some other factors play an important part. Sue and Zane (1987) distinguish between *ascribed* and *achieved credibility*. Ascribed credibility is that status given to the counselor by the client that is often due to sex, age, experience, and similarity of life experiences and attitudes. For example, in some cultures, an older person is ascribed more credibility than a younger person.

Achieved credibility refers to the counselor's skills and demonstrated abilities. If the counselor cannot be ascribed much credibility with an individual from a special population, he or she may be able to achieve it over time. For example, a therapist who is *not* recovering from alcohol or substance abuse will be ascribed very little credibility by clients in treatment programs for these problems. If the counselor possesses special knowledge and skills, however, it may be possible to achieve some measure of acceptance among substance abusers. According to Sue and Zane, the counselor can achieve credibility by

- Conceptualizing problems in a way that is congruent with the client's beliefs and values. For example, it has been suggested that framing a problem as medical, rather than psychological, is more acceptable to an Hispanic client (Meadow, 1982). It has also been suggested that African American clients prefer educational and practical strategies for dealing with problems to methods that focus only on feelings (Parker, 1988).
- Conceptualizing goals of treatment in a way that is acceptable and understandable to the client.
- Identifying client activities that are compatible with one's cultural back-

ground or life experiences. For example, asking an Asian woman to become more assertive with her father could conceivably weaken the therapist's credibility since that might be unthinkable to the client; whereas asking a priest to mediate a family problem with a Catholic family would lend credibility.

Giving

Giving is a term coined by Sue and Zane. It means providing the client with some immediate experience of relief due to treatment. In some ways this approach is similar to crisis intervention, although it does not mean that therapy must necessarily be short term. According to the authors, besides increasing credibility, giving may prevent early termination and decrease scepticism about Western forms of treatment by those who are culturally different.

CHAPTER SUMMARY AND CONCLUSIONS

This chapter addressed three challenges that face clients in their attempts to establish a workable client/counselor relationship: transference, countertransference, and client/counselor difference in culture and background. Beyond the counseling relationship, these issues also influence the effectiveness of counseling techniques.

Although psychoanalytic practitioners encourage the development of transference reactions in their patients, modern therapists do not see the resolution of transference as an inevitable part of every counseling relationship. Because it sometimes involves powerful feelings, every therapist should be prepared to help clients resolve transference issues when they do arise. The most common reactions include hostility, dependency, and strong affection. The technique of interpretation is the primary therapeutic tool to be used; however, client issues must be fully explored. Although countertransference is not a method or technique to aid the client, countertransference feelings can disrupt the client/counselor relationship. It is the job of the therapist to keep a watch on his or her own feelings to determine if they are strong enough to interfere with the client's goals. There are also occasions when authentic expression of counselor feelings can be helpful to the client.

Cultural and other differences between client and counselor have become highlighted in recent years. In this chapter, I have tied the importance of considering the needs of special populations with an overriding theme in the book—that counseling should be tailored to the client. When viewed from this perspective, the counselor must strive to understand the client fully in order to gain special knowledge and to be open in one's attitudes. In addition, there are many similarities among persons stigmatized or disempowered by society, and the counselor's job is to be open to completely altering strategies to help clients achieve their unique goals.

FURTHER READINGS

Gelso, C. J., & Carter, J. A. (1985). The relationship in counseling and psychotherapy: Components, consequences and theoretical antecedents. *The Counseling Psychologist, 13,* 155–243. Gelso and Carter's article is a landmark since it translates the notion of transference into terms more acceptable to nonanalytic therapists. It places transference in its theoretical and historical context but also is very practical in its suggestions for practitioners.

Larson, P. C. (1982). Counseling special populations. *Professional Psychology, 13,* 843–858. This article gives an overview of the recommendations from the literature for successful counseling with members of special populations from ethnic minorities to sexual orientation and disability. The article argues that counselors who are effective with these populations must believe in the positive value of diversity, possess special training, and have a capacity for dialectical thinking.

Ritchie, M. H. (1986). Counseling the involuntary client. *Journal of Counseling and Development, 64,* 516–518. Martin Ritchie's article describes a number of tactics to test the voluntariness of therapy and to persuade clients to work despite the demands of an institution, court, etc. Ritchie couches his arguments in an ethical framework that helps counselors think about their duties and responsibilities to the growing population of clients who have been forced into therapy.

REFERENCES

Atkinson, D. R., Poston, W. C., Furlong, M. J., & Mercado (1989). Ethnic group preferences for counselor characteristics. *Journal of Counseling Psychology, 36,* 68–72.

Baptiste, D. A. (1987). Psychotherapy with gay/lesbian couples and their children in "stepfamilies": A challenge for marriage and family therapists. *Journal of Homosexuality, 3,* 223–238.

Basch, M. F. (1980). *Doing psychotherapy.* New York: Basic Books.

Beukenkamp, C. A. (1956). Beyond transference behavior. *American Journal of Psychotherapy, 10,* 467–470.

Campbell, J., & Witmer, J. M. (1991). Working with special populations: Guidelines for treatment and counselor education. Manuscript submitted for publication.

Cavanagh, M. E. (1982). *The counseling experience.* Monterey, CA: Brooks/Cole.

Corey, G., Corey, M. S., & Callanan, P. (1988). *Issues and ethics in the helping professions* (3rd ed.). Monterey, CA: Brooks/Cole.

Devoe, D. (1990). Feminist and nonsexist counseling: Implications for the male counselor. *Journal of Counseling and Development, 69,* 33–36.

Dyer, W. & Vriend, J. (1973). Counseling the reluctant client. *Journal of Counseling Psychology, 20,* 240–246.

Ellis, A. (1985). *Overcoming resistance: Rational-emotive therapy with difficult clients.* New York: Springer.

Fine, R. (1975). *Psychoanalytic psychology.* New York: Jason Aronson.

Fremont, S., & Anderson, W. P. (1986). What client behaviors make counselors angry?: An exploratory study. *Journal of Counseling and Development, 65,* 67–70.

Gelso, C. J., & Carter, J. A. (1985). The relationship in counseling and psychotherapy: Components, consequences and theoretical antecedents. *The Counseling Psychologist, 13,* 155–243.

Kell, B. L., & Mueller, W. J. (1966). *Impact and change: A study of counseling relationships.* Englewood Cliffs, NJ: Prentice-Hall.

Larson, P. C. (1982). Counseling special populations. *Professional Psychology, 13*, 843–858.

Lazarus, A. A. (1981). *The practice of multimodal therapy.* New York: McGraw-Hill.

Lazarus, A. A. (1986). Multimodal therapy. In J. C. Norcross (Ed.), *Handbook of eclectic psychotherapy* (pp. 65–93). New York: Brunner/Mazel.

Lloyd, A. P. (1987). Multicultural counseling: Does it belong in a counselor education program? *Counselor Education and Supervision, 26*, 173–175.

Malan, D. (1976). *The frontier of brief psychotherapy.* New York: Plenum Press.

Margolis, R. L., & Rungta, S. A. (1986). Training counselors for work with special populations: A second look. *Journal of Counseling and Development, 64*, 642–644.

Meadow, A. (1982). Psychopathology, psychotherapy and the Mexican-American patient. In E. E. Jones and S. J. Korchin (Eds.), *Minority mental health* (pp. 331–362). New York: Praeger.

Murray, E. J. (1986). Possibilities and promises of eclecticism. In John C. Norcross (Ed.), *Handbook of eclectic psychotherapy* (pp. 398–415). New York: Brunner/Mazel.

Paolino, T. J. (1981). *Psychoanalytic psychotherapy: Theory, technique, therapeutic relationship and treatability.* New York: Brunner/Mazel.

Parker, W. M. (1987). Flexibility: A primer for multicultural counseling. *Counselor Education and Supervision, 26*, 176–180.

Parker, W. M. (1988). Becoming an effective multicultural counselor. *Journal of Counseling and Development, 67*, 93.

Pedersen, P. B. (1987). Ten frequent assumptions of cultural bias in counseling. *Journal of Multicultural Counseling and Development, 14*, 16–24.

Pedersen, P. B. (1988). *A handbook for developing multicultural awareness.* Washington, DC: American Association for Counseling and Development.

Pedersen, P. B. & Pedersen, A. (1989). The cultural grid: A complicated and dynamic approach to multicultural counseling. *Counseling Psychology Quarterly, 2*, 133–141.

Ritchie, M. H. (1986). Counseling the involuntary client. *Journal of Counseling and Development, 64*, 516–518.

Rogers, C. R. (1957). The necessary and sufficient conditions of therapeutic personality change. *Journal of Consulting Psychology, 21*, 95–103.

Russell, M. N. (1986). Teaching feminist counseling skills: An evaluation. *Counselor Education and Supervision, 25*, 320–331.

Singer, E. (1970). *Key concepts in psychotherapy* (2nd ed.). New York: Basic Books.

Smith, E. M. J. (1985). Ethnic minorities: Life stress, social support and mental health issues. *The Counseling Psychologist, 13*, 537–579.

Smith, E. J. (1981). Cultural and historical perspectives in counseling blacks. In D. W. Sue (Ed.), *Counseling the culturally different.* New York: Wiley.

Strupp, H. H., & Binder, J. L. (1984). *Psychotherapy in a new key: A guide to time-limited therapy.* New York: Basic Books.

Sue, D., & Sue, D. M. (1989). Multicultural counseling. *Counseling and Human Development, 22*, 1–21.

Sue, D. W. (1981). *Counseling the culturally different: Theory and Practice.* New York: Wiley.

Sue, S. & Zane, N. (1987). The role of culture and cultural techniques in psychotherapy. *American Psychologist, 42*, 37–45.

Sullivan, H. S. (1954). *The psychiatric interview.* New York: Norton.

Wachtel, P. L. (1977). *Psychoanalysis and behavior therapy: Toward integration.* New York: Basic Books.

Watkins, C. E., Jr. (1986). Transference phenomena in the counseling situation. In W. P. Anderson (Ed.), *Innovative counseling: A handbook of readings.* Alexandria, VA: American Association of Counseling and Development.

Weiner, M. F. (1979). *Therapist disclosure: The use of self in psychotherapy.* Boston, MA: Butterworth Press.

Weinrach, S. G. (1990). A psychosocial look at the Jewish dilemma. *Journal of Counseling and Development, 68*, 548–550.

Wolberg, B. J. (1973). *Dictionary of behavioral science.* New York: Van Nostrand Reinhold.

Wolberg, L. R. (1954). *The technique of psychotherapy.* New York: Grune & Stratton.

Wolf, A. (1950). The psychoanalysis of groups. *American Journal of Psychotherapy, 4*, 525–558.

Yalom, I. (1985). *Theory and practice of group psychotherapy.* New York: Basic Books.

CHAPTER FOUR

Assessment

KEY CONCEPTS

▼ *Assessment aids in understanding the causes of client problems, in gauging suicide risk and risk of violence, in determining the client's strengths and coping skills, and in setting the stage for treatment planning by uncovering core issues.*

▼ *Observation is an informal means of assessing the client's problems and involves awareness of client speech, grooming, posture, and other behaviors as well as the counselor's emotional reaction to the client.*

▼ *Questions are probes that can be used to investigate and explore problems or to challenge and influence the client.*

▼ *The genogram is an example of an assessment method used to generate information about the client's family history, relationships, and current composition.*

▼ *Diagnosis using the DSM-III-R is a well-accepted method of summarizing assessment results about the client. Its drawbacks include its basis as a mental illness model and the negative effects of labeling.*

▼ *One system for drawing together assessment results is the BASIC ID model of Lazarus. This model uses a behavioral/theoretical base to explain client symptoms but assesses a wide range of client excesses and deficits in the behavioral, emotional, physical, cognitive, interpersonal, and biological realms.*

▼ *The REPLAN system advanced in this book focuses on the assessment of client problems and the client's reaction to them. The REPLAN worksheet is divided into four parts: the client's statement of the problem; a biopsychosocial, or mental health, assessment; a summary of assessment hypotheses made by the therapist; and the mutually agreed-upon treatment goals.*

INTRODUCTION

Definitions

Assessment is a term that describes the activity of gathering information about clients and their problems. It is a process that begins at the first contact; however, as Figure 4.1 depicts, it tends to become the central focus after the client/counselor relationship has become rooted. Assessment includes diverse counselor activities, such as observation and evaluation of the client, asking questions,

FIGURE 4.1
Stages of the counseling relationship.

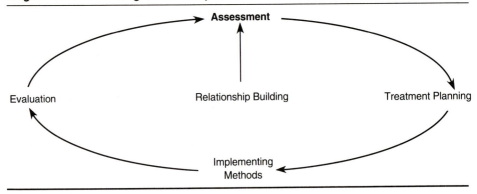

reading client journals and writings, and other informal methods of gathering background history and gauging current functioning.

Testing is a category of assessment. It is the practice of administering standardized tests of achievement, personality, and special abilities, such as intelligence. Testing may also mean using projective tests, such as the Thematic Apperception Test or the Rorschach Test, that involve presenting an ambiguous stimulus to the client and recording and coding responses. Space does not allow for an adequate treatment of the topic of testing. The interested reader is referred to three very practical texts: *Appraisal Procedures for Counselors and Helping Professionals* by Robert J. Drummond (1988), *Handbook of Psychological Assessment* by Gary Groth-Marnat (1988), and *Assessment of Children* by Jerome Sattler (1988).

Diagnosis is a separate and distinct activity from assessment. It is the art and science of classifying individuals into categories, depending on the results of testing, informal assessment, and clinical data. Assessment does not necessarily lead to diagnosis. It is possible to gather information about a client and the client's problems without labeling the person.

Although diagnosis and testing have become controversial both in the schools and in therapy, all clinicians use some assessment procedures. They record data about the client, and out of this, they make hypotheses, assumptions, and predictions and form treatment plans. The most controversial issues with regard to assessment involve the unethical use of test data and the use of pejorative diagnostic labels.

Goals and Purposes of Assessment

For the counselor, the main purpose of assessment is to plan differential treatments for clients. If this purpose is not achieved, assessment is both unethical and useless. Some standard reasons for using tests and other assessment methods are discussed in the following paragraphs.

Assessment Helps to Identify the Causes of Problems

Once causes of problems are pointed out, therapy can then be aimed at eliminating or reducing the causes of problems. For example, a client may find out through self-monitoring that stressful days at the office are associated with excessive smoking and coffee drinking. Hypothetically, the client might reduce intake of these substances and determine if they are adding to the stress. This example is instructive since it shows the reciprocal nature of causes. A person under stress might be inclined to drink more coffee and smoke more cigarettes which in itself leads to more stress and anxiety. Helping the client reduce stress might lead to less abuse of these substances. Assessing substance use and the amount of stress would help the client to understand the connection between the two causes of stress.

Unfortunately many problems presented by clients do not benefit from delving into causes, especially if these causes are in the distant past. Many individuals have a great deal of insight into the causes of their problems but still can not shake them. Very often the problem behavior has become "functionally autonomous," or disconnected from the original cause. For example, a client who was poor when he was young became very fixed on making and saving money. Later, when he was quite well-to-do, he could not free himself of his desire to amass more and more.

Assessment Helps to Predict Future Client Behavior

Among those behaviors that the therapist is most interested in predicting are suicidal intent, potential for violence, and the client's likelihood of staying in treatment. In addition, assessment procedures, including observation and history taking, can help predict client/counselor compatibility, the client's level of commitment to counseling, and the client's probable behavior toward the counselor. For example, an understanding of a Vietnamese client would need to include a thorough grasp of cultural and familial patterns since these would affect the client's orientation toward authority.

Assessment Helps the Client Understand Problems

Not only can assessment help the client understand problems more fully, it can reveal the relationship of the presenting complaint to other problem areas. For instance, when a client complains that his love relationship is undergoing upheaval due to his inability to achieve intimacy, the therapist would find it useful, if not essential, to assess the quality of his other relationships and to examine commonalities.

Assessment Provides Valuable Historical Data

It is often the case that clients cling to outmoded and ineffective coping strategies learned in adolescence or another life period. The historical data gathered through assessment reveals important patterns in client behavior.

Assessment Surveys Client Strengths

Besides assessing client problems, assessment procedures can be aimed at finding client skills, positive attributes, and psychological fortitude, which enhances self-esteem. Several personality tests, such as the Personal Orientation Inventory, the California Psychological Inventory, and the Myers-Briggs Type Indicator, to name a few, contain a good balance of positive indicators along with more pathological or deficit data about the client.

Assessment Makes Clients Cognizant of Problems Outside of Current Awareness

It is very difficult to get clients to own problems identified only by the therapist. Yet, through the assessment process, the client may be asked to examine troubling issues that have been consciously or unconsciously set aside. Take, for example, the college student who comes to therapy at the behest of his girlfriend after he had slapped her at a fraternity party. Assessment of the client's drinking behavior points to alcohol dependence. Although the client may be resistant, the assessment process can be a catalyst that forces the client into recovery or at least into the first stages of an awareness of the problem. Awareness of one's discomfort provides the impetus for the change process to begin. Assessment is one way of increasing emotional arousal and thereby stimulating change.

Assessment Makes the Therapist Aware of Undivulged Problems

Here, it is largely the therapist who benefits from the use of assessment procedures. Frequently beginning therapists fail to assess suicidal information and substance abuse if they see no overt signs in the interview. Assessment procedures can help reassure the therapist that the therapy is aimed at crucial issues. One major reason for using formalized or structured assessment and testing is to back up the interview data: to ask the question, "Have I missed signs of suicide, violence, substance abuse, or psychosis?"

SELECTED ASSESSMENT METHODS EXPLAINED

Observation

Yogi Berra once said, "You can observe a lot just by watching." His statement underlines the fact that observation has become something of a lost art. It also suggests that to observe well, conscious effort is required. The art of observation is rarely practiced nor are the results of observation taken seriously enough. Recently, a physician watching a national figure on television phoned in and encouraged the individual to seek medical help for cardiac problems. Unfortunately, the person died before seeking treatment. A trained and practiced observer can generate hypotheses about clients based on experience and careful attention. For example, the counselor can detect depression and anxiety in the faces of clients and infer socioeconomic status from clothing and appearance. Often these guesses are wrong. Still these observations are hypotheses that should be entered into the therapist's data bank along with the results of formal assessment.

The fictional detective Sherlock Holmes relied on inferences (which he called deductions) based on his keen observations. In *The Sign of the Four* (Conan Doyle, 1929), Holmes discusses with Watson the two different processes involved in his art, observation and deduction (pp. 7–8):

> Observation shows me that you have been to the Wigmore Street Post Office this morning but deduction tells me that when there you dispatched a telegram . . . Observation tells me that you have a reddish mold adhering to your instep. Just opposite to the Wigmore Street Office they have taken up the pavement and thrown up bare earth which lies in such a way that it is difficult to avoid treading upon it . . . the earth there is of this particular reddish tint which is found, so far as I know, nowhere else in the neighborhood. So much for observation, the next is deduction . . . Why of course I know that you had not written a letter since I sat opposite you all morning. What could you go into a post office for but to send a wire? Eliminate all other factors and what remains is the truth.

Like Holmes, Sigmund Freud was aware of the importance of observation and deduction. Freud believed that evidence of unconscious motivation was available in the everyday activities of clients, including unconscious movements and slips of the tongue (parapraxes). For example, Freud described clients with marriage problems who twisted their wedding rings throughout the session. From these unconscious acts, underlying effects can be deduced.

In this age, we are a little less inclined to take at face value the deductions of the therapist without verifying them with the client. In the example of the wedding ring above, there are several possible reasons for this behavior. Therapist hypotheses are guesses, not deductions. Instead of arriving at a single conclusion, the assessment process of observation involves documenting one's observations and forming a list of hypotheses about the client that, when linked to other information, may show a general pattern or theme. The next paragraphs list some aspects of appearance and behavior that are sometimes obtained via observation by the clinician.

What to Observe

Speech

Note all aspects of a client's speaking voice. Does the client's voice whine or soothe? Is the client's tone slow and monotonous or excessively labile? Does the client have an accent of any kind? Is the client's speech hurried or forced? Does the client have a speech impediment of any kind? Does the client speak without listening?

Client's Clothing

Does the client wear expensive, stylish, well-coordinated, seductive, old, or out-moded clothing? Is there anything odd or unusual about it? Does the client reflect a particular style (artistic, conservative, etc.)? Is clothing appropriate to the weather (several layers on a hot day), and is it appropriate to the occasion? Does the client wear a little jewelry or a great deal? Does the client wear appropriate amounts of makeup? Does the client wear glasses or a hearing aid?

Grooming

Is the client clean? Does the client exhibit body odor and a general disregard for personal hygiene? Even if the client shows concern for cleanliness, is there a disorganized appearance to the hair and clothing suggesting disorderliness, depression, or lack of social awareness?

Posture, Build, and Gait

What is the client's posture in the session? What is the position of the shoulders and head? Does the client sit in a rigid or a slouched position or with head in hands? Does it reflect the present emotional state, or is the client's posture indicative of a more long-term state of anxiety, tension, or depression?

Build refers to the body habitus. Is the client physically attractive? Is the client obese, muscular, or thin? Are there any unusual physical characteristics, such as excessive acne, physical disabilities, or prostheses?

Gait means the person's manner of walking. Does the client's manner of walking reflect an emotional state, such as depression or anxiety? Is the client tentative and cautious in finding a seat? Does the client's walk seem to indicate confidence or low self-esteem?

Facial Expressions

Facial expressions include movements of the eyes, lips, forehead, and mouth. Shakespeare wrote that "the eyes are the windows of the soul." Note if the client maintains direct eye contact or avoids it. Do the eyes fill with tears? Does the client smile or laugh during the session? Is the brow wrinkled?

Other Bodily Movements

Frequently clients are anxious during therapy sessions and may smoke excessively. Others twist tissue and still others tap restlessly with fingers or toes or legs, or they exhibit tics of one sort or another. One important way in which people express themselves is through their hand movements. Fritz Perls, the founder of Gestalt therapy, was fond of making clients aware that their hand movements expressed their general condition (Perls, 1959, p. 83).

General Appearance

In writing an assessment of the client, it is sometimes useful to note initial holistic impressions, which may become less noticeable as therapy progresses. For example, "The client appeared much older than his stated age," "The client appeared to be very precise, neat and carefully considered all of his statements," "I had the feeling that the client was a super salesman." Holistic thinking helps the counselor become aware of personal feelings evoked in the interaction as well. This topic is considered in the next section.

Feelings of the Counselor

Basing his observations on Harry Stack Sullivan's (1947) theories, Timothy Leary (1957) hypothesized that we react automatically and unconsciously to the communications of others. Our reaction in turn triggers their next response. We tend to instinctively react in a positive, friendly manner to individuals whom we find attractive. They, in turn, become open and friendly toward us and the cycle continues. These "interpersonal reflexes" (Shannon & Guerney, 1973) occur outside of awareness and are rarely discussed. Since these reflexes are part of the client's interpersonal behavior, it is incumbent on the therapist to become aware of their effect on the therapist's feelings and behavior. The counselor's job is not to meet the social expectations of the client and fall into those typical patterns. The therapist must be willing to examine the effects of the client's reflexes on his or her feelings and behavior and to explore them with the client.

In his book, *The Silent Language of Psychotherapy,* Ernst Beier (1966) suggests that the feelings of the therapist are the instruments that can help the clinician detect the effect the client has on other people. If the clinician becomes annoyed, is it possible that most of the client's social contacts have the same feeling? What would motivate the client to push people away? Is the client aware of his or her effect on others?

Questioning

Gladding (1992) describes two types of interviews: an information-oriented one and a relationship-oriented type. I have always found that using the initial interview to question the client is relatively unproductive. This can be saved for the end of the session when rapport is strong and questions are met with greater openness. Arnold Lazarus tends to used the first session to understand the client's concerns, begin some initial tasks, and sends the client home with a lengthy questionnaire to fill out.

Asking too many questions was criticized in chapter 2 as being apt to strain the relationship between client and therapist. On the other hand, introductory questions are helpful in signaling the transition to the assessment phase of counseling once a relationship seems to have been initiated. Listed below are some common questions asked by therapists early in the assessment phase in order to begin focusing on problems. The last two questions in the list are behaviorally oriented questions suggested by Lazarus (1981).

> "How can I help you?"
> "Where would you like to begin?"
> "What prompted you to make today's appointment?"
> "Has something happened in the last few days or weeks that persuaded you that help was needed?"
> "What is it that you want to stop doing or do less of?"
> "What is it that you want to begin or do more of?"

Questioning is an important part of the assessment process since answers to direct and indirect questions are part and parcel of taking personal and sexual histories, conducting genograms, and allowing the client to elaborate his or her construction of the problem.

Tomm's Model of Therapeutic Questions

Beyond these openings, a counselor's use of questions can become more sophisticated than simple requests for information or invitations for self-disclosure. Tomm (1987a, 1987b) has proposed a general model that classifies questions based on four dimensions of therapist intent: investigative, exploratory, corrective, or facilitative.

Investigative Intent.   Questions with investigative intent are *linear questions* that ask who, what, where, and when. A common question along these lines would be, "How did you feel when she said she was not free on Saturday night?" It implies a cause and effect based on a linear model. These kinds of questions are consistent with a functional analysis of the kind behaviorists often employ. Such probing questions can elicit information quickly but may seem invasive and judgmental to the client.

Exploratory Intent.   The intent of *circular questions* is to explore. Like linear questions, they seek information—information about recurrent interpersonal events. Such questions assume a circular model of causality, meaning that events reciprocally influence and cause each other. Coyne's (1976) theory, for example, recognized that depressed individuals alienated people with their depression and that this alienation made them feel worse. Using our example from above, a circular question might be, "When you became silent and sad after your girlfriend said she needed to spend some time alone, what effect do you think this had on her?"

Circular questions may also ask about differences between events to further clarify connections. For example, "What is the difference between this relationship and previous ones?" or, "How is this fight that you had with your girlfriend different from your fight with your mother last week?"

Corrective Intent.   A *strategic question* is a question with corrective intent. Strategic questions are attempts to stop the client's behavior and persuade him or her to change in a particular way. For example, the client says, "I want to quit drinking." The therapist says, "What stops you from quitting?" The therapist is trying to influence the client toward a particular course of action. Such questions are often called confrontations or leading questions.

Facilitative Intent.   Finally, Tomm identifies questions which he calls *reflexive questions*. These questions assume both a circular model of causality and yet are attempts to influence the client. It is hoped that these questions will trigger the client to find his or her own solutions. Unlike exploratory questions, the intent is not to orient the therapist to the client's world but to push the client to dig deeper. For example, a therapist might say, "If you continue your drinking, what do you expect will be the effect on your relationship with Jane?"

Examples of four question types are presented in the following table:

Linear question   What sorts of things cause you to experience stress?

Circular question	When you are feeling this kind of stress, how do people react to you?
Strategic question	Client: I can't stand up to my boss. Counselor: Don't you mean, 'I won't stand up to my boss'?
Reflexive question	Do you think your relationship with your mother would be different if you believed she could never really change?

Questions used in therapy overlap between categories but the value of Tomm's model is that it recognizes that questions have underlying assumptions. They reflect the counselor's belief system about the causes of problems (linear versus circular) and produce different results (gathering information or orienting versus influencing).

Genograms

Description

The *genogram* is a drawing of the client's family tree. The genogram is a specific format that helps to describe family history, functioning, and relationships graphically. Murray Bowen, a family therapy pioneer (1978, 1980) popularized the use of the genogram. His approach to therapy looked at familial influences spanning at least three generations. He used the genogram as a vehicle to hypothesize what sorts of problems might occur in a family based on their histories (J. Wright, personal communication, April 1990). This multigenerational viewpoint yielded such a vast quantity of data that a simple organizational tool was needed to represent the relationships between several individuals.

There is no quantification system that requires the therapist to use scoring methods outside of the session nor is there any standard way to draw genograms. McGoldrick and Gerson (1985) have developed an approach that has become something of a standard in family therapy. The approach in this book is slightly different from theirs and more suited to an eclectic approach. In the next few pages genogram symbols will be described. It is suggested that the reader draw several genograms to become familiar with the method.

What to Look For in a Genogram

It is recommended that the genogram be used to answer specific questions about an individual, couple, or family system. For example, Bowen was interested in how the family related emotionally and the degree of differentiation or individuality that the family allowed its members. A genogram might also be used in order to find family influences on career choice (Dickson & Parmerlee, 1980; Okiishi, 1987), alcoholism, or abuse. Some of the possible reasons for using a genogram include the following:

1. To represent the strengths and weaknesses in relationships between family members
2. To understand the present household composition and the relationships among the client's household, previous marriages and past generations

3. To discover the presence of family disturbances that might be affecting the client, including alcoholism, abuse, divorces, suicides, schisms and skews in marital relationships, mental illness in the family, etc.
4. To uncover sex-role and other family expectations on the client
5. To assess economic and emotional support resources for the client
6. To identify repeated patterns in the client's relationships
7. To determine the effects of birth order and sibling rivalry on the client
8. To make the client and counselor aware of family attitudes concerning health and illness
9. To identify extrafamilial sources of support
10. To identify cultural and ethnic influences on the client
11. To trace family patterns of certain preferences, values, and behaviors, such as legal problems, sexual values, obesity, and job problems
12. To identify problem relationships, competitive and triangulated individuals (persons who play a divisive or other key role in a relationship between two others)
13. To document historical traumas, such as suicides, deaths, abuse, and losses of pregnancies, whose effects might surface much later

Methods for Using Genograms

Using the symbols in Figure 4.2, the counselor draws the client's genogram according to the skeletal form in Figure 4.3. Figure 4.4 is an example of a completed genogram, which was drawn using the skeletal form. A pencil is preferred since erasures and additions are made throughout the session. Many therapists use large pieces of newsprint so that they can include more information. One method is to draw the initial skeleton on legal size paper and then make three or four photocopies. With each copy, the counselor may make notes on a different aspect of the client's functioning. A drawback is that the session must be interrupted while copies are made.

Once the skeletal genogram is drawn, the therapist selects one or more questions to be answered. Using one of the copies of the completed skeleton, the therapist accumulates additional data from the client about family members portrayed in the genogram. Let us suppose the genogram is being used to ask, "Does the client have a family history that predisposes him or her to alcohol problems?" The drinking patterns of the family members, including those members who might have died of alcohol-related accidents or illnesses, can be documented next to their symbols on the genogram. This can be a powerful method for increasing the client's cognitive and emotional awareness of the problem.

Another method developed by Flannagan (personal communication, September 26, 1989) is to draw the skeletal genogram and overlay it with plastic transparencies. Each transparency holds a different set of information about the client, such as occupations of family members, most influential family members, sexual history, or substance abuse. Using two or more overlays, one could ask the question, "What is the effect of influential family members on career choice?" or, "What is the effect of family sexual values and history on the client's current behavior?" Transparencies can be photocopied for record-keeping purposes, then erased and reused.

FIGURE 4.2
Genogram symbols.

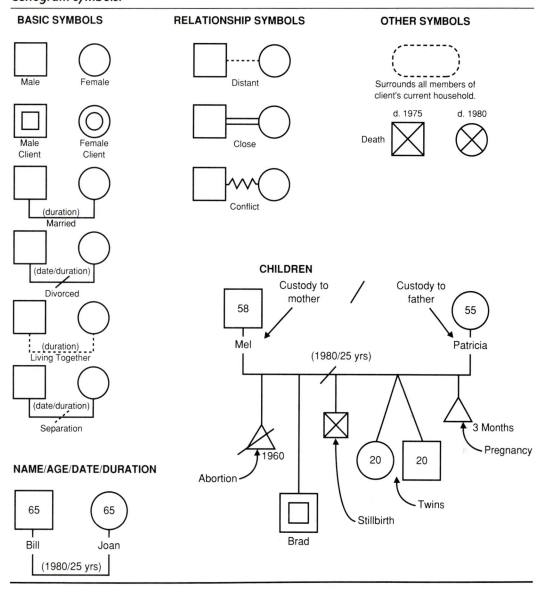

Following the period of questioning and recording, the client and counselor immediately discuss the findings of the genogram to determine if any patterns or situations need to be added to the client's problem list and to identify goals for upcoming therapy sessions. In future sessions, it may be important to update the genogram, as changes may occur in the client's family. Changes in the family can have wide-ranging impacts on other relationships and arenas of client functioning.

FIGURE 4.3
Genogram skeleton.

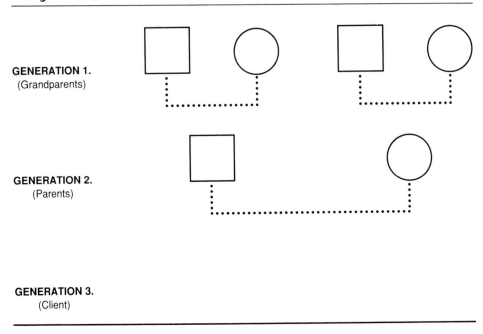

GENERATION 1.
(Grandparents)

GENERATION 2.
(Parents)

GENERATION 3.
(Client)

SYSTEMS FOR SUMMARIZING ASSESSMENT DATA

In this section, three ways of organizing collected data will be examined. The first is the American Psychiatric Association's system for classification of mental disorders, the *Diagnostic and Statistical Manual, Third Edition, Revised (DSM-III-R)*. The second is the BASIC ID from multimodal therapy, which was alluded to earlier. The third is the REPLAN system, which is advanced in this book as an eclectic approach that can be modified to suit the theoretical leanings of the practitioner.

Use of Diagnosis and *DSM-III-R*

When the issue of diagnosis arises, the only classification system for mental disorders currently under consideration is the *Diagnostic and Statistical Manual (DSM-III-R)* of the American Psychiatric Association. Table 4.1 is an abbreviated version of the major categories of *DSM-III-R*. It is widely used because its categories follow a disease model that insurance companies can easily comprehend. It is also easily translated into categories of the *International Classification of Diseases (ICD-9)*, which are recognized by medical institutions. Most insurance companies require a *DSM-III-R* diagnosis before paying for mental health treatment.

DSM-III-R and its immediate predecessor, *DSM-III,* are considered to have more reliable diagnostic categories than earlier versions of this manual. It is also

FIGURE 4.4
Example of a genogram.

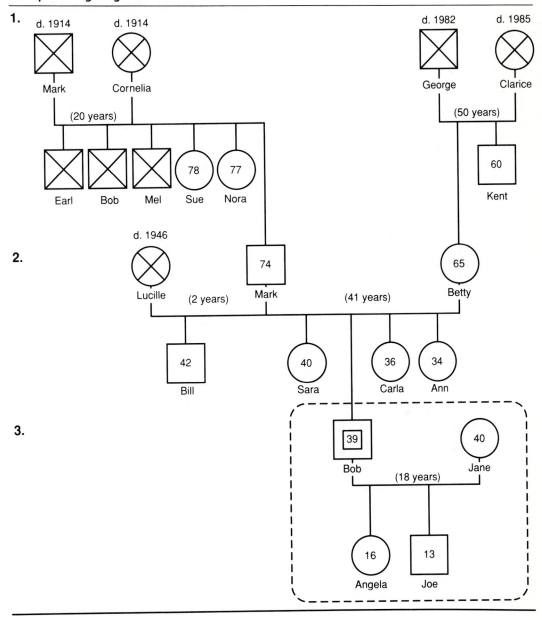

TABLE 4.1 (pp. 96–101)
DSM-III-R *classification: Axes I and II categories and codes.*

All official *DSM-III-R* codes are included in *ICD-9-CM*. Codes followed by a * are used for more than the *DSM-III-R* diagnosis of subtype in order to maintain compatibility with *ICD-9-CM*.

A long dash following a diagnostic term indicates the need for a fifth digit subtype or other qualifying term.

The term *specify* following the name of some diagnostic categories indicates qualifying terms that clinicians may wish to add in parentheses after the name of the disorder.

NOS = Not Otherwise Specified

The current severity of a disorder may be specified after the diagnosis as

	currently
mild	meets
moderate	diagnostic
severe	criteria

in partial remission (or residual state)
in complete remission

DISORDERS USUALLY FIRST EVIDENT IN INFANCY, CHILDHOOD, OR ADOLESCENCE

DEVELOPMENTAL DISORDERS
Note: These are coded on Axis II.

Mental Retardation

317.00	Mild mental retardation
318.00	Moderate mental retardation
318.10	Severe mental retardation
318.20	Profound mental retardation
319.00	Unspecified mental retardation

Pervasive Developmental Disorders

299.00	Autistic disorder
	Specify if childhood disorder
299.80	Pervasive developmental disorder NOS

Specific Developmental Disorders

Academic skills disorders

315.10	Developmental arithmetic disorder
315.80	Developmental expressive writing disorder
315.00	Developmental reading disorder

Language and speech disorders

315.39	Developmental articulation disorder
315.31*	Developmental expressive language disorder
315.31*	Developmental receptive language disorder

Motor skills disorders

315.40	Developmental coordination disorder
315.90*	Specific developmental disorder NOS

Other Developmental Disorders

315.90*	Developmental disorder NOS

TABLE 4.1
(continued)

Disruptive Behavior Disorders

314.01	Attention-deficit hyperactivity disorder
	Conduct disorders
312.20	group type
312.00	solitary aggressive type
312.90	undifferentiated type
313.81	Oppositional defiant disorder

Anxiety Disorders of Childhood or Adolescence

309.21	Separation anxiety disorder
313.21	Avoidant disorder of childhood or adolescence
313.00	Overanxious disorder

Eating Disorders

307.10	Anorexia nervosa
307.51	Bulimia nervosa
307.52	Pica
307.53	Rumination disorder of infancy
307.50	Eating disorder NOS

Gender Identity Disorders

302.60	Gender identity disorder of childhood
302.50	Transsexualism
	Specify sexual history: asexual, homosexual, heterosexual, unspecified
302.85*	Gender identity disorder of adolescence or adulthood, non-transsexual type
	Specify sexual history: asexual, homosexual, heterosexual, unspecified
302.85*	Gender identity disorder NOS

Tic Disorders

307.23	Tourette's disorder
307.22	Chronic motor or vocal tic disorder
307.21	Transient tic disorder
	Specify single episode or recurrent
307.20	Tic disorder NOS

Elimination Disorders

307.70	Functional encopresis
	Specify primary or secondary type
307.60	Functional enuresis
	Specify primary or secondary type
	Specify nocturnal only, diurnal only, nocturnal and diurnal

Speech Disorders Not Elsewhere Classified

307.00*	Cluttering
307.00*	Stuttering

Other Disorders of Infancy, Childhood, or Adolescence

313.23	Elective mutism
313.82	Identity disorder
313.89	Reactive attachment disorder of infancy or early childhood

TABLE 4.1
(continued)

307.30	Stereotype/habit disorder
314.00	Undifferentiated attention-deficient disorder

ORGANIC MENTAL DISORDERS

Dementias Arising in the Senium and Presenium

Primary degenerative dementia of the Alzheimer type, senile onset

290.30	with delirium
290.20	with delusions

SEXUAL DISORDERS

Paraphilias

302.40	Exhibitionism
303.81	Fetishism
302.89	Frotteurism
302.20	Pedophilia

    Specify same sex, opposite sex, same sex and opposite sex
    Specify if limited to incest
    Specify exclusive type or nonexclusive type

302.83	Sexual masochism
302.84	Sexual sadism
302.30	Transvestic fetishism
302.82	Voyeurism
302.90*	Paraphilia NOS

Sexual Dysfunctions

Specify psychogenic only or psychogenic and biogenic
(Note: If biogenic only, code on Axis III)
Specify lifelong or acquired
Specify generalized or situational

Sexual desire disorders

302.71	Hypoactive sexual desire disorder
302.79	Sexual aversion disorder

Sexual arousal disorder

302.72*	Female sexual arousal disorder
302.72*	Male erectile disorder

Orgasm disorders

302.73	Inhibited female orgasm
302.74	Inhibited male orgasm
302.75	Premature ejaculation

Sexual pain disorders

302.76	Dyspareunia
306.51	Vaginismus
302.70	Sexual dysfunction NOS

Other Sexual Disorders

302.90*	Sexual disorder NOS

TABLE 4.1
(continued)

SLEEP DISORDERS

Dyssomnias

	Insomnia disorder
307.42	related to another mental disorder (nonorganic)
780.50*	related to known organic factor
307.42*	Primary insomnia
	Hypersomnia disorder
307.44	related to another mental disorder (nonorganic)
780.50*	related to known organic factor
780.54*	Primary insomnia
307.45	Sleep-wake schedule disorder

Specify advanced or delayed phase type, disorganized type, frequently changing type

	Other dyssomnias
307.40*	Dyssomnia NOS

Parasomnias

307.47	Dream anxiety disorder (nightmare disorder)
307.46*	Sleep terror disorder
307.46*	Sleepwalking disorder
307.40*	Parasomnia NOS

FACTITIOUS DISORDERS

	Factitious disorder
301.51	with physical symptoms
300.16	with psychological symptoms
300.19	Factitious disorder NOS

IMPULSE CONTROL DISORDERS NOT ELSEWHERE CLASSIFIED

312.34	Intermittent explosive disorder
312.32	Kleptomania
312.31	Pathological gambling
312.33	Pyromania
312.39*	Trichotillomania
312.39*	Impulse control disorder NOS

ADJUSTMENT DISORDER

	Adjustment disorder
309.24	with anxious mood
309.00	with depressed mood
309.30	with disturbance of conduct
309.40	with mixed disturbance of emotions and conduct
309.28	with mixed emotional features
309.82	with physical conditions
309.83	with withdrawal
309.23	with work (or academic) inhibition
309.90	Adjustment disorder NOS

TABLE 4.1
(continued)

PSYCHOLOGICAL FACTORS AFFECTING PHYSICAL CONDITION

316.00   Psychological factors affecting physical condition
                        Specify physical condition on Axis III

PERSONALITY DISORDERS
Note: These are coded on Axis II.

Cluster A

301.00   Paranoid
301.20   Schizoid
301.22   Schizotypal

Cluster B

301.70   Antisocial
301.83   Borderline
301.50   Histrionic
301.81   Narcissistic

Cluster C

301.82   Avoidant
301.60   Dependent
301.40   Obsessive compulsive
301.84   Passive aggressive
301.90   Personality disorder NOS

V CODES FOR CONDITIONS NOT ATTRIBUTABLE TO A MENTAL DISORDER THAT ARE A FOCUS OF ATTENTION OR TREATMENT

V62.30   Academic problem
V71.01   Adult antisocial behavior

V40.00   Borderline intellectual functional (Note: This is coded on Axis II)

V71.02   Childhood or adolescent antisocial behavior
V65.20   Malingering
V61.10   Marital problem
V15.81   Noncompliance with medical treatment
V62.20   Occupational problem
V61.20   Parent-child problem
V62.81   Other interpersonal problem
V61.80   Other specified family circumstances
V62.89   Phase of life problem or other life circumstance problem
V62.82   Uncomplicated bereavement

TABLE 4.1
(continued)

ADDITIONAL CODES

300.90	Unspecified mental disorder (nonpsychotic)
V71.09*	No diagnosis or condition on Axis I
799.90*	Diagnosis or condition on Axis I

V71.09	No diagnosis or condition on Axis II
799.90	Diagnosis or condition on Axis II

Source: Reprinted with permission from the *Diagnostic and Statistical Manual of Mental Disorder, Third Edition, Revised.* Copyright 1987 American Psychiatric Association.

considered to be atheoretical with regards to etiology (the origins and causes of a disease). Central to the *DSM-III-R* is the notion of *mental disorder,* which is a clinically significant syndrome that meets the diagnostic criteria of the manual and that occurs in an individual and is associated with distress disability or an increased risk of suffering. This notion infers a dysfunction that should be treated.

Another implication of the *DSM-III-R* is that it changed the act of interviewing and assessment from an "insight-oriented" process to a "symptom-oriented" process (Othmer & Othmer, 1989). Previously, the interviewing style (especially for psychiatrists) had been to identify deep conflicts and to interpret them for clients. The aim of symptom-oriented interviewing is to classify client symptoms and then to base treatment on the resulting diagnosis. This new system of diagnosis changed the therapeutic function from an analytically oriented process of uncovering to an activity characterized by observation and classification, at least in the early stages of therapy.

While most of the changes noted above have been heralded as improvements by mental health professionals, many clinicians still balk at using the *DSM-III-R* for ethical and theoretical reasons. Some of the arguments on both sides of the diagnosis issue are discussed below.

DSM *Diagnosis: For and Against*

Argument for the Use of *DSM* Diagnosis.   *DSM-III-R now uses a multiaxial system that classifies individuals not on one but on five different levels.* It is also possible to put multiple diagnoses on each axis. This multiaxial system was designed to provide a more comprehensive view of an individual and to avoid using a single label to describe a person. The five axes are as follows:

Axis I   Clinical syndromes or presenting problems
Axis II   Developmental disorders, such as learning disabilities and personality
              disorders (relatively inflexible patterns of behavior)
Axis III   Physical problems

Axis IV   Level of psychosocial stress (based on a six-point scale)

Axis V   Global Assessment Scale (a 90-point scale of psychological, social, and occupational functioning)

Below is an example of a typical *DSM-III-R* diagnosis. The numbers of the diagnostic categories on Axis I and II have been deleted. The numerical ratings on Axis IV and V have also been omitted for simplicity. Learning how to use the classification system takes formal training and several years of experience. This simple example should allow the reader to gain a feel for the system.

Axis I   Major depression, recurrent, severe without psychotic features (principal diagnosis)
Parent-child problems

Axis II   Dependent personality

Axis III   Hypertension

Axis IV   Extreme (death of spouse)

Axis V   Major impairment in work (patient cries at work, oversleeps, cannot concentrate)

Using DSM-III-R, a clinician can indicate various levels of diagnostic certainty rather than assigning a definite label to a client's condition. A clinician can defer diagnosis; designate a "V" code, indicating that the syndrome is present but not severe enough to cause dysfunction; or identify the problem as either a psychotic or nonpsychotic disorder causing dysfunction, when information is not sufficient to be more specific. In addition, the clinician may indicate the general class of a disorder, such as depression, when there is not enough assessment data to indicate the exact type. Also on Axis II, the therapist may indicate the presence of personality traits that in themselves may not be sufficient to indicate a diagnosis but that may add to the understanding of the client.

The DSM-III-R provides clinicians with a common language. The common language of *DSM-III-R* allows clinicians from different backgrounds to speak in the language of psychiatrists. Very often decisions about placement and treatment of clients cannot be made without a diagnostic label. For example, a substance abuse treatment center may need to exclude individuals with a diagnosis of schizophrenia.

Using a common language can aid research activities to determine prognoses of various client groups. Without common diagnoses, it is difficult to test new treatments for psychological conditions. The *DSM-III-R* categories specify strict criteria about who may be included and excluded in research programs. This leads to greater usefulness of research results since the client group that benefits from a treatment is clearly specified.

The Case Against the Use of Psychiatric Diagnosis.   *DSM-III-R diagnoses tend to make us lose sight of the client's individuality.* No matter how many axes describe the client, he or she is usually reduced to Axis I or Axis II, the primary clinical concerns or a personality disorder. In short, many of the disadvantages of labeling discussed by Rosenhan (1973) remain despite the fact that the system of classification has become more reliable. Even caring clinicians find themselves describing their clients as borderline, dependent, etc.

Diagnostic testing can be a time-consuming process that does not help the client. Diagnosis has been criticized when it becomes the "diagnosis of existing status" (Anastasi, 1968, p. 105). This occurs when diagnosis is used to assess the client's current condition but holds no promise for treatment. Once, as part of the diagnostic process, a colleague gave a battery of tests to one of my clients while I conducted the therapy. The battery took about 10 hours to administer, score, and interpret. When the psychological report was ready a couple of weeks later, I had already completed four sessions with the client. Most of the useful material identified by the testing was also obtained in the first and second counseling sessions. Much of the test data was inaccurate, although a small portion added credence to some of my hypotheses and, in one or two incidences, suggested possibilities for further exploration that I had not considered. By the fourth counseling session, the client was making substantial progress on one of his problems, but it became clear that the 10 hours spent in testing was not going to produce any substantial addition to the client's treatment. There are many instances when the direction of therapy is quite unclear and the client's condition is mysterious. At such times, taking the time for exhaustive testing can be quite useful.

Diagnostic labels may be difficult to remove. Most diagnoses are made early in treatment and are rarely revised. Client records reflect diagnoses, which are passed on from one therapist to the next. Some diagnoses may be harmful to a client's attempts to gain employment or advancement. Assessment of the client and the client's problems should actually be an ongoing process, constantly undergoing revision as the counselor gains new information. More importantly, the counselor should share this new information with the client so that the goals of therapy are clear to both parties.

The DSM-III-R categories that deal with family problems, parent/child conflicts, and phase-of-life problems are given "V" codes, meaning that no mental disorder is present. "V" areas are not reimbursable by insurance companies and therefore therapists are financially motivated to give more severe diagnoses.

BASIC ID Assessment

In chapter 1, some time was spent describing Arnold Lazarus's system of multi-modal therapy. The assessment of the client is a vital part of that system. One method Lazarus (1981) uses to collect data is to send the client home with a lengthy history form (12 pages or so), thus saving time in the initial interview to cover other ground. The form is commercially available through Research Press. In the first few sessions, the client is assessed across each of the modalities of the BASIC ID. The therapist asks questions about each modality, using information obtained from the questionnaire to note deficiencies and excesses and their frequency, duration, and intensity, where possible.

To illustrate this process more clearly, consider the example of Kathy, a 22-year-old woman who was referred by her physician for treatment of an eating disorder (binging and purging syndrome). The BASIC ID assessment of the client, which was completed by the end of the second session, is illustrated here:

Behavior

1. Overeating in binges 3 times per week, involving a range of 5 candy bars to as many as 40 cookies
2. Self-induced vomiting after each binge
3. Impulsive spending

Affect

1. Mild anger at self for "lack of control"
2. Moderate feelings of guilt following binges

Sensation

1. Sore throat much of the time
2. Bloated feeling following binges
3. Neck and shoulder tension

Images

1. Image of body as "chunky"
2. Imagines being alone or abandoned
3. Imagines scenes of "being loved totally"

Cognitions

1. I am fat and unattractive
2. I am "wild" and impulsive
3. I should make others happy and not be angry

Interpersonal

1. Husband is 15 years older and tends to make decisions for her
2. Has few intimate friends; none are women
3. Clashes with father; competitive with only sister; close to mother

Drugs/Physical

1. Takes birth control pills
2. Regular and reasonable exercise
3. Denies any alcohol or drug use for two years

Treatment Planning in Multimodal Therapy

During and following the assessment of the BASIC ID, the multimodal therapist notes connections between each of the seven modalities to try to understand the chain of events that produces the client's problem behavior. This "triggering sequence" is unique to the client. Let us suppose that, in Kathy's case, the following sequence was hypothesized from an assessment of the BASIC ID:

1. Client is at home alone in the evening when husband works.
2. Client feels bored and lonely.
3. Client goes to the cupboard and eats 30 pieces of candy.
4. During the binge, the client senses oral pleasure and satisfaction.
5. These sensations produce images of being loved as a child.
6. The client experiences bloated sensations in her stomach.
7. The client images herself as "fat."
8. The client says to herself, "I am fat and unlovable."
9. The client induces vomiting.
10. Following the vomiting, the client thinks to herself that she is strong and virtuous for cleansing her body of calories.
11. Later, the client feels anger directed at herself for being "out of control."

Interventions in multimodal therapy were planned to disrupt the behavioral cycle by simultaneously treating each of the affected modalities. In Kathy's case, recommendations could include reducing the client's irrational ideas and maladaptive images using behavioral self-management techniques, improving marital communication, examining self-esteem issues, examining historical parent/child issues, and establishing a more realistic body image.

THE REPLAN SYSTEM

A recurring proposition in this book is that focusing on client problems in assessment and treatment rather than focusing solely on personality factors is the most useful therapeutic approach. Many of the problems inherent in testing misuse and client resistance to appraisal can be overcome by the clinician who clearly explains that testing and assessment procedures are aimed at clarifying the problems upon which the client wishes to work. Let me give an example. A relatively inexperienced counselor came to me for supervision. She was seeing a young woman who complained of depression, feelings of anger, and problems within her marriage, which were apparently due to having been sexually abused as a child. The client mentioned that she had a number of different ways of acting, depending on whom she was with, so the novice counselor read a book about multiple personality disorders. My supervisee wanted to refer the client to a special program for the treatment of multiple personalities. An interesting aspect of the problem was that the supervisee felt that the client's stated problems were somehow different from the "real problem"—being a multiple personality. We eventually agreed that because of the positive nature of the therapeutic relationship, the counselor should continue to work on the client-identified problems (which were just as real), rather than search for a label or a syndrome. This anecdote is related to underscore the orientation of the REPLAN system—that arriving at a diagnostic formulation or personality profile is not as useful as identifying problems and beginning to work on them. Of course, each person brings a unique angle to various problems based on history, cultural background, values, etc. This provides the starting point for the assessment process in the REPLAN system. The problem is the focal point, and information from the client is incorporated as it relates to the problem area.

Assessment in the REPLAN System

In chapter 2, the point was made that the relationship must be firmly established to form trust and provide an atmosphere where the problem can be freely addressed. Next, in Phase II, the assessment process, the therapist must try to "hear" the problem from the client's own perspective and gather data. Figure 4.6, entitled "Goal-Planning Worksheet," shows that the first step in identifying client problems is to ask the client to describe the situation in his or her own words. This statement is then taken down as close to verbatim as possible. The reason for this word-for-word record keeping is that is has been found that clients' problems, when translated through the ears of the therapist, tend to lose their uniqueness, becoming stripped of their personal and cultural meaning. The client's words are vitally important since they tell us how the problem is conceptualized. Consider the client who describes herself as "a bad wife" because her husband and children resent her new job. The therapist may be tempted in this situation to reformulate the problem as a lack of assertiveness. In this case, I believe that interpreting the client's problem as lack of assertiveness would miss something very crucial. It is very important to explore the client's notions of what is a good and a bad wife. It may be that the client will be able to resolve this issue by discovering that a good wife balances her personal needs with those of others. Perhaps the client will select some completely different solution, but the therapist may lose the client unless the words of the client are fully explored.

So, the first step in the assessment process is to ask the client to describe as fully as possible all aspects of the problem. The counselor listens, builds the relationship, and tries to discern the personal meaning of the client's problem. Rather than focusing on what the "real problem" is, the therapist, in the REPLAN system, attempts to assess what the client brings to this problem.

Next the therapist selects assessment procedures to gain additional information or to achieve a broader knowledge of the client's situation. Some therapists will involve the client in the decision about what assessment devices to employ. At the very least, the counselor should be sensitive to the client's history and feelings regarding tests and measurements. The REPLAN system does not articulate a particular set of assessment procedures. Rather it relies on a skilled counselor to individualize the assessment process based on the client needs and according to general categories.

The REPLAN Worksheet

The REPLAN system divides assessment into four parts. Part I is the client's statement of the problem written as close to verbatim as possible. This statement can be elaborated in later sessions. Part II (see Figure 4.5) is a biopsychosocial (Donovan, 1988) or mental health assessment of the client that contains informa-

FIGURE 4.5 (pp. 107–108)
Part II: Biopsychosocial or Mental Health Assessment.

---

1. **ABCD³ Assessment (Affective, Behavioral, Cognitive, Diet/Drugs/Disabilities)**

Affective: _____

_____

_____

Primary Emotional States (Excesses and Deficits): _____

Fears: _____

Anger: _____

Sadness: _____

Interest/excitement: _____

Joy/contentment: _____

Major Emotional Disorders (Depression, Anxiety, etc.): _____

Behavioral: _____

_____

_____

Behavior Deficits or Excesses: _____

Antecedents and consequences of behavior that evoke or maintain problem behaviors: _____

_____

Frequency, intensity, and duration of the behavior problems: _____

_____

Cognitions: _____

_____

_____

Rational and irrational thoughts: _____

Imagery: _____

FIGURE 4.5
(continued)

Distorted thinking patterns: _____

D³: Drugs/Diet/Disabilities: _____

_____

Drug and alcohol use and abuse: _____

Evaluation of dietary intake, including caffeine and nicotine (recognition of any physical or intellectual disabilities or physical differences): _____

_____

2. Social/Cultural Orientation (This category is a compilation of data regarding the client's social milieu and cultural values. Common assessment instruments include autobiographies, sociometry, sexual history, and genograms.)

Relationships with friends: _____

Family history and current family functioning: _____

_____

Family cultural background and language: _____

_____

Social class and education of parents: _____

_____

Religious orientation and degree of orthodoxy: _____

_____

3. Client Developmental Information [Developmental information as part of the assessment includes not only the history of weaning, toilet training, and other maturational milestones but may also include data collected according to the theories of cognitive development à la Piaget (1960), Loevinger's ego development (Loevinger, Wessler & Redmore, 1978), Kohlberg's cognitive moral development (1980), interpersonal development (Selman, 1971), and career development (Super, 1963). Testing in this area may focus on specific areas of psychobiological development, including intelligence (e.g., Wechsler scales of intelligence), neurological development (Bender Visual-Motor Gestalt Test), social maturity and adaptive behavior (Vineland Social Maturity Scale), career maturity (Career Maturity Inventory), etc.]

_____

FIGURE 4.6 (pp. 109–110)
Goal-planning worksheet: Example of a REPLAN assessment.

I. Client's Statement of the Problem

"It's not just my career, it's everything. I'm not really sure why I'm in school or what I'm doing here. I don't feel like my friends really care about me. My parents are divorced. I went home last week, and the house just doesn't seem the same. My father is living with his girlfriend in Sarasota and that doesn't feel like home at all. I thought I wanted a music career, but now I'm not sure if that's only what other people wanted for me. I'm working at a restaurant now, and I know that's not what I want to do for the rest of my life."

II. Biopsychosocial or Mental Health Assessment

1. ABCD[3] Assessment (Affective, Behavioral, Cognitive, Drugs/Diet/Disabilities)

Beck Depression Inventory, Self-Directed Search, Autobiography, and California Psychological Inventory administered 10/28. Results attached.

Note: Highly artistic in dress and expressed interests. Personal grooming has declined according to client. Client denies drug, alcohol use, has poor diet, and no physical problems, medications or disabilities.

2. Social/Cultural Orientation (Family, Ethnic Background, Social Class, Religion, Social Relationships, Support System)

See genogram (attached). White middle-class, protestant upbringing, "not very religious," few close friends, more males than females. Was quite close to grandmother, who died last year. Is close to older brother who is in army. No best friend. Has several acquaintances at work. Feels she is too shy to make friends. Lacking parental support. Sees therapist as major influence.

3. Client Developmental Information

Age 18, completed one year of college, few relationships have worked out, including romantic and roommate. Client sees herself as unusual, concerned with "meaning of life questions and not trivialities." Major issues include leaving home, career development, and moral issues, including the feeling that she has been inappropriate sexually, apparently in an attempt to gain intimacy. Has strong interest and concern for others. Would guess client functions mainly at Kohlberg stage 3. Certainly still concerned with psychosocial issues of identity versus inferiority. Associated with identity problems is the feeling that she is not connected to any family, culture, or group of people.

III. Assessment Results (Therapist Conclusions)

A. Holland Code of Artistic, Social, Conventional
B. Low-achievement orientation
C. Anger and confusion over family problems
D. Well-developed moral sense and concern for others
E. Need for intimacy

FIGURE 4.6
(continued)

F. Lacks assertiveness
G. Identity confusion in several areas, religion, career, etc.
H. At risk for drug/alcohol abuse
I. Poor interpersonal relationships
J. Probably above-average intellectual abilities
K. Strong need for belonging

IV. This section of the assessment pulls together the findings into a treatment plan. This process is described in the next chapter.

---

tion regarding affective, behavioral, cognitive data, and drugs, diet and disabilities: the ABCD³ or ABCD cubed section for short. Besides the results of formal assessment devices (tests, for example), informal data from the clinical interview are included. Part III is a sumary of assessment results stated as hypotheses. A *DSM-III-R* diagnosis might be one way of summarizing the therapist's findings. Here also the therapist notes the general patterns and themes emerging from the client's assessment. Part IV is the mutually agreed-upon goals that have been derived from the assessment process.

CHAPTER SUMMARY AND CONCLUSIONS

According to the model proposed in this book, assessment is the second major step in the process of counseling. It builds on the foundation of the therapeutic relationship, which provides the trust needed to open doors of communication. This chapter has promoted the concept that assessment should not be standardized but should be adapted to explore and clarify the unique problems of each client. A variety of methods of data collection are available to the clinician, including the results of psychological tests as well as informal techniques of questioning and observation and the interactive formats of the genogram. Once data has been collected, it must be summarized if it is to guide the formation of treatment plans. Three methods were discussed in this chapter: the psychiatric system (*DSM-III-R*), the BASIC ID of multimodal therapy, and the REPLAN system. The REPLAN system is an eclectic model that suggests focusing on identified problems as the starting point for the assessment as opposed to a personality-focused approach.

FURTHER READINGS

Rosenhan, D. L. (1973). On being sane in insane places. *Science, 180,* 250–258. This study reports the experience of "pseudo-patients" who came to hospitals complaining of a single symptom (e.g., auditory hallucinations) and who were almost without exception diagnosed as schizophrenic. Their normal behavior in the hospital was seen as pathological by the staff. Rosenhan's article has been hotly debated and, despite later criticisms, has been deemed to be an important factor in bringing about reforms in the *Diagnostic and Statistical Manual* of the American Psychiatric Association culminating in *DSM-III*.

Bradley, L. J. (1988). Developmental assessment: A life-span process. In R. Hays & R. Aubrey (Eds.), *New directions for counseling and human development* (pp. 136–157). Denver, CO: Love. This chapter makes a case for considering social, moral, career, ego, and cognitive development in assessment despite the age of the client. One of the outstanding features of the chapter is the review of psychological tests, which might prove useful to the mental health professional in establishing client development.

Nelson, R. O. (1983). Behavioral assessment: Past, present and future. *Behavioral Assessment, 5,* 195–206. As the title suggests, Nelson's article is a description of assessment from a purely behavioral point of view. For those unfamiliar with these methods, this article is an excellent starting point.

REFERENCES

American Psychiatric Association (1987). *Diagnostic and statistical manual of mental disorders* (3rd ed., revised). Washington, DC: Author.

Anastasi, A. (1968). *Psychological testing* (3rd ed.). New York: Macmillan.

Beier, E. (1966). *The silent language of psychotherapy.* Chicago, IL: Aldine.

Bowen, M. (1978). *Family therapy in clinical practice.* New York: Jason Aronson.

Bowen, M. (1980). *Key to the genogram.* Washington, DC: Georgetown University Hospital.

Conan Doyle, A. (1929). *Conan Doyle's best books.* (Vol. 2). New York: P. F. Collier & Son.

Coyne, J. C. (1976). Depression and the response of others. *Journal of Abnormal Psychology, 85,* 186–193.

Dickson, G. L., & Parmerlee, J. R. (1980). The occupational family tree: A career counseling technique. *The School Counselor, 28,* 131–134.

Donovan, D. M. (1988). Assessment of addictive behaviors: Implications of an emerging biopsychosocial model. In D. M. Donovan & G. A. Marlatt (Eds.), *Assessment of addictive behaviors* (pp. 3–48). New York: Guilford Press.

Drummond, R. J. (1988). Appraisal procedures for counselors and helping professionals. Columbus, OH: Merrill.

Gladding, S. L. (1992). *Counseling: A comprehensive profession* (2nd ed.). Columbus, OH: Merrill.

Groth-Marnat, G. (1988). *Handbook of psychological assessment* (2nd ed.). New York: Van Nostrand Reinhold.

Kohlberg, L. (1980). The cognitive-developmental approach to moral education. In V. L. Erickson & J. Whiteley (Eds.), *Developmental counseling and teaching.* Monterey, CA: Brooks/Cole.

Lazarus, A. A. (1981). *The practice of multimodal therapy.* New York: McGraw-Hill.

Leary, T. (1957). *Interpersonal diagnosis of personality.* New York: Ronald.

Loevinger, J., Wessler, R., & Redmore, C. (1978). *Measuring ego development* (Vols. 1–2). San Francisco: Jossey-Bass.

McGoldrick, M., & Gerson, R. (1985). *Genograms in family assessment.* New York: W. W. Norton.

Okiishi, R. W. (1987). The genogram as a tool in career counseling. *Journal of Counseling and Development, 66,* 139–143.

Othmer, E., & Othmer, S. C. (1989). *The clinical interview using DSM-III-R.* Washington, DC: American Psychiatric Press.

Perls, F. S. (1959). *Gestalt therapy verbatim.* New York: Bantam Books.

Piaget, J. (1960). The general problem of the psycho-biological development of the child. In J. M. Tanner and B. Inhelder (Eds.), *Dis-*

cussions on child development (Vol. 4). New York: International Universities Press.

Rogers, C. R. (1951). *Client-centered therapy.* Boston: Houghton Mifflin.

Rosenhan, D. L. (1973). On being sane in insane places. *Science, 180,* 250–258.

Sattler, J. M. (1988). *Assessment of children* (3rd ed.). San Diego, CA: Jerome M. Sattler.

Selman, R. L. (1971). Taking another's perspective: Role-taking in early childhood. *Child Development, 42,* 1721–1734.

Shannon, J. & Guerney, B. G., Jr. (1973). Interpersonal effects of interpersonal behavior. *Journal of Personality and Social Psychology, 26,* 142–150.

Sullivan, H. S. (1947). *Conceptions of modern psychiatry.* Washington, DC: William Alanson White Psychiatric Foundation.

Super, D. E. (1957). *The psychology of careers.* New York: Harper.

Super, D. E. (1963). *Career development: Self concepts theory.* New York: College Entrance Examination Board.

Tomm, K. (1987a). Interventive interviewing: Part I. Strategizing as a fourth guideline for the therapist. *Family Process, 26,* 3–13.

Tomm, K. (1987b). Interventive interviewing: Part II. Reflexive questioning as a means to enable self healing. *Family Process, 26,* 167–183.

CHAPTER FIVE

Goal Setting and Treatment Planning

KEY CONCEPTS

▼ *Psychotherapy requires an explicit contract between client and counselor that spells out expectations, provides focus for the counseling session, and increases client involvement.*

▼ *Therapy goals should be determined jointly by client and counselor, bringing together the client's unique perspective and the counselor's expertise and objectivity.*

▼ *It is important that contracts be formulated as goals or as positive restatements of problems. Goals do not need to be quantifiable, but they should be clearly understood by both client and counselor.*

▼ *Many goals need to be simplified or boiled down into workable statements. Then they should be placed in priority order to finalize the contract.*

▼ *Once a contract is established, it is the counselor's task to identify therapeutic strategies or techniques to help the client realize his or her goals.*

▼ *The diagnostic treatment planning method, DO A CLIENT MAP, is one method of treatment planning based on client diagnosis according to DSM-III-R.*

▼ *The REPLAN system uses the concept of curative factors to help plan the treatment process by first identifying the crucial curative factors for the therapy and then generating a number of strategies that may be employed to help the client change in the intended direction.*

INTRODUCTION

In chapter 2, the first phase of counseling—establishing a trusting relationship that allows the client to express difficult problems and encourages the client to feel safe enough to go further in the process of change—was discussed. Chapter 3 examined potential problems in the relationship. Next, chapter 4 looked at the therapist's first responsibilities: to observe, collect information, and make inferences. Information gathered about the client and the client's problem in the assessment process and the development of a good working relationship make possible the next phase of the process—developing a treatment plan.

Even in developing a treatment plan, the therapeutic relationship emerges as an important issue. A viewpoint expressed in this chapter is that the therapeutic alliance is not merely an exchange of warm feelings between client and counselor. Nor is it only the client pouring out his or her feelings with the counselor determining the correct diagnosis. It involves shared tasks and goals. A contract or a mutual work project, as we will describe it here, is an explicit and simple statement of therapeutic goals.

KEY QUESTIONS ABOUT CLIENT GOALS

This chapter is designed to help the counselor assist the client in developing focused, realistic, and compatible goals and in ordering them by priority. The chapter begins by looking at some key questions about client goals:

- Why do we need a contract?
- Should we be identifying problems or setting goals?
- How does formulating goals help the counseling process?
- Must goals be in writing?
- Whose goals should therapy address?
- Who owns the problem?
- How will we know when therapy is finished?
- What kinds of goals?

In the second half of the chapter, some time will be spent discussing skills that can help the client boil down the problem, place goals in priority order, and select treatment strategies.

Why Do We Need a Contract?

According to Goodyear and Bradley (1986), all relationships are in some way contractual since they involve either agreed-upon goals or unspoken expectations. Eric Berne, the founder of transactional analysis, felt that the therapeutic relationship should never be entered into without a contract. Without a contract, therapy becomes aimless, and the possibility for game playing exists (Berne, 1972). For example, therapy may be initiated to mollify some third party, such as family members or the courts.

Claude Steiner (1974) claims that the therapeutic contract outlines responsibilities for both the client and the counselor. Like legal contracts, a therapy contract contains four basic requirements:

1. Mutual consent
2. Consideration, or exchange (the client receives competent services; the counselor receives money or credit for time spent)
3. Competency (the client must be mentally competent and old enough to understand the contractual arrangement)
4. Lawful object (the contract cannot be in violation of a law or public policy)

Without these contractual requirements, therapy may be ineffective, unethical, or illegal.

There is another reason that a mutual work project or contract must exist. Contracts can more deeply involve the client in treatment. One study (Evans,

1984) found that the degree to which the client participates in goal setting is directly related to the degree to which the client is committed to attaining goals. This may be especially true for clients who feel that treatment goals are forced upon them. In this same vein, another study (Barbrack & Maher, 1984) bears deeper examination. These researchers divided adolescent clients into four groups. Group 1 formulated goals conjointly with the counselor. Group 2's goals were set by the counselor alone. The clients were informed of their counseling goals but did not participate in formulating them. Group 3's goals were set by the counselor, but clients were not informed that any therapy goals had been set. No therapy goals at all were developed for Group 4. The study found that goal attainment was highest in Groups 1 and 2, where clients were cognizant of their therapy goals. Group 1 (those who participated in goal setting) also showed the highest satisfaction with treatment. In summary, clients who are included in the goal-setting process are more likely to achieve their goals and feel satisfied with the results of therapy.

Besides involving the client in the counseling process, other writers have suggested that, for goals to be effective, they must be explicit and clearly focused. According to Dyer and Vriend (1977), counseling goals are most potent when they are

1. Mutually agreed upon by counselor and client
2. Specific
3. Relevant to self-defeating behavior
4. Achievement and success oriented (versus eliminating or reducing)
5. Quantifiable and measurable
6. Behavioral and observable
7. Understandable and can be clearly restated

Should We Be Identifying Problems or Setting Goals?

O'Hanlon and Weiner-Davis (1989) feel that psychotherapy has evolved in three stages. Having been born as an amalgam of philosophy, medicine, and psychology, psychotherapy's original emphasis was on the past, looking at *causes and explanations* of behavior. Sometimes clients do indicate that they want to know why they feel a certain way; however, even after gaining a good deal of understanding and insight into the origins of their difficulties, clients often find it difficult to change (Goodyear and Bradley, 1986).

In the 1960s psychotherapy's emphasis changed from past to present—a more here and now orientation. The therapies of that time, especially Gestalt, behavioral, and rational emotive therapies, primarily concerned themselves with the treatment of *present problems* or *symptoms and their maintenance.*

O'Hanlon and Weiner-Davis (1989) indicate that the newest change in psychotherapy is a future orientation that is concerned with how problems are *solved.* They suggest that an important task for the therapist is to dissolve the client's idea that there is a problem or at least to negotiate a "solvable problem with the client" (pp. 57–58). According to Haley (1976), therapy often fails because therapists accept problem statements containing mystical terms such as a *symbiotic mother/*

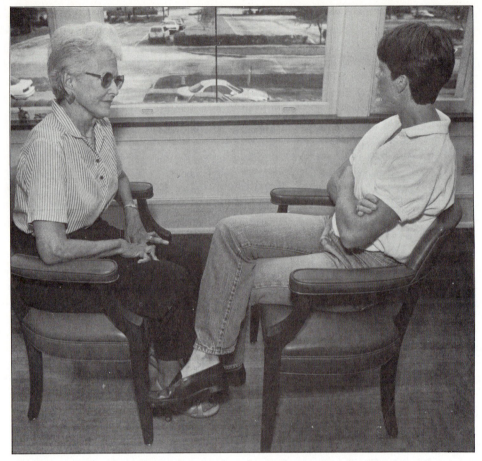

Clients may resist setting goals, but it is advantageous for counselors to change the focus of therapy sessions from the negative examination of problems to the positive attainment of goals.

daughter relationship or *borderline personality*. These labels may come from client statements or therapist diagnoses. To be useful for the client, diagnoses must be transformed from problems into workable statements or goals.

One way for clients to change their thinking about problems is for the counselor to be firm about only negotiating goals. For example, when the client says, "I have a problem with my mother," the therapist's response is, "How would you like it to be?" The therapist continues to encourage very specific, future-oriented thinking until the client develops a realistic and specific goal statement. There are many advantages to accepting only goal statements. Among these are instilling hope in the client and changing the focus of therapy sessions from examination of problems (negative) to the attainment of goals (positive).

How Does Formulating Goals Help the Counseling Process?

Cormier and Cormier (1991, p. 217) have discussed the purposes of goals in the counseling process. According to these authors, developing clear counseling goals helps to modify client expectations about what can realistically be accomplished in counseling. In addition, at least six other favorable outcomes accrue from a joint process of counselor/client negotiation of goal statements:

1. By selecting individual goals for the client, the therapy is more likely to be aimed at the client's needs rather than derived from the therapist's theoretical orientation alone.
2. When goals are clearly understood by client and counselor, the counselor can determine if he or she possesses the requisite skills to continue with the counseling or if a referral is needed.
3. Many clients have problems imagining or envisioning success. Visualizing a positive outcome has the tendency to focus the client's resources and energies and increase hope.
4. Goals provide a rational basis for selecting treatment strategies in counseling;
5. Goals help counselors determine how successful counseling has been for the client. Goal statements provide feedback to the client as well who can be asked to evaluate the outcome of therapy based on the degree to which goals have been achieved.
6. Like assessment procedures, simply setting goals can be therapeutic. The client who is clear about the goals will be able to work on these goals in and out of therapy. The setting of a goal also motivates the client to work harder in therapy.

Must Goals Be in Writing?

The contract or work project does not need to be a written document, but many therapists do ask their clients to sign an agreement for treatment and a written treatment plan. Some advantages to using a written contract include the following:

1. A contract provides a record of therapy progress.
2. An explicit contract motivates the client and therapist to work towards goals.
3. With clearly defined goals, clients feel less confused and more hopeful that solutions can be achieved.
4. Therapeutic goals place responsibility for goal attainment on the client rather than on some outside party or solely on the therapist.
5. Contracts encourage the client to return to counseling by requiring a commitment (Thomas & Ezell, 1972).

Besides a clear statement of agreement as to therapy goals, a therapy contract may include the following elements:

1. Fees and costs of all services

2. Expected length of treatment
3. Length of sessions
4. Policies for lateness or missed appointments
5. Policies concerning contacting the therapist outside of business hours

Whose Goals Should Therapy Address?

In practice, client goals are usually established either by the client, the counselor (based on diagnosis and assessment), or by some other interested partner. A fourth alternative is a mutual client/counselor goal-setting process that blends the viewpoint of the client with the objectivity and professional observations of the counselor. Before examining this alternative, let us look a little closer at the options of client-centered goal setting and goal setting by some third party.

Client-Centered Goal Setting

Goal attainment is increased by identifying goals that the client really wants to achieve (Goodyear & Bradley, 1986). When goals are set only by the client, however, the plan will miss the counselor's professional insights and may lead to the pursuit of superficial or unrealistic goals. If the counselor takes the position that the client's goals are paramount, another problem surfaces: What if the client's goals are unacceptable to the counselor? Besides value issues, there are cases where the client lacks insight about an aspect of a problem that is crucial to the client's improvement. As an expert, the counselor has a duty to help the client focus on central problems that will lead to lasting or more generalized improvement (Weinberger, 1982). For example, a female client once presented an initial statement of her problem as a "bad marriage." She was tired of being dominated by her husband, although she had been married only 18 months. She went on to say that she had an ongoing conflict at work with her boss, who was too demanding, and that another major problem was her mother, who was always telling her what to do. The client wished assistance in dissolving this, her third, marriage. In this case, the counselor suggested that the client's difficulties were more general than just the marital issue. The therapist felt that unless the client learned to develop better communication skills and to improve her assertiveness in general, she would continue to have relationship problems. The therapist offered a contract to deal with the general problem first before addressing the marital issue in particular, and the client agreed.

Goal Setting by a Third Party

Therapy aimed at achieving the goals of a third party, such as parents or school officials, is often difficult. Since neither client nor counselor participates in the goal-setting process, they may not feel personally involved or motivated to achieve these aims. Let us pursue this third party problem in the example of a client who has been referred by a probation officer following an incestuous relationship. The probation officer wants the client treated for sexual dysfunction to ensure that this kind of thing does not happen again. The client is divorced now and has had no contact with his teenage daughter, the incest victim. At this point, the client's concerns are forming new relationships and dealing with family members' rejection. He is not willing to rehash the incestuous relationship in therapy. In such cases, the counselor is obligated to decide whether to help the client with his stated goals or to become an agent of the state and accept the probation officer's goals. Many counselors recognize the needs of society, but the notion of a contract delineated earlier means that the counselor must decide for whom he or she works; that is, who is the client. This kind of situation is quite common (Ritchie, 1986), and clients pressured into therapy by a third party may be as much as one third of all new clients (Haley, 1989). For this reason, therapists must be clear about whose goals will be the focus of therapy. The point of these two examples is that, from practical and ethical points of view, goal setting involving both client and counselor provides the best opportunity for successful therapy. As we will see in the section on boiling down the problem and ordering goals, one way of dealing with problems that have been identified by the therapist or by some third party is to place those goals lower on the client's list of priorities, waiting until the relationship is firmly established before tackling them.

Who Owns the Problem?

Thomas Gordon (1975) formulated a key question for the treatment planning stage of the counseling relationship: Who owns the problem? The question can be most clearly answered by determining who is emotionally upset by the problem. The emotional reaction not only provides the motivation to seek help, but acts as a red flag for the counselor by identifying the person most affected. If both members of a couple are upset, the couple will own the relationship problem and may seek counseling. The man who complains about his employer's stinginess owns the problem and must decide how to solve the problem either by seeking another job, becoming more assertive, or modifying his feelings and perceptions to better handle the situation. It is unlikely that the employer owns the problem since he or she is probably not upset by stinginess toward others.

One of the reasons this is such a crucial question is that, early on in their practice, counselors can easily be sidetracked into helping a client change some other person: spouse, employer, or significant other. Nowhere is this more likely than in the case of the alcoholic family. At first, the affected family members seek professional help to try to control the drinking of the alcoholic member. Sometimes this can be accomplished by forcing or coercing the alcoholic into treatment. Eventually, though, the counselor must confront other family members with the fact that they are troubled and need to deal with their own emotional disturbance and develop their own goals. The family members eventually realize the senselessness of trying to stop the alcoholic's drinking and instead try to regain self-esteem and handle their own negative feelings, regardless of the alcoholic's behavior. The proper view of problem ownership is a central theme of Alcoholics Anonymous and is crystallized in their prayer, "God grant me the courage to change the things I can change, serenity to accept the things I cannot change, and the wisdom to know the difference."

CASE EXAMPLE _____

A 60-year-old woman came to therapy, complaining that her 40-year-old son was irresponsible with money. She always seemed to be bailing him out. She was both resentful and worried about his spendthrift ways, wanting suggestions about how to get her son to become more responsible. She was angry and under financial pressure; whereas her son experienced little concern. Fortunately, the client was able to grasp the fact that she owned the problem. Only then was she able to reduce her tendency to pay her son's bills and, of course, she became less resentful in the process. Interestingly, this action had the effect of producing a financial pinch for the son, who then began managing his finances better.

_____

This example shows that the counselor's first efforts in setting goals should be to focus on those problems owned by the client rather than being railroaded into attempts to change others. Sometimes in the process, healthier behaviors like working on one's own problems have the benefit of forcing others to contemplate change.

How Will We Know When Therapy Is Finished?

This question can be answered in several ways. Some therapists use a time-limited approach, where the client attends counseling only for a certain amount of time or a certain number of sessions. In this method, therapy is over when the time is up, typically between 6 and 20 sessions (Grayson, 1979). Time limits motivate both client and counselor to achieve therapy goals within a specified period. Counselors with long waiting lists have found this to be useful in managing their case loads. Time-limited therapy appears to be just as effective as therapy without these limits (Muench, 1965).

Another commonly accepted method is for the therapist or the client to unilaterally declare that therapy is completed. Clients are frequently terminated despite their protests if the therapist feels that the client has obtained the maximum benefit from counseling, is becoming too dependent on the therapist, or if the therapist feels problems have been solved. Even more usual is the tendency for clients to terminate therapy on their own.

Just as it has been recommended that treatment goals be jointly formulated by counselor and client, it makes sense for therapy to be concluded through mutual agreement. Therapy is over when the client and counselor agree that mutually derived goals have been met, that therapy goals cannot be met in the current relationship, or that a transfer is necessary. When goals have been accomplished, therapy is concluded. It continues only if there is a new contract to pursue additional aims.

What Kinds of Goals?

Goals may be formulated in at least two ways: behaviorally (with quantifiable goals) or semantically (with goals that both parties understand). In the paragraphs that follow, some advantages and disadvantages of each are discussed.

Behavioral Goals

Behaviorists have long advocated identifying discrete problem behaviors and keeping quantitative records of client progress (Krumboltz, 1966). A major benefit of such a system includes a clear contract between client and counselor regarding the reasons and goals of therapy. An example of a behavioral treatment plan follows.

Client's Stated Goal.   The client would like to increase comfort and decrease anxiety in social situations. The client's job entails several social functions each week, and they are necessary for his employment.

Target Behaviors (Described in Frequency, Duration, and Intensity).   The client would like to be able to attend a social gathering, hold two or more conversations (frequency), at least one of these with a woman, stay for a period of more than one hour (duration), and maintain a subjective distress level (SUDS) of 3 or 4. (The SUDS level is the client's feelings of discomfort in the situation and is measured on a 10-point scale of intensity, with 10 being the most uncomfortable and 1 being mildly uncomfortable.)

Baseline (Current Level of Target Behaviors).   The client states he can stay at a party for about 15 minutes before he leaves. He can hold a brief conversation with a male coworker but has not recently talked to a woman in this setting. He currently experiences a SUDS level of 8 or 9 during social conversations with any woman.

Treatment Plan.   The client's treatment plan has three components:

1. Relaxation training and covert desensitization using imagery specific to the client's problems. This training will be complete when the client is able to maintain a low level of distress in imagined situations and can achieve a high degree of relaxation.
2. Client will be given weekly homework assignments to attempt conversations with people outside of the target setting and to record duration of the contact and the SUDS level.
3. Client will attend one social gathering per week and will be asked to record the frequency and duration of each visit and the intensity of his discomfort, increasing his time at these functions by five-minute increments.

A benefit of the behavioral approach is that the client becomes aware that therapy is an incremental learning process and that progress comes as a series of small steps, not in one miraculous cure. Success in small steps can lead to a greater sense of efficacy and hope to continue the process of change.

One drawback to the behavioral approach is that clients and counselors are usually not fond of keeping charts and graphs. Also, focusing on a single observable behavior tends to take the focus away from other important situational variables, such as family dynamics. For example, bed-wetting may be mainly a symptom of family conflict or feelings of neglect. Another problem of the behavioral approach is that clients may reach goals yet remain dissatisfied, feeling that the general problem still has not been solved. The client needs to see the connection between small behavioral steps and the original reasons for coming to therapy. The process of defining goals and a variety of subgoals (Cormier & Cormier, 1991) is a laborious and time-consuming process that both clients and counselors seem to regard with some skepticism.

At the other end of the spectrum, some therapists never clearly identify client problems, and each session has no relationship to the previous ones. This here-and-now method has its benefits since it makes the counseling responsive to the current needs of the client. On the other hand, many sessions can be wasted on mundane and transitory issues while the major goals of treatment are forgotten. Such therapy may take longer than other types of therapy, and the client may become discouraged.

Semantic Goals

A middle position between quantifiable goals and no goals at all are those that both client and counselor can understand and that can be easily restated. It is still possible to have clear goals without reducing them to extremely small, observable units. One obvious pitfall is that the therapist can be trapped into accepting goals that are too broad or vague. A rule of thumb in developing a contract is that it should be extremely simple, so simple that an "eight year old could understand it" (Steiner, 1976). In other words, even if counseling goals are not quantifiable, they can still be concrete (Goodyear & Bradley, 1986). For example, the counselor might not want to accept the following goal: "I want to improve my relationship with my mother." The counselor might be willing, though, to accept the following revision: "Well, I would like to be more assertive when she starts trying to give me advice."

The process by which semantic goals are identified and clarified is reflexive and interactive. In essence, the development of semantic or reflexively derived goals involves

1. Identifying problem areas through assessment
2. Transforming problems into broad goal statements
3. Responding to and having input into the client's goals
4. Agreeing on a set of therapy goals
5. Continuously evaluating and refining goal statements

BOILING DOWN THE PROBLEM AND ORDERING GOALS

John Dewey said that a question well asked is a question half-answered. Although some clients come to a therapist with clearly defined problems, more often they present tangles of feelings, people, and events that can easily sidetrack both client and counselor. Rule (1982) describes three types of elusive goals: unfocused, unrealistic, and uncoordinated.

Unfocused goals are goals that are either not in conscious awareness or are too broad. It is also unclear where unfocused goals fit in the hierarchy of therapeutic priorities. These goals are hard to put into workable form. An example of an unfocused goal is this type of client statement: "I don't really know what's wrong;

it's just that I am uneasy with everything." *Unrealistic goals,* on the other hand, are vaguely stated desires for "happiness" or for having things "back the way they used to be in our marriage." Finally, *uncoordinated goals* are seemingly incompatible with each other or with the client's personality. Before accepting a client's goal statement, the client's goals must be

1. In a workable form
2. Realistic
3. Ordered according to priority (central or core goals must take precedence over goals of lesser importance)

In summary, then, the therapeutic task at this juncture is to boil down problems, to change problems into realistic goal statements acceptable to client and counselor, and to place them in priority order.

Boiling Down the Problem

Boiling down the problem is my way of describing the process of changing problem statements into workable goals. Egan (1990) describes this process as helping the client move through four stages:

1. Declaration of intent
2. Mission statements
3. Specific aims
4. Concrete and specific goals

Stage 1: Declarations of Intent

At this stage, the client shows an interest in changing something in his or her life. An example of a declaration of intent would be, "It has recently become clear to me that I can't go on like this." In the early stages of the relationship, the counselor is inclined to get the client to expand on this statement in order to explore, observe, assess, and to firmly establish the supportive relationship. The therapist may respond to the client's declaration by paraphrasing its content.

Client [declaration of intent]:
> It has recently become clear to me that I can't go on like this.

Counselor [paraphrase of content]:
> You've come to a point where you need to make a change.

Eventually, the therapist and client feel the need to shift gears and to begin the work of implementing change. To do this, the therapist uses directives or questions that continually narrow the focus. The following dialogue is an example of boiling down the problem when the client presents a declaration of intent.

Client: It has recently become clear to me that I can't go on like this.

Counselor [question with exploratory intent]:
> Go on, like what?

Client: Living in this situation at home. My wife, all the pressure at work. No one at work understands what I'm going through, and I'm tired of making excuses.

*Counselor [counselor uses the words **pressure** and **situation** to match the terms the client selected in describing the problem]:*
Where is most of the pressure in this situation coming from?

Client: I'd have to say it's in the marriage. That's most of it. A lot of things revolve around that.

Counselor [counselor verifies that the marriage is a central problem]:
If the marriage were better, other things would be improved, too.

Client: Yeah. I'd certainly be able to concentrate better at work.

Counselor [boiling down the problem]:
What is it about your marriage that bothers you so much that you can't stop thinking about it?

Client: I'm always thinking she is being, you know, unfaithful. I know she isn't, but she says I'm always checking on her. Then she gets mad.

Counselor: So, one way of stating the problem is that you are very often worried about whether your wife is seeing someone else to the point that your work is affected and your wife is often annoyed at you.

Client: That's it.

Stage 2: Mission Statements

Now that the problem has been isolated, the next step is to change the problem into a goal statement. Egan (1986) calls this phase of problem formulation mission statements. Counselors help clients develop mission statements by asking them to look to the future, to imagine how things would be if the problem were solved. Let us continue the dialogue already started to illustrate this counselor activity.

Counselor: How would you like it to be?

Client: Well, I'd like to be able to go to work without wondering if she were running around. And, when I get home, we could go out more like we did before the kids came. Not every night. I work hard and sometimes I'm just too tired. And we could go out without a fight.

Stage 3: Specific Aims

Now that the client has imagined some possible positive outcomes, the third step in boiling down the problem is what Egan calls specific aims. The counselor can facilitate movement from mission statements to specific aims by restating the client's goals more specifically and asking the client to agree or disagree. Second, the counselor asks the client to identify the most important aspects of the problem and to set others on the back burner for the time being. The dialogue continues with the counselor continuing to ask the client to develop specific aims.

Counselor [restating]:
Okay, let me see if I understand. You'd like to be able to concentrate on your job, and, second, you'd like to go out together occasionally and have a good time. Is that it?

Client: It has been a long time since we went out and had a good time. Yeah, that would be great. The worst thing, though, is always wondering what she's up to.

Counselor: So, it's most important to be able to concentrate better at your job rather than working on having a good time when you two go out together.

Client: Yeah, because I can't even have a good time if I'm wondering if she is looking at other guys.

Stage 4: Concrete and Specific Goals

The fourth stage Egan identifies is Concrete and Specific Goals. In this final stage of the boiling down process, the counselor asks the client to even more specifically identify the conditions under which therapy would be considered complete. An important aspect of this is to make certain that the client's goals are realistic. The dialogue continues as follows:

Counselor: So, how would you know if things were improved enough to stop coming to counseling?

Client: I'd never think about her while I was at work. I'd never call her or her mother to check up on her.

Counselor: That sounds like perfection. Like a magical cure. I guess my question should have been, "How much change would need to occur before you felt that things were improved enough that your work isn't affected anymore." Am I correct that better work performance is the real goal?

Client: OK, I'd like to be able to wait until lunch break to phone her, and I'd like to stop these thoughts running around in my head so that I don't make mistakes on the assembly line. I'd like to have a better quality record.

Here, the counselor can continue to press the client to set even more specific or even quantifiable goals and to challenge the client to act. For example, the client may set a goal to increase his performance record, to lengthen times between calls to his wife, or to increase positive (nonworrying) thoughts about her.

Ordering Client Goals

Boiling down the problem might yield a long list of possible goals. A laundry list of this type might be thorough, but it can also be confusing and unwieldy. Instead, it becomes important to identify and accomplish a few important tasks first. Some general rules that help the counselors decide the priority of client problems are presented here.

1. *Help the client manage crises first*—Generally speaking, crises that are lower on the Maslovian hierarchy of needs (food, clothing, shelter, and security needs) take precedence over crises in higher needs categories, such as relationships (Bruce, 1984).

2. *Focus on goals that the client feels are crucial even if they do not appear to be serious*—Sometimes therapists talk about "goblet issues," referring to client problems that are raised early in treatment but that appear to be only an entree into therapy. Carl Rogers said that clients talk about "the thing next to the thing," meaning that clients may, in the beginning, present calling cards or pseudoproblems until the therapeutic relationship is developed enough to bring out more important issues.

3. *In the absence of a crisis, initially tackle problems that have a high probability of success*—Whenever small goals are achieved, the client will be encouraged to continue with more difficult or more time-consuming projects (Egan, 1990). As Milton Erickson once said, "Therapy is often a matter of tipping the first domino" (Rossi, 1980, Vol. 4, p. 454).

4. *Goals for which the client has little motivation should be placed lower on the list*—Counselors can accept goals for which the client has little motivation, but they should be saved until the time when the client has solved pressing problems or has become more committed to therapy.

5. *Advocate goals that will lead to general improvement in the client's life rather than Band-Aids*—The counselor should be concerned with the client's longer term welfare. After crises are dealt with, the counselor should encourage the client to look at recurring patterns and their causes.

TREATMENT PLANNING

Treatment planning is the art of selecting treatment strategies once therapy goals have been negotiated. Treatment strategies are the *steps* to be taken in reaching these goals. In general, the professional counselor must rely on the results of research and clinical experience as a guide for selecting treatment strategies. Another source of direction for the therapist is a theoretical model. The reader will recall that an eclectic model, multimodal therapy, was described earlier. Multimodal therapy promotes selecting treatment strategies based on strengths and weaknesses in the various modalities of client functioning, including behavior, affect, cognition, etc. In this section, we will look at two models: Linda Seligman's diagnostic treatment planning (1990) and the REPLAN system, both of which develop a set of guidelines to help generate strategies for accomplishing therapy goals.

The Diagnostic Treatment Planning Model

Seligman's model relies on the concept of psychiatric diagnosis compatible with the *DSM-III-R*. Seligman has described her model as being similar to an hourglass: a wide variety of assessments is made that then narrow to a single diagnosis that, in turn, broaden again into a number of interventions strategies gleaned from various theoretical orientations. To this extent, the model is eclectic.

The diagnostic treatment planning model uses a mnemonic device in the acronym DO A CLIENT MAP. Filling out each portion of the client map is the method for completing a treatment plan. Table 5.1 shows the elements of the plan. Table 5.2 shows an example of a typical treatment plan using the model.

TABLE 5.1
Outline of DO A CLIENT MAP.

Elements of the Model	Description
D—Diagnosis	*DSM-III-R* diagnosis on all five axes
O—Objectives	Goals of treatment
A—Assessments	Assessments needed (e.g., testing)
C—Clinician	Therapist characteristics that would be helpful in treatment
L—Location of treatment	For example, inpatient versus outpatient
I—Interventions	Specific treatment strategies based on diagnosis
E—Emphasis of treatment	Cognitive, affective, supportive, directive, etc.
N—Nature of treatment	Individual, couple, group, family
T—Timing	Frequency, duration, and pacing of therapy sessions
M—Medications needed	Need for medication evaluation by medical personnel.
A—Adjunct services	Referrals, support groups, education
P—Prognosis	Amount of change or improvement expected with this disorder

The REPLAN System of Treatment Planning

REPLAN is the comprehensive, goal-directed, treatment planning model around which this book is organized. It relies on the notion of common curative factors, which have been described earlier. These curative factors are thought to be the reason why specific counseling techniques work. All counseling methods seem to include one or more of these curative factors. Once the client's goals are known and isolated, one or more of these curative factors emerges as the main focus of treatment. The selection of focus is based on the assessment process, which identifies client goals, general patterns or themes, and the individual needs of the client.

When compared to the multimodal approach, the REPLAN system focuses more on the client's problems rather than on his or her psychological and physical symptoms. Seligman's diagnostic treatment planning method, on the other hand, replaces this phase of the process by arriving at a tentative diagnosis. This diagnosis then directs the treatment process. For example, the diagnosis of major depression should point to the use of some standard treatment methodologies for this disorder. Although nothing in the REPLAN system eliminates the use of diagnosis, it is not the center of treatment planning, but a method for communication with other health professionals. The REPLAN system is distinguishable from other forms of treatment planning because it focuses on a relatively few number of client goals, using strategies associated with one or two curative factors. This approach has the benefit of helping clients achieve a few goals at a time rather than planning an elaborate treatment regimen. The approach is not incompatible

TABLE 5.2
Client map of Susan B.

Client Map of Susan B.

Diagnosis.   Axis I: V62.89—Phase of life problem; V62.20—Occupational problem
            Axis II: V71.09—No diagnosis or condition
            Axis III: No physical disorders
            Axis IV: Psychosocial stressors: Departure of youngest child for college.
                    Severity: 2—mild, acute
            Axis V: Current Global Assessment of Functioning: 80; highest GAF past
                    year: 85

Objectives.   (1) Develop rewarding and realistic career goals and plans
            (2) Increase comfort and ability to deal with new phase of life

Assessments. Strong-Campbell Interest Inventory, Myers-Briggs Type Indicator

Clinician. Supportive and accepting yet action oriented, knowledgeable about career
    counseling

Location. Outpatient, college counseling center with community services

Interventions. Emphasis is on career counseling in the context of a supportive
    therapeutic relationship designed to build self-esteem and clarify goals and direction

Emphasis. High in supportiveness, low in directiveness, emphasis on cognitions (self-
    doubts) with a secondary focus on behavior and affect

Nature. Primarily individual therapy with a few couples sessions

Timing. Short-term, weekly sessions, moderate pace

Medication. None needed

Adjunct services. Support group for reentry women

Prognosis. Excellent

Source: From *Selecting Effective Treatments: A Comprehensive Systematic Guide to Treating Adult Mental Disorders* (pp. 74–75) by L. Seligman, 1990, San Francisco, CA: Jossey-Bass. Copyright 1990 by Jossey-Bass. Reprinted by permission.

with long-term therapy, but it approaches client problems as distinct goals that must be regularly evaluated and replanned. Replanning is necessary since it is very often the case that client goals shift as some problems are resolved. Clients and counselors both gain greater insight through the realization that some goals are more important or irrelevant after some progress has been made.

The two basic steps in REPLAN treatment planning are

1. Formulate mutually agreed-upon treatment goals, as a result of assessment, that are understandable to both client and counselor. These goals are then boiled down to a workable form and placed in priority order.
2. Use the curative factors (relationship, enhancing efficacy and self-esteem, practicing new behaviors, lowering and raising emotional arousal, activating expectations and increasing hope, and providing new learning experiences) to generate a list of possible treatment strategies or techniques to achieve the

goals. The counselor accomplishes this by asking himself or herself two questions: "What curative factors are most likely to help the client reach therapy goals? What strategies, methods, or techniques will be most effective and acceptable to the client?"

To illustrate the model, let us look at a case example of a 25-year-old single white male, a chemist, who is shy and wishes to meet and date women but has not been successful. The client reports, in his statement of the problem, that anxiety in social situations is his main problem. Through assessment, the counselor knows that he is well motivated, a religious Protestant, and an only child. Together client and counselor agree upon the following goal (goal 1): ask two women for dates during the next two months.

Based on assessment and her own theoretical orientation, the counselor believes that the client would be best served by an action orientation to reduce his anxiety. The counselor reviews the six curative factors to help direct the counseling and chooses two areas that she feels will help the client reach his goals:

R

E

Practicing New Behaviors

Lower/Raise Emotional Arousal

A

N

In this example, the counselor chose two curative elements to target, practicing new behaviors and lowering the client's emotional arousal (anxiety). Once the major curative factors are identified, the counselor selects strategies aimed at both areas. An example of a treatment plan, with a set of strategies or steps to address the first curative factor, is presented here:

Curative Factor	**Strategy**
Practicing new behaviors	1. Practice self-disclosure and listening skills with therapist and a friend.
	2. Role-play with therapist, asking someone out for a drink.
	3. Ask male friend out for a drink.
	4. Ask female friend out for a drink.

In summary, the notion of curative factors helps the counselor select which general approach would be most helpful in addressing the client's problems. The use of curative factors also stimulates thinking about possible techniques to employ. Part of the rationale for this kind of approach is that it encourages the therapist to consider a variety of planned interventions and to consider ordering these interventions in advance. Each session is not necessarily planned in advance, though, since some steps in the process might take longer than one session or several steps might be accomplished at the same time.

TABLE 5.3
REPLAN strategy worksheet.

Counselor asks self the following questions: (1) Which general curative factors are most likely to lead to improvement for this client? (2) What particular strategies will be most effective and acceptable to the client?

Curative Factor	Strategy
1. Decrease Depression and Suicidal Thoughts	
*R	A. Continue relationship building; encourage self-disclosure
*E	B. Ask client to generate list of positive self-statements—homework
	C. Challenge client's irrational self-downing
P	
L	
*A	D. Explain the cyclical nature of depression; encourage client to see
N	it as time limited
2. Resolve Family Problems; Make Brief Comfortable Contacts	
R	
E	
*P	A. Ask client to practice assertiveness skills in session
L	
A	
*N	B. Refer client to ACOA meeting to help client gain insight into
	family

Table 5.3 is a REPLAN strategy worksheet that shows how a counselor might select techniques to address specific problems of depression and family dysfunction.

CASE EXAMPLE USING THE REPLAN SYSTEM

Earlier, it was explained that the process of counseling actually begins in the center with the therapeutic relationship. Then it moves to assessment and treatment planning before implementing and evaluating strategies or techniques (Figure 5.1). A case example that takes the reader through the three stages of the counseling process that we have discussed thus far (viz., relationship building, assessment, and treatment planning) follows. The purpose of this example is to link together these three stages of the counseling relationship by examining a real case, which is used with the client's permission and disguised for the client's protection.

The Case of Chad

Relationship

Chad, a very attractive, extroverted 21-year-old man, was referred to counseling by his mother who was concerned about him. He had previously been treated for

FIGURE 5.1
Stages of the counseling relationship.

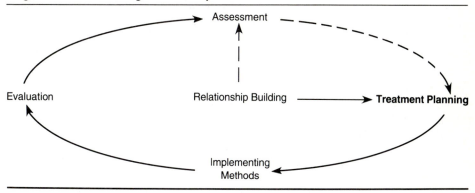

depression two years ago by a psychologist and had been relatively happy with that experience. It, therefore, took little time to gain his trust as a client since he was comfortable with the process of counseling. Chad's sadness and frustration suggested that he was well motivated. From the counselor's point of view, the relationship was very positive: Chad was very open and forthcoming and seemed very cooperative. There seemed to be mutual liking and respect. Some transference was expected since the therapist was a slightly older male, and Chad's concerns somewhat focused on his problematic relationship with his father; however, no issue was made of transference feelings since they did not seem to impinge on the relationship.

Assessment

Figure 5.2 shows the REPLAN assessment for Chad, according to the process described in chapter 4.

Implementation of Treatment

Based on the assessment, the counselor determined that the client's suicidal potential was low and decided not to evaluate for medication immediately. The client was also averse to the use of medication. The client's family had expressed concern about this method of treatment as well. It was decided that one curative factor in the REPLAN system would be the most crucial in the first stage of treatment. The client needed to increase feelings of self-esteem (E). The counselor believed that client needed to decrease negative self-evaluation and described a technique for substituting positive for negative thinking. At the fourth session, as suggested in the treatment plan, progress was evaluated. It appeared that the client was not completing homework assignments although the therapeutic relationship had grown stronger. In discussion with the client, it appeared that messages from his family over the phone had discouraged the client from using the cognitive techniques recommended by the therapist. The therapist then called a family meeting. Mother, grandmother, an uncle, and Chad attended. When Chad's family understood the rationale for the treatment, they agreed to it;

FIGURE 5.2
REPLAN assessment for Chad.

I. **Client's Statement of the Problem:**

I've had this problem for several years. But now it seems to be coming to a head. My father left the family when I was 4 or 5, and I have felt responsible for taking care of my mother and sister since then. Recently, I have been depressed and have even considered suicide. Because of my over-sleeping and depression, I haven't been going to work and I'm going to lose my part-time job. I am also failing my two courses at the community college, and I am in a financial pinch. I might get thrown out of school if I don't start going to class and studying.

II. **Biopsychosocial or Mental Health Assessment:**

1. ABCD³ Assessment (Affective, Behavioral, Cognitive, Diet/Drugs/Disabilities)

Affective: The client appears sad, with periods of crying. He does not meet *DSM-III-R* criteria for major depression. He shows interest in several normal activities and plans. He shows a great deal of anger and hostility toward his father, who makes no attempt to contact the client or the family. The Beck Depression Inventory and the Suicide Prevention Scale suggest that the client's depression is not severe and that his potential for suicide is low. These scales will be read-ministered periodically.

Behaviors: The client has been avoiding going to class. He has been working steadily but over-sleeps and does not study. He becomes most depressed when he thinks about his family. These behaviors have become evident in the last six weeks since school began. Previously, he was functioning well for about six months.

Cognitions: The client's thinking shows evidence of irrational thinking, especially with regard to his father whom he demands should love him and pay more attention to him. His view of the future, himself, and the world is largely negative. He tends to idealize his mother and vilify his father. He is sometimes troubled by images of beating his father but says he would never do that.

D³ (Drugs/Diet/Disabilities): The client admits that he drank heavily as a freshman student but denies alcohol use at this time. He denies ever having used any other drugs. His diet by his report is poor due to a lack of motivation to cook for himself and eating much of the time in fast food restaurants. The client has no physical disabilities or differences. At the first interview, he was suffering from a head cold.

2. Social/Cultural Assessment

Relationships with Friends: The client has few friends nearby. He lives with a roommate in an apartment, and they "tolerate each other." The fact that he withdrew from school previously has meant that many of his friends have graduated. His friends back in his home community are very important to him. The client has been reluctant to form any serious relationship with a woman since he feels certain his family wishes him to marry a woman from his own background.

Family History and Current Family Functioning: A genogram of the client would show that he is the eldest of two children born to an Indian couple whose marriage was arranged in Delhi, India, in 1970. He was born in America. His younger sister is 17 years old. The family's cultural background is Indian. They speak Hindi in the home. The client's maternal grandmother lives with

FIGURE 5.2
(continued)

the mother and sister. The client's mother is involved in running an export business with her brother but finances are tight. By American standards, the client's family is lower middle class. They are rather orthodox Hindus and are vegetarians.

3. Client Developmental Information

Despite the client's age of 21, he is still apparently struggling with the developmental issues of autonomy and identity. Independence from family is not normally a relevant goal for someone of the client's cultural background. The client is, however, very Americanized, having lived here since birth. The issue of how much independence he wishes to have from the family is very relevant. He feels that he is now ready to form a serious relationship with a woman.

III. **Assessment Results (Counselor Hypotheses):**

Based on interview and testing, the following hypotheses were generated:

1. Client is suffering from moderately severe depression and has one or two suicidal thoughts per day.
2. Client's depression contributes significantly to school and work problems.
3. Client has unresolved family problems, including feelings of anger towards father.
4. Client feels sense of responsibility for his family and this seems to interfere with accomplishing personal goals.
5. The client's situation of straddling two cultures is an identity issue that, when resolved, could enhance feelings of self-esteem.

IV. **Treatment Plan (Client and Counselor Contract):**

1. Counseling will be aimed at reducing depressive feelings and suicidal thoughts.
2. Counseling will be aimed at resolving family problems so that client can make comfortable contacts with his family.
3. Counseling will attempt to assist the client in achieving greater comfort with cultural identification.

Follow up Plan: This plan will be reevaluated in session #4 or on 2/12/92.

Date   /   /
Counselor Signature _____ Client Signature _____

however, the family also believed that some evil influence might be causing the depression and they planned to hold a purification service in the client's house and asked the counselor to attend. The counselor agreed and thereafter was more successful in getting the client to discourage his own depressive thinking. During this time, the family consulted with the counselor on a weekly basis by phone. The counselor was then able to get them to agree to more positive phone interactions with the client. A final aspect of the treatment was to encourage Chad's involvement with an Indian cultural group in the nearby city. After about four months, the client's depression was significantly improved as was the client's relationship with his family.

CHAPTER SUMMARY AND CONCLUSIONS

The first part of the chapter posed and addressed some critical questions about goal setting and treatment planning. Goal setting is seen as a critical step in cementing the therapeutic partnership and in transforming the focus of counseling from problems to solutions. Through the process of establishing mutually acceptable goals, the counselor involves the client in the process of counseling. Finally, the setting of goals helps both client and counselor anticipate the conclusion of therapy as a time when goals have been reached. The second half of this chapter looked at several skills that the counselor must use in order to change client problems into workable goal statements. The counselor must learn to boil down client statements into specific aims. In addition, the counselor must order the client goals according to priorities, such as the existence of a crisis, the importance of the goal to the client, the likelihood of success, the amount of client motivation, and the relation of the goal to the central or core issues.

Treatment planning involves selecting specific techniques or strategies to accomplish client goals. The REPLAN system suggests that the counselor use the curative factors to select a general direction for treatment efforts and then to identify the techniques to be used. Alternately, the counselor might use a diagnostic treatment planning model, such as DO A CLIENT MAP or a BASIC ID assessment to provide the guiding principles. In any case, counselors can no longer ignore the importance of the client's membership in a special population when planning treatment and attempting to implement counseling methods and techniques. Becoming aware of an individual's special needs and background is a practical matter for counselors who want to be successful in an increasingly diverse society.

From here, the book will begin to examine specific counseling techniques. Chapters 6 through 10 each address a different curative factor by examining several techniques that seem to share that common element.

FURTHER READINGS

Ivey, A. E. (1991) *Developmental strategies for helpers*. Pacific Grove, CA: Brooks/Cole. In this book, Ivey continues to promote his developmental counseling and therapy (DCT) theory over the traditional pathology model. In this book, he ties together the theory with suggestions on how to apply techniques to developmental blocks. Ivey highlights multicultural issues and even suggests developmental interventions for clients with personality disorders.

Omer, H. & Alon, N. (1989). Principles of psychotherapist strategy. *Psychotherapy, 26,* 282–289. This article uses a strategic therapy framework à la Erickson. The authors describe 10 rules for choosing psychotherapeutic methods. The focus of the article is on how to select methods according to chosen goals and how to minimize failure by assuring client acceptance of both goals and strategies.

Seligman, L. (1990). *Selecting effective treatments: A comprehensive, systematic guide to treating adult mental disorders.* San Francisco, CA: Jossey-Bass. Linda Seligman's book, uses the diagnostic treatment planning approach, which incorporates assessment, diagnosis, and treatment planning as interdependent activities. The book suggests treatment strategies for most major mental disorders.

REFERENCES

Barbrack, C. R., & Maher, C. A. (1984). Effects of involving conduct problem adolescents into the setting of counseling goals. *Child and Family Behavior Therapy, 6,* 33–43.

Berne, E. (1972). *What do you say after you say hello?* New York: Grove Press.

Bruce, P. (1984). Continuum of counseling goals: A framework for differentiating counseling strategies. *Personnel and Guidance Journal, 62,* 259–263.

Cormier, W. & Cormier, L. S. (1991). *Interviewing strategies for helpers: Fundamental skills and cognitive behavioral interventions.* Pacific Grove, CA: Brooks/Cole.

Dyer, W. W., & Vriend, J. (1977). A goal-setting checklist for counselors. *Personnel and Guidance Journal, 55,* 469–471.

Egan, G. (1986). *The skilled helper* (3rd ed.). Monterey, CA: Brooks/Cole.

Egan, G. (1990). *The skilled helper* (4th ed.). Pacific Grove, CA: Brooks/Cole.

Evans, M. H. (1984). Increasing patient involvement with therapy goals. *Journal of Clinical Psychology, 40,* 728–733.

Goodyear, R. K. & Bradley, F. O. (1986). The helping process as contractual. In W. P. Anderson (Ed.), *Innovative counseling: A handbook of readings* (pp. 59–62). Alexandria, VA: American Association for Counseling and Development.

Gordon, T. (1975). *P.E.T.: Parent effectiveness training.* New York: Peter H. Wyden.

Grayson, H. (1979). *Short term approaches to psychotherapy.* New York: Human Sciences Press.

Haley, J. (1976). *Problem solving therapy: New strategies for effective family therapy.* San Francisco, CA: Jossey-Bass.

Haley, J. (1989, May). Strategic family therapy. Symposium conducted at Stetson University, DeLand, FL.

Krumboltz, J. D. (1966). Behavioral goals for counseling. *Journal of Counseling Psychology, 13,* 153–159.

Muench, G. (1965). An investigation of the efficacy of time-limited psychotherapy. *Journal of Counseling Psychology, 12,* 294–298.

O'Hanlon, W. H., & Weiner-Davis, M. (1989). *In search of solutions: A new direction in psychotherapy.* New York: W. W. Norton.

Ritchie, M. H. (1986). Counseling the involuntary client. *Journal of Counseling and Development, 64,* 516–518.

Rossi, E. (1980). *Collected papers of Milton Erickson on hypnosis* (Vols. 1–4). New York: Irvington.

Rule, W. R. (1982). Pursuing the horizon: Striving for elusive goals. *Personnel and Guidance Journal, 61,* 195–197.

Seligman, L. (1990). *Selecting effective treatments: A comprehensive, systematic guide to treating adult mental disorders.* San Francisco, CA: Jossey-Bass.

Steiner, C. (1974). *Scripts people live.* New York: Grove Press.

Steiner, C. (1976, April). *Radical psychiatry.* Symposium conducted at the University of Dayton, Dayton, OH.

Thomas, G. P., & Ezell, B. (1972). The contract as counseling technique. *Personnel and Guidance Journal, 51,* 27–31.

Weinberger, A. (1982). The "consumer" in psychotherapy. *Canadian Psychology, 2,* 37–41.

CHAPTER SIX

Enhancing Efficacy and Self-Worth

KEY CONCEPTS

▼ *A positive self-concept is recognized by mental health professionals as both a desired outcome of counseling and a sign of therapeutic success. Conversely, low self-esteem is associated with a number of client problems and psychological conditions.*

▼ *Self-esteem is comprised of a global sense of self-worth and also a feeling of efficacy or mastery associated with the ability to accomplish specific tasks.*

▼ *Low self-esteem for many clients may have started early in life due to negative messages from others. These messages are reinforced through internal repetition. In addition, low self-esteem can be the result of irrational beliefs, poor or distorted body image, or inadequate or other faulty information about the self.*

▼ *Self-monitoring is an activity that asks the client to dispassionately evaluate some attribute and record the results of the observation. Feedback from others can also be a valuable, often untapped source of data.*

▼ *Reducing negative self-talk is a method for eliminating counterproductive self-criticism. It is often the next logical step after self-monitoring. Once the client has identified self-defeating internal dialogue, it must be challenged and disputed in a way that is compatible with the client's belief system.*

▼ *Assertiveness training is a broad term given to describe a set of social skills that help to build self-esteem. These skills include such things as giving and receiving compliments, refusing requests, and asserting one's rights. Verbal and nonverbal behaviors can be learned that increase assertiveness and social efficacy.*

▼ *Responding to criticism is a method for sorting out useful feedback from destructive criticism and is an important skill that compliments reducing self-critical behaviors.*

INTRODUCTION

In the REPLAN system developed in this book, the letter *E* represents the second curative factor, enhancing efficacy and self-esteem (Figure 6.1). There is wide agreement that a positive self-concept is a keystone of mental health and that raising self-esteem is a fundamental task of psychotherapy (Frey & Carlock, 1989; Kurpius, Rockwood & Corbett, 1989; Walz, 1990). Low self-esteem has been identified as a cause or contributing factor in many psychological diagnoses and symptoms, especially anxiety (Rosenberg, 1962), depression (Wilson & Krane,

139

FIGURE 6.1
Six curative factors in the REPLAN system.

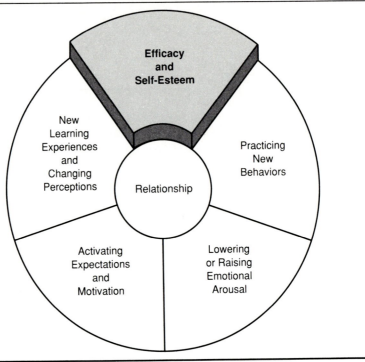

1980), stress, dependency, pathological guilt, borderline personality (Ingham, Kreitman, Miller & Sasidharan, 1986), and substances abuse (Brehm & Back, 1968). Cognitive therapists have postulated that depressions have a common psychological substrate called the *cognitive triad*. The triad consists of three major viewpoints: negative view of one's experiences, negative view of the future, and negative view of the self (Beck, Rush, Shaw & Emery, 1979).

COMPONENTS OF SELF-ESTEEM

Self-esteem has two aspects: efficacy (competence) and self-worth (Branden, 1969, 1971; Witmer, 1985). Efficacy has best been described in the psychological literature by Bandura (1982). *Efficacy* is an expectation that one can perform a specific task. For example, when an experienced driver sits behind the wheel of a car, he or she feels a sense of confidence or expectation that driving a car is a manageable task. Efficacy is tied to specific activities, though it may generalize to similar situations. It is also subject to modification by experience. Having an auto accident could undermine one's sense of efficacy as a driver. For the most part, this chapter describes methods for enhancing self-worth, but greater social efficacy is the important result of assertiveness training that is presented at the end.

FIGURE 6.2
Stages of the counseling relationship.

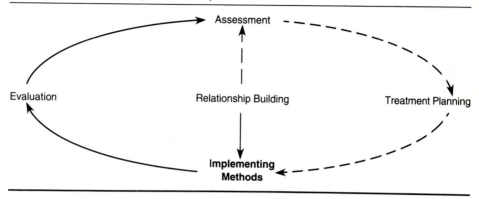

Self-worth on the other hand, is a global experience of self-esteem: the feeling that one has the right to exist and is worthy to live. It has sometimes been described as the tension felt by an individual between the perceived and ideal self (Campos, 1986; Rogers, 1961). It is the sum total of one's attitudes about the self, including a sense of efficacy related to tasks. It is the fundamental feeling of being OK or not OK (Berne, 1972).

It is possible to feel competent or efficacious at a number of tasks and still experience low self-worth. As therapists, we often meet intelligent, attractive, skilled individuals whose major problems are deeply held negative beliefs about themselves and the accompanying negative feelings. Psychotherapists attempt to help clients modify both the global sense of worth (mainly through implementing cognitive methods) and feelings of competence through the direct teaching of skills (Figure 6.2).

While raising self-esteem is recognized as a vital target of psychotherapy and counseling, changing the self-concept can be disorienting for the client. A realistic look at one's strengths and weaknesses may produce anxiety. In order to maintain a positive self-image, defense mechanisms may come into play to preserve the self-concept even at the expense of ignoring positive and new information. This tendency brings to mind two opposing forces in human growth identified by Witmer (1985). Defensive functions, such as seeking balance, withdrawal, quietude, and equilibrium, are necessary for survival. Pulling oneself into a shell is an adaptive function. But as the saying goes, the turtle must stick out its neck if it wants to go anywhere. Growth involves risk and the exploration of new information.

Before looking at specific methods for raising self-esteem, let us examine how defense mechanisms relate to self-esteem. After that, we will look at some sources or causes of low self-esteem in clients. Recognition of the power of the forces that help to maintain the current self-concept should help the clinician recognize the need for a respectful and patient attitude toward changing aspects of the self-concept.

Defense Mechanisms: Guardians of Self-Esteem

Defense mechanisms are psychological techniques designed to reduce anxiety and protect self-esteem. Excessive use of defense mechanisms is considered unhealthy since, by definition, they avoid or distort reality rather than cope with it. Defense mechanisms may not be all bad, though. Denial, for instance, has been found to be quite useful in emergencies and in handling other stressful situations (Grayson, 1986; Lazarus & Golden, 1981; Lazarus & Folkman, 1984). Epstein (1983) has postulated that defense mechanisms serve to pace or to slow down the experience of anxiety so that individuals are not forced to face more arousal than they can cope with. In any case, it is important for the clinician to recognize the overuse of defense mechanisms since overuse can point to low self-esteem. Table 6.1 shows some defense mechanisms and their functions. Most of them are commonly described elsewhere with the exception of substance abuse. Substance abuse appears here merely to recognize a common way in which people attempt to reduce anxiety and bolster self-esteem and for which they may eventually seek counseling.

Helping Clients Recognize Defense Mechanisms

The major method for confronting clients with defensive reactions might be called *the suggestive question.* It is a blend of interpretation and confrontation (i.e., it makes a suggestion about the reason for the client's behavior and at the same time focuses on the unproductive nature of the behavior). Two counselor responses that use the suggestive question to make the client aware of defensive maneuvers are given here:

Counselor's Response to Compensation:

Because your sister was so good in school, you decided to excel in sports. Now I'm wondering if your belief that you are no good at academics is entirely accurate or something you just didn't develop?

Counselor's Response to Avoidance/Withdrawal:

It sounds to me as if you have decided to give up on the relationship because you have been hurt before. Even though you don't know what might come of it, you'd rather stop now and avoid the potential pain. Is that right?

In summary, client defensive responses are designed to preserve self-esteem, but they typically trade growth for safety. The counselor must not always insist on growth but should bring defensiveness into awareness and let the client decide how to proceed. Setting viable goals and examining defended areas is necessary, as the examples clearly illustrate. Defenses serve a purpose, though: to maintain and support self-esteem. They should not be callously pulled away but deliberately and respectfully explored.

TABLE 6.1
Some common defense mechanisms and their functions.

Defense Mechanism	Function in Maintaining Self-Esteem
Avoidance/withdrawal	Escaping responsibility (No attempt, no failure)
Denial	Refusing to admit to problems
Fantasy	Imagining self as powerful and achieving
Substance abuse	Creating grandiose and powerful self-image
Rationalization	Denying failure by giving excuses
Projection	Denying negative traits and feelings in the self and ascribing them to others
Compensation	Denying inferiority by achieving in other areas.

Sources of Low Self-Esteem

Drivers

Commonly mentioned causes of low self-esteem are messages received during childhood that become internalized images or phrases about the self. In transactional analysis, the individual's life plan or script is thought to be transmitted from the parents along with accompanying injunctions such as, "You'll never amount to anything," "Don't trust anyone," etc. Some of these injunctions or themes become preeminent and rule a person's life. These ruling injunctions are called *drivers* because they broadly motivate or drive behavior (Kahler, 1977). The person attempts to maintain self-esteem by attempting to live up to the standards of parents and others. Unfortunately, these internalized sentences may not be relevant to the present, healthy, nor even possible to uphold.

An example of an impossible driver is "Be perfect." For example, a client once told me that she never plays the guitar even though she enjoys it because she cannot afford lessons nor can she stand to make mistakes. She had been raised with the injunction that "Anything worth doing is worth doing right." In reality, some things, like playing the guitar, are worth doing sloppily if one enjoys them. Perfectionism keeps people from trying new things and from enjoying activities that they perform less than flawlessly.

Table 6.2 shows physical, psychological, and behavioral manifestations of some common drivers. A therapist can recognize the manifestations of a driver in a client by the behaviors associated with it. One term in the table that needs clarification is *Discount*, which indicates the negative message or put-down associated with the driver.

Irrational Ideas

Irrational ideas are a second source of low self-esteem (Daly & Burton, 1983). *Irrational ideas* are destructive beliefs about the world that cause us to suffer

TABLE 6.2
Drivers: sources of negative self-image.

Drivers	Compliance (Inner Feelings)			Important Behavior			
	Physical	Psychological: Internal Discount	Words	Tones	Gestures	Posture	Facial Expressions
Be perfect	Tense	"You should do better."	"Of course." "Obviously." "Efficacious." "Clearly." "I think."	Clipped, righteous	Counting on fingers, cocked wrist, scratching head	Erect, rigid	Stern
Try hard	Tight stomach, tense shoulders	"You've got to try harder."	"It's hard." "I can't." "I'll try." "I don't know."	Impatient	Clenched, moving fists	Sitting forward, elbows on legs	Slight frown, perplexed look
Please me	Tight stomach	"You're not good enough."	"You know." "Could you." "Can you." "Kinda."	High whine	Hands outstretched	Head nodding	Raised eyebrows, looks away
Hurry up	Antsy	"You'll never get it done."	"We've got to hustle."	Up and down	Squirms, taps fingers	Moving quickly	Frowning, eyes shifty
Be strong	Numb, rigid	"You can't let them know you're weak."	"No comment." "I don't care."	Hard monotone	Hands rigid, arms folded	Rigid, one leg over	Plastic, hard, cold

Source: "Driver Chart" in "The Miniscript" by Taibi Kahler from *Transactional Analysis After Eric Berne.* Copyright © 1977 by Graham Barnes. Reprinted by permission of HarperCollins Publishers.

emotionally but that are so firmly entrenched that they are difficult to challenge and expunge. Albert Ellis (1973) ascribes low self-esteem to a set of "nutty beliefs" about ourselves and the world. He asserts that it is not a black cat that makes us afraid but our belief that a black cat causes bad luck. Similarly, if we rid ourselves of irrational beliefs and develop more realistic ones, we relieve ourselves of emotional turmoil. Although we each probably have something unique about our belief systems, Ellis found that some irrational ideas are quite common. The list of seven shown here are especially widespread. Interestingly, irrational ideas are often promulgated by the cultural media; books, magazines, and the lyrics of popular songs.

1. The idea that it is a dire necessity for an adult human to be loved or approved of by virtually every significant other person in his or her life.
2. The idea that one should be thoroughly competent, adequate, and achieving in all possible respects to consider oneself worthwhile.
3. The idea that certain people are bad, wicked, or villainous and that they should be severely blamed or punished for their villainy.
4. The idea that it is awful and catastrophic when things are not the way one would like them to be.
5. The idea that human unhappiness is externally caused and that people have little or no ability to control their terrors and disturbances.
6. The idea that it is easier to avoid than to face life's difficulties and self-responsibilities.
7. The idea that one's past history is an all important determiner of one's present behavior and that, because something once strongly affected one's life, it should definitely continue to do so (Ellis, 1973, p. 37).

Body Image

Psychological literature tells us that attractiveness is a valuable social asset (Adams, 1977). But many individuals, especially women, seem to equate attractiveness with self-worth (Greenspan, 1983). An individual may have a negative body image because of a physical disability, a difference, or a lack of attractiveness by media standards. On the other hand, a distorted body image is a common symptom of many psychological syndromes, especially eating disorders, resulting in the evaluation that one is fat or unattractive despite evidence to the contrary (Baird & Sights, 1986). A belief that one must be perfect is probably behind this powerful dissatisfaction that propels starvation, causes self-induced vomiting in extreme cases, and engenders low self-esteem, anger, and distress even in those without major emotional problems (Thompson & Thompson, 1986). To deal with the perfectionism associated with body image, therapists have adopted strategies such as

1. Using cognitive restructuring by asking the client to describe the perfect body and then compare his or her own body to this description. The client is then confronted with the fact that the self-description is not far from the ideal.
2. Helping the client to focus on aspects or positive qualities of the self that do not require a perfect physical appearance.

3. Having the client describe childhood experiences that involved the importance of appearance, from early memories to parental statements and asking the client to be specific and to identify those individuals from whom this learning took place.

Because the perceived need for a perfect body is so powerful, cognitive methods may not be effective (K. Myers-Sutter, personal communication, January, 1991). Instead, more use of emotional arousal has been suggested to attack these notions.

Body image correlates with self-esteem. Those with high self-worth generally feel good about their bodies. Those who do not like their bodies tend to be negative about themselves. The body also serves as a mirror of self-esteem. Table 6.3 shows some bodily, or physical, cues counselors may use to identify low and high self-esteem in clients.

Attributions

A final and somewhat more complex way of looking at sources of low self-esteem is derived from the psychological literature concerning attribution. *Attributions* are ways of assigning causality to the behaviors or cognitions of other people or oneself. Where we assign credit or blame for our successes and failures has an important effect on self-esteem.

One of the more useful versions of attribution theory was advanced by Weiner, Frieze, Kukla, Reed, Nest, and Rosenbaum (1971), revised by Weiner (1979), and translated for therapists in an article by Kurpius, Rockwood, and Corbett (1989). Let us look at it in light of the case of a middle manager named Sheila, who was demoted from an executive position in her company. The theory suggests that Sheila can attribute her failure along three dimensions. In the first place (the *locus of control* dimension), Sheila might attribute her failure to either external or internal sources. She might feel that she did not have the intelligence or did not try hard enough to perform the job (internal). Alternately, she may have felt that the job itself was too demanding, that too much was asked of her, or that she was unlucky somehow (external). The second dimension is called *stability*. She may have attributed her failure to lack of native intelligence, a rather *stable* (as well as an internal) characteristic, as opposed to a lack of effort, which might change and is therefore *unstable* (and, in this case, also internal). Thus far we can see that Sheila's feelings about herself would be different if she attributed her failure to the internal, stable cause of not being intelligent enough as opposed to an external, unstable cause such as the company's deciding to reduce the number of executives as part of a reorganizational scheme. It is important to note that in Sheila's case, it is not crucial what reasons the company gives but what attributions Sheila makes for her demotion.

The final aspect of Weiner's theory suggests that Sheila may attribute her failure to controllable or uncontrollable qualities. If she feels intelligence was the reason for her failure, that is an *uncontrollable* cause; whereas a lack of effort is *uncontrollable*. According to Weiner, attributing her failure to internal, stable, and uncontrollable causes like intelligence decreases efficacy and self-worth. Along these same lines, Forsterling (1984) concludes that attributing success to internal

TABLE 6.3
Physical cues to self-esteem.

Bodily Cues	High Self-Esteem	Low Self-Esteem
Chest	Soft but solid	Sunken, constricted
Eyes	Bright	Dull
Skin tone	Smooth	Erupted
Breathing	Full	Shallow
Muscle tone	Elastic	Tight or flaccid
Proportion of body	Segments coordinated	Top-bottom split, uncoordinated
Gait	High, bouncy	Burdened
Neck	Pliable	Rigid
Head	Moves easily	Does not move freely; immobile; movements jerky
Pelvis	Swings freely	Frozen
Alignment of body	Aligned	Off-center
Hands	Well cared for, smooth, nails clean and trimmed; expressive	Rough, nails bitten or dirty; hidden out of sight
Movements	Coordinated	Awkward
Shoulders	Relaxed	Slumped/raised
Actions	Supported by total body, moving from the "center," flowing	Incomplete, chaotic
Posture	Relaxed, spine straight	Slumped or rigid
Arms	Animated	Hang lifelessly
Jaw	Relaxed	Juts out
Total body energy	Vibrant	Dull

Source: From *Enhancing Self-Esteem*, Second Edition (p. 337) by Diane Frey and C. Jesse Carlock, 1989, Muncie, IN: Accelerated Development. Reprinted by permission.

attributes and failures to unstable sources, like bad luck or insufficient effort, tends to preserve self-esteem.

With this knowlege, how can the counselor help the client who has an attributional style that leads to lowered self-esteem? In Table 6.4 Kurpius, Rockwood, and Corbett (1989) look at three common client problems, along with their associated attributional styles, and suggest interventions for raising self-esteem. In this table, three key terms under "Client Problems" need clarificaiton. The first of these terms, *learned helplessness,* refers to a state of acceptance and the failure to try in what appear to be unalterable circumstances because of previous experiences, even if change may now be possible. *Self-handicapping* is a strategy involving attributing all failures to one's handicap, such as "I am an alcoholic," and attributing all successes to the self. It protects self-esteem by eliminating guilt from

TABLE 6.4
Attributional interventions.

Client Problems	Attributional Styles	Interventions
Learned helplessness (depression; low self-esteem)	Attributes success to external, unstable causes (e.g., luck); attributes failures to internal, stable causes (e.g., ability)	Change attributions for success to ability; change attributions for failure to internal, unstable causes (e.g., misguided effort)
Self-handicapping strategies (protection of precarious self-esteem)	Maintains attributional control by attributing failures to self-handicaps and successes to self	Increase awareness of competencies; counter irrational thinking about evaluative feedback; examine self-handicap as a coping strategy
Victimization	Maladaptively blames victimization on one's *character*	Provide support; discourage characterological self-blame; accept *behavioral* self-blame as a way to maintain personal control

Source: From "Attributional Styles and Self-Esteem: Implications for Counseling by D. Kurpius, G. F. Rockwood, and M. O. Corbett, 1989, *Counseling and Human Development, 21*(8) pp. 1–12.

internal attributions. Finally *victimization* refers to lives that have been disrupted by extreme circumstances. In a counseling situation, one often encounters individuals who are struggling with how to assign blame after having been the victims of serious assaults, illnesses, or catastrophes. The authors recommend that individuals who present with problems of learned helplessness should be encouraged to take credit for successes that result from their abilities. Those using self-handicapping strategies should be encouraged to become aware of strengths and asked to explore the self-handicap. Those who have been victimized should be encouraged to accept responsibility for behaviors that maintain or cause their problems and to eliminate self-blame.

Up to this point, some causes and symptoms of low self-esteem have been outlined. It has been suggested that self-esteem is composed of a global sense of self-worth and feelings of efficacy with reference to specific skills or situations. Some of the things that contribute to negative self-concept include body image, irrational beliefs, drivers, and attributional style. In the next section, we will look at some methods for developing self-esteem.

METHODS AND TECHNIQUES FOR DEVELOPING SELF-ESTEEM

Self-Monitoring: Overview and Purpose of the Method

Earlier in the chapter it was stated that irrational beliefs and drivers are created early in life and represent habitual or automatic attitudes about the self. Therefore, the first step in enhancing self-esteem is to obtain accurate information about the self and, second, to become aware of automatic negative statements that are repeated with minimal awareness. The Johari window (Luft, 1969) is a way of explaining that information about the self comes from two sources: things we observe and the observations of other people (Figure 6.3). The window has four panes:

I. Information known both to others and to the self (public area)
II. Information known to others but not to the self (blind spot)
III. Information not known to others but known to the self (private)
IV. Information not known to others or the self (unknown)

According to the model, self-disclosure widens the public area and shrinks the private area. Feedback from others helps to make the blind spot smaller and to increase the public area. This enlarging of the public area through gathering information from others and sharing the self with others is thought to increase self-esteem and mental health in general (Jourard, 1968). This process of gathering information about the self is not only the initial step in changing negative aspects of behavior but is also a strengthening process due to the acquisition of knowledge of one's positive attributes as well.

A major problem with accepting feedback from others is that it is very often discounted by the client. If the counselor falls into the social role of attempting to increase self-esteem by complimenting the client's positive traits, ordinarily the information is rejected. Experienced clinicians find that one of the best ways of increasing the client's knowledge about the self is to assign self-monitoring or self-assessment tasks. Since the client may have been laboring under false assumptions about the self for many years, resistance to change may be strong.

There are a number of techniques to increase client information about the self. They share the common methodology of attempting to dispassionately and scientifically examine the client's behavior and give useful feedback or to confront the client with his or her own self-evaluations. As a representative method of the self-monitoring process, we will now examine the use of the self-monitoring card.

A Representative Self-Monitoring Method: The Self-Monitoring Card

A 3-by-5-inch or 4-by-6-inch card is a useful and readily available tool for accumulating daily information on a client goal. Keep in mind that the therapist's goal is not to prod the client into changing any perceptions at first, but merely to increase attention and allow increased awareness to motivate change. Human beings tend to accommodate painful experiences. Bringing this discomfort into consciousness tends to bring about change. This phenomenon, called *psychological reactance*, was

FIGURE 6.3
The Johari window.

	Known to self	Not known to self
Known to others	I Public area	II Blind spot
Not known to others	III Hidden area	IV Unknown area

Source: From *Of Human Interaction* (p. 13) by J. Luft, 1969, Palo Alto, CA: National Press.
Reprinted by permission.

discovered serendipitously by early behaviorists who asked individuals to keep track of a habit, such as smoking, to assess a starting point or baseline. It turned out that just by monitoring the behavior, it began to lose its strength and decrease at least temporarily (cf., Maletzky, 1974). A great deal of smoking, for example, is done without much awareness. It might be done while listening to the radio and driving the car. By asking the person to write down every cigarette smoked, the individual becomes conscious of each occurrence and is reminded of the negative consequences of smoking. Self-criticism, too, is often habitual and automatic and is also thought to decrease in frequency when monitored. The method for self-monitoring this behavior involves the five following steps:

1. *Identifying the target behavior to be monitored when it occurs*—Identifying a target behavior is the result of counselor/client discussions and negotiation. To begin with, the client should be certain that there is a clear understanding of the behavior and what is to be counted. For example, does the client with bulimia count a binge of only five cookies or just one of two dozen? Sometimes clients do not see success until they completely eliminate a behavior or perfectly acquire a new behavior. It is for the counselor to assist the client in coming up with a measuring system that will be easy and workable and that will reflect client progress easily.

2. *Marking each occurrence of the behavior*—Since most people are not good observers of behavior, an accurate baseline assessment of behavior can be very revealing. If you ask someone how many times per day he or she engages in self-criticism, the answer will likely be quite inaccurate. Precise information can be very surprising to the client. It is quite common to find extreme distortions in judgement using this method. Counting alone may not be sufficient for monitoring some behaviors. It may be necessary to use a SUDS (subjective units of discomfort scale) rating from 0 to 100 of the

TABLE 6.5
Self-criticism monitoring card for Joe — day 1.

No.	Time	Self-Statement	Feeling	SUDS
1.	8:15	I'll never get all this work done.	Discouraged	85
2.	9:00	I didn't do a good job on that report.	Disgust	50
3.	10:00	I'll never be good at this job. I'm just average and that's all.	Self-Pity	60
4.	10:35	I'm daydreaming again. Why am I so lazy?	Anger	35
5.	12:00	I offended the secretary again. Why can't I just keep my mouth shut.	Anger	45
6.	1:00	I feel fat after eating so much. I'm turning into a blimp.	Disgust	35
7.	2:40	Another day almost done, and I've completed nothing.	Anger	40
8.	3:30	My desk is a mess. What a slob!	Discouraged	50
9.	5:15	Even my car is full of trash. I wish I were more organized.	Anger	25

SUDS = subjective units of distress

0 100

No emotional distress　　　　　　　　　　　　　　　　　　　Extreme emotional distress

Emotions = fear, anger, sadness, guilt, interest-excitement/(boredom), joy

Summary
9 = negative self-statements; average SUDS = 47 (approx.)
Most prevalent emotion = self-anger/disgust

emotional intensity of the behavior. This rating is helpful since progress may first be noticed before the number of actual occurrences decreases (i.e.,when the intensity of self-criticism decreases).

3. *Noting any concomitant emotional responses*—One option with the self-monitoring card is to help the client begin to make the connection between self-criticism and negative emotional states. The client is educated regarding the primary emotional experiences—anger, fear, sadness, guilt, interest/excitement, and joy (Witmer, 1985)—or the short-hand transactional analysis version—sad, mad, glad, and afraid.

4. *Using charts and graphs*—These adjuncts to self-monitoring can aid the client in gaining accurate knowledge about the frequency, duration, or intensity of target behaviors (Fremouw, Wiener & Seime, 1987). Table 6.5 illustrates a self-monitoring card. Figure 6.4 is a graph of the occurrences of the targeted behavior and the SUDS levels of the same client taken from his self-monitoring cards. SUDS levels and negative self-statements are graphed on the same page to visually gauge the correlation (e.g., if days with higher average SUDS levels might also be days with higher numbers of negative self-statements.

5. *Changing negatives into positives when possible*—Decreasing a negative behavior does increase self-esteem, but the acquisition of a positive behavior is even

FIGURE 6.4
Graph of critical self-statements and daily SUDS levels for Joe.

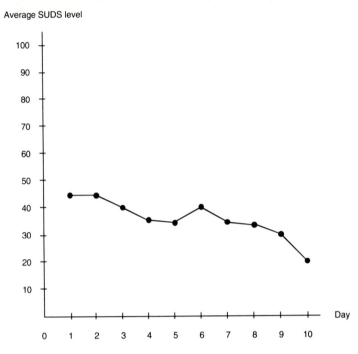

Average SUDS level

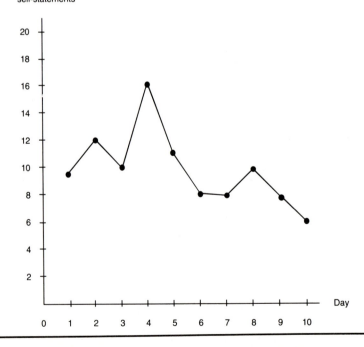

Negative
self-statements

more strengthening. Once the client becomes aware of self-criticism, it may be useful to help the client to monitor the number of occasions when he or she is able to intervene and produce a counteracting positive statement about the self. This is related to the Adlerian concept of *catching yourself.* Catching yourself can be introduced informally in the counseling session by suggesting something like this to the client:

> *Counselor:* During this next week, there will be several times when you know that you are lapsing into self-criticism, but you will be able to catch yourself and insert a more positive statement. Just be aware of how well you're able to do this and we'll talk about it next time.

Problems and Precautions with Self-Monitoring

The major problem that exists in using self-monitoring with outpatient clients is compliance. While initially enthusiastic, some clients will lack the necessary organizational skills or motivation to do accurate and regular self-monitoring. Attempting to achieve compliance by entreating the client to recognize the importance of achieving accurate data may help, but this strategy may be unsuccessful if the client is unconvinced or unwilling to participate. Surprisingly some clients are eager and enthusiastic about collecting data.

A second precaution or problem with self-monitoring noted by Sharpley (1986) is that when client results are presented graphically, there are many unsupported hypotheses that may result from eyeballing the data. Furthermore, not all clients are data people, and they may not be interested in or encouraged by graphic evidence.

Variations on Self-Monitoring

Listing Good Things/Bad Things. An in-office method for increasing client awareness of self-concept is the simple exercise of asking clients to alternately list 10 good things about themselves and 10 things they would like to change. For many clients, it becomes obvious that they can easily engage in self-criticism, but they have a more difficult time identifying positive traits.

Group Therapy. Group therapy provides one of the best opportunities for growth in self-esteem. Perhaps the most important learning comes from the feedback of others, which increases knowledge about the self and one's strengths and weaknesses (Yalom, 1985). At the same time, clients in group therapy find that their flaws are not unique.

A structured exercise called "First Impressions" is often used to establish a norm of feedback and self-disclosure in the group. The exercise is usually done in the second or third group meeting. Participants individually volunteer to receive first impressions from the group. One at a time, group members share their initial ideas about an individual and perhaps contrast their first impressions with current ones. Those who give feedback are encouraged to be specific and as honest as possible. The therapist can be the first to give feedback, modeling the sort of specific, balanced feedback that is most helpful.

The individual who volunteers to receive feedback listens intently but refrains from responding until the end. Some clients find it difficult not to make some sort of rejoinder and become defensive even to positive feedback. The counselor can later make the client aware of this tendency, and once feedback has been received from the entire group, the client can be encouraged to explore his or her reactions to everything that has been said. This kind of awareness exercise often helps clients focus on interpersonal behaviors they would like to change as well as increasing awareness of their strengths.

When other group members give feedback, the therapist's job is to make certain that the feedback given is not harmful to the receiver. Group members should challenge each other, but some feedback is unfair and useless to the receiver. Feedback is helpful only if it concerns something that can be changed (Egan, 1990). To be valuable, feedback should

1. Make the person aware of positive behaviors.
2. Make the person aware of areas where correction is needed.
3. Be brief.
4. Focus on behaviors rather than personality traits.

Marriage Counseling.   One outcome of successful marriage counseling is heightened self-esteem (Greene, 1986). There is a connection between feeling good about a relationship and feeling good about oneself. Divorce, separation, and marital discord are accompanied by feelings of failure and lowered self-esteem. When couples are in conflict, they also tend to focus on negative aspects of their partners, to talk about these traits, and to try to change them. Although it is important to face areas of conflict directly, it is sometimes more helpful for the counselor to ask couples to become aware of the good things about their partners. This has the dual purpose of increasing the partner's self-esteem and of cementing the marital relationship enough so that problems may be worked through.

Early marriage counseling sessions may need the kind of bonding and positive focus described above. One method for accomplishing this is to ask each partner in turn to describe the positive traits of the other. The therapist then explores with the couple their reaction to the exercise. Couples are frequently surprised after a long period of fighting that some positive regard and respect still exist. Others find this exercise difficult and resist it because of anger over the misdeeds of their partners. The therapist asks the couple to lay aside this anger for the moment and become aware only of the reasons for staying in the relationship. Although couples sometimes feel that they can read each other's minds, they are often surprised at their partner's compliments. The technique is an elementary one for building the bridge necessary to continue early dialogue in marriage counseling. It also has its pitfalls. The major counseling mistake is conveying that the therapy will never get around to the serious concerns and criticisms that the couple has and will focus only on the positive aspects of the relationship.

Personal Experiments.   Much of human psychological suffering is due to misconceptions about oneself and one's effects on others. Most people do not challenge their ideas about themselves that were formed early in life. Therapists frequently hear these types of statements:

- I can't draw. I'm not much of an artist.
- I'm not very smart.
- I am ugly.
- Women don't find me attractive.
- I'm not good with money.

One way of challenging these beliefs is through personal experiments, to assign homework that collects empirical data concerning the client's statements. For example, the client may ask a friend to show his picture to 10 women and to rate his attractiveness on a 10-point scale. Beforehand, the client predicts the average rating. In a way, this experiment is fixed since the therapist usually knows that the client's rating will be lower than the actual results. The technique is used to provide the client with new information to combat misconceptions and negative views of the self.

CASE EXAMPLE

Joe is a 29-year-old administrator for an insurance company who has come to counseling for problems associated with "stress." He has borderline high blood pressure, is often tense and angry after work, and is rude to his fiancée. He plays racquetball competitively. Last week, he purposefully broke a $100 racquet after a bad shot. He wishes to control his anger and feel less "stressed" at work. During the assessment, the counselor identified negative self-statements as a major cause of the client's stress and felt that, in general, the most useful path for Joe was to increase self-esteem. Joe agreed but also felt he needed better organizational skills. The initial therapy plan was therefore a two-pronged attack: to decrease self-criticism and to develop better time management and organization skills. Joe enrolled in a three-day time management workshop sponsored by his company and, at the same time, began a self-monitoring activity, as shown in Table 6.5. Figure 6.2 is a graph of Joe's SUDS levels and negative self-statements over the first 10 days. Using a self-monitoring card, Joe found that he was producing anger by his self-statements, which were first aimed at himself and sometimes discharged on innocent bystanders. Joe agreed to continue to monitor his self-statements for two more weeks and noticed a marked diminishing of his self-criticism. In Joe's case, there seemed to be a correspondence between his self-criticism and his emotional SUDS levels. Self-monitoring also confirmed that anger toward others and toward himself was the major emotion he was experiencing.

Reducing Negative Self-Talk Through Countering: Overview and Purpose of the Method

Before one can experience self-worth, it is often necessary to silence the internal critic, the "voice in the head" that reproaches and finds fault. This critic is probably created early in life through the learning of irrational beliefs and drivers (McKay & Fanning, 1987). These irrational beliefs and drivers persist later in life as silent sentences that the individual repeats to himself or herself overtly or

---

Feedback Checklist #3
Self-Monitoring

1. To what extent was the counselor able to help the client identify and simplify the target behavior to be monitored?

Not at All	*A Little*	*Somewhat*	*Moderately*	*A Great Deal*
1	2	3	4	5

2. How well did the counselor instruct the client to monitor every occurrence of the behavior, explaining the need for accuracy and the definitions of a SUDS level?

Not at All	*A Little*	*Somewhat*	*Moderately*	*A Great Deal*
1	2	3	4	5

3. To what extent did the counselor explain the connection with emotional responses and help the client understand and label feelings?

Not at All	*A Little*	*Somewhat*	*Moderately*	*A Great Deal*
1	2	3	4	5

4. How well did the counselor explain the use of graphs and charts and help the client understand the use of a self-monitoring card?

Not at All	*A Little*	*Somewhat*	*Moderately*	*A Great Deal*
1	2	3	4	5

---

covertly. These thoughts tend to occur automatically. For example, before giving a speech, the following thought might occur: "I am going to get up and make a fool of myself." According to cognitive therapy, these negative thoughts lead to negative emotions of anger, depression, and lowered expectations of the self. Thus, before self-esteem can be built, it is often necessary to reduce the power of the internal critic and to modify these self-statements (Dowd, 1985).

The Countering Method

Step 1: Identify and Explore Negative Self-Talk. Once a problem of negative self-talk has been identified, it is then critical to determine the nature and frequency of the negative self-statements and the conditions under which they occur. For this purpose, the client is asked first to engage in self-assessment or self-monitoring activities to determine the frequency and types of self-downing behavior. Typically, the client carries an index card in a pocket, wallet, or purse and notes each time any self-criticism occurs. The client is asked to be objective and not to make any determination as to the validity of the self-criticism.

The self-criticism card serves two functions; it gives client and counselor more data about the problem, and it helps the client make the connection between negative self-statements and the feeling states they produce. The client can then begin to see that instead of providing valid criticisms, the internal monologue is producing negative emotions.

Step 2: Examining the Function of the Client's Self-Criticism.   Once the client has completed at least a week's worth of self-monitoring, the major negative thought patterns and core beliefs about the self may be identified from the compiled results of the self-monitoring task. Often three or four general ideas come to the surface:

- I am not disciplined and never get anything accomplished.
- I am disorganized.
- I'll never be able to reach my goals.

Before these beliefs can be successfully eliminated, it may be important to hold discussions with the client, attempting to understand the source of these beliefs. It must be remembered that clients hold onto these beliefs through habit and self-protection, nor do they easily let go of them. There is evidence, for example, that some individuals use negative self-evaluations for "self-handicapping," meaning that by believing in a disability, such as test anxiety, a person can avoid labeling themselves as stupid or lazy (Smith, Snyder & Handleman, 1981; Tucker, Vuchinich & Sobell, 1981).

One way to explore this area is for clients to evaluate the negative thoughts on the list and ask themselves, "What does this negative thought help me do or feel?" or, "What does this negative thought help me avoid?" If a client finds, for instance, that she harasses herself in order to avoid shock and hurt when someone else criticizes her work, she will begin to grasp the defensive quality of her behavior and may become more motivated to change it. She may also discover that she wishes to work on becoming less sensitive to the criticism of others.

Step 3: Developing Effective Counters.   *Counter* is a term coined by McMullin (1986) to describe the production of a self-statement that is incompatible with the critical thought. According to McMullin, the counter can be a phrase, a sentence, or a single word such as nonsense. The counter talks back and disputes the self-criticism. The best counters are those that fit the client's values and philosophy. Together client and counselor brainstorm a number of possible counters, and the client selects several to try. An example of a self-criticism and the list of counters generated by client and counselor follows:

Self-Criticism	Counters
I am stupid.	1. You've always performed well in school: there's no evidence for this.
	2. *Feeling* stupid doesn't mean you *are* stupid.
	3. That's something my Dad always told me. But it's not true!
	4. Not true!

Step 4: Reacting to New Self-Statements and Modifying.   The final stage in the process of eliminating self-criticism is to evaluate the effectiveness of the counters that the individual has practiced since the last counseling session. The client will likely need more than one week to feel a sense of effectiveness since much self-criticism takes place without full awareness. In a short time, the client should

be able to identify an effective counter or two for each core belief. It must be emphasized that there is a great deal of individuality in terms of which counters will be effective.

One method for evaluating the effectiveness of a counter is to practice the technique with the client. The client verbalizes the self-criticism, such as "I am a failure at everything I do," and then notes on a 100-point SUDS scale the amount of discomfort in the resulting feeling. Next, the client verbalizes a counter and records the amount of reduction in the discomfort following its use. This teaches the client to evaluate the effect of counters and to use those which are most powerful.

Problems and Precautions of Countering

Ineffective counters should be discarded, and the client should be prepared for the fact that some counters are more potent than others. The client can be asked to modify the counter slightly in any way that might refine it or make it more effective. The counselor should also suggest any personal words or phrases that might cue more self-confidence. For example, one client found that introducing each counter with "Clearly . . ." gave the counter more power for her.

Counters should be realistic. They should not be simply positive thinking but should actually dispute the negatives. A statement such as "Every day in every way, I'm getting better and better" is a pep talk without real substance.

Some negative self-statements are quite persistent, and it may take months to eliminate insidious automatic thoughts. For this reason, therapy may have to include follow-up visits to check on progress.

McMullin (1986) suggests that the counter should be in the same mode as the thought it is disputing. Negative visual images should be countered with positive visual images. Angry thoughts should be countered with compassionate ones and "passive thoughts with assertive ones" (p. 5). Also, shorter counters tend to be more effective than longer ones.

Variations on Countering

Thought Stopping. Sometimes clients are troubled by unwanted thoughts and images that create anxiety and depression and damage self-esteem. Unwanted thoughts and images may be remembered scenes of failure or concern about upcoming events. Compared to the developing of counters, *thought stopping* can be considered more of an emergency measure to halt the flow of negative messages. Generally, the technique is described in the office and practiced by the client as homework. Three steps in the thought-stopping technique have been identified (Davis, Eshelman & McKay, 1980; Lazarus, 1971; Witmer, 1985):

1. Stating the thought
2. Creating a startling interruption
3. Substituting the thought

Once the thought has been identified, the client is asked to label and state it either mentally or aloud: for example, "I am seeing her laughing at me again." This repetition brings the thought into clearer focus.

The client creates a startling response strong enough to force the negative thinking out of awareness. One practical method when practicing thought stopping privately is to yell "Stop!" as loud as possible. In public, a mental, "Stop!" is the next best alternative. Some counselors suggest snapping a rubber band around the wrist along with a mental "Stop!" to produce the interruption.

The client finally inserts a positive thought to replace the irrational, self-downing thought. This can be either a spontaneous or a planned counter that the client produces to counteract the negative thought. For example, when the client berates himself by saying, "How could I let that deal slip away!" a replacement thought might be, "There's nothing I can do about the past except to learn from it."

CASE EXAMPLE

Jane was a 35-year-old woman who believed that she was a bad luck charm. She described a life full of loss, including the death of her first husband, the poor health of her present husband, and a devastating auto accident that disfigured one of her children. She was, at that time, working for a travel agency that was having severe financial problems. She admitted that she was responsible in some unknown way for all of these events. She was experiencing a sort of chronic mild depression and avoided forming close relationships with people. Close relationships might mean that friends could become the next victims of her bad luck. With the counselor's help, she was able to identify the following core beliefs:

- I am the cause of other people's misfortunes.
- Nothing I ever do works out.

Through discussion with the therapist, the client was able to determine that she attributed the ups and downs in her life to fate and saw nothing positive coming out of her own efforts (external, uncontrollable, and unstable attributions). Paradoxically, she was convinced that she had the power to affect other people's lives. She was an intelligent woman who grasped the incompatibility of these two beliefs. With the therapist's help, she developed a set of 20 counters. She kept a list of the five most effective in her purse and reviewed them when disappointments occurred. Two of her most effective counters were

1. I could hurt other people if I tried. But I'm not trying!
2. I could show compassion to others when they are in trouble, not simply wallow in my own guilt. It's not helpful.

Assertiveness Training: Overview and Purpose of the Method

Assertiveness training is a term that was most popular in the 1970s (Alberti & Emmons, 1974; Rathus, 1975; Smith, 1975). Assertiveness refers to a broad set of social skills used to enhance self-esteem. It has been used successfully with a wide variety of client concerns, including marriage problems, depression, sexual dysfunction, aggressive behavior, substance abuse, and dependency (Gambrill, 1985; Tanner & Holliman, 1988). More recently, the term *assertiveness training* has been

---

Feedback Checklist #4
Countering

1. How effective was the counselor in helping the client identify the nature and frequency of negative self-statements?

Not at All	*A Little*	*Somewhat*	*Moderately*	*A Great Deal*
1	2	3	4	5

2. To what extent did the counselor help the client examine the function and source of negative self-statements?

Not at All	*A Little*	*Somewhat*	*Moderately*	*A Great Deal*
1	2	3	4	5

3. To what degree was the counselor able to help the client develop a list of counters?

Not at All	*A Little*	*Somewhat*	*Moderately*	*A Great Deal*
1	2	3	4	5

4. To what extent did the counselor attempt to determine the compatibility of the counters with the client's values, philosophy, and the nature of the negative thoughts?

Not at All	*A Little*	*Somewhat*	*Moderately*	*A Great Deal*
1	2	3	4	5

5. How much did the counselor help the client evaluate the effectiveness of counters and modify them based on the evaluation?

Not at All	*A Little*	*Somewhat*	*Moderately*	*A Great Deal*
1	2	3	4	5

---

replaced with *social skills training*. This change reflects a recognition that assertion is not as simple as standing up for one's rights or saying "No." Today, when we speak about assertiveness training in clinical practice, we are talking about specific admixtures of a number of social skills, especially

- Giving and receiving a compliment
- Greeting others and initiating conversation
- Refusing requests and saying no
- Disclosing oneself to others and making contact
- Asking for information
- Asserting beliefs, preferences, requests and rights (Witmer, 1985)

Until now, a rather simple idea, that social behavior can be classified as either submissive (nonassertive) or aggressive, had been advanced (Alberti, 1977). And assertiveness, the target cluster of behaviors, had been described as falling in the middle of a continuum between nonassertion and aggressiveness. Although it may be useful educationally to explain assertiveness as a compromise between submission and dominance and as a balance between meeting one's own needs and those of others, it has been found that assertiveness is also very situation specific. A woman who is a very assertive director of a large business may be very nonassertive with her parents. Individuals who come to counseling for assertiveness training may be exposed to some general principles but should then move to identifying specific characteristics unique to their situations.

Verbal Behaviors Associated with Assertiveness

One of the most basic assertive behaviors is the use of the word *I* instead of *you*. When using *I* at the beginning of a statement such as "I am bothered by your smoking," one takes responsibility for the statement and, at the same time, avoids a *you* statement that might make the other person defensive. Other examples of *I* statements include

- "I disagree with you" rather than "You are wrong."
- "I get angry when . . ." rather than "You make me angry."
- "May I have one of those programs?" rather than "You forgot me."

Another way of thinking about assertive behaviors is acknowledging that different strengths or levels of assertion are needed for different situations. At the first level, a polite request is attempted: "I'm having trouble hearing the movie, would you mind speaking more quietly?" Notice that the request describes the situation in nonjudgemental terms and specifies what is wanted of the other person. If the assertive request does not have the desired effect, it may be necessary to increase the power of the request. This is done by adding feelings to the polite request, as in the following statement: "I feel very uncomfortable when you tell racist jokes and I wish you wouldn't." In extreme situations, it may be necessary to indicate the consequences if the behavior continues: for example, "I find this situation with my stereo very frustrating and I would like you to refund my money. If you don't, I will talk to the manager about this."

Nonverbal Behaviors Associated with Assertiveness

A number of body postures is often associated with assertiveness.

Eye contact.   Maintaining direct eye contact is an effective way of expressing sincerity. Looking away or looking down, in this culture, suggests a lack of confidence or deference to the other as the authority.

Body posture.   An assertive body posture involves squarely facing the other person, sitting or standing appropriately close, and perhaps leaning forward slightly with head erect.

Touch.   Touch can be used in making a request since it gains the attention of the listener. When denying a request, a touch can lessen the feelings of rejection.

Gestures.   Gestures add emphasis to the message and can be descriptive and visually communicative. On the other hand, extensive gesturing can be a distraction. Clients should be given feedback when gestures are lacking, overused, and instead become nervous distractions.

Facial expression.   Facial expression should be appropriate to the message one is sending. The therapist should help the client become aware of discrepancies between verbal messages and facial expressions.

Voice tone, inflection, and volume.   These aspects of voice should reflect the kind of message one is trying to convey. Usually, a well-modulated conversational tone accompanies assertion. Speaking softly will water down an assertive message and a loud dominating voice may also negate assertion by activating the other person's defenses.

Assertive Methods of Responding to Criticism

Earlier we discussed silencing the internal critic as a means of increasing self-esteem. A specific assertiveness method that relates directly to self-esteem is learning how to respond to the criticisms of others. No matter how firm one's convictions are, they may be subject to modification by significant others, including bosses, parents, spouses, friends, and even children. If this criticism is not constructive, it can damage self-esteem.

Step 1: Preparing and Educating the Client.   Before the client can be taught the method of responding to criticism, some preparation is required to familiarize the client with the theory behind assertiveness training. This also helps to gain the client's trust and assistance in learning the method. The exact preparation is based on the client's level of knowledge and the specific goal he or she is trying to accomplish. The preparation can be done by the counselor in the office as a kind of didactic presentation or through homework reading assignments.

Preparation might include presenting the refusal of criticism as an *assertive right*. Smith (1975) listed 10 such rights. The following list incorporates some of Smith's ideas and might be given to a client who is learning how to handle criticism from others:

1. You have the right to change your mind.
2. You have the right to try something and make mistakes.
3. You have the right to say, "I don't know."
4. You have the right to make a request.
5. You have the right to refuse a request.
6. You have the right to refuse destructive feedback.
7. You have the right to be illogical when making decisions.

Besides these rights, a number of irrational beliefs may be implicated in a person's nonassertive or aggressive behavior. Typically, they include blaming others or believing that others are fragile and will be easily hurt. The therapist should certainly examine the possibility of irrational beliefs when dealing with problems of assertiveness.

Related to this, the client may need to learn that other persons' perceptions are subject to error. Just as five witnesses at an auto accident will have differing versions of the same collision, another's criticism is based on his or her vantage point and does not represent the whole truth. Learning that everyone's viewpoint is valid, including one's own, may help to strengthen self-esteem and aid in reducing anger towards those who criticize us.

One hope is that the client can begin to see criticism as valuable and not just something to tolerate. There may be aspects of criticism that are constructive even if uttered in the most unpalatable of circumstances. The client should be encouraged to take a detached attitude toward criticism and see it as a potential learning experience. In order to do this, the client must be able to distinguish between destructive and constructive criticism. Destructive criticism tends to be global, using the words *always* and *never*. It is hard to accept because exceptions easily come to mind. Destructive criticism also includes attempts to make the other person feel guilty. Manipulation through guilt may be effective, but it breeds resentment. Also destructive are uncontrolled outbursts of anger, lengthy monologues, and name calling. Although the person who expressed the anger may feel better, the feelings are dumped onto the other individual who may also respond defensively and be unable to find anything useful in the feedback. Finally, destructive criticism may take the form of resentments from the past. It is useless and even detrimental to evoke feelings of guilt about something that cannot be changed. All of these forms of destructive criticism are harmful to the self-concept if they are accepted at face value.

More often than not criticism contains a germ of truth that an individual may examine and benefit from. According to Egan (1990), constructive criticism

1. Includes noticing positive as well as negative aspects of a performance
2. Is brief and specific
3. Does not require the other person to change instantly but acknowledges that change takes time
4. Involves an openness to the other person's viewpoint and is stated tentatively to recognize this
5. Includes a commitment to negotiate and take positive action to solve the problem

While clients cannot expect that they will receive constructive criticism at all times, they can learn to ask for this type of feedback.

Step 2: Assessment.   Once a general orientation toward assertiveness is completed, the focus must move to specific areas of concern. Initially an assessment must be done that includes descriptions of the problem situations the client wishes to work on and the client's current verbal and nonverbal behavior in these settings. The counselor should collect statements from the client about his or her behavior. If possible, additional descriptions from a cohort, such as a spouse or coworker, should be solicited.

Step 3: Identifying Personal and Environmental Obstacles.   This is a follow-up to the educational step. Here the therapist asks the client to identify what specific feelings (e.g., anxiety) or negative thoughts are likely to intrude in the acquisition of the target behaviors. The client is also urged to identify problems in the environment, such as uncooperative and difficult people, or inappropriate social environments, such as access to privacy for conversations.

Step 4: Identifying Personal and Environmental Supports.   Because social skills associated with assertiveness may be rather complex, it is vital to encourage or reinforce the client along the way. Luckily, much assertive behavior is its own reward since we begin to get more of what we want when using it. Early in the process, though, it may be very useful to ask the client to engage in brief, encouraging reminders to the self. Even if the assertive goals are not accomplished, practicing assertive behaviors is itself a goal of therapy and indicates personal growth.

At the same time, the client is asked to seek out other individuals who in their social contexts can act as supports to his or her assertive efforts. The client asks these confederates to give feedback when positive changes in target behaviors are noticeable.

Step 5: Developing a Hierarchy of Situations Based on Client Skill and Comfort. Let us take the example of an individual whose boss is always criticizing her work as a graphic artist. The client believes she is a hardworking and talented artist and feels the criticism is destructive and unjustified. She develops a list of behaviors she would like to attempt and orders them from the easiest and most comfortable to accomplish to the most difficult as follows:

1. Remind the boss that the idea he is criticizing is not hers
2. Remind the boss that the design she is working on was approved by him
3. Disagree with the boss's criticism but agree to change the product
4. Disagree with the boss and politely argue for her own viewpoint

Step 6: Identifying Specific Verbal and Nonverbal Behaviors to Be Acquired. Once the assessment has been accomplished, the therapist and client identify the goals or target behaviors, both verbal and nonverbal, for each of the behaviors on the hierarchy. This is an interactive process since it combines the therapist's experience with the client's specific knowledge of the situation and the persons involved.

Step 7: Presenting a Model. When the client has learned specific assertive behaviors, the therapist provides a model for each target on the hierarchy. These models may be live performances by the therapist, audio or videotaped presentations, written scripts, or films. Written scripts are ideal assertive conversations concocted and written down by the therapist and client together. The client is not asked to follow the scripts exactly during *in vivo* practice, but scripts do help clients to learn key phrases and to anticipate the arguments of others. In group counseling situations, other clients may provide excellent models. A number of client fears are overcome by observing responses to criticism that are not necessarily adversarial contests.

Step 8: Rehearsal and Feedback. Once the client has seen a positive model, he or she must build confidence in the ability to perform the behavior in real life. Practicing behaviors with the therapist or group in a role-playing situation is the first step before attempting to implement the first behavior on the hierarchy. Following the practice attempt, the therapist or group members give specific feedback for improvement or reinforcement. Homework assignments are aimed at the first level of the hierarchy, moving forward as the client becomes comfortable with each behavior. Feedback from individuals in the environment who have been monitoring the client's behavior should also be reported.

Problems and Precautions of Assertiveness Training

Sometimes clients complain that though they may look assertive (display the appropriate nonverbals), they do not feel assertive and are scared or angry during their practice of assertive behaviors. It can be explained that, at first, one simply tends to go through the motions before actually feeling the results. Clients should judge the effectiveness of assertiveness on the feelings of accomplishment following a successful trial. In Alcoholics Anonymous there is a maxim, "Fake it 'til you make it." The saying implies that acquiring a behavior sometimes precedes positive feelings. Smiling will make you feel happier and acting assertive will bring about self-confidence.

Because assertiveness training has become popularized and misused, occasionally clients will feel that assertiveness training is inconsistent with their values, especially religious ones. Counselors need to be sensitive to this criticism. Another way of presenting this model is as a social skill designed to ensure that both members in a relationship find satisfaction rather than dominate each other. Clients may believe that the aim of assertiveness training is to turn them into very aggressive persons who only look out for #1. This is why the education phase of the method is crucial in combatting any misconceptions.

Gambrill (1985) reports that assertive people are not always viewed as positively as are submissive people. This might mean that assertiveness, if only aimed at getting one's needs met or at standing up for one's rights, may have longer term negative effects. The squeaky wheel may get the grease, as the saying goes, but it may also engender resentment. Assertiveness training, as it is now practiced, is more likely to emphasize the use of tentativeness, politeness, and a more humble attitude, especially when dealing with longer term relationships. Placing "consequences" on a recalcitrant store clerk may be effective, but it may be counterproductive with family and friends.

Variations on Assertiveness Training

Broken Record Technique. This technique is one if the most widely taught assertive behavior sequences. It is especially useful when a person is being criticized or nagged, and it is primarily a defensive response. The method involves repeating one's feelings, needs, or major points over and over even though the other person may be trying to enlarge or change the topic.

Fogging. Fogging is a method that has been very effective for some clients, especially when dealing with family members or others who want to give unsolicited advice or criticism. The technique is simply to let it go in one ear and out the other. The client actively listens to the advice giver but is taught to internally dispute or ignore the suggestion.

Probing. Related to the technique of fogging, probing means asking the other person to explain the criticism fully and explore completely all of the nuances but without agreeing to the criticism. Instead of defensiveness or disgust, one presents an interested and concerned demeanor. For example, a client once reported that her friend criticized her driving. She learned the technique of probing and asked the friend to tell her in detail what frightened her. The client admitted to the therapist that she gained some valuable information about her driving but did not feel sad or discouraged by it since the feedback became very specific via the probing technique.

Making a Contract in Group.   Group assertiveness training can be more than a didactic presentation. Clients can gain practice in assertiveness by identifying specific assertive behaviors they wish to work on and by attempting to apply these behaviors in all interactions with group members. Let us suppose that an individual wants to learn how to handle criticism from others. He or she can contract with the group to solicit feedback from group members whenever possible. By accepting a contract, the group member works on specific assertiveness behaviors in all group activities.

CASE EXAMPLE

Nina was a 76-year-old woman whose husband died one year previously. Since that time, she appeared to have coped well with living alone and was generally content except with what she felt was the oversolicitous attitudes of her family and friends. She enjoyed reading late into the night and resented the constant suggestions of her daughter that she needed to get out of the house more. She had recently felt very angry at her minister's suggestion that she go on a cruise. Although she felt anger and resentment, she made little attempt to communicate her feelings to others.

The counselor explained to Nina that refusing a nagging request is an art. The therapist helped her look at her current behavior, which amounted to feeling angry and avoiding that person for days. She identified an obstacle: her own personal belief that she would hurt someone deeply if she asked them to desist. Nina felt that her son would understand her dilemma and would help her if he could. He agreed with her that she had a right to refuse or ignore the requests of others.

With the therapist's help, she identified three situations on a hierarchy. The most difficult situation was to ask her daughter to stop calling three or four times per day. The therapist presented a role play in the office in which the counselor portrayed some polite ways of achieving the target behavior and the client played the other person to gauge how it would feel to be on the receiving end of an assertive response. Roles were then reversed to allow the client to be assertive in her own unique way. She was given feedback on her performance by the therapist. Interestingly, the opportunity for a confrontation with her daughter occurred only one week after therapy began and before the other items on the hierarchy had been attempted. The client evaluated her own behavior as very successful but felt that her daughter might need some further reminders.

CHAPTER SUMMARY AND CONCLUSIONS

Self-esteem is defined as having two components: self-worth and efficacy. This chapter was mostly concerned with methods for raising self-worth. Low self-worth is the result of a number of factors but is a commonly identified problem of clients

Feedback Checklist #5
Assertiveness

1. How well did the counselor educate and prepare the client to learn the skill?

Not at All	*A Little*	*Somewhat*	*Moderately*	*Very Well*
1	2	3	4	5

2. To what extent was the client's current nonassertive behavior discussed and evaluated?

Not at All	*A Little*	*Somewhat*	*Moderately*	*A Great Deal*
1	2	3	4	5

3. How much did the counselor identify personal and environmental obstacles and supports?

Not at All	*A Little*	*Somewhat*	*Moderately*	*A Great Deal*
1	2	3	4	5

4. How well did the counselor enumerate the hierarchy of target behaviors based on client comfort?

Not at All	*A Little*	*Somewhat*	*Moderately*	*Very Well*
1	2	3	4	5

5. To what degree was the client presented with appropriate models of the target behavior?

Not at All	*A Little*	*Somewhat*	*Moderately*	*A Great Deal*
1	2	3	4	5

6. To what extent was the client able to engage in rehearsal and obtain feedback?

Not at All	*A Little*	*Somewhat*	*Moderately*	*A Great Deal*
1	2	3	4	5

with a number of psychological conditions. The first part of this chapter took some time to explore sources of low self-worth and identified drivers or injunctions learned early in life, irrational ideas, body image, and attributional style as important determinants.

The second half of the chapter looked at three methods for enhancing self-esteem. The first of these methods, self-monitoring, is a rather scientific method that involves the client in gathering objective data about the self. The second method, a cognitive therapy technique called *countering*, aims at reducing negative self-talk or internal dialogue. The third, a technique taken from assertiveness training, is called responding to criticism. The first method of self-monitoring brings about greater awareness of strengths and weaknesses; the second method reduces negative internal messages; and the third technique eliminates unhelpful criticism from others. In the countering and assertiveness techniques, ways are suggested to build in positive, coping self-statements as other negative self-statements are eliminated.

FURTHER READING

Frey, D., & Carlock, C. J. (1989). *Enhancing self esteem* (2nd ed.). Muncie, IN: Accelerated Development. This book was written by two prominent psychotherapists, one a Gestalt therapist, and one who works primarily with children and families. The book contains a variety of activities for individuals and groups that have been tested by the authors. The book pays special attention to women's issues related to self-esteem but is relevant to almost any setting where counselors work.

Kurpius, D., Rockwood, G. F., & Corbett, M. O. (1989). Attributional styles and self-esteem: Implications for counseling. *Counseling and Human Development, 21* (8), 1–12. This article is the main focus of one issue in a counseling newsletter. The authors use vignettes to illustrate client situations that involve low self-esteem and review literature on self-handicapping, learned helplessness, and victimization. The article deals primarily with attribution theory and its relevance to self-esteem.

Witmer, J. M. (1985). *Pathways to personal growth: Developing a sense of worth and competence.* Muncie, IN: Accelerated Development. Witmer's book is a miniature encyclopedia of personal growth based on the "third force" framework: that improved self-concept is the goal of counseling and personal development. The book is well documented and re-searched. It addresses stress, coping and wellness, values, communication, developing healthy beliefs, and other significant paths to growth.

REFERENCES

Adams, G. R. (1977). Physical attractiveness re-search: Toward a developmental social psy-chology of beauty. *Human Development, 20,* 217–239.

Alberti, R. E., & Emmons, M. L. (1974). *Your perfect right: A guide to assertive behavior.* San Luis Obispo, CA: Impact.

Alberti, R. E. (Ed.) (1977). *Assertiveness: Innova-tions, applications, issues.* San Luis Obispo, CA: Impact.

Baird, P., & Sights, J. R. (1986). Low self-esteem as a treatment issue in the psychology of anorexia and bulimia. *Journal of Counseling and Development, 64,* 449–451.

Bandura, A. (1982). Self-efficacy mechanism in human agency. *American Psychologist, 37,* 122–147.

Beck, A. T., Rush, A. J., Shaw, B. F., & Emery, G. (1979). *Cognitive therapy of depression.* New York: Guilford Press.

Berne, E. (1972). *What do you say after you say hello?* New York: Grove Press.

Branden, N. (1969). *The psychology of self esteem.* Los Angeles, CA: Nash.

Branden, N. (1971). *The disowned self.* New York: Bantam Books.

Brehm, M., & Back, W. (1968). Self image and attitude towards drugs. *Journal of Personality, 36,* 299–314.

Campos, A. (1986). Self-ideal congruence as a measure of self-esteem. *Psychological Reports, 58,* 729–730.

Daly, M. J., & Burton, R. L. (1983). Self-esteem and irrational beliefs: An exploratory investi-gation with implications for counseling. *Jour-nal of Counseling Psychology, 30,* 361–366.

Davis, M., Eshelman, E. R., & McKay, M. (1980). *The relaxation and stress reduction workbook.* Richmond, CA: New Harbinger.

Dowd, E. T. (1985). Self statement modification. In A. S. Bellack, & M. Hersen, *Dictionary of behavior therapy techniques* (p. 200). New York: Pergamon.

Egan, G. (1990). *The skilled helper* (4th ed.). Pa-cific Grove, CA: Brooks/Cole.

Ellis, A. (1973). *Humanistic psychotherapy.* New York: McGraw-Hill.

Epstein, S. (1983). Natural healing processes of

the mind: Gradual stress inoculation as an inherent coping mechanism. In D. Meichenbaum & M. S. Jaremko (Eds.), *Stress reduction and prevention* (pp. 39–65). New York: Plenum.

Forsterling, F. (1984). Attributional retraining: A review. *Psychological Bulletin, 98,* 495–512.

Fremouw, W. J., Wiener, A. L., & Seime, R. J. (1987). Self-monitoring forms for bulimia. In P. A. Keller & S. R. Heyman (Eds.), *Innovations in clinical practice: A source book* (Vol. 6, pp. 325–332). Sarasota, FL: Professional Resource Exchange.

Frey, D., & Carlock, C. J. (1989). *Enhancing self esteem* (2nd ed.). Muncie, IN: Accelerated Development.

Gambrill, E. (1985). Assertiveness training. In A. S. Bellack & M. Hersen (Eds.), *Dictionary of behavior therapy techniques* (pp. 7–9). New York: Pergamon.

Grayson, P. A. (1986). Disavowing the past: A maneuver to protect self-esteem. *Individual Psychology: Adlerian Theory, Research and Practice, 42,* 330–338.

Greene, G. J. (1986). The effect of the relationship enhancement program on marital communication and self-esteem. *Journal of Applied Social Sciences, 10,* 78–94.

Greenspan, M. (1983). *A new approach to women and therapy.* New York: McGraw-Hill.

Ingham, J. G., Kreitman, N. B., Miller, P. M., & Sasidharan, S. P. (1986). Self-esteem, vulnerability and psychiatric disorder in the community. *British Journal of Psychiatry, 148,* 373–385.

Jourard, S. M. (1968). *Disclosing man to himself.* New York: Van Nostrand Reinhold.

Kahler, T. (1977). The miniscript. In G. Barnes (Ed.), *Transactional analysis after Eric Berne* (pp. 220–241). New York: Harpers College Press.

Kurpius, D., Rockwood, G. F., & Corbett, M. O. (1989). Attributional styles and self-esteem: Implications for counseling. *Counseling and Human Development, 21* (8), 1–12.

Lazarus, A. A. (1971). *Behavior therapy and beyond.* New York: McGraw-Hill.

Lazarus, R. S., & Folkman, S. (1984). *Stress, appraisal, and coping.* New York: Springer Publishing.

Lazarus, R. S., & Golden, G. (1981). The function of denial in stress, coping and aging. In E. McGarraugh & S. Kiessler (Eds.), *Biology, behavior and aging.* New York: Academic Press.

Luft, J. (1969). *Of human interaction.* Palo Alto, CA: National Press.

Maletzky, B. M. (1974). Behavior recording as treatment: A brief note. *Behavior Therapy, 5,* 107–111.

McKay, M., & Fanning, P. (1987). *Self-esteem.* Oakland, CA: New Harbinger.

McMullin, R. E. (1986). *Handbook of cognitive therapy techniques.* New York: W. W. Norton.

Rathus, S. A. (1975). Principles and practices of assertiveness training: An eclectic overview. *The Counseling Psychologist, 5,* 9–20.

Rogers, C. R. (1961). *On becoming a person: A therapist's view of psychotherapy.* Boston, MA: Houghton Mifflin.

Rosenberg, M. (1962). The association between self-esteem and anxiety. *Journal of Psychiatric Research, 1,* 135–152.

Sharpley, C. F. (1986). Some arguments against analyzing client change graphically. *Journal of Counseling and Development, 65,* 156–159.

Smith, M. J. (1975). *When I say no, I feel guilty.* New York: Bantam.

Smith, T. W., Snyder, C. R., & Handelman, M. M. (1981). On the self-serving function of an academic wooden leg: Test anxiety as a self-handicapping strategy. *Journal of Personality and Social Psychology, 42,* 314–321.

Tanner, V. L., & Holliman, W. B. (1988). Effectiveness of assertiveness training in modifying aggressive behaviors in young children. *Psychological Reports, 62,* 39–46.

Thompson, J. K., & Thompson, C. M. (1986). Body size distortion and self-esteem in asymptomatic, normal weight males and females. *International Journal of Eating Disorders, 5,* 1061–1068.

Tucker, J. A., Vuchinich, R. E., & Sobell, M. B. (1981). Alcohol consumption as a self-handicapping strategy. *Journal of Abnormal Psychology, 90,* 220–230.

Walz, G. (1990). *Counseling for self esteem.* Alexandria, VA: American Association for Counseling and Development.

Weiner, G. (1979). A theory of motivation for some classroom experiences. *Journal of Educational Psychology, 71,* 3–25.

Weiner, B., Frieze, I., Kukla, A., Reed, L., Nest, B., & Rosenbaum, R. M. (1971). *Perceiving the causes of success and failure.* Morristown, NJ: General Learning Press.

Wilson, A., & Krane, R. (1980). Change in self esteem and its effect on symptoms of depression. *Cognitive Therapy and Research, 4,* 419–421.

Witmer, J. M. (1985). *Pathways to personal growth: Developing a sense of worth and competence.* Muncie, IN: Accelerated Development.

Yalom, I. R. (1985). *The theory and practice of group psychotherapy* (3rd ed.). New York: Basic Books.

CHAPTER 7

Practicing New Behaviors

KEY CONCEPTS

▼ *Behavior change is often considered to be an important outcome of therapy. It has also been discovered that by changing behaviors, concomitant alterations occur in affect and cognition.*

▼ *Imagery as a counseling method has become popular in recent years and has been found to be compatible with a number of counseling theories. Imagery can be used to rehearse desired behaviors. It can provide a first practice of a new behavior in a nonthreatening manner.*

▼ *Role playing is a practice technique that involves recreating the context of a desired behavior right in the therapist's office. Major contributions to this technique have come from psychodrama and the behaviorists. This technique allows the therapist to obtain first-hand knowledge about the client's behavioral style, and the client benefits from rehearsal and feedback.*

▼ *Homework assignments are given to clients to prolong treatment between sessions. Assignments should be individually tailored to the client and may involve self-monitoring activities. Strategic interventions involve tasks that disrupt the client's familiar, nonproductive patterns.*

INTRODUCTION

Psychotherapy can be conceived of as an educational process (Guerney, Stollack & Guerney, 1971; Schutz, 1982; Young & Rosen, 1985). This way of thinking necessarily changes the emphasis of therapeutic work. As an educator, the counselor cannot be content to help the client lay aside old behaviors or gain insight into a new way of being. Clients must overcome the force of habit and establish a pattern of new behaviors through practice (Figure 7.1). Although some theoretical orientations posit that insight precedes behavioral change, it has been the experience of many therapists who adopt this psychoeducational point of view that changing behavior may also lead to changes in thinking and in emotion. Let us consider a couple of examples of how behavioral change or practice can precede cognitive and emotional changes in the client.

173

FIGURE 7.1
Six curative factors in the REPLAN system.

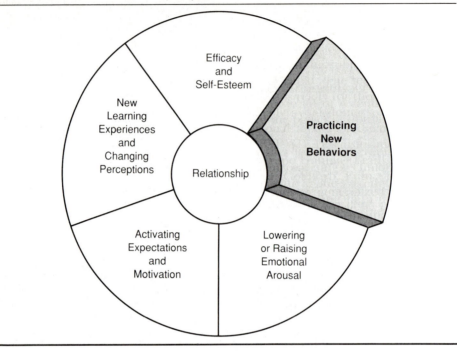

Example 1

A young white man who has learned to be prejudiced against Hispanics is forced (behavioral change) to work on a project as an equal with two Hispanic partners. By treating them as equals, he comes to believe they are equal (cognitive change) and later experiences a diminished emotional reaction to Hispanics (affective change).

Example 2

A 60-year-old man was forced into a 30-day hospitalization for alcoholism by his physician. He was abstinent during his stay. Even though he received no treatment beyond regular medical care, his abstinence changed his feeling that he could not control his drinking. He started to view himself as strong enough to quit drinking altogether. Abstinence (behavioral practice) from a bad habit, even if against one's will, decreases the psychological craving and loosens the emotional dependency.

The process of change may start with emotional quieting or arousal, changing cognitions (e.g., developing insight) or by practicing some new behavior. The eclectic counselor selects the treatment modality that best fits the client with the idea in mind that the most lasting change probably includes changes in cognition, emotion, and behavior.

SELECTING THE LEVEL OF PRACTICE

The notion of practice in our educational institutions begins with instructor modeling, followed by in-class practice and homework assignments. The process of acquiring a new behavior or a new thinking skill in psychotherapy is much the same. The best learning initially occurs when practice takes place in a safe environment, where natural conditions are closely simulated. Eventually, the client must practice new behaviors *in vivo,* that is, in a real life situation.

In this chapter we will look at three specific methods for practicing new learning gained during counseling and psychotherapy:

1. Imaginal rehearsal
2. Role playing
3. Homework

These three methods exist on a continuum, with imaginal rehearsal being an exclusively mental practice, role playing being even closer to real life, and *in vivo* homework as the final step. It has been my experience that difficulties in homework are due to a lack of practice at the imaginal or role-playing level. If difficulties are encountered, one rule of thumb is to return to a lower level of practice on the continuum. For example, a client who is having difficulties with *in vivo* assignments should be exposed to more role playing before further outside assignments are given.

METHODS AND TECHNIQUES FOR PRACTICING NEW BEHAVIORS

Imaginal Rehearsal: Overview and Purpose of the Method

Both Freud and Watson were reported to have had very little visualizing ability. Perhaps that is why imagery, as a counseling technique, went underground for many years, banished by both psychoanalytic and behavioral revolutions, only resurfacing in the works of cognitive-behaviorists such as Albert Ellis, Meichenbaum, and Cautela in the 1960s. These writers tend to view problem behavior as either partially or fully caused by faulty thinking processes involving internal language (e.g., "I am going to fail") or by negative imagery. Whether positive imagery provides a rehearsal for a new behavior or whether it merely increases self-confidence has not been agreed upon. Still, imagery has been found to enhance performance, and it is making a comeback as a primary therapeutic tool (cf., Fezler, 1989). It is a mainstay of Covert Conditioning (Cautela & Bennett, 1981), Neurolinguistic Programming (Bandler & Grinder, 1976), Multimodal Therapy (Lazarus, 1977; Lazarus, 1982), Systematic Desensitization (Wolpe,

1958), Rational-Emotive Therapy (Maultsby & Ellis, 1974), Reality Therapy (Parr & Peterson, 1983), humanistically oriented counseling (Gladding, 1986) and many others.

The broad and various uses of imagery include increasing awareness of self and others, future planning and career development, gaining control over undesirable behavior, treating physical illness, improving learning, skill development and performance, reducing stress and enhancing health, and increasing creativity and problem solving in everyday living (Pope, 1982; Sheikh, 1983; Witmer & Young, 1985; Witmer & Young, 1987). A few of the client problems currently treated with imagery include bulimia (Gunnison & Renick, 1985), career indecision (Sarnoff & Remer, 1982; Skovholt, Morgan & Negron-Cunningham, 1989) posttraumatic stress disorder (Grigsby, 1987), and parenting decision making (Skovholt & Thoen, 1987).

In this section, we will be looking at imagery for improving or developing a skill in therapy sessions. Mental, or imaginal, rehearsal has sometimes been termed *covert rehearsal* (Bellack, 1986). The term *covert* in this context means hidden or invisible, as contrasted with the word *overt*, which means outer or observable.

The purpose of imaginal rehearsal is to allow the client to practice the acquisition of a skill, especially when an actual enactment is not feasible. Actual enactment may not be feasible because the client's emotional state is such that confronting the real life situation may be too stressful. Moreover, imaginal rehearsal can take place anywhere, not only in the therapist's office, and clients sometimes want help when no time is available for lengthy practice sessions. For example, the client might inform the therapist that his mother is coming to visit within the week and he wishes to handle this stressful confrontation. In addition, imagery rehearsal can be accomplished in minutes and can be repeated several times in one hour with the therapist available to provide feedback.

The Method of Imaginal Rehearsal

Step 1: Identify the Target.   The first task of client and counselor is to cooperatively reduce the client's goal into a list of skills (target behaviors) that are required to perform the desired task successfully. For example, the goal of asking someone out for a date might include the following skills:

1. Making a phone call
2. Greeting the other person
3. Describing the proposed activity
4. Asking the other person to join the client in the activity

Those who are adept at social skills might find the list above simplistic and rather clinical. It may come as a surprise to some readers that therapists are commonly asked by clients to help them acquire simple social skills such as making small talk, telling friends how they feel about them, or asking for a raise.

Step 2: Preparing the Client for Imagery.   Imaginal rehearsal is ideally performed in a quiet environment with eyes closed. The counselor may reassure the client that the technique is not hypnosis but an active rehearsal process. The purpose is explained as a method of learning to avoid or to eliminate negative images of failure and to develop positive, successful ones.

Step 3: Imagining Each of the Target Behaviors.   The client is reminded of the first target behavior and visualizes performing it in a specific situation where it is likely to be actually employed. From there, the counselor asks the client to visualize each successive aspect of the behavior, moving ahead only when the client can vividly imagine each step. During this process, it is important to carry on a dialogue with the client to make certain that the client has a clear understanding of each step in a sequence of behaviors and can accurately and vividly imagine it.

Step 4: Imagining a Successful Sequence.   Once each step has been visualized, the client is then guided through the entire sequence by the counselor, who also describes a successful completion of the desired behavior. The description is done in present tense as if the therapist were telling a story. At various points the therapist points out target behaviors, saying, for example, "Now you are shaking hands with the interviewer while maintaining eye contact."

Step 5: Reinforcement.   At the end of the first complete visualization, the client receives a covert reinforcement, an imagined reward or happy ending to firmly establish the behavior. For example, the therapist might end the exercise by saying, "You leave the job interview saying to yourself, 'I did the best I could and that feels good.' "

Step 6: Practice.   In subsequent trials in the office, the client imagines the scenario until each component of the behavior and a positive outcome can be vividly pictured. The client should not focus on negative or troubling imagery but, instead, simply work on developing positive images.

Step 7: Identifying Obstacles.   Following the imaginal rehearsal, the client should be asked to list obstacles that might arise in the actual use of the behavior and to identify ways to cope with them. In subsequent sessions, the client visualizes successfully coping with these obstacles through the acquisition of skills or hard work, not through the intervention of some helper. The client is asked not to imagine magical or improbable outcomes. Most importantly, the client is asked to imagine a successful completion of the target, not necessarily a perfect outcome. The client's sights should be focused on coping, not on perfection.

Problems and Precautions with Imaginal Rehearsal

1. Imagery tends to evoke a much fuller experience of remembered events than simply talking about them. Some clients may be overwhelmed by these feelings and may require support from the therapist especially if the imagery involves painful events from the past. The focus of the technique described here is on positive future performance, but occasionally memories of past failures intrude.
2. Clients differ in their capacity to produce imagery. The ability of individuals to produce vivid images can be tested and improved by methods described by Lazarus (1977). In my experience, about 10% of clients in group settings report an inability to sustain mental imagery long enough for counseling purposes. Some clients feel inadequate because of this, and it is important to explain that the technique is not essential for counseling to take place. Other rehearsal methods are available.

3. Some clients resist imagery because of anxiety, embarrassment, or fear of losing control. They may feel that they are being hypnotized and object to it. Sometimes lack of vividness or the inability to imagine may be a form of resistance. Clients can be reassured that learning to develop imagery can lead to greater control.

4. Imagery techniques are not appropriate for individuals reporting hallucinations or delusions.

5. Some children may overuse fantasy and story telling as an escape. They may wish to use magical images rather than acquiring social tools to deal with problems.

Variations on Imaginal Rehearsal

Covert Modeling.   In individual counseling, covert modeling is a technique used to increase the probability of a new behavior occurring. It consists of the use of an imagined model who successfully performs the target behavior. This kind of imagery may be especially effective with children, who are familiar with symbolic models from television and books. The behavior is either punished or rewarded in the imaginary situation, depending on whether the behavior is to be encouraged or eliminated (Kazdin, 1978).

Group Fantasy.   In a technique called group fantasy, the leader asks group members to fantasize individually and then to describe their picture of the group to other members when they have reached a mature working stage. A typical fantasy might be expressed this way: "I see us helping someone in the group who is hurting and that person feels free to cry and is safe." When members have shared their fantasies of their ideal group, the leader asks the members to discuss what behaviors would be necessary to adopt in order to create a climate where these fantasies can be realized.

Imagery Techniques in Marriage Counseling.   Peggy Papp (1987) uses an imagery technique in marriage counseling where both members of the couple in turn describe the marriage in symbolic terms. For example, the wife may describe the marriage as being like two icebergs floating in the ocean. The wife then elaborates on her description of the iceberg image, as if it were occurring in the present, and reveals the feelings that it evokes. The husband may react to her image. The purpose of the technique is to assess the relationship in a nonrational way and hopefully to bypass some resistances and defenses. Carrying this technique a bit further, the counselor might ask both members to visualize a picture of themselves as they would like their relationship to become. Later the couple begins to identify ways of reaching that imagined state.

CASE EXAMPLE _____

Dan is a 20-year-old man who recently returned from alcohol treatment. He has come to counseling to work on his anxiety about drinking in social situations. He has some trouble relaxing but is a good visualizer. In male/female encounters, his anxiety peaks when he reaches the part of the conversation where he would like to ask the woman out for a date or a second meeting. He says that he has no idea how people generally initiate this question and that he feels foolish. In the past, Dan used alcohol as a "social lubricant." He does not remember, though, exactly how he went about asking for a date when he was intoxicated, but he admits that he felt he needed to be "pretty loaded" in order to ask someone out. The counselor hypothesized that in addition to imaginal rehearsal, Dan needed to dispute some irrational beliefs. For example, Dan thought that it would be devastating if a woman said, "No." He also needed to learn relaxation skills to decrease his anxiety enough to practice some new behaviors.

During the first two sessions, Dan learned a basic relaxation method and began to place possible rejection in its proper perspective. Two sessions were then held during which he was able to imagine successfully asking out a woman he had met at Alcoholics Anonymous. At first, he was unable to control negative images, which included feeling depressed by the rejection and even wanting a drink. After three trials, he was able to reward himself for his courage when he imagined a rejection. He was given homework to practice the scene one time per day for one week before attempting the first behavioral trial.

Feedback Checklist #6
Imaginal Rehearsal

1. How well was the counselor able to make a list of target behaviors leading to a mutually agreed-upon goal?

Not at All	*A Little*	*Somewhat*	*Moderately*	*Very Well*
1	2	3	4	5

2. How well did the counselor prepare the client and help the client relax?

Not at All	*A Little*	*Somewhat*	*Moderately*	*Very Well*
1	2	3	4	5

3. To what degree was the counselor able to help the client move smoothly through the visualization of the target behaviors and provide covert reinforcement?

Not at All	*A Little*	*Somewhat*	*Moderately*	*A Great Deal*
1	2	3	4	5

4. How well did the counselor deal with obstacles or variations in the client's imagery?

Not at All	*A Little*	*Somewhat*	*Moderately*	*Very Well*
1	2	3	4	5

5. To what extent did the counselor help develop follow-up plans and homework assignments for the client?

Not at All	*A Little*	*Somewhat*	*Moderately*	*A Great Deal*
1	2	3	4	5

Role Playing: Overview and Purpose of the Method

Role playing is a technique commonly used by therapists in social skills training and especially in practicing feared behaviors. It involves practicing a behavior in a contrived situation with the therapist playing auxiliary or observer roles. It may also take place in a group with other participants acting as assistants or as an audience.

Role playing in psychotherapy was introduced by the creative genius, J. L. Moreno, a Viennese psychiatrist who formulated the psychodrama. Moreno has been called the "Father of Group Therapy" because he was one of its first practitioners and because he developed a number of important group techniques. But Moreno was a very controversial figure. He had a revolutionary bent, sometimes expressed in virulent attacks against psychoanalysis and other forms of therapy. It is probably for this reason that his contribution to counseling is largely unacknowledged. On one occasion, following a lecture by Freud, Moreno is said to have responded, "Well, Dr. Freud, I start where you leave off. You meet people in the artificial setting of your office. I meet them on the street and in their home, in their natural surroundings. You analyze their dreams. I try to give them the courage to dream again . . . " (Moreno, 1964, pp. 5–6). Moreno's response reflects his belief, as well as the beliefs of the behaviorists, that counseling should involve learning in as naturalistic a setting as possible.

Part of what Moreno objected to in traditional therapies was the separation of a client's problems from the natural environment, just as a religious sculpture or painting cannot be fully appreciated in a museum but must be seen in a church or temple. Moreno is said to have held the first (ever) group therapy sessions with prostitutes in a Berlin park where they usually assembled.

Since it is not always possible to see individuals in their natural contexts, the psychodramatic method proposes to recreate an individual's joys and sorrows on the psychodramatic stage (Starr, 1977). Moreno's famous dictum was, "Show me, don't tell me!" He felt that most "talk therapies" relied on the client's descriptions of problems. Since we cannot reach into the subjective experience of the person through words, we should transfer the mind onto the stage where the person's total behavior, including thoughts, feelings, and intuitions, are observable and changeable.

A second reason Moreno liked role playing was that it allowed for a more complete expression of the client's experience. Moreno felt that life happens too much or too little, too fast or too slow. Psychodramatic role playing can slow down life and allow it it be fully appreciated and experienced.

Finally, Moreno believed that spontaneity was intimately connected to mental health. People do not act spontaneously when they repress or withhold feelings and actions. Moreno believed that this type of blocking behavior occurred because the individual had not developed a well-formed role for expressing these feelings. Expressions that are out of character for us tend to be explosions rather than useful communications. We must learn a new constellation of behaviors in order to let these feelings out. This new set of thoughts, feelings, and actions is called a *role*. The personality can be described as the sum total of one's roles. One of the best ways to learn a new role is to see someone else perform the role and then try it out for oneself. This can be done first in a psychodrama.

To illustrate this point further, I can recall the case of a rather successful man who felt that he had "lost control" of his life. By this he meant that he could not find a way to stand up to his boss or his wife, whom he felt dominated him. On the one hand, he felt powerless because of inhibiting his desire to take greater charge of his personal decision making. On the other hand, he did not wish to alienate those whom he loved and respected. In a group psychodrama, the client was able to project himself into the future and see himself in a more powerful role with family and work superiors. To envision this took some work and some extensive modeling by a member of the group whom the client respected. That individual was able to step into these future situations as they were being played out and showed the client some ways to handle them. With the group's support, the client practiced some new behaviors with the group in order to get the feel of his new role.

Elements of Role Playing

The technique of role playing is a limited form of psychodrama and usually involves an encounter between two individuals or two or more different parts of the self. Role playing can be performed by a single individual (called the *protagonist*) who plays all of the roles in the drama or with the help of other individuals called *auxiliaries*. Before going further, it will be helpful to define some additional terms since the technique hinges on a number of elements that may be unfamiliar to most readers.

Encounter.   Moreno coined the term *encounter* to mean the experience of walking a mile in another's shoes or seeing through the eyes of another person. In role playing, the individual may reverse roles and take on the perspective of a significant other. After confronting one's father with some unfinished business, the client might be directed to take the role of the father and respond to the charges.

Stage.   The *stage* can be any defined space with rudimentary props to increase the realism of the experience.

Soliloquy.   In a *soliloquy*, the protagonist speaks inner thoughts and feelings, as if alone, in free association (uncensored monologue) along with expressive movement. The soliloquy provides the counselor and/or the group with information about the protagonist, including irrational beliefs and incongruent behavior.

Doubling.   The double is a group member or therapist who literally stands behind the protagonist/client during the acting out of the scene and expresses the unexpressed thoughts or feelings of the client. This is done at the therapist's bidding to provide for increased awareness and more complete expression at times when the client is blocked or has reached some sort of impasse. The double talks for the client, hopefully bringing out some of the client's deeper experiences and feelings. Following the doubling, the protagonist repeats those phrases of the double that seem accurate to the client.

Three Phases of Psychodramatic Role Playing

Psychodrama has always been conceived of as having three phases: warm-up, action, and sharing (Yablonsky, 1976). Kipper (1986) and others have suggested a

Role playing is often accomplished with the help of other individuals called auxiliaries.

fourth phase, involving a cognitive integration that we might call *analysis*. In this section, each of the three phases of psychodynamic role playing are described with analysis considered as part of the sharing stage. While these phases are most distinct in a group setting, the process is similar in an individual counseling setting.

Warm-Up.   The *warm-up* is any activity that helps the client get in touch emotionally with the experience he or she is trying to express. The warm-up decreases stage fright and allows the protagonist to develop readiness and involvement in the process. Most of us have warm-ups, or rituals, we use to prepare us for action. For example, the high diver mentally rehearses a dive (a mental starter, or trigger) and the runner does stretching exercises (a physical starter). In role playing, proper warm-up is crucial to the success of the technique. The process helps to move the protagonist toward increasingly more complete levels of expression. Warm-up might include asking the protagonist to discuss the situation, to reverse roles with one of the important people in the drama, or to use a physical starter, such as pacing back and forth, or a mental starter, such as a soliloquy.

The phrase *moving from the periphery to the center* is connected to the notion of a warm-up. It is a rule of thumb or a reminder to the therapist to begin with tangential events before moving to more significant or central issues. For example, if the role play involves returning home to see a dying grandfather, the psychodramatist would not begin with the deathbed confrontation but would move the client through several less potent scenes. In this case, these scenes might include driving to the house while reminiscing about the relationship or replaying previous encounters between the two. This method also gives the director (counselor or therapist) more information about the client and the client's relationships and life circumstances. During these peripheral encounters, the warm-up increases confidence so that the client will be able to react more spontaneously to later and more crucial events.

Action.   The *action* phase consists of segments or scenes that are strung together by the director in order to allow the individual to fully explore the connections or themes in situations where similar events have taken place. The technique of *scene setting* is the preliminary part of the action phase. It involves allowing the protagonist to set up the stage to resemble the actual setting where the incident took place or where the behavior will possibly occur in the future. The protagonist is given free rein to use available props and to orient the stage in whatever way feels comfortable. The director helps the protagonist define the stage, designate the time of day and date, describe the situation verbally, use props, and identify important people to be portrayed. Using auxiliaries chosen by the protagonist, the director moves the individual through a variety of connected scenes. These scenes may lead to examining the unfinished past, and the individual may experience a catharsis as withheld feelings come out.

The final part of the action phase is called *closing the stage*. Here, the director helps the protagonist move from imaginary scenes back to the real situation, regain emotional stability and comfort, develop a sense of optimism and understanding, and establish future plans. This is often accomplished through a *monodrama,* a technique whereby the protagonist discusses the meaning of the psychodrama with himself or herself in a soliloquy or by explaining the meaning of the psychodrama to an empty chair that represents some aspect of the self.

Sharing and Analysis.   Originally, the *sharing* phase of psychodrama was designed to allow the individual to reenter the group counseling situation; that is, to get out of the spotlight that the action phase entails. In this phase, the other group members relate personal experiences evoked by the protagonist's drama. This technique reinvolves the audience and helps the protagonist feel less alone and exposed.

Eventually, a *feedback* or *analysis* session can be held to help the individual cognitively assimilate the drama. Often, though, the protagonist/client is in an emotionally aroused state immediately following the psychodrama and is not ready to process additional information or feedback.

Behavioral Role Playing

Fairly recently role playing has been adopted by behaviorists and given the term *behavior rehearsal* (Lazarus, 1985). Unlike homework assignments, behavioral rehearsal, or behavioral role playing, takes place in the office under the aegis of a therapist. Behaviorists are less likely to reenact early conflict and are more likely to use role playing strictly as practice. Cognitive-behaviorists may replay significant events in order to understand the client's thinking processes and to help the client deal with difficult people. Contrasted with psychodramatic role playing, behavioral methods, however, do not focus on emotional arousal but instead are based on learning theory. The source of reinforcements and rewards comes initially from the therapist, who praises the client at each step. Later, the behavior is rewarded by successful outcomes and through self-praise for handling a difficult situation. Behavior rehearsal is usually divided into four stages (Kipper, 1986):

1. Preparing the client
2. Selecting the target situation
3. Rehearsing the behavior
4. Practicing the new behavior in real life situations

In the opening stage, it is crucial to ascertain that the client agrees with the need for the technique. Next, the counselor helps relax the client and tries to deal with feelings of embarrassment or uneasiness that often accompany first trials.

The second stage is the scene-setting phase. The client describes the place where the problem behavior manifests itself, or the client is unable to perform the appropriate behavior.

The third stage follows the behavioral sequence called *shaping* where the counselor rewards the client with praise at each successive step toward the final goal. The therapist may use role reversal to allow the client to experience the role of the antagonist in social situations. The therapist may also play the part of a significant other to let the client try out some assertive skills in an experimental fashion.

In the last stage, the client is finally urged to practice the new behavior *in vivo* and to record the experiences of these trials for discussion at the next counseling session.

The Role-Playing Method

Regardless of the theoretical orientation of the counselor, role playing is one of the most effective means of bringing past experiences into the here and now. The immediate observation and feedback, whether in groups or individually, allow for actual practice, not simply talking about problems. At a deeper level, role playing and role reversal can help the individual to become more fully aware of feelings and to explore the phenomenological world of the significant people in his or her life.

The method described below is a generic role-playing technique for practicing new behavior. To make the method easier to understand, a hypothetical example is unfolded throughout the explanation. The client, named Marie, is anxious because she has to give a presentation to her board of directors concerning progress on her yearly goals.

Step 1: Warm-up   In the warm-up, the technique of role playing is previewed and explained to the client. Using the principle of proceeding from the periphery to the center, the warm-up begins by asking the client to discuss aspects of her job that she will be presenting, details of the workplace, and other tangential topics. The most important aspect of this step is for the client and counselor to describe the target behavior specifically. In this case, the client wanted to

1. Maintain eye contact with her audience.
2. Speak from notes in a loud, clear voice.
3. Smile when questions are asked.
4. End the session by thanking the audience.

Step 2: Scene Setting.   When the client had discussed the situation and appeared more or less relaxed, she was invited to describe her own office (peripheral) and later the board meeting room (central). The counselor then directed the client to stage the boardroom, using the counselor's office furnishings. The client was encouraged to point out various environmental features to establish the scene.

Step 3: Selecting Roles.   The client identifies important people in the scene and briefly describes them. In a group setting, other members of the group would be assigned to these roles. In an individual session, empty chairs represent these significant persons. In this example, Marie was asked to role-play her boss to get a sense of his demeanor and attitude. She was also asked to point out the chairs of some of the other board members.

Step 4: Enactment.   At this point, the counselor asks the client to briefly portray the target behavior as described in the warm-up. The scene begins in her office and culminates with the client's entrance into the "boardroom." The counselor acts as coach during the first run-through, prompting the client to practice each identified behavior. If the client experiences any difficulty in this action phase, the counselor may consider modeling the appropriate behavior. Following the modeling, the counselor asks the client to try it in her own way. Modeling may take some of the pressure away and may give the client confidence and a sense of control.

Step 5: Sharing and Feedback.   The therapist shares feedback with the client on the client's performance. The feedback should be specific, simple, observable, and understandable to the client. It should mainly reinforce positive aspects of the behavior. In our example, the counselor would tell Marie, "Your voice was very strong and clear. I think you got your points across very well. I would like to see even more eye contact with the board members during the next run-through."

Step 6: Reenactment.   Reenactment is a repetition of the target behavior from entrance to exit. The sequence is repeated until the client feels that she has fulfilled her own goals for the meeting and the therapist is confident that each of the behaviors in the target list have been mastered.

Step 7: Follow-up.   At the next session, the client is asked to report practice results. Marie practiced the behavior by giving the presentation to some family members and described this to the counselor. Further role-playing practice may be given during the session, if necessary.

Problems and Precautions of Role Playing

1. The most frequently encountered difficulty with the role-playing technique is stage fright. This is the reason for the emphasis on warm-up. Resistance to the technique is ordinarily the result of insufficient preparation time, the client's lack of confidence, or inadequate reassurance by the therapist. Several sessions may be necessary before a client will agree to engage in role playing.

2. A second and related problem is the tendency on the part of the therapist to overdirect the client. As much as possible, the client's spontaneity should be encouraged, and the client's own solutions should be supported. The counselor's job is to facilitate and assist.

3. Because of the power of the technique, both the counselor and the client may be unprepared for the strength of the emotion or affect that is evoked. This is especially true when traumatic scenes from the past are reenacted. The counselor must be comfortable enough with the strong show of emotion to experience and work through these scenes and flexible enough to move away from these enactments if the client so wishes. A rule of thumb is that a counselor should never try to force the client to face what he or she is unwilling to face. Good clinical judgment includes the ability to discern which clients are prepared to role play painful historical events.

4. Because most clinicians are trained as "intrapsychic" and linguistic thinkers, we sometimes have trouble working in dramatic terms. In the usual counseling session, the client who is encouraged to describe an encounter might say, "I am angry because she neglected me." In a role-playing session, the client would be instructed to show me how you expressed your anger to her." By creating a dramatic situation, the counselor learns a great deal about the quality and context of the behavior rather than just the client's description of it.

Variations on Role Playing

The Mirror Technique in Group Therapy.   In a variation on role playing called the *mirror technique,* the client steps out of the drama at a moment when a crucial behavior occurs. For example, a client may wish to confront his mother regarding her behavior. In role-playing the situation, the counselor notices that the client becomes very timid, that he avoids eye contact with his "mother," and that his voice softens to a whisper. A volunteer from the group is asked to step into the client's role for a moment and to replay the client's behavior toward his mother. During the reenactment, the client watches himself in this psychological mirror. It may be necessary to encourage a little exaggeration on the part of the auxiliary in order to highlight the behavior of the client. The counselor can facilitate this by pointing out various behaviors such as lowered voice volume, averted gaze, etc.

Next, the client discusses and critically evaluates the behavior with the counselor and the rest of the group. Once the client understands the target behaviors, the therapist asks one of the group members to model for the client, assertively replaying the scene while again the client watches. Finally, the client performs a new behavioral sequence, using new learning and the feedback and modeling provided by the group members.

Assuming the Viewpoint of the Other in Marriage and Family Counseling.
One of the most common and frustrating problems for a counselor in a family
counseling session is the inability of family members to understand each others'
points of view. The result is that family members often end up restating their own
opinions about problems over and over again. Gottman (1976) termed this the
summarizing self syndrome. The following is an excerpt of a session with an actual
couple with small children who had been married for seven years. The husband
had been taking time after work to spend with a fatherless boy in the Big Brother
program. The wife was in college, had primary responsibility for their two young
children, and needed time to study at night.

Donna: I am tired of your coming home late at night when I have the children to
take care of and all this work to do. I need some help.

Steve: I promised I would spend some time with Roger, and I have to follow
through with it.

Donna [summarizing self syndrome]:
Can't you see how much I have to do. I need your help at night.

Steve [summarizing self syndrome]:
Well, I promised. I can't let the kid down.

In both exchanges the clients failed to acknowledge the point of view of the
other person as if it had not registered. One way out of this dilemma is the use of a
role reversal technique. In this case, the counselor initially asked each party to
state his or her side of the conflict and to identify feelings as well as to advance
arguments for that point of view. Each partner was asked to listen carefully to the
other.

Next, each partner reversed roles and played the opposing point of view as
genuinely and convincingly as was possible. The counselor stopped the interaction when one person seemed to be inaccurately portraying the other's position.
For example, the counselor called a halt at one point and said, "Donna, is Steve's
last statement a fair summary of what you've been trying to say?" The enactment
was then repeated until both parties felt that the other had correctly presented
their point of view. Finally, the clients resumed their natural roles and once again
attempted to resolve the conflict. This time the couple recognized the validity of
the other's viewpoint and a compromise was arranged.

If each member in a dispute is able to fully assume the viewpoint of the other,
rapprochement can take place. Proper preparation of the clients is needed in
order to encourage them to try to take the other perspective. Normally one person
or both experience some reluctance or fear associated with surrendering his or
her vantage point.

CASE EXAMPLE

Carol was a 37-year-old married woman with one child. She and her counselor
agreed to work on her extreme reluctance to leave home even for a few hours to
go to the grocery store. She experienced fear and panic attacks in public situations. She had not been shopping in two years and had lost respect for herself as a
contributing member of her family. Following two sessions of history taking and a
medical evaluation (the client incorrectly believed she had a heart condition), the

counselor and client, using the REPLAN system, agreed that she needed assistance in dealing with low self-esteem and, second, that she needed to practice going out in public. The client was found to have a number of dysfunctional beliefs, including "I am weak." Work was begun to reduce this counterproductive thinking, but the major effort was aimed at helping the client practice getting out of the house. The role-playing technique was explained to her, and a treatment plan was established with the major goal being an unaccompanied shopping trip.

In the first role-playing rehearsal, Carol enacted driving by the store in her car and then returning home. During the car ride, she was encouraged to speak her feelings and thoughts in a monologue. She expressed her anger at herself for being weak. During the same session, she imagined returning to the store, entering it, and buying one small item. Although she felt pleased that she was able to finish the scene, she was somewhat anxious on completion.

The remainder of the session was spent in analyzing some of her negative self-talk and in learning to keep track of her subjective units of distress (SUDS) level. One of her negative thoughts was "What if I have a heart attack in the store?" We then discussed the use of a thought-stopping method to expunge that kind of disruptive pattern. Progress was slow, involving an interplay between decreasing negative thinking and encouraging *in vivo* practice. The client was given successively more difficult outings to practice and was eventually given the assignment of a weekly shopping trip. For each excursion, she was asked to submit a slightly higher weekly shopping bill as a measure of increased time spent in the store. She began with one purchase and eventually was able to complete an entire shopping list.

Homework: Overview and Purpose of the Method

Homework has been identified as a crucial tool in effective psychotherapy (Beck, Rush, Shaw & Emery, 1979; Ellis, 1962; Shelton & Ackerman, 1974). *Homework* refers to any tasks or assignments given to clients to be completed between sessions (Last, 1985). Some tasks are used for assessment purposes; others are used simply to increase client awareness (Martin & Worthington, 1982). In this section, the main emphasis will be on homework that is used to practice new behaviors. These new behaviors are normally learned during the therapeutic session and may be modeled or rehearsed there before the homework is assigned.

Later in the book, client progress notes will be discussed. The final section of the suggested format for progress notes lists homework assignments and plans that client and counselor agree to work on between sessions. Review of homework provides a point of beginning for the next session. Each new session can begin with a discussion of the progress and the problems encountered in the assignment. Many counselors have relied too much on older traditions that concentrated solely on listening and waiting in the early sessions. As brief therapy becomes increasingly a standard, more psychotherapists are recommending early interventions and assigning homework tasks immediately (de Shazer, 1985; Driscoll, 1984; O'Hanlon & Weiner-Davis, 1989).

Feedback Checklist #7
Role Playing

1. How well did the counselor explain the role-playing technique and other methods to enhance client warm-up?

Not at All	*A Little*	*Somewhat*	*Moderately*	*Very Well*
1	2	3	4	5

2. How well did the counselor set the scene by asking the client to define the space and arrange for props?

Not at All	*A Little*	*Somewhat*	*Moderately*	*Very Well*
1	2	3	4	5

3. How well did the counselor help the client portray important individuals to be enacted?

Not at All	*A Little*	*Somewhat*	*Moderately*	*Very Well*
1	2	3	4	5

4. How well was the counselor able to help the client through a complete enactment of the target behaviors?

Not at All	*A Little*	*Somewhat*	*Moderately*	*Very Well*
1	2	3	4	5

5. How well did the counselor aid the client in refining the behavior through reenacting the scene?

Not at All	*A Little*	*Somewhat*	*Moderately*	*Very Well*
1	2	3	4	5

6. Was the counselor able to provide feedback to the client and provide for follow-up sessions to monitor progress?

Not at All	*A Little*	*Somewhat*	*Moderately*	*Very Well*
1	2	3	4	5

Reasons for Using Homework

A major advantage of using homework assignments is that it provides follow-up or treatment continuance between sessions. When one realizes that a client spends 1 hour out of 112 waking hours per week in counseling, it is easy to see how counseling can be diluted by other activities. Homework assignments, especially if they require some daily work, can enhance treatment considerably (Shelton & Ackerman, 1974; Shelton & Levy, 1981).

Second, homework assignments turn insights and awareness into tangible behaviors and prevent therapy from being only a place to unload one's feelings. Transfer of training is facilitated by applying descriptions and models of behavior to real life situations.

Homework practice also begins the shift of control from the therapist to the client. If the client attributes progress to his or her own effort in outside assignments, greater efficacy and self-esteem will result.

The Homework Method

Step 1: Review Client Goals.   Before assigning homework, the counselor and client should review the most important goals of therapy and be certain that homework assignments are aimed in this direction.

Step 2: Client and Counselor Identify Activities That the Client Needs to Practice.   For example, if the client is attempting to decrease depression, the identified goals might be to increase physical activity or reduce self-downing thoughts.

Step 3: The Counselor Describes Several Options About How the Goals May Be Met.   In the example above, the counselor might use his or her experience to describe some physical activities that some clients have found to be helpful, including a regular aerobics class, a regular one-mile walk, yoga instruction, an exercise program on television, etc.

Step 4: The Client and Counselor Negotiate an Acceptable Plan.   The client is encouraged to modify or to expand the counselor's suggestion. The counselor's job is to continue to challenge the client to identify the plan that is most likely to work for him or her and to make the plan simple enough so that success is assured.

Step 5: The Client Makes a Commitment to the Plan.   The success of the assignment hinges on the client's commitment and enthusiasm for the plan. The counselor must be flexible enough to discard the plan and return to Step 3 (describing options) if the client is not committed to the assignment.

Step 6: The Counselor Reiterates the Assignment and Challenges the Client to Act.   The certainty of the therapist that the assignment can be met and will be helpful goes a long way in increasing the client's willingness to follow through. Besides this, the therapist must be sure that the client fullly understands the assignment and should invite questions. The therapist should end the session by encouraging the client to complete the homework, saying "I am confident that this assignment, though small, is a very important first step and I look forward to discussing the results next session."

Step 7: Follow-up.   At the follow-up stage, the counselor and client devise a reporting system so that the client can deliver a progress report at the next session. No matter what homework is employed, the client can collect data regarding practice attempts in a notebook or on file cards. At the minimum, the client should record the date, the type, and the amount of homework. Other record-keeping options are for the client to note any difficulties in practice. The therapist can help the client by charting improvements and by correcting any inaccuracies noted in client self-reports.

Problems and Precautions with Homework

1. Homework assignments that have a high probability of success should be chosen (Dyer & Vriend, 1977). This is true especially early in the counseling relationship in order to keep the client's hope alive. Also, by promoting

small, easily completed goals, the client begins to learn that most change is gradual, not an overnight phenomenon.

2. Homework strategies should be individually tailored for each client (Haley, 1978). Too often the counselor uses a standard format or form that, to the discouraged client, may feel impersonal. By stretching one's creativity, some assignments can incorporate more than one of the client's goals. If the client likes to read, reading self-help books as homework might work well. If the client enjoys writing, some compatible assignment could be devised.

3. Regularity of practice is important. It would be better, for example, if the client performed a visual rehearsal for 10 minutes, one time per day than once a week for an hour. Clients should be asked to monitor practice and to bring in records to gauge compliance.

4. Homework should be simple and fit easily into the life-style of the client. Complicated homework involving extensive record keeping may not be completed.

5. Homework should, at times, involve graduated tasks—tasks that increase in difficulty or discomfort as the client progresses. Clients usually have a feel for when they are ready for more challenging tasks and for tasks that are presently beyond them.

Variations on Homework

Bibliotherapy. *Bibliotherapy*, or the use of books as adjuncts to therapy, extends therapy beyond session hours. The plethora of self-help books now on the market is evidence of a growing awareness that psychological literature can bring about change; however, much of the offerings in trade books is oversimplified, based on opinion or a few anecdotes. Before recommending a book for a client, the therapist should have read the book and selected it based on the client's personal attributes. At each session, the therapist should discuss the client's reading and go over important points, perhaps even asking a few relevant questions as to how the assignment fits the client's current dilemma.

Although it is not possible to provide an exhaustive list of good bibliographic materials here, resources for selecting books and manuals are available (cf., Glasgow & Rosen, 1978). A very good stress management workbook-and-tape set, *Kicking Your Stress Habits* (Tubesing, 1979), is available. David Burns's (1980) *Feeling Good* contains an excellent cognitive approach to depression that the average person can easily grasp. A number of other books, such as Arnold Lazarus's (1982) *Personal Enrichment Through Imagery*, are now available on audiotape and can be listened to while driving or relaxing.

Besides informing the client, bibliotherapy can provide covert practice by exposing the client to a fictional or historical model of a desired behavior. Clients may identify with case studies or with fictional characters who face similar problems. The "Big Book" of Alcoholics Anonymous contains a number of true accounts of individuals who successfully overcame drinking problems.

Aides.   One way to increase the efficacy of homework practice is to enlist the help of a client's friend, spouse, or family member as an *aide* who provides either feedback or support for completing assignments. Generally, an aide comes to therapy sessions with the client. The counselor specifically identifies the aide's role as either support or feedback. Let us say that the client is attempting to become more assertive. The aide would be given specific verbal and nonverbal behaviors to observe and would report observations to the client. Alternately, the aide might simply be enlisted to provide support or to accompany the client while he or she completes assignments. The client who is attempting to exercise regularly may use an aide as a regular walking partner. The aide would help the client increase regularity and provide encouragement from session to session. The major pitfall of using aides is that they must be supervised by the therapist. Sometimes aides are too helpful and wish to take excessive responsibility for the client. If this behavior cannot be modified, the client should proceed alone.

Strategic Tasks.   Strategic therapists call homework assignments *tasks*. There are a number of variants, but there are also some standard tasks (O'Hanlon & Weiner-Davis, 1989). These therapists believe that tasks can produce change even if they are irrational. Haley (1989) listed some ways in which strategic therapists give tasks to families:

1. Tell them directly what you want them to do.
2. Use a paradox, such as "I want you to have two arguments this week." (Paradox is described more completely later.)
3. Give advice.
4. Let the therapist become a coach and use homework as practice.
5. Give the family an ordeal. Although not harmful, an *ordeal* is a task that is as hard on the family as are the symptoms. Sometimes an ordeal can even be absurd. Haley (1989) gives the example of telling a family to get in the car, go 17.3 miles, stop, and find a reason for being there.
6. Assign penance or something that makes up for guilt.

One of the standard tasks or *formula interventions* of strategic therapists is called *Write, read, and burn* (de Shazer, 1985). It involves writing down obsessive or depressing thoughts, reading them, and then burning the pages as a means of exorcising them.

Another technique that originated in strategic family therapy is the *surprise task* (O'Hanlon & Weiner-Davis, 1989). The therapist gives instructions to a couple to do one or two things that will surprise the other person between now and next session but not to tell him or her what was done. The surprises are then discussed at the next meeting. The surprise task helps break up old patterns and introduces a sense of play into the relationship. Clients who are troubled by recurrent behavior patterns may be given a more open-ended task: do domething different (de Shazer, 1985).

One permutation of the surprise task is replacing negatives with positives. A client once complained that even though he knew that the relationship was destructive, whenever his old romantic partner called, he almost automatically responded to her wish to get together. As a homework assignment, he was given the task of developing a set of positive alternatives to acquiescing to her requests.

The list of alternatives included calling up a friend, going to a movie, going to see his parents, going for a run, and asking someone out for a date. He decided to attempt two of these behaviors. The method was successful in developing new coping behaviors and, at the same time, provided a delay before jumping into a counterproductive behavior pattern.

CASE EXAMPLE

Maureen was a 20-year-old only child, living away from home, whose parents appeared to be on the verge of divorce. She came to counseling complaining that she was always in the middle and that each parent would call to tell her about the other's failings. In her attempts to placate both sides, Maureen became anxious and depressed and had trouble working at her job as a switchboard operator. She experienced periods of crying, had feelings of helplessness, and expressed sympathy for both parents. Maureen initially framed her problem as "how to help my parents cope with their divorce."

Before accepting this as a goal, the therapist completed a genogram on the client. From this the therapist hypothesized that the client was being *triangulated* by her parents, who complained to her rather than working out their differences. In the second session, Maureen agreed that what she wanted to do was to maintain a relationship with both parents, be supportive of both, and not to listen to their complaints about each other. This goal was compatible with her overall wish to become more independent. On this basis, the therapist agreed to the contract.

It was agreed that Maureen needed to learn some assertive behaviors that she could use on the phone with each parent. Although she had agreed to the contract, the therapist noted some hesitancy on Maureen's part. On confronting this resistance, Maureen admitted that she was very much afraid that she might offend and alienate one parent or the other and that he or she would break off contact. She also felt that her mother desperately needed to talk to someone. The therapist outlined several possible strategies for the client including, terminating the phone call when the conversation moved into unacceptable territory and suggesting therapy for the parents and several others. Maureen agreed that she would practice a standard assertive format that involved (1) expressing her love for the parent, (2) asking the parent to talk about something else; and (3) changing the conversation herself if the criticism continued. She also indicated that, in the case of her mother, she would locate a counselor in the mother's vicinity and encourage her to seek help there. Once Maureen became committed to the plan, some rehearsal via role playing was done in the office until she was adept at handling a number of variations. On one occasion Maureen took on the role of her mother, experiencing what it would be like to receive an assertive message. She was then given a reporting sheet on which to write down her responses during her phone calls that week and how she felt emotionally each time. The counselor encouraged Maureen to follow through with the plan and asked her to call if any problems arose. Maureen returned the following week with mixed success. She had been able to accomplish her goals with her father, but when her mother cried, she felt sympathetic and reverted to her old stance. Client and counselor agreed that she needed to talk with her mother personally, and Maureen went home for a visit to arrange counseling for her mother. Eventually, Maureen was able to approximate her goal of getting out of the middle. She noted a significant drop in their complaining and a decrease in stress for her.

Feedback Checklist #8

Assigning Homework

1. To what extent were client goals reviewed before homework was assigned?

Not at All	*A Little*	*Somewhat*	*Moderately*	*A Great Deal*
1	2	3	4	5

2. How well was the counselor able to help the client identify activities that the client needs to practice?

Not at All	*A Little*	*Somewhat*	*Moderately*	*Very Well*
1	2	3	4	5

3. To what extent was the counselor able to suggest ways in which goals might be met?

Not at All	*A Little*	*Somewhat*	*Moderately*	*A Great Deal*
1	2	3	4	5

4. How well was the counselor able to negotiate an acceptable plan with the client and obtain a commitment?

Not at All	*A Little*	*Somewhat*	*Moderately*	*Very Well*
1	2	3	4	5

5. How well did the counselor review the assignment and challenge the client to act?

Not at All	*A Little*	*Somewhat*	*Moderately*	*Very Well*
1	2	3	4	5

6. How well did the counselor devise an appropriate reporting system to be reviewed at the next session?

Not at All	*A Little*	*Somewhat*	*Moderately*	*Very Well*
1	2	3	4	5

CHAPTER SUMMARY AND CONCLUSIONS

Practice is used in psychotherapy and counseling to put insights into action and to help clients successfully experience new behaviors in a protected environment. Three levels of practice were described in this chapter: imaginal, role playing, and homework, or *in vivo* practice. Each has its appropriate use, but imaginal and role-playing practice may be considered initial steps that lead to eventual *in vivo* practice. Therapists who utilize practice methods will likely increase the generalization of therapy to real life contexts and will extend therapy and therapeutic gains beyond the therapy hour.

FURTHER READINGS

Bellack, A. S., & Hersen, M. (1985). *Dictionary of behavior therapy techniques*. New York: Pergamon. This book contains about 150 behavior therapy methods. Each is described in a page or two with relevant references for further research. Some of the therapies described that are relevant to practice include aversive behavioral rehearsal, contingency contracting, covert rehearsal, and massed practice.

Kipper, D. A. (1986). *Psychotherapy through clinical role playing*. New York: Brunner/Mazel. Kipper's book, written for therapists, is a thorough description of all aspects of role playing. It includes both behavioral and existential/psychodramatic approaches.

REFERENCES

Bandler, R., & Grinder, J. (1976). *The structure of magic* (Vol. 2). Palo Alto, CA: Science and Behavior Books.

Beck, A. T., Rush, A. J., Shaw, B. F., & Emery, G. (1979). Integration of homework into therapy. In A. T. Beck, A. J. Rush, B. F. Shaw & G. Emery, *Cognitive therapy of depression* (pp. 272–294). New York: Guilford.

Bellack, A. S. (1986). Covert rehearsal. In A. S. Bellack & M. Hersen (Eds.), *Dictionary of behavior therapy techniques*. New York: Pergamon.

Burns, D. D. (1980). *Feeling good*. New York: William Morrow.

Cautela, J. R., & Bennet, A. K. (1981). Covert conditioning. In R. Corsini (Ed.), *Handbook of innovative psychotherapies*. New York: Wiley.

de Shazer, S. (1985). *Keys to solution in brief therapy*. New York: Norton.

Driscoll, R. (1984). *Pragmatic psychotherapy*. New York: Van Nostrand Reinhold.

Dyer, W., & Vriend, J. (1977). *Counseling techniques that work*. New York: Funk & Wagnalls.

Ellis, A. (1962). *Reason and emotion in psychotherapy*. New York: Lyle Stuart.

Fezler, W. F. (1989). *Creative imagery: How to visualize in all five senses*. New York: Simon & Schuster.

Gladding, S. T. (1986). Imagery and metaphor in counseling: A humanistic course. *Journal of Humanistic Education and Development, 25,* 38–47.

Glasgow, R. E., & Rosen, G. M. (1978). Behavioral bibliotherapy: A review of self-help behavior therapy manuals. *Psychological Bulletin, 85,* 1–23.

Gottman, J. (1976). *A couple's guide to communication*. Champaign, IL: Research Press.

Grigsby, J. P. (1987). The use of imagery in the treatment of posttraumatic stress disorder. *Journal of Nervous and Mental Disease, 175,* 55–59.

Guerney, B., Stollak, G., & Guerney, L. (1971). The practicing psychologist as educator: An alternative to the medical practitioner's model. *Professional Psychology, 11,* 276–282.

Gunnison, H., & Renick, T. F. (1985). Bulimia: Using fantasy-imagery and relaxation techniques. *Journal of Counseling and Development, 64,* 79–80.

Haley, J. (1978). Ideas which handicap therapists. In M. Berger (Ed.), *Beyond the double blind: Communication and family systems, theories, techniques with schizophrenics* (pp. 24–36). New York: Brunner/Mazel.

Haley, J. (1989, April). *Strategic family therapy*. Symposium given at Stetson University, Deland, FL.

Kazdin, A. E. (1978). Covert modeling: The therapeutic application of imagined rehearsal. In J. L. Singer & K. S. Pope (Eds.), *The power of human imagination*. New York: Plenum Press.

Kipper, D. A. (1986). *Psychotherapy through clinical role playing*. New York: Brunner/Mazel.

Last, C. G. (1985). Homework. In A. S. Bellack & M. Hersen (Eds.), *Dictionary of behavior ther-*

apy techniques (pp. 140–141). New York: Pergamon.

Lazarus, A. (1977). *In the mind's eye: The power of imagery for personal enrichment.* New York: Rawson.

Lazarus, A. A. (1982). Personal enrichment through imagery [Cassette Recording]. New York: BMA Audio Cassettes/Guilford Publications.

Lazarus, A. A. (1985). Behavior rehearsal. In A. S. Bellack & M. Hersen, (Eds.), *Dictionary of behavior therapy techniques* (p. 22). New York: Pergamon Press.

Martin, G. A., & Worthington, E. L. (1982). Behavioral homework. In M. Hersen, R. Eisler & P. M. Miller (Eds.), *Progress in behavior modification* (Vol. 13, pp. 197–226). New York: Academic Press.

Maultsby, M., & Ellis, A. (1974). *Techniques for using rational emotive imagery (REI).* New York: Institute for Rational Living.

Moreno, J. L. (1964). *Psychodrama: Vol. 1* (3rd ed.). Beacon, NY: Beacon House.

O'Hanlon, W. H., & Weiner-Davis, M. (1989). *In search of solutions.* New York: Norton.

Papp, P. (1987, May). Symposium given at the American Association of Marriage and Family Therapists, Orlando, FL.

Parr, G. D., & Peterson, A. V. (1983). The use of imagery in reality therapy. *Journal of Reality Therapy, 2,* 2–6.

Pope, K. S. (1982). A primer on therapeutic imagery techniques. In P. A. Kellar & L. G. Ritt (Eds.), *Innovations in clinical practice: A sourcebook* (Vol. 1, pp. 67–77). Sarasota, FL: Professional Resource Exchange.

Sarnoff, D., & Remer, P. A. (1982). The effects of guided imagery on the generation of career alternatives. *Journal of Vocational Behavior, 21,* 299–308.

Schutz, W. (1982). Holistic education. In I. R. Corsini (Ed.), *Handbook of innovative psychotherapies* (pp. 378–388). New York: Wiley.

Sheikh, A. (Ed.) (1983). *Imagery: Current theory, research and application.* New York: Wiley.

Shelton, J. L., & Ackerman, J. M. (1974). *Homework in counseling and psychotherapy.* Springfield, IL: Charles C. Thomas.

Shelton, J. L., & Levy, R. L. (1981). *Behavioral assignments and treatment compliance.* Champaign, IL: Research Press.

Skovholt, T., & Thoen, G. A. (1987). Mental imagery in parenthood decision making. *Journal of Counseling and Development, 65,* 315–316.

Skovholt, T. M., Morgan, J. I., & Negron-Cunningham, H. (1989). Mental imagery in career counseling and life planning: A review of research and intervention methods. *Journal of Counseling and Development, 67,* 287–292.

Starr, A. (1977). *Psychodrama: Rehearsal for living.* Chicago: Nelson Hall.

Tubesing, D. (1979). *Kicking your stress habits.* Duluth, MN: Whole Person Press.

Wolpe, J. (1958). *Systematic desensitization through reciprocal inhibition.* Stanford, CA: Stanford University Press.

Witmer, J. M., & Young, M. E. (1985). The silent partner: Uses of imagery in counseling. *Journal of Counseling and Development, 64,* 187–190.

Witmer, J. M., & Young, M. E. (1987). Imagery in counseling. *Elementary School Guidance and Counseling, 22,* 5–16.

Yablonsky, L. (1976). *Psychodrama: Resolving emotional problems through role playing.* New York: Basic Books.

Young, M. E., & Rosen, L. S. (1985). The retreat: An educational growth group. *Journal for Specialists in Group Work, 10,* 157–163.

CHAPTER EIGHT

Lowering and Raising Emotional Arousal

KEY CONCEPTS

▼ *Lowering and raising emotional arousal are key processes in therapeutic change. Raising arousal motivates the client and gives a direct experience of withheld feelings. Lowering arousal leads to dramatic relief of symptoms.*

▼ *If repressed emotions are thought to stem from incomplete actions (unfinished business), therapy aims at allowing feelings to be reexperienced and completed.*

▼ *Systematic desensitization is a well-established technique drawn from the behavioral tradition that combines guided imagery and relaxation training to help clients overcome strong emotional reactions, especially fears and anger.*

▼ *The empty chair technique is a Gestalt therapy method that encourages the expression of emotions in order to overcome conflicts. Central to the technique is allowing the individual to contact both sides of a polarity and thereby to achieve integration.*

▼ *Free association is one of the oldest psychoanalytic methods for achieving emotional catharsis and insight. Outside of orthodox psychoanalysis, its use today is in helping clients recognize the meaning of projective drawings and symbols found in dreams and guided imagery.*

▼ *Also included in the chapter is a description of seven general methods for enhancing emotional awareness in counseling, including attending, refocusing, present centeredness, expression analysis, intensifying, symbolizing, and establishing intents.*

INTRODUCTION

Emotional Arousal: The Curative Factor

Frank (1985) named his fourth curative factor *arousing emotions.* His findings suggested that emotions supply the motivation for change. Feelings of suffering and pain also turn the client toward the therapist and promote compliance with treatment. Frank and his colleagues found that subjects who were emotionally stimulated with ether and adrenalin were susceptible to changes in attitudes imposed by the experimenters but that these changes were transitory (Hoehn-Saric, 1978). This led Frank to believe that although emotional arousal may be an important catalyst for change, other factors may be at work in maintaining the change. In other words, new learning (cognitive) and practice (behavioral) factors may be necessary to promote long-lasting effects.

199

Other writers, such as Fenichel (1945), have suggested that emotional arousal, or *catharsis,* as it is known in psychoanalysis, demonstrates to the client that he or she has repressed strong emotions and that they are real. It is a confirmation by direct knowledge of the efficacy of psychotherapy, a real experience versus an intellectual insight. This is also affirmed by Gestalt therapy, which recognizes the energy and vitality when clients are able to focus on the here and now rather than lapsing into aboutism. *Aboutism* is the tendency to distance the self from experience by talking *about* it (Polster & Polster, 1973, p. 9). Counseling should not only be a rehashing of past experiences.

Catharsis also has the effect of *palliation,* or reducing emotional arousal (Conoley, Conoley, McConnell & Kimzey, 1983; Meichenbaum & Cameron, 1983; Nichols & Zax, 1977). Following emotional arousal is a second relief stage involving emotional equilibrium or lowering of arousal. The eventual effect of crying, for example, can be a lessening of sadness or grief. The first stage is associated with sympathetic arousal, and the second stage with parasympathetic action. (Nichols & Efran, 1985).

Another reason for the effectiveness of emotional arousal in psychotherapy is simply that emotions are salient. They have been called "hot cognitions" (Greenberg & Safran, 1988). In other words, the emotional aspects of a problem are the most prominent to the client. Dealing directly with the emotions is persuasive to the client since it brings about an immediate sense that core issues are being dealt with.

Lowering and Raising Emotions in the REPLAN System

The conceptualization of lowering and raising emotional arousal as a curative factor in the REPLAN system (Figure 8.1) differs from Frank's ideas since Frank pointed to arousal as the key factor in therapeutic change. In the mind of this author, lowering arousal is compatible with emotional arousal because the therapist's final goal is to help the client achieve emotional balance. Arousing emotions is one way to achieve a decrease in negative affective states. My inclusion of techniques that reduce emotional arousal is primarily for educational and organizational purposes. These quieting methods seem to provide a good contrast with cathartic techniques.

ROLE OF EMOTIONS IN THERAPEUTIC CHANGE

The development of a well-socialized person involves learning to restrain emotions. Direct affective expression is often labeled as a sign of social immaturity. While emotional health does involve restraint, it also involves a recognition of one's emotions and learning to find alternative methods of expression (Witmer, 1985).

It has long been known that emotional arousal, when too intense, inhibits performance, and when arousal is too weak, performance is also affected nega-

FIGURE 8.1
Six curative factors in the REPLAN system.

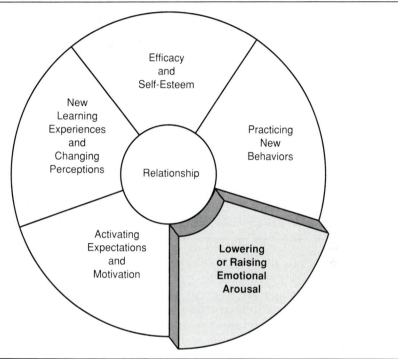

tively (Yerkes-Dodson Law). It has been the experience of many clinicians that clients who change in therapy come to therapy with a great deal of emotional arousal or find their emotions aroused in the therapy process. Although a few clients seek counseling in order to make a good life better or to prevent potential problems, most come due to some emotional pain they are seeking to ease.

Emotions as Catalysts

Kurt Lewin talked about therapeutic change being an "unfreezing and refreezing" process, meaning that the client's old viewpoints must be heated up with emotions in order to change. After this "corrective emotional experience" the client "refreezes," or solidifies, in a slightly different state. McMullin (1986) calls this phenomenon the "melted wax theory." As a cognitive therapist, McMullin thinks that beliefs must be changed in order to bring about emotional and behavioral alterations. Emotional arousal can be used to provide the heat needed to melt down old beliefs so that they may be reformed. Emotional arousal seems to intensify memories. It is hypothesized that lessons learned in therapy when emotions are aroused make a deeper impression on the client.

Emotions as Actions

One other way of thinking about emotions is that they are action tendencies (Greenberg & Safran, 1988). Anger prepares the body to fight and fear is a preparation for flight. Awareness of emotions includes awareness of desired actions as well as the vocal and conscious/intuitive experiences of feelings (Izard, 1977). Perls (1977, p. 119) related this to the notion of a gestalt when he said

> The gestalt wants to be completed. If the gestalt is not completed, we are left with unfinished situations, and these unfinished situations press and press and press and want to be completed. Let's say if you had a fight, you really got angry at that guy, and you want to take revenge. This need for revenge will nag and nag and nag until you have become even with him. So there are thousands of unfinished gestalts.

Moreno, psychodrama's founder, termed the action component of repressed feelings *act hunger*. A psychodramatic example may help to explain this concept more completely.

CASE EXAMPLE ————————————————————————————

A man came to psychodramatic therapy with "a few things he wanted to get off his chest." He had come home a few months earlier and found his wife in bed with another man. His response was to leave the house and not return for several days. Still, he experienced a great deal of rage and self-contempt. In role-playing the situation, the psychodramatist encouraged the man to act out his feelings and to express the actions he wished he would have taken on that night. After some consideration, he decided that bodily throwing her out of the house was what he had really wanted to do. This scene was recreated using fellow group members, and the man was able to express his intense feelings of anger at his impotency in the situation. After the scene was completed, he acknowledged that this was what he wanted to do at the time but, in retrospect, he was glad that he did not follow through. He experienced a sense of relief at having gotten this unfinished act out of his system.

This example demonstrates that emotions are not simply pools of stored emotions but also involve the holding back of expressive actions.

HISTORY OF CATHARSIS IN PSYCHOTHERAPY AND COUNSELING

The earliest records of cathartic methods are found in Ancient Greek drama. The word *katharsis* indicates a purging or purification experienced after the display of emotions. The effectiveness of traditional uses of cathartic methods is documented in the history of religious rituals, confession of sins, mesmerism, drug induced emotional states, and rituals of mourning.

Freud's view of catharsis (Breuer & Freud, 1895/1955) was that neurosis was caused by repressed affect, or withheld emotions that needed to be released. He later rejected this "hydraulic theory" in favor of the "conflict theory," which postulated that emotions are caused by a conflict between psychic structures rather than a buildup of unconscious emotions. Initially, his work with Breuer led Freud to believe that discharging painful emotions under hypnosis was the curative factor. He became disillusioned with both hypnosis and catharsis when he found that they did not lead to sustained change. Patients seemed to discharge emotions and still did not understand them. Freud became more interested in the role of memories as causes of dysfunction. He began to investigate free association as a replacement for hypnosis and emphasized working through emotions over abreaction or catharsis. He saw the unleashing of affect as a by-product of uncovering memories rather than an end in itself.

Post-Freudian Methods

In modern psychotherapy, catharsis is an undeniable curative factor present in virtually every form of therapy. Terms that refer to this phenomenon include abreaction, emotional insight, corrective emotional experience, affective expression, emotional awareness, and releasing blocked emotions. Emotional arousal has been activated through hypnosis and drugs (Wolberg, 1977), psychodramatic methods (Moreno, 1958), guided imagery (Witmer & Young, 1985), reflective listening in client-centered therapy, confrontation, deprecating and devaluating feedback in Synnanon groups, free association in psychoanalysis, the empty chair technique of Gestalt therapy (Polster & Polster, 1973), focusing (Gendlin, 1969), flooding, implosive therapy (Stampfl & Levis, 1967), bioenergetics (Lowen, 1967), primal therapy (Janov, 1970), reevaluation counseling (Jackins, 1962), provocative therapy (Farelly & Brandsma, 1974), and many others.

Emotional Flooding

Prochaska (1984) identified several schools of thought that he called "emotional flooding therapies." Among them are Janov's primal therapy (1970), bioenergetics (Reich, 1945), and implosive therapy (Stampfl & Levis, 1967). All three share roots in the psychoanalytic tradition, which focused on unleashing affect from early traumas. They all rely on techniques that directly evoke intense emotions. *Bioenergetics* focuses on body manipulation, postures, and breathing techniques to unlock blocked energies. *Primal therapy* involves stimulating early memories and reexperiencing them. Rebirthing, a newer therapeutic fad, is a spin-off from primal and Reichian therapies. In *rebirthing*, clients relive the trauma of the birth process through a role-playing experience intensified with special breathing techniques (Orr & Ray, 1977). *Implosive therapy* combines flooding and psychodynamic ideas. The technique of *flooding* involves exposing the client to the feared stimulus either directly or through imagery. The implosive method uses intense and even revolting imagery techniques to heighten emotional arousal.

Most therapists who evoke strong emotions as part of the therapy do not use these emotional flooding therapies. These techniques are considered quite controversial. Several authors (Frank, 1985; Greenberg & Safran, 1988; Nichols & Efran, 1985) besides Freud have suggested that expressing affect alone is not sufficient for real progress: it leads only to temporary relief. Despite the popular appeal of emotional flooding, a change in thinking and behavior is also needed to sustain therapeutic movement.

Lowering Emotional Arousal

It could be said that all psychotherapy techniques temper emotional arousal to some extent. Even methods that enhance the therapeutic relationship help to decrease fear and anxiety. Early interest in lowering emotional arousal centered on phobias and fears and later on decreasing sadness. More recently, anger and anxiety, the two most prominent emotions of a busy society, have been thoroughly examined. Some of the better known methods in use today for lowering emotional arousal are systematic desensitization (Wolpe, 1958), progressive relaxation (Jacobson, 1938), coping skills training, confession/ventilation (Menninger, 1958), emotional support (Gilliland, James & Bowman, 1989), stress inoculation (Novaco, 1977), biofeedback training, and meditation (Carrington, 1978). These techniques are often combined and offered in a psychoeducational format as stress reduction or coping skills training courses. Combined coping skills training is thought to be as effective as other methods (Yorde & Witmer, 1980).

Coping Skills Training

Cognitive behaviorists who study stress and coping have developed interesting insights into this process (Lazarus & Folkman, 1984). According to their views, stress is the result of an appraisal by the organism that some threat, harm, or loss is likely to be experienced. The uncomfortable emotional arousal suggests that coping mechanisms should be employed. Coping can be of two types: *problem focused* or *emotion focused* (palliative). On the one hand, a person can attempt to change behavior or to escape or avoid the stressful transaction with the environment. On the other hand, the person can reduce emotional arousal.

Some coping attempts are more effective than others. For example, avoidance of a feared stimulus may be effective in the short run but, in the long term, it may eventually be self-defeating. Defense mechanisms, such as denial, may be emotional palliatives, but they also distort reality.

In summary, emotional equilibrium has been identified as a sign of mental health and emotional disturbance as the opposite. A goal of therapy has always been to bring emotions into expression and under control. Therapists have traditionally used emotional arousal for these purposes, and many cathartic techniques are still in use. More recently, lowering emotional arousal has become an important part of many therapies through the introduction of quieting techniques such as meditation, relaxation, and stress-coping and biofeedback training.

In the section on methods and techniques in this chapter, we will look at three areas. First, systematic desensitization, a method for lowering emotional arousal, will be explained. Second, we will examine the empty chair technique, a Gestalt method for emotional arousal. Finally, we will explore several techniques for increasing emotional arousal. We have entitled these techniques emotional awareness methods to indicate that not all of them were designed to produce high levels of emotional arousal. Each of these methods is more or less a standard way that therapists make clients aware of unexpressed or withheld feelings.

METHODS AND TECHNIQUES OF LOWERING OR RAISING EMOTIONS

Systematic Desensitization: Overview and Purpose of the Method

Systematic desensitization was developed by Wolpe in 1958 and has been a standard tool for reducing emotional arousal since the 1960s. Its primary use has been to diminish fear, though it has been a tool for anger reduction as well (Warren & McLellarn, 1982). Systematic desensitization is one of the best-researched techniques available to the practitioner (cf., Gatchel, 1980; Lazarus, 1961; Paul 1966; Rimm & Masters, 1974). One review of 25 studies (Berman, Miller & Massman, 1985) concluded that cognitive and desensitization therapies are roughly comparable in efficacy. The method is somewhat complex and demanding, involving specific training for the client in relaxation, imagery, hierarchy construction, as well as daily homework assignments. These components are useful on their own however, and are integral to more modern cognitive behavioral interventions. Variations of the method are considered later in the chapter.

What Is Systematic Desensitization and How Does It Work?

Systematic desensitization is a method for slowly weakening fear and anxiety responses associated with a stimulus (object or situation). This is done by pairing imagined scenes depicting aspects of the feared stimulus with a positive, relaxed state achieved through deep muscle relaxation.

Wolpe contended that the method works because of *reciprocal inhibition* (the replacement of a fear response with an incompatible response, relaxation). The counter-conditioning process builds an association between a previously feared situation and a positive feeling of relaxation. Over time, the anxiety-provoking stimulus loses its potential to evoke anxiety. A simpler way of saying this is that one emotion (relaxation/pleasure) can be used to counteract another (anxiety) (Mckay, Davis & Fanning, 1981).

Other explanations have been proposed for the efficacy of the technique. One behavioral version suggests that exposure to the feared stimulus reveals to the client that the stimulus has no real potential for harm. The anxiety response is no longer reinforced and, thus, it is extinguished (Lomont, 1965; Levin & Gross, 1985). Some have found that clients change because of insight gained during the systematic desensitization process (Kuhlman, 1982). Another researcher proposes that learning the skill of relaxation helps the client cope with anxiety in the feared situation (Goldfried, 1971). Still another suggests that desensitization brings about cognitive changes. Clients reduce anticipatory anxiety as they begin to change expectations about fearful circumstances (Meichenbaum, 1977).

Clients Who May Benefit from Systematic Desensitization

Obviously clients who are fearful of particular objects or activities are candidates for systematic desensitization. Most of the research on this subject has focused on minor fears, but major phobias have also been treated. The technique is not a format for assertiveness or social skills training. It is really for those who already possess the skills to perform but who continually avoid doing so. In addition, desensitization has been applied to interpersonal anxiety reduction, fears of rejection, ridicule, of being alone (Mckay et al., 1981). Desensitization has been successful with nightmares (Schindler, 1980), rape trauma (Frank, Anderson, Stewart & Dancu, 1988), and anorexia nervosa (Goldfarb, Fuhr, Tsujimoto & Fischman, 1987). It is not indicated for conditions of generalized anxiety. Selecting clients for desensitization is well discribed in an article by Deffenbacher and Suinn (1988). They especially recommend desensitization for phobias, situational anxiety, such as test-anxious behavior, and conditioned aversion reactions.

Method of Systematic Desensitization

There are several formats for systmatic desensitization. The one described here is closest to that advanced by Goldfried (1971). The emphasis of this version is on helping the client learn to become aware of bodily sensations of tension and to use these to cue relaxation. This method differs from Wolpe's original format in several ways. Goldfried's model concentrates on learning to cope with anxiety: it allows the client to construct a single hierarchy of anxiety-provoking situations rather than a different hierarchy for each feared condition. The emphasis is on learning to reduce anxiety rather than to reduce fear of a particular stimulus situation.

Step 1: Preview, Explain, and Assess.   Before beginning the process of systematic desensitization, it is crucial to educate the client fully regarding the process. Preparation and motivation are necessary because the anticipated length of treatment using the technique is about six sessions and it requires dedication on the part of both participants. The client should be told that success is usually attributable, in large part, to the homework and follow-up that takes place after training is complete.

   If the client is not aware of the use of a SUDS scale (subjective units of discomfort), it should be explained. At the beginning and the end of each session, the counselor uses the SUDS scale to gauge generalized relaxation, with 100 being the most tense or fearful and 0 being completely free of anxiety. The SUDS scale is also used in constructing the hierarchy of fearful situations that the client addresses.

   A very important aspect of the preparation is to determine if the client is able to achieve some degree of relaxation in the therapy setting and if the client can produce reasonably vivid imagery. Some clients with extreme anxiety become too uncomfortable with the process of relaxation even to sit with eyes closed for several minutes. Some report increases in anxiety as they begin to relax. In a few clients, it may take two or three sessions to overcome fears of relaxation through gradually increasing the relaxation period and homework. One brief way of testing the client's ability to image is to ask the client if he or she can sustain the following images for 10 seconds:

1. The sight of a bowl of fruit (visual)
2. The feel of sandpaper on one's fingertips (tactile)
3. The sound of a barking dog (auditory)
4. The smell of a bouquet of roses (olfactory)
5. The taste of warm soup (gustatory)

After each stimulus, the counselor asks if the client was able to sustain the image over the entire interval. Next, a description of each image is obtained from the client. The amount of detail is a clue to the vividness of the image perceived. A rule of thumb is that if a client has difficulty sustaining the image or describes only minimal imagery in three or more of the sense modalities, additional imagery practice is needed before desensitization can proceed. The assessment provides some information to the counselor about the modalities that are easiest for the client to imagine: visual, auditory, kinesthetic, etc. Clients who produce only minimal or no imagery might be better served by developing an alternative treatment plan.

Step 2: Identifying the Situations Associated with Emotional Arousal. The most important part of gathering this information is to be as complete and as thorough as possible. Use of client self-monitoring (described previously) for at least one week is highly recommended. The client is given a stack of index cards and is instructed to write down each anxiety-arousing situation encountered during the week. Each situation is briefly noted on a separate card. In the upper right-hand corner, the SUDS level at the time it was noticed is also recorded. Some clients have great difficulty assigning a SUDS level. In this case, it may be useful to ask for a designation of high, medium, or low instead. Some clients seem to comprehend a 10-point scale more easily than a 100-point SUDS scale.

During the counseling interview the client and counselor add more cards for situations that they have identified during their discussions. One way of eliciting this information is to ask the client to describe step by step several circumstances where the emotion is evoked. For example, the client who has trouble going into crowded places might begin with thinking about going to the shopping mall, driving there in the car, finding a parking space, walking to the entrance, etc. Each of these actions represents separate steps and separate cards. The client is also encouraged to quiz friends and family members to see if they can remember relevant experiences.

An additional source of information is the client's response to the Fear Survey Schedule (Wolpe & Lang, 1964), a self-report questionnaire that lists common fearful situations, or the Fear Inventory (McKay et al., 1981, pp. 80–82). Cards can be filled out for any new items identified in this way. To develop a comprehensive list, at least 12 cards are needed, but 15 to 20 is optimal. The difference in

SUDS level between cards should be approximately 5 to 10 points. If larger gaps exist, client and counselor should develop additional items to insert.

Finally two or three 0-SUDS-level items should be developed. These are cards with descriptions of scenes that are either emotionally neutral or relaxing. These cards provide a sort of trial run before moving into the emotionally arousing items. Relaxing scenarios are also a positive way to end each desensitization session.

Step 3: Develop a Hierarchy of Emotionally Arousing Events.   When working with a very discrete or simple fear, the hierarchy is often ordered naturally since fear increases as one approaches the feared object in time or space. In the coping model described here, the order is based on the SUDS score since the client is being asked to move toward more and more difficult imagined scenes as skill in relaxation is developed.

The cards obtained in the listing process are ordered from highest SUDS level to lowest, with 0-point items on top of the pile and the most arousing cards at the bottom. If a high, medium, and low designation has been used, the client is asked to order the cards in each of the three categories from highest to lowest.

Step 4: Teach Relaxation.   Edmund Jacobson's progressive relaxation technique (1938) was, for many years, the favored method for teaching clients deep muscle quieting for systematic desensitization. Jacobson's method, if faithfully followed, teaches the client to identify and relax every major muscle group in the body, a procedure that may actually take several months. Abbreviated versions of this technique have been used successfully (cf., Gatchel & Baum, 1983; McKay et al., 1981).

The following paragraphs describe a simple muscle relaxation technique developed by Witmer (1985) that has been used with both groups and individuals.

The subject is asked to find the most comfortable position with eyes closed. This may be sitting or lying, but in either case, there should be support for the head. The procedure is best practiced without the distractions of glaring lights. The client is instructed to speak as little as possible and to avoid unnecessary movement except as needed to obtain a more comfortable position. The legs and arms should not be crossed.

The procedure involves progressively tightening and then relaxing each muscle group in turn. The client is encouraged to hold each tensed muscle six or seven seconds until the experience of tightness is fully felt. Cramps and spasms may result, though, if the posture is held too long.

During the tension of the muscle group, the client is to focus attention on that area, simultaneously relaxing other parts of the body and holding the breath. Following the tensing of the area, the client is then told to exhale and relax fully and completely. This relaxation is accompanied with slow, deep, diaphragmatic breathing and should last 20 seconds or so. The tension and relaxation of that same muscle group is then repeated before moving on.

The first administration of the relaxation technique should be recorded on cassette for the client, or a standardized commercially available version of the technique should be obtained. Some relaxation recordings are sold in several sequential cassettes. I believe it is better to use a single cassette that takes the client through a complete relaxation each time. A single recording seems to produce results more quickly and is less confusing for the client to use.

Table 8.1 contains instructions for tensing and relaxing various muscle groups in the body according to a modified Jacobsonian system. A complete administration can be completed in about 20 minutes or so.

TABLE 8.1 (pp. 209–211)
Instructions to the client for tensing and relaxing muscle groups.

Major Muscle Group and Area of Tension	Tensing and Relaxing Instructions
1. Hands and Arms	
Hand: The back of your hand, fingers, and the wrist	Tense the muscles in the right hand and lower right arm by making a tight fist. Hold for at least five seconds. Feel the tension. Now relax. Notice the difference between the tensing and relaxing. Repeat the same procedure. Now do the same thing with your left hand. Finish by tensing and relaxing both hands together.
Lower Arm: The forearm and the wrist	Hold both arms out in front of you with palms up, bend the hands down. Feel the tension in the hand, wrist, and forearm. Then relax. Repeat the same procedure. Now extend your arms out in front of you but with palms down. Bend your hands up. Feel the tension. Relax. Repeat the same procedure. Now let both arms hang loosely at your side.
Upper Arm: The bicep muscles	Start with your right arm. Bend the elbow, touch your shoulder with your fingers, and tense the bicep just like you want to show off your muscles. Feel the tension, then relax and notice the contrast. Repeat the same procedure. Now do the same thing with your left arm. Finish by tensing, then relaxing both arms together. Now let both arms hang loosely at your side.
2. Head, Face, and Throat	
Forehead and Scalp: The entire forehead and scalp area	Wrinkle your forehead by raising your eyebrows as high as you can. Feel the tension in the forehead and scalp area. Now relax, notice the difference between tension and relaxation. Repeat the procedure. Next frown by pulling your eyebrows down as far as you can. Feel the tension, then relax. Repeat the same procedure. Let go of all tension, then relax. Repeat the same procedure. Let go of all tension in the forehead and scalp area. Feel the smoothness of the muscles.
Eyes and Nose: The eyelids and muscles around the eyes, nose, and upper cheeks	Squeeze your eyes shut and at the same time wrinkle up your nose. Feel the tension, then relax. Repeat the procedure. Next roll your eyes left and right, up and down or rotate them both directions. Finish by opening your eyes as widely as you can, then relaxing them. Now feel the relaxation of muscles around your eyes.

TABLE 8.1
(*continued*)

Major Muscle Group and Area of Tension	Tensing and Relaxing Instructions
Mouth and Jaw: The area around the mouth and the lower face	Bite your teeth together and pull the corners of your mouth back. Feel the tension, then let go. Now press your lips tightly together and extend them as though you are sucking a straw. Feel the tension and relax. Next open your mouth widely, then relax. Now pull your mouth to the left side of your face, then to the right. Repeat any of the above exercises until this part of your face is deeply relaxed.
Throat and Jaw: Muscles inside the mouth and throat	Push your tongue against the roof of your mouth. Feel the tension, then relax. Clench your jaw tightly, then relax.
Entire Head and Facial Area	Try a final tensing and relaxing by making a face. Scrunch up your face so your eyes squint, your nose is wrinkled up and your mouth is pulled back. Now your face feels smooth and relaxed as you let go of any tension left over.
3. Neck and Shoulders *Neck:* The muscles in the back of the neck, at the base of the scalp, and across the shoulders	Drop your chin down against your chest. Press down hard enough so you feel tension under your chin and at the back of your neck. Now lift your head and press it backward. Roll your head to the right, then forward to your chest, then to the left and back to where you started. Go slowly and gently. Repeat this at least twice in the same direction. Next, do the same exercise in the other direction. Relax with your head in a normal position, stretching it in whatever way you need for working out remaining tension spots.
4. Chest, Shoulders, and Upper Back *Muscles in the Chest, Shoulders, and Upper Back Area*	Take a deep breath, hold it and at the same time pull the shoulders back, trying to make the shoulder blades touch. Feel the tension around your ribs, shoulders, and the upper back. Exhale slowly and feel the relaxation as you return to a natural position. Now pull your shoulders as far forward as you can, then as far up, as far back, and as far down as you can, making a kind of circular motion. Repeat this at least twice. Feel the tension and relaxation. Next go in the opposite direction in your rotation of the shoulders. Sense the looseness and relaxed feeling in this part of your body.
5. Lower Back, Stomach, and Hips *Lower Back:* The muscles across the lower back area	Begin by taking a deep breath and sitting up straight. Pull the shoulders back and arch your back so your stomach sticks out. Exhale and let all the air and tension flow out. Repeat this procedure. Next bend forward arching your back the other way with your head down to your knees and your hands touching the floor. Feel the muscles stretching. Return to a

TABLE 8.1

(continued)

Major Muscle Group and Area of Tension	Tensing and Relaxing Instructions
	normal sitting position and feel the relaxation. Repeat the procedure.
Stomach and Hips: The muscles in the abdominal area and hips	Take a deep breath and hold it as you make your stomach muscles hard. Just tighten them up as though you were going to hit yourself in the stomach. You should feel a good deal of tightness in the stomach area. Breathe out and feel the relaxation as you do let go of this tension. Repeat the procedure. Next breathe out as far as you can, feeling the tension in your stomach area as you hold your breath. Now let go and allow yourself to breathe naturally, noticing the difference between tension and relaxation.

6. Hips, Legs, and Feet

Major Muscle Group and Area of Tension	Tensing and Relaxing Instructions
Hips and Upper Legs: The muscles in the upper and lower parts of the thighs	Gently hold fast to the bottom of your chair. Press your heels down hard on the floor. Feel the tension around your hips and the hardness of the large upper leg muscles. Relax and notice the difference between tension and relaxation. Repeat the procedure.
Lower Legs: The muscles from the knees to the ankles	Hold both legs straight out in front of you. Point your feet and toes away from your head. Feel the tension in your legs and on top of your feet. Relax and drop both feet on the floor. Now extend your legs again, but point your feet and toes toward your head. Feel the tension in the calf muscles and around your ankles. Relax and drop both feet. Notice the relaxed feeling.
Feet: The muscles around the ankles, over the top of the feet, the arch and ball of the feet, and the toes	Extend both toes pointed away from you. Then turn both feet inward and at the same time curl your toes. Gently tense the muscles just enough to feel the tension and relax. Now try moving each foot in a circulation motion, feeling the stretching and tensing. Relax. Repeat but reverse the direction and relax! Try spreading your toes, then relaxing, letting all the tension go out of your feet. Now put both feet flat on the floor, take a deep breath and relax.

7. Body Review

Major Muscle Group and Area of Tension	Tensing and Relaxing Instructions
	Scan your whole body and recognize how it now feels more relaxed. Let the muscles of your body relax even more as you do a body scan from head to toe. Muscles that still feel a bit tight can be tensed, then relaxed.
	Next, try tensing your whole body at one time. Take a deep breath and feel the tension all over your body. Hold for several seconds, then let go. Let all the air out and feel the deep relaxation coming over your entire body. The tension is flowing out like the air escaping from a balloon. Enjoy the relaxed feeling.

Source: From *Pathways to Personal Growth: Developing a Sense of Worth and Competence* (pp. 391–394) by J. M. Witmer, 1985, Muncie, IN: Accelerated Development. Reprinted by permission.

The client is asked to practice the relaxation technique twice daily, usually upon arising and in bed before falling asleep. The practice must begin one or two weeks before the implementation of the densensitization process. The client is to note which of the six target areas are the sources of the greatest tension and to report this to the therapist.

The most important phase of the lesson is the body review. This "body scan" is an important aspect of desensitization since the client will be asked to return to specific and discrete areas of tension during the procedure and relax them. The client is instructed that the final part of the body review, which involves tensing the whole body, is also a simple way of achieving relaxation at times when the full process cannot be implemented.

Step 5: Pairing Relaxation and Scene Presentation.   This step has several components. First, the counselor helps the client relax to a SUDS of 10 or less following instructions given in previous sessions. Next, the client and counselor agree on a signal (usually nonverbal) to be used by the client when the imagined scene evokes anxiety. Traditionally, therapists have asked clients to lift an index finger about one inch. Some use a verbal signal, such as the word *now,* to indicate the presence of anxiety and *gone* to indicate full relaxation. I prefer that the client turn one or both palms up when the scene evokes anxiety and palms down when relaxation accompanies the image. The amount of time spent with palms down is recorded on the card.

The actual scene presentation phase begins as the counselor reads the initial card to the client. The first card or two are 0 items designed to prime the client in the relaxation process. Eventually, the first real card from the hierarchy is read. If the client signals anxiety, the counselor instructs the client as follows: "Hold the image and relax away all of the tension. Signal when you are able to lower the tension to a 10 or less." The counselor records the length of full relaxation and the SUDS level associated with each scene on the situation card (see Figure 8.2). The SUDS level is reported by the client after the trial.

If after several trials, the client has difficulty in maintaining relaxation, additional training in that area will be needed before proceeding. Another method is to ask the client to do a body scan during the emotionally arousing imagery and to identify areas that are particularly tense. During the next presentation, the client is told to focus relaxation efforts primarily on those body parts.

After each trial, the counselor should institute a brief hiatus of 30 seconds or so before the next presentation. The client is then returned to a state of full relaxation and the same instructions are given. Successful completion of a card is achieved when the client is able to hold the arousing image with a low SUDS level for 40 seconds or so on at least two trials. Once the client and counselor agree that imagery and relaxation can be maintained consistently, it is time to move on to the next item. Scene presentations in subsequent sessions begin with the last situation card that was successfully completed.

Step 6: Practice.   Following each desensitization session, homework tasks should be assigned to be completed on a daily basis. Relaxation training, the first step, can be learned in one to two weeks by most individuals. The client is given audiotaped instructions, which are best played through small headphones. The client is also

FIGURE 8.2
Situation card for systematic desensitization.

Situation Card Number 8							SUDS: 45	

Situation Title: Talking with my ex-wife about the kids.

Description: You are walking up the sidewalk to the house where she lives and you are wondering how she will react to your being there. You are also wondering if she will be alone.

TRIAL #	1	2	3	4	5	6	7	8
RELAXED	6"	4"	19"	15"	23"	40"	40"	
SUDS	45	60	50	30	20	15	10	

encouraged to identify cues in the environment that will act as reminders for relaxation, such as stopping at a traffic light or looking at the clock. Some therapists recommend that clients affix adhesive dots obtained from office supply stores to watches and computer screens as cues. In brief moments throughout the day, one can do a body scan and quick tension/relaxation.

Once desensitization begins, the procedure of holding images and relaxing away the tension should be practiced at least two times daily by the client. For this, a duplicate set of cards is made up, and the client records dates and results of practice. The client is not to move ahead in the hierarchy during practice but is to go over items covered during the last session.

Eventually, *in vivo* tasks should be introduced. Whether this should begin while desensitization is going on or after its completion is a matter of judgment for the therapist. A new set of cards that draws items from the original pool is arranged hierarchically, and the client is asked to enter that feared situation alone or accompanied, gradually lengthening the amount of time in that setting.

Problems and Precautions with Systematic Desensitization

1. The major precaution in systematic desensitization has already been alluded to. If the client does not become fully proficient in the relaxation technique, little success will come from the desensitization sessions.
2. For clients who cannot visually imagine well, the therapist may attempt to use some other sense modality. For example, some clients find that a scene can be more easily imagined in terms of dialogue or internal monologue. An example of such an item might be, "Then I think, 'What if a fire broke out in the theater?'" This description is used on the situation card rather than a description of the setting.

3. Homework practice must be closely monitored. Clients who assiduously avoid fearful situations will show a great deal of reluctance to practice.
4. Once a hierarchical listing of arousal situations has been determined, it should not necessarily be followed slavishly. Some rearrangement is almost always necessary when it is determined that one scene is more stressful than another.

Variations on Systematic Desensitization

In Vivo **Desensitization.** One important variation on systematic desensitization, *in vivo* desensitization, has already been mentioned. This method is very often used with severe phobias. Here the client is gradually exposed to real situations rather than imagined ones and is taught to implement cognitive and relaxation techniques. A hierarchy is constructed, and the client begins to face each setting in turn. Clients may enter these situations alone, with a friend, or accompanied by the therapist at first. The therapist or a friend helps to model the appropriate behavior and provides support initially. If the client is accompanied, it is important that the next step on the hierarchy has the client visiting that place alone.

Desensitization in Different Formats. Desensitization can be administered in a number of different formats. It has been provided in group settings using standardized instructions for individuals who share a common fear. Generally, group desensitization works best for relatively minor anxieties (cf., Osterhouse, 1976). Computerized desensitization programs have also been used successfully with phobias (Chandler, Burck, Sampson & Wray, 1988; Lang, Melamed & Hart, 1970).

Stress Inoculation. Applying the gradual exposure of systematic desensitization to stress-related problems is called *stress inoculation* (Meichenbaum & Cameron, 1983). It is a combined coping skills training method that the authors originally designed to provide phobic clients with additional skills. Stress inoculation training initially referred to a three phase operation:

1. An educational phase that introduced the relationship between cognitive, affective, and physiological components of the individual's behavior
2. A skills training phase that involved the teaching of two basic competencies, coping self-statements and self-directed relaxation
3. An application phase in which the person tested out skills in a simulated condition

This process was found to be more effective than systematic desensitization for phobia treatment (Meichenbaum & Cameron, 1974).

Recently stress inoculation has become more generic with the possibility of modifying it to a variety of subject populations and emotions. Phase one is now termed *conceptualization* and includes an assessment procedure that teaches clients to gather their own data through self-monitoring. Phase two, *skills acquisition and rehearsal* involves training in both problem-focused and emotion-focused coping. It also includes rehearsal using imagery and role playing. Phase three, now called *application and follow-through,* uses graded *in vivo* exposures to stressors and follow-up review sessions.

Stress inoculation is now being applied to other emotions besides fear. Novaco (1977, 1983) has pioneered stress inoculation for depression and anger. His methods for anger control involve both emotional palliatives, such as relaxation training and coping self-statements, as well as learning cognitive methods for redefining anger.

CASE EXAMPLE

Marita was a 50-year-old Malaysian woman who had been in the United States for over 20 years. She had been raised as a Roman Catholic and had always wanted to be a nun until she met her American husband and got married. She saw her marriage as a minor act of defiance to her faith and parents. She now complained of severe marital problems, especially because her husband disapproved and seemed jealous of her close involvement with the parish priest and with the church in general.

She came for counseling following an overnight hospitalization for an anxiety attack that had occurred in a small aircraft during a flight with a family friend. She was placed on a minor tranquilizer and released. The incident was especially troubling since she very much wished to travel back to Malaysia later in the year in order to see her ailing mother. This episode had, for the first time in her life, made her afraid to fly.

The process of systematic desensitization was explained to the client and she appeared to have little difficulty learning the relaxation technique, which she practiced for a week using an audiotape. She seemed to have very vivid imagery but often had trouble blocking out the memory of images associated with her "attack." Four desensitization sessions were held before the client could hold images associated with flying without evoking much anxiety. Two follow-up sessions were held, during which the client, accompanied by a friend, drove to the airport and watched planes take off. Finally, she attended two airline-sponsored group education classes for "white knuckle fliers." The client was finally able to make a transatlantic flight by herself and was with her mother when she died. After the trip, the client returned again for a follow-up session. She reported a significant increase in her ability to be assertive toward her husband and made it clear to him that she planned to continue with her church work. She claimed she was free of all anxiety symptoms and said, "Now, I am ready to live my own life."

Techniques for Emotional Awareness: Overview and Purpose

Besides the two techniques described at length in this chapter, systematic desensitization and the empty chair, there are a number of more limited methods that should be examined. They may not be considered techniques to be used and learned separately but can be incorporated in the flow of a normal counseling session when it has been determined that the client's goal would respond best to such methods. Clients who persist in denying the experiences of anger, grief, or sadness or who fail to express positive feelings are most likely to benefit from awareness techniques.

Feedback Checklist #9
Systematic Desensitization

1. How well did the counselor educate the client about the process of desensitization?

Not at All	A Little	Somewhat	Moderately	Very Well
1	2	3	4	5

2. Was the client's ability to produce vivid images assessed?

Not at All	A Little	Somewhat	Moderately	Very Well
1	2	3	4	5

3. How complete was the investigation of situations that might produce emotional arousal (discussions, inventories, self-monitoring)?

Not at All	A Little	Somewhat	Moderately	Very Complete
1	2	3	4	5

4. To what extent was the counselor able to help the client develop a hierarchy of arousing events on cards and to indicate a SUDS score for each?

Not at All	A Little	Somewhat	Moderately	Very Well
1	2	3	4	5

5. How well did the counselor instruct the client in the basic method of muscle relaxation?

Not at All	A Little	Somewhat	Moderately	Very Well
1	2	3	4	5

6. In the scene presentation phase, check those items successfully completed by the counselor. Note any comments after each component:

_____ a. Initial relaxation _____

_____

_____

_____ b. Signalling procedure established _____

_____

_____

_____ c. Image is read to client by the counselor _____

_____

_____

_____ d. The client is instructed to hold the image as anxiety appears and relax away the tension _____

_____ e. The counselor records the length of time the client is able to maintain image with a SUDS level of 10 or less _____

_____ f. Counselor returns client to state of full relaxation and helps the client through a body review to seek out areas where tension persists _____

_____ g. The counselor provides a brief latency period or break between trials _____

_____ h. The counselor presents the situation card again until the client is able to hold the image and relax away tension to a SUDS of 10 or less _____

_____ i. The counselor moves to the next step on the hierarchy when the client can successfully complete two trials of an item _____

7. How well did the counselor describe and prepare the client for relevant homework assignments involving the most recently practiced situations on the hierarchy?

Not at All	A Little	Somewhat	Moderately	Very Well
1	2	3	4	5

The use of these methods is predicated on the concept that emotional awareness is essential to growth. Through the expression of emotions, one develops a greater understanding of one's own motivations and goals. As Branden (1971, p. 28) says, "One does not destroy an emotion by refusing to feel it or acknowledge it; one merely disowns a part of one's self." Certainly there are times when emotions need to be lessened, as we have discussed. But a good part of a therapist's early efforts are aimed at "unfreezing" the client and enhancing self-disclosure, and a focus on emotions is the requisite first step. Many clients are reluctant to experience emotional awareness or arousal because they fear that simply acknowledging such feelings is tantamount to acting upon them. A general description about how the counselor may increase emotional awareness can be summarized in the following four steps:

1. The counselor observes the client's attempt to move away from the emotion. This may take a myriad of forms including a change of topic, blocking of speech, stuttering, fidgeting, and other nonverbal changes including facial sagging, tightening, and the presence of tears in the eyes.
2. The counselor stops the client's movement away from the emotion. This may mean interrupting the flow of the interview, a response that is not in keeping with social conventions.
3. The counselor invites the client to become aware of the emotion. The counselor asks the client to focus on the emotions underlying the story the client is telling, to explore the meaning of that emotion, and to express it as fully as possible.
4. The counselor challenges the client to follow through on the discoveries made through awareness of the emotion. If, for instance, the client is experiencing guilt over neglecting his children, he should be encouraged to develop a plan to change the behavior.

Free Association

The technique of free association has been associated exclusively with psychoanalysis. Freud developed the technique through his interactions with the famous client, Anna O. She had told Freud that she had not expressed herself fully because she was not certain what he wanted to hear (Kaplan & Sadock, 1988). He thereafter encouraged her to talk about anything she wished without censoring it.

The main purpose of free association is to enhance the production of unconscious material, especially memories of childhood traumas. The recollection of such memories is likely to produce a cathartic reaction. Freud found that clients tend to block the return of memories. This led him to postulate the existence of defense mechanisms. He called the patient's unwillingness or inability to remember *resistance*. Interpretation of the client's resistance to free association became the major task of the therapist. To this day, the method of free association remains the fundamental rule of orthodox psychoanalysis.

Albert Ellis, who practiced first as a lay analyst, described free association as one of the most superficial therapeutic techniques. It is only fair to point out, though, that the ultimate goal of free association is not only to produce emotional arousal but to eventually help the client work through or to apply the insights gained.

Using free association is a somewhat time-consuming process, and most modern therapists are unwilling to spend two or three sessions a week for several years to allow the client to adapt to the process and to eliminate the censorship that seems to be innate.

The method is usually practiced with the client reclining on a couch and the therapist sitting behind or beside the client. Originally, the therapist intruded very little except to draw forth words, memories, and emotions from the client. This rule of strict neutrality has changed in recent years, and the dynamic therapist is much more active. In modern versions of psychoanalysis, there is less reliance on free association and more on face-to-face interviews. Analysts now more often use observation, reflection, and interpretation to enhance the client's exploration (Baker, 1985). Use of free association outside of psychoanalysis is almost nonexistent today.

Despite its recent neglect among counselors, free association has several potential uses in therapy. Of course, free association is the basis for enhancing client responses to projective tests like the Rorschach and the Thematic Apperception tests, but it can also be utilized in ordinary therapy sessions. For example, a client may be helped to understand symbolic material produced during guided imagery or in a dream. There are a number of guided imagery techniques that ask the client to bring back an object (symbol) from an imaginary quest to a forest, mountain, or underground cave. Often the symbol apparently has very little meaning to the client, but when the client is asked to free associate or just ramble about other things that might be associated with that object, some interesting feelings and meanings sometimes become apparent. In a group guided imagery session, one of my clients, a college senior, found that she kept returning to the image of a key ring. Using the free association method, the client listed all of the things she might associate with a set of keys. She talked about her new car, about the doors that the keys of knowledge would open, and so on. Finally she halted and said that she realized that the key ring was heavy. All of the keys were iron and looked just like her father's keys. With encouragement from the therapist, she became aware of her growing fear of leaving behind her childhood and of accepting the looming weight of adult responsibilities and a life that would be just like that of her parents.

Other Counseling Methods for Increasing Emotional Awareness

According to Greenberg & Safran (1988), there are seven therapist activities or principles that can help clients focus on the emotional aspects of their experience.

Attending to Feelings.   *Attending to feelings* refers to all attempts by the therapist to focus the client's attention on the feeling aspects of his or her statements. It includes, of course, the Rogerian technique of reflecting feelings described earlier and all other attempts by the therapist to halt the client's intellectualization and to enhance affective awareness. For example, the therapist might observe that the client has brushed by or glossed over the feeling aspects of a problem and asks, "What are you experiencing now?" "What are you aware of right now?" "How does that statement feel to you?"

Refocusing.   *Refocusing* means constantly asking the client to "own" his or her own experience. One way we tend to distance ourselves from our feelings is to use global terms. Refocusing is the technique of asking the client to change his or her language to reflect responsibility for a feeling. This may include asking the client to use *I* or *me* instead of *one* or *you*. Global language is used to isolate us from feelings of blame and guilt (Gysbers & Moore, 1987). For example, a client might say the following:

> *Client:* It's a pain in the neck sometimes when my "ex" comes into the shop. But you learn to take it after a while.

A refocusing response by the counselor might look something like this:

> *Counselor:* Can you say that again please and own it. Like, 'When my ex comes into the shop, I still feel the pain sometimes.' "

Present-Centeredness.   Based on Gestalt therapy principles, the therapist is encouraged to use the *poignancy criterion.* This means that the therapist asks the client to attend to those aspects of the problem that are the most emotionally upsetting right now. The counselor may ask, "What part of the situation is bothering you the most."

The second aspect of present-centeredness is that the therapist then draws the client into the experience of that feeling in the here and now by attending and focusing. When the client describes a scene from the past, the therapist responds by saying, "And how does that feel right now as you describe it to me."

Expression Analysis.   *Expression analysis* means bringing awareness to the way in which the client expresses the problem. It involves calling the client's attention to nonverbal productions, such as voice tone, gestures, eye movement, bodily tension, or movement. The therapist may simply encourage the client to pay attention to a particular area by saying, "Are you aware that you are clenching your jaw?" It may also involve homework activities to help the client determine the extent of the emotion in other settings.

Intensifying.   Another available avenue for increasing emotional experience is to ask the client to *intensify* an ongoing emotion after it has been identified. For example, clients are asked to hit or pound on pillows or to wrestle or push against each other in group activities.

Batacas are "pillow bats" developed and sold specifically to provide a safe weapon for these intensifying techniques. The client may be asked to establish firm footing and to use the bataca or a pillow to slap or hit a chair. The client takes long deep breaths and can be told to loudly repeat a particularly meaningful phrase that may further arouse or deepen the experience. Normally the client is encouraged to maximize and to exaggerate emotional expression. The technique can be frightening to the client and to other group members. Education of clients beforehand, supervision, and extensive experience by the practitioner are the minimal requirements for the ethical practice of this method; however, such techniques are still experimental and not supported by research.

Enacting is a related method whereby the client experiences more of the feeling by verbally or physically acting out the emotion. For example, an individual may be encouraged to repeat the statement *I hate you!* several times loudly or may be asked to demonstrate feelings of isolation or dependency physically by moving alone to another part of the room or clinging to another group member. The psychodramatic version of the technique is called *physicalizing* and may involve several members in group counseling. For example, a young mother in a group therapy session was able to intensify her feelings of being trapped by the enactment method. Several of the other members played her children and each was given a phrase by the client that summarized that child's demands. These auxiliaries were then instructed to lightly pull and tug the client while uttering their demands. The method was very effective in helping the client become aware of both her feelings of being needed and of being trapped and restrained.

Symbolizing.   *Symbolizing* techniques are employed when it is felt that verbalizing might intellectualize the experience too much and detract from it. It means encouraging a tangible expression of feelings through drawing, painting, writing poetry, movement, or the production of expressive sounds. Many of these techniques can be used in a group setting or may be done as homework (Gladding, 1992, pp. 436–458). The use of a "feelings journal" is an example of such a method. Here the client is simply instructed to record daily experiences and especially to identify the accompanying emotions.

Establishing Intents.   This seventh set of activities, *establishing intents,* is for helping the client complete actions that are evoked by emotional expression. When it seems that the client is in touch with underlying feelings, the therapist attempts to focus on what the client wants to do next. The motive power of the emotion has been released and needs a direction. Therapists encourage this tendency by challenging clients to develop plans and goals with the following kinds of interventions:

- What do you need?
- What do you want?
- Where do you go from here?

The Empty Chair Technique of Gestalt Therapy: Overview and Purpose of the Method

Gestalt therapy was developed by Frederick S. Perls (1893–1970), a charming and charismatic therapist. Perls died at the height of his popularity and left much of the theoretical work to his followers, such as Zinker (1977), Polster and Polster (1973), Simkin (1976), and Passons (1975). The theory behind Gestalt therapy cannot be explained in a few short paragraphs; so, the reader is referred to the resources cited above and to the *Gestalt Journal* (cf., Harman, 1982) for more in-depth coverage. Gestalt therapy is a relatively small theoretical school. The training of Gestalt therapists takes place at the Gestalt Institutes, which are located in major cities across this country. Among counselors, at least, Gestalt therapy does not seem to have gained many adherents recently (Young & Feiler, 1989) and may be on the decline. However, many methods and techniques of Gestalt therapy are in wide use. Besides the empty chair, Gestalt therapists engage in dreamwork, ask clients to change their language to become more responsible, give clients directives to verbalize feelings, and use frustrating and confrontational methods.

Experiencing Polarities in Gestalt Therapy

There is a Japanese story about a Zen master and his student. The student was accused of being extremely stingy. Hearing this, the master held up a fist and asked the novice, "What do you call a man whose hand is always like this?" The student replied, "Crippled!" Opening his empty palm, the master again asked, "And what do you call a man whose hand forever remains in this position?" The student replied, "Handicapped!" After seeing this demonstration, the student is said to have had no more problems with generosity.

This example reflects the Gestalt principle of *integration of polarities,* which is a first-order therapeutic goal (Gilliland et al., 1989). The integration of polarities is consistent with the idea that the therapist helps the client in the process of being what one is rather than identifying with one's strivings. A conflict between values, actions, thoughts, and feelings is dealt with in Gestalt therapy by expressing both aspects of the problem at about the same time.

The idea is that when one aspect of the self is overemphasized, the polar opposite tends to emerge. Just as in the interpersonal sphere, if one parent is too strict, the other becomes too lenient. Within an individual and interpersonally, an extreme tendency brings out the other end of the continuum. In analytic terms, repression leads either to acting out or to depressive inaction—what might be called an impasse. The integration of opposites helps the individual overcome the tying up of vital energies and is the reason for using the empty chair technique.

The technique of the empty chair was borrowed by Perls from psychodrama, but Perls modified the method for distinctively Gestalt purposes. As mentioned above, its use is indicated in cases where an individual is in conflict with two opposing tendencies. Polster and Polster (1973) give the example of a woman who feels *helpless* because of her *anger.* In a dialogue between these two emotions using the empty chair, the helpless side eventually realizes the strength the anger provides and yet fears the destructiveness of rage. By the end of the interview, the client is able to imagine a personal strength that is not destructive. Some common polarities experienced by clients include

1. Extreme dependency versus being rejecting and independent
2. Constantly fearful of disapproval versus complete disregard of others' feelings
3. Extremely trusting and gullible versus very suspicious
4. Being overly emotional versus extreme rationality
5. Being sexually abstinent versus being sexually promiscuous
6. Between what I should do versus what I want to do (Perls called this the top dog/underdog split)

The Gestalt Empty Chair Method

Step 1: Preview and Explain.   Like role playing, the empty chair technique is novel to most clients and some warm-up will be necessary. The counselor's explanation of the reasons for using the method may take away some of the mystique, but it may also eliminate some of the natural resistance that the method engenders. One way of overcoming this is to ask the client to silently meditate or think about the polarity and to recall a scene that exemplifies the client feeling or behaving in these two ways. The client should try to become fully aware of feelings elicited by these two sides. This warm-up procedure is also enhanced by acknowledging to the client that it may seem strange at first but that ordinarily the stage fright diminishes.

The technique requires that an empty chair be placed directly in front of the client. In the next steps, the client is asked to verbally and nonverbally express one pole of the continuum while sitting in each chair.

Step 2: Deepening the Experience.   The counselor asks the client to choose one side based on which side of the polarity he or she feels the most strongly about or is most easily able to access. At this point, the client should be given some time to get in touch with that feeling and should be told to "allow the experience to deepen." Another way that the counselor helps the client deepen the experience is to constantly refer the client to the present tense (present-centeredness). When the client says, "I could have cried," the therapist responds, "Are you aware of that sadness now?"

Step 3: Expression.   The counselor first asks the client to describe the most prominent or salient polarity in terms of the thoughts, feelings, and experiences that are associated with it (poignancy criterion). The client is instructed to maximize the expression by using and even by exaggerating gestures and voice tone. The counselor may ask the client to repeat a particular phrase several times if it seems particularly relevant and if it seems to deepen feelings or summarize the client's position. The emphasis should be on showing one's experience rather than describing it. This is possible only if the client stays in the present tense.

When the counselor feels that the client has come to a stopping point, the client is directed to move to the empty chair. A stopping point is decided by the counselor. When the client seems to have run out of words, repeats the same statements, has gotten stuck, or seems to have fully expressed that position he or she has reached a stopping point.

Step 4: Counter Expression.   Sitting in the opposite chair, the client responds directly, emotionally, and as completely as possible to the first expression or argument. The client attempts to switch to the pole opposite the original argument and this time to express the antithesis bodily, emotionally, verbally, and fully. Again, the counselor attempts to heighten the client's emotional experience by trying to deepen the experience, encouraging the client's gestures and key phrases, and by repeating the client's statements with a stronger voice tone. When the client says, "I am so angry, I could scream," the counselor may either repeat the phrase with more emphasis, "You're angry enough to scream!" or might even say, "Let's hear that scream."

Step 5: Repetition.   The switch between the two poles of the conflict is repeated until the client or counselor feels that both aspects have been fully expressed. During this switching, the two sides may begin to develop a resolution, compromise, or a solution. The client need not feel that this must occur; it is only an occasional benefit of the method. Whether dramatic insight occurs or not, the advantage of the empty chair is that the client is now operating with full knowledge of both tendencies and will make more conscious choices.

Step 6: Commitment.   Even if the problem has not reached a complete resolution, the client is encouraged to agree to a plan of action that at least involves investigating both facets of the problem situation. Let us say that the client's conflict involved the dichotomy between constant dependency on others when making a decision and sulking independence. A homework assignment might be made that asks the client to use each of these two strategies on two separate occasions and then to report the results.

Problems and Precautions with the Gestalt Empty Chair

1. As in role playing, the biggest hurdle to overcome is the client's anxiety over looking foolish. Most clients expect therapy to be a matter of sitting in a chair or lying on a couch as the therapist poses meaningful questions. Techniques like the empty chair run contrary to the client's image. No matter how well it is previewed or explained, expressive methods such as this are often rejected. The counseling relationship must be very firmly established before the client is willing to experiment. Some therapists might deal with this as resistance. Others may wait for a more opportune moment to introduce the therapy or select another method more amenable to the client.

2. It is sometimes tempting to allow the client to move from the original position even if that side of the polarity has not been fully expressed. It has been my experience that it is generally best to keep the client in the original chair despite some frustration rather than returning to this side later. In the first precaution above, the client is giving up prematurely. This precaution suggests that the therapist may also be tempted to give up or give in too soon.

3. The expression of strong emotion makes some clients feel overwhelmed, out of control, and "crazy." The counselor should use reassurance to help the client recognize that the method normally brings out these strong feelings but that these feelings will subside. Clients who have limited control over their emotions and those whose defense mechanisms and coping skills are limited (such as those who tend to be explosive) are not candidates for this technique.

   Following the expression of great affect, a few clients may need support for several hours or days. It has been the author's experience that clients often feel that expressive and emotional releases are helpful, but initially they can be frightening. I recently treated a young woman who had previously attended a group that focused almost entirely on emotional expression. For several days after the workshop, she was very upset and even considered suicide. The group had met at a hotel as a weekend workshop. When the group ended, the leader made no arrangements for follow-up or support. When the client revealed her emotional state, she was only encouraged to attend another group the following weekend. Beyond the ethical implications, this example shows that some therapists use expressive techniques without developing an integrated treatment plan. In my own experience, the techniques of psychodrama and Gestalt awareness methods are relatively easy to learn. But emotional expression, by itself, does not substitute for the availability of a therapist who is willing to help the client utilize emotional insights and transform his or her life.

4. Counselors who are newly learning the method will certainly require the supervision of an experienced therapist.

5. Clients who are experiencing severe emotional turmoil, such as phobias, schizophrenia, bipolar disorder, major depression, etc., should not be subjected to the technique. Its major benefit lies in helping individuals contact emotional experiences that may have been pushed out of awareness.

Variations on the Gestalt Empty Chair

Fantasy Dialogue.   Occasionally clients will complain of somatic symptoms, such as a headache or stomach distress, that seem to be associated with the presenting conflict. Using a variation of the empty chair, the counselor may ask the client to hold a fantasy dialogue with the affected body part. One finding from this technique might be to determine the advantages that the symptom has for the client. A colleague and I once treated a 50-year-old woman who experienced great weakness in her arms. Despite a medical examination and neurological workup, no physical reason for the symptoms could be found. Although we suspected that the symptom had some special meaning for the client, it was through a fantasy dialogue with her arms that the client became aware of her growing resentment at having to care for her ailing mother. Bringing this to the client's awareness and helping her develop more of a life of her own helped to resolve this symptom.

Forced Catastrophes.   Some people live in a world where they are always expecting the worst to happen. The fact that the worst rarely happens does not stop them from preparing for it just the same. The technique of *forced catastrophes* demands that the client face the worst nightmare scenario complete with the accompanying emotions.

A colleague of mine once treated a man who constantly avoided feelings of anger. He was very afraid that he would lose control of his anger and that he would explode. The therapist gave him the assignment to spend four hours thinking about his anger and experiencing it as deeply as possible. He was even told that, if the opportunity presented itself, he was to explode. He was to set no controls, such as locking the doors to his apartment. The rationale was given that the client had spent many months fearing this disaster and it might as well be experienced as soon as possible. The client eventually agreed and performed the experiment without exploding. He reported that it was difficult to sustain the anger over the entire half-day period. He experienced a rapid diminishing of symptoms thereafter. McMullin (1986) recommends this technique as something of a last resort for some depressed and passive clients but suggests that it may backfire with anxious individuals. Certainly such methods should only be attempted by a skilled practitioner who possesses complete knowledge of the client's psychological makeup.

Hot Seat.   The empty chair technique and the term *hot seat* are often used interchangeably (Ivey & Simek-Downing, 1980). The hot seat is really a group

Feedback Checklist #10
The Empty Chair

1. To what extent did the counselor preview and explain the technique to the client as a way of enlisting the client's cooperation?

Not at All	*A Little*	*Somewhat*	*Moderately*	*A Great Deal*
1	2	3	4	5

2. How well did the counselor provide a way for the client to get in touch with feelings surrounding the problem situation?

Not at All	*A Little*	*Somewhat*	*Moderately*	*Very Well*
1	2	3	4	5

3. The counselor was able to facilitate the full emotional expression of both sides of the client's conflict.

Not at All	*A Little*	*Somewhat*	*Moderately*	*Very Well*
1	2	3	4	5

4. The counselor was able to help the client move between argument and counterargument, making a transition at appropriate times.

Not at All	*A Little*	*Somewhat*	*Moderately*	*Very Well*
1	2	3	4	5

5. The counselor helped the client achieve a full recognition of both sides of the conflict by repeating the argument and counterargument.

Not at All	*A Little*	*Somewhat*	*Moderately*	*Very Well*
1	2	3	4	5

6. The counselor helped the client achieve a sense of closure by developing a plan to integrate both sides of the conflict.

Not at All	*A Little*	*Somewhat*	*Moderately*	*Very Well*
1	2	3	4	5

technique in which one member is worked with individually by the therapist. This was Perls's normal way of working in a group, but it does not represent the only Gestalt approach to group work (Polster & Polster, 1973). Generally, the technique is quite confrontational (hence the name). The person in the hot seat (an empty chair next to the therapist) experiences a heightened sense of anxiety and a feeling of being on the spot. The person may disclose a great deal in the process, and the leader may use additional exercises or experiments for the client to enact with the rest of the group. The case example that follows shows how this can be accomplished. Although it refers mainly to the hot seat technique, it shows the underlying method of helping the client express emotional polarities.

CASE EXAMPLE

In a group run by a Gestalt therapist, a quiet and shy client volunteered for the hot seat. After the therapist mimicked her shyness in a slightly exaggerated fashion, he asked her to "make the rounds," telling each member of the group, "I am very shy and I don't want to hurt your feelings." The group members became angered at the therapist for subjecting this quiet young woman to the humiliating experience. The client completed the exercise anyway and made the following statement, "When I heard you defending me, I knew that's what I wanted you to do. I suddenly realized, that's what my shyness does! It gets people to take care of me and I'm sick of that. I can take care of myself." By exaggerating the shyness, the client began to become aware of the aggressive end of the continuum and from that awareness a sense of personal power developed as she moved closer to middle ground.

CHAPTER SUMMARY AND CONCLUSIONS

This chapter addressed the curative factor of lowering and raising emotional arousal. The aim of such methods is to help clients express and achieve closure with emotions that have been suppressed or that are in need of reduction. Cathartic techniques have long been used in psychotherapy, but this chapter argued that implementing catharsis in isolation or as the sole means of therapy is not the practice of experienced therapists and may not allow the client to integrate these experiences fully into changes in thoughts and actions. Such techniques can be dangerous especially when used outside of the supervision of a trained clinician. One arousing technique was considered in depth: the empty chair technique. A number of emotional awareness techniques were also described that help clients become aware of and focus in on emotional aspects of problems during the normal course of therapy.

This chapter also discussed emotional palliatives, or quieting techniques, and as an example, the classic method of systematic desensitization was explained. Other group and individual methods were considered, including coping skills training, a psychoeducational method. The process of helping individuals overcome emotional disturbance involves determining if the goal is to reduce unwanted emotions or to comlete unfinished actions by expressing emotions. Through both quieting and expressing techniques, the counselor helps the client achieve emotional balance.

FURTHER READINGS

Fretz, B., Kluge, N., Ossanna, S., & Jones, S. (1990). Intervention targets for reducing pre-retirement anxiety and depression. *Journal of Counseling Psychology, 36,* 301–307. The authors describe the stages immediately following retirement (honeymoon, disenchantment, reorientation, stability, and termination). They also point out developmental and environmental factors that affect retirement adjustment, including social isolation and lack of information, both financial and concerning the aging process.

Glick, B. & Goldstein, A. P. (1987). Aggression replacement training. *Journal of Counseling and Development, 65,* 356–362. This article reviews methods for lowering aggression in psychoeducational formats. The focus of the article is on techniques for dealing with hostile or assaultive adolescents. There is a review of anger control training, moral education, and the authors' aggression replacement training model, which is based on Goldstein's structured learning approach.

Nichols, M. P., & Efran, J. S. (1985). Catharsis in psychotherapy: A new perspective. *Psychotherapy, 22,* 46–58. Nichols and Efran's article traces the historical use of catharsis, from Freud to the mid 1980s. Their approach argues for self-expression but sees blocked emotions primarily as blocked actions rather than as memories or "foreign bodies lodged in the human psyche and requiring purgation."

REFERENCES

Baker, E. L. (1985). Psychoanalysis and psychoanalytic psychotherapy. In S. J. Lynn & J. P. Garske (Eds.), *Contemporary psychotherapies: Models and methods* (pp. 19–68). Columbus, OH: Merrill.

Berman, J. S., Miller, R. C., & Massman, P. J. (1985). Cognitive therapy versus systematic desensitization: Is one treatment superior? *Psychological Bulletin, 97,* 451–461.

Branden, N. (1971). *The disowned self.* New York: Bantam.

Breuer, J. & Freud, S. (1895/1955). Studies on hysteria. In J. Strachey (Ed.), *The complete works of Sigmund Freud, Standard Edition* (Vol. 2). London: Hogarth.

Carrington, P. (1978). *Learning to meditate: Clinically standardized meditation* (instructor's manual). Kendall Park, NJ: Pace Educational Systems.

Chandler, G. M., Burck, H., Sampson, J. P., & Wray, R. (1988). The effectiveness of a generic computer program for systematic desensitization. *Computers in Human Behavior, 4,* 339–346.

Conoley, C. W., Conoley, J. C., McConnell, J. A., & Kimzey, C. E. (1983). The effect of the ABC's of rational emotive therapy and the empty-chair technique of Gestalt therapy on anger reduction. *Psychotherapy: Theory, Research and Practice, 20,* 112–117.

Deffenbacher, J. L., & Suinn, R. M. (1988). Systematic desensitization and the reduction of anxiety. *Counseling Psychologist, 16,* 9–30.

Ekman, P. & Friesen, W. V. (1969). Nonverbal leakage and clues to deception. *Psychiatry, 32,* 88–105.

Farelly, F., & Brandsma, J. (1974). *Provocative therapy,* Cupertino, CA: Meta.

Fenichel, O. (1945). *The psychoanalytic theory of neurosis.* New York: W. W. Norton.

Frank, J. D. (1985). Therapeutic components shared by all psychotherapies. In M. J. Mahoney & A. Freeman (Eds.), *Cognition and psychotherapy* (pp. 49–79). New York: Plenum Press.

Frank, E., Anderson, B., Stewart, B. D., & Dancu, C. (1988). Efficacy of cognitive behavior therapy and systematic desensitization in the treatment of rape trauma. *Behavior Therapy, 19,* 403–420.

Gatchel, R. J. (1980). Effectiveness of two procedures for reducing dental fear: Group administered desensitization and group education and discussion. *Journal of the American Dental Association, 101,* 634–637.

Gatchel, R. J. & Baum, A. (1983). *An introduction to health psychology.* Reading, MA: Addison-Wesley.

Gendlin, E. T. (1969). Focusing. *Psychotherapy: Theory, Research and Practice, 6,* 4–15.

Gilliland, B. E., James, R. K., & Bowman, J. T. (1989). *Theories and strategies in counseling and psychotherapy.* Englewood Cliffs, NJ: Prentice-Hall.

Gladding, S. T. (1992). *Counseling: A comprehensive profession* (2nd ed.). Columbus, OH: Merrill.

Goldfarb, L. A., Fuhr, R., Tsujimoto, R. N. & Fischman, S. E. (1987). Systematic desensitization and relaxation as adjuncts in the treatment of anorexia nervosa: A preliminary study. *Psychological Reports, 60,* 511–518.

Goldfried, M. R. (1971). Systematic desensitization as training in self-control. *Journal of Clinical and Consulting Psychology, 37,* 228–234.

Greenberg, L. S., & Safran, J. D. (1988). *Emotion in psychotherapy.* New York: Guilford.

Gysbers, N. C., & Moore, E. J. (1987). *Career counseling: Skills and techniques for practitioners.* Englewood Cliffs, NJ: Prentice-Hall.

Harman, R. L. (1982). Gestalt therapy theory: Working at the contact boundaries. *Gestalt Journal 5,* 39–48.

Hoehn-Saric, R. (1978). Emotional arousal, attitude change and psychotherapy. In J. D. Frank, R. Hoehn-Saric, S. D. Imber & A. R. Stone (Eds.), *Effective ingredients of successful psychotherapy.* New York: Brunner/Mazel.

Ivey, A. E. & Simek-Downing, L. (1980). *Counseling and psychotherapy: Skills, theories and practice.* Englewood Cliffs, NJ: Prentice-Hall.

Izard, C. E. (1977). *Human emotions.* New York: Plenum.

Jackins, H. (1962). *Elementary counselor's manual.* Seattle, WA: Rational Island.

Jacobson, E. (1938). *Progressive relaxation* (2nd ed.). Chicago, IL: University of Chicago Press.

Janov, A. (1970). *The primal scream.* New York: Dell.

Kaplan, H. I., & Sadock, B. J. (1988). *Synopsis of psychiatry: Behavioral sciences, clinical psychiatry.* Baltimore, MD: Williams & Wilkins.

Kuhlman, T. L. (1982). Symptom relief through insight during systematic desensitization: A case study. *Psychotherapy: Theory, Research and Practice, 19,* 88–94.

Lang, P. J., Melamed, B. G., & Hart, J. A. (1970). Psychophysiological analysis of fear modification using an automated desensitization procedure. *Journal of Abnormal Psychology, 76,* 220–2343.

Lazarus, A. A. (1961). Group therapy of phobic disorders by systematic desensitization. *Journal of Abnormal and Social Psychology, 63,* 504–510.

Lazarus, R. S. & Folkman, S. (1984). *Stress, appraisal and coping.* New York: Springer.

Levin, R. B., & Gross, A. M. (1985). The role of relaxation in systematic desensitization. *Behaviour Research and Therapy, 23,* 187–196.

Lomont, J. F. (1965). Reciprocal inhibition or extinction? *Behavior Research and Therapy, 3,* 209–219.

Lowen, A. (1967). *The betrayal of the body.* New York: Collier.

Mckay, M., Davis, M., & Fanning, P. (1981). *Thoughts and Feelings: The art of cognitive stress intervention.* Richmond, CA: New Harbinger.

McMullin, R. (1986). *Handbook of cognitive therapy techniques.* New York: W. W. Norton.

Meichenbaum, D. (1977). *Cognitive behavior modification.* New York: Plenum.

Meichenbaum, D. H., & Cameron, R. (1974). The clinical potential of modifying what clients say to themselves. *Psychotherapy: Theory, Research and Practice, 11,* 103–117.

Meichenbaum, D. H., & Cameron, R. (1983). Stress inoculation training: Toward a general paradigm on training coping skills. In D. H. Meichenbaum & M. E. Jaremko (Eds.), *Stress reduction and prevention* (pp. 115–157). New York: Plenum.

Menninger, K. (1958). *Theory of psychoanalytic technique.* New York: Harper & Row.

Moreno, J. L. (1958). *Psychodrama* (Vol. 2). New York: Beacon House.

Nichols, M. P., & Efran, J. S. (1985). Catharsis in psychotherapy: A new perspective. *Psychotherapy, 22,* 46–58.

Nichols, M. P., & Zax, M. (1977). *Catharsis in psychotherapy.* New York: Gardner Press.

Novaco, R. W. (1977). Stress inoculation: A cognitive therapy for anger and its application to a case of depression. *Journal of Consulting and Clinical Psychology, 45,* 600–608.

Novaco, R. W. (1983). Stress inoculation therapy for anger control. In P. A. Keller & L. G. Ritt (Eds.), *Innovations in clinical practice: A source book* (Vol. 2, pp. 181–201). Sarasota, FL: Professional Resource Exchange.

Orr, L. & Ray, S. (1977). *Rebirthing is the new age.* Milbrae, CA: Celestial Arts.

Osterhouse, R. A. (1976). Group systematic desensitization of test anxiety. In J. D. Krumboltz & C. E. Thoreson (Eds.), *Counseling methods* (pp. 269–279). New York: Holt, Rinehart & Winston.

Passons, W. R. (1975). *Gestalt approaches in counseling.* New York: Holt, Rinehart & Winston.

Paul, G. L. (1966). *Insight versus desensitization in*

psychotherapy. Stanford, CA: Stanford University Press.

Perls, F. S. (1977). *The Gestalt approach: An eye witness to therapy.* Palo Alto: Science and Behavior Books.

Polster, E., & Polster, M. (1973). *Gestalt therapy integrated.* New York: Brunner/Mazel.

Prochaska, J. (1984). *Systems of psychotherapy.* Chicago, IL: Dorsey.

Reich, W. (1945). *Character analysis.* Orgone Institute.

Rimm, D. C. & Masters, J. C. (1974). *Behavior therapy: Techniques and empirical findings.* New York: Academic Press.

Schindler, F. E. (1980). Treatment by systematic desensitization of a recurrent nightmare of a real life trauma. *Journal of Behavior Therapy and Experimental Psychiatry, 11,* 53–54.

Simkin, J. (1976). The development of Gestalt therapy. In C. Hatcher & P. Himmelstein (Eds.), *The handbook of Gestalt therapy.* New York: Jason Aronson.

Stampfl, T. G., & Levis, D. J. (1967). Essentials of implosive therapy: A learning-theory–based psychodynamic behavioral therapy. *Journal of Abnormal Psychology, 72,* 496–503.

Warren, R., & McLellarn, R. W. (1982). Systematic desensitization as a treatment for maladaptive anger and aggression: A review. *Psychological Reports, 50,* 1095–1102.

Witmer, J. M. & Young, M. E. (1985). The silent partner: Uses of imagery in counseling. *Journal of Counseling and Development, 64,* 187–189.

Witmer, J. M. (1985). *Pathways to personal growth: Developing a sense of worth and competence.* Muncie, IN: Accelerated Development.

Wolberg, L. B. (1977). *The technique of psychotherapy.* New York: Grune & Stratton.

Wolpe, J. (1958). *Psychotherapy by reciprocal inhibition.* Stanford, CA: Stanford University Press.

Wolpe, J., & Lang, P. J. (1964). A fear survey schedule for use in behavior therapy. *Behaviour Research and Therapy, 2,* 27–30.

Yorde, B. S., & Witmer, J. M. (1980). An educational format for teaching stress management to groups with a wide range of stress symptoms. *Biofeedback and Self Regulation, 5,* 75–90.

Young, M. E., & Feiler, F. (1989). Theoretical trends in counseling: A national survey. Unpublished manuscript.

Zinker, J. (1977). *Creative process in Gestalt therapy.* New York: Brunner/Mazel.

CHAPTER NINE

Activating Client Expectations and Motivation

KEY CONCEPTS

▼ *Demoralization, discouragement, and learned helplessness are all descriptors of a condition that indicates lowered expectations, loss of hope, and a lack of motivation for change.*

▼ *The Adlerian concept of encouragement involves attitudes and behaviors that include a positive focus, a belief in equality, respect for the client, and the ability to push and challenge the client.*

▼ *Paradoxical methods are apparently contradictory advice given to the client to accomplish therapeutic goals. Paradox is an advanced technique for use when usual methods are ineffective.*

▼ *Resistance is a somewhat controversial term that refers to all client behavior that appears to be irrelevant to therapeutic goals. Lack of progress by the client is a common source of therapist frustration.*

▼ *Resistance may be combatted directly. It may also be overcome by accepting and defusing it. Means may be found to tip the balance, motivating the client through increasing rewards and increasing discomfort with old behavior.*

INTRODUCTION

In this chapter, we will take a closer look at the curative factor involved in instilling hope, increasing expectations, and overcoming barriers to change (Figure 9.1). We will also examine the notion of demoralization advanced by Frank (1985). According to Frank, overcoming demoralization is the therapist's major task. Over the years, client demoralization has been described in several ways, including learned helplessness, discouragement, and resistance. Many techniques have also been developed to counteract demoralization. In this chapter, we will look specifically at the Adlerian technique of encouragement, the use of paradox, as well as a number of methods for dealing with resistance to change.

FIGURE 9.1
Six curative factors in the REPLAN system.

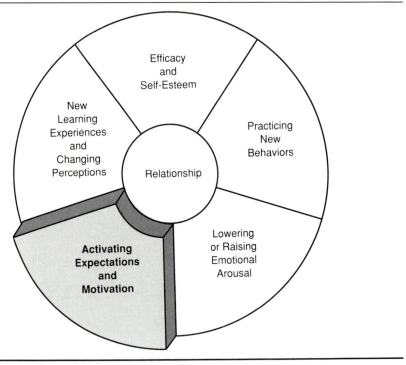

THE DEMORALIZATION HYPOTHESIS

According to Jerome Frank (1985), those who seek counseling are demoralized. *Demoralization* is described by Frank as a "state of mind characterized by one or more of the following: subjective incompetence, loss of self-esteem, alienation, hopelessness (feeling that no one can help), or helplessness (feeling that other people could help but will not" (p. 56). According to this view, clients seek not only to alleviate problems and symptoms but to decrease feelings of discouragement. In a nutshell, Frank uses the term to convey a sense of incompetence coupled with psychological distress.

The Demoralization Hypothesis Expanded

Demoralization is well known among psychotherapists. Adlerians call it *discouragement.* Seligman (1975) identified an aspect of demoralization called *learned helplessness,* a state in many ways analogous to depression. Learned helplessness was discovered in animal research and later in human research. Seligman found that persons exposed to unsolvable problems became so discouraged that their later performance on solvable problems was negatively affected.

Frank believes that anxiety, depression, and loss of self-esteem (the most common presenting symptoms) are the result of demoralization. Frank also proposes that symptoms and mental demoralization interact. On the one hand, client problems or symptoms are worsened by a sense of discouragement and isolation. For example, some minor physical problem may be seen as inconsequential by one person, whereas the demoralized individual takes it as a further indication of the hopelessness of his or her situation. On the other hand, overcoming a problem helps to eradicate demoralization.

Are Methods That Combat Demoralization Simply Placebos?

Many clients improve radically early in psychotherapy. This has been attributed to the *placebo effect,* a medical analogy that has been unfortunately applied to the psychological realm. Placebo implies that the client can be fooled by the therapist and that client symptoms are imaginary. According to the placebo effect, well-established factors (Patterson, 1973) in social influence—attractiveness, trustworthiness, and high expectations—are akin to sugar pills. Another and perhaps better way of conceptualizing early client improvement is the ending of demoralization and the activation of hope and expectations for change (cf., Frank, Nash, Stone & Imber, 1963). It is the expectation itself that is healing. Faith is powerful medicine (Siegel, 1986).

METHODS AND TECHNIQUES FOR ENHANCING CLIENT EXPECTATIONS

Encouragement: Overview and Purpose of the Method

Witmer (1985) points out that a close analysis of the word *encouragement* shows that it means *to cause to have heart.* Encouragement is closely aligned with Alfred Adler's school of psychotherapy, individual psychology, as it is properly called. Encouragement, in the Adlerian sense, is the major method by which the therapist helps the client overcome demoralization or discouragement. Rather than being a specific method, it is a set of techniques that the counselor uses throughout therapy to coax the client away from discouraging beliefs and a self-centered world built on private logic. Ultimately, encouraging techniques develop social interest in the client, who is then able to make authentic contact with others.

Importance of Encouragement

In a national survey conducted by the author (Young & Feiler, 1989), encouragement was the second most often used counseling technique. It was utilized by 90% of the mental health counselors and counselor educators surveyed. A related technique, positive reinforcement, was the fifth most often used technique. It was selected by 75% of those who answered the survey. We cannot be certain from these data that all respondents were operating under the same definition of

TABLE 9.1
Comparison of encouragement and praise/reinforcement.

Dimension	Encouragement	Reinforcement
Purpose	To motivate, inspire, hearten, instill confidence	To maintain or strengthen a specific behavior
Nature	Focuses on inner direction and internal control; emphasizes personal appreciation and effort more than outcome	Focuses on outer direction and external control; tends to emphasize material appreciation; emphasizes outcome
Population	All ages and groups	Seems most appropriate for children, situations with limited self-control and development, and conditions of specific problem behavior
Thoughts/Feelings/ Actions	A balance of thinking, feeling, and actions with feeling underlying the responses; i.e., satisfaction, enjoyment, challenge	Attending primarily to an action (behavioral) response that is observable
Creativeness	Spontaneity and variation in how encourager responds; encouragee has freedom to respond in spontaneous and creative ways; however, it may be difficult to understand the expectations of the encourager	Reinforcer responds to very specific behavior in a specific way; reinforcee is expected to respond in a specific and prescribed way; little doubt about the expectations of the reinforcer; helpful in establishing goals
Autonomy	Promotes independence, less likelihood of dependency upon a specific person or thing; more likely to generalize to other life situations	Tends to develop a strong association, perhaps dependence, between a specific reinforcer and a behavior; less likely to generalize to other life situations

Source: From *Pathways to Personal Growth* (p. 142) by J. Melvin Witmer, 1986, Muncie, IN: Accelerated Development. Reprinted by permission.

encouragement; however, the survey is supportive of the notion that this class of methods is essential to therapists.

While encouragement is widely used, it is not normally taught as a separate method in most texts. One reason for this neglect might be that methods that increase client optimism, hope, and expectations have been linked with the power of positive thinking and the popular market in success tapes and books. Another reason for this may be that many approaches, such as the client-centered theory of Carl Rogers, include an affirming attitude toward the client as part and parcel of the theory. Finally, encouragement does not seem to follow a precise set of steps, and it involves attitudes of the therapist as well as specific therapist behaviors.

Praise Versus Encouragement

Table 9.1 shows a comparison of the concepts of reinforcement from the behavioral tradition and the Adlerian concept of encouragement. Both praise (positive reinforcement) and encouragement have their uses. In general, encouragement is designed to inspire, to foster hope, to stimulate, and to support (Pitsounis & Dixon, 1988); whereas praise is designed to increase the likelihood that a specific behavior will be repeated. Encouragement focuses on developing autonomy, self-reliance, cooperation, rather than competition (it avoids comparisons), and an internal locus of control (Hitz & Driscoll, 1988). Praise strengthens a behavior when it occurs.

Who Benefits Most from Encouragement?

According to Losoncy (1977), persons who are dependent, depressed, cut off from social support systems, and who suffer from low self-esteem respond to encouragement. Discouraged clients show an excessive need for attention, for power, for control of situations and people, and for revenge. They avoid participation and responsibility, and are perfectionistic, closeminded, and dishonest (Losoncy, 1977).

Types of Encouraging Responses

Fourteen types of encouraging behaviors have been identified from the writings of Dinkmeyer and Losoncy (1980), Losoncy (1977), Witmer (1985), and Sweeney (1989) as effective therapist interventions.

1. Acknowledge efforts and improvement.
2. Concentrate on the present capacities, possibilities, and conditions rather than past failures.
3. Focus on client strengths.
4. Show faith in the client's competency and capabilities.
5. Show an interest in the progress and welfare of the client.
6. Focus on those things that interest or excite the client.
7. Ask the client to evaluate his/her own performance rather than comparing it to another standard.
8. Show respect for the client and the client's individuality and uniqueness.
9. Involve the self through honest disclosure.
10. Offer assistance as an equal partner in the counseling process.
11. Use humor.
12. Provide accurate feedback on deeds rather than on personality.
13. Confront discouraging beliefs.
14. Lend enthusiasm and ask for commitment toward goals.

Summarizing these fourteen interventions may oversimplify the Adlerian concept, but it may give some general direction to therapists and improve the understanding of the method. I have divided these interventions into three major therapist activities: focusing on the positive, emphasizing equality and individuality, and pushing with enthusiasm.

Focusing on the Positive and the Changeable.   Lionel Tiger (1979) has written about the biological nature of optimism, the tendency to view the world as a benign, friendly source of support. Most writers agree, though, that optimism can be learned and is a hoped-for outcome of psychotherapy and a definition of mental health. Witmer, Rich, and Barcikowski (1991) have discovered a link between optimistic attitudes and stress reactivity. Their research reveals that persons who cope better with stress are more likely to possess optimistic attitudes. The work of Simonton and Mathews-Simonton (1978) with cancer patients has pointed to the potential health benefits of optimism. Most recently the work of Bernard Siegel (1986) has interested millions in the power of optimistic attitudes in dealing with medical crises.

Interventions 1 through 4 are grouped together into the therapist activity of focusing on the positive because they show the encouraging technique of changing the client's attention from the deficits in one's life to one's strengths. Further, encouragement means noticing the successes and showing faith in the client's ability to succeed. An important aspect of this activity is shifting the client's discussions from the past to the present. Consider the following dialogue:

Client: I feel like I've totally messed up my future.

Counselor: Tell me what you really enjoy doing.

Client: What? . . . Oh, well, I really enjoy working in the garden. [The client goes on to describe the feelings he enjoys and the counselor encourages him.]

Counselor: How do you feel now?

Client: Better. But I always feel better when I think about good things like that.

Counselor: "Yes, so do I. I prefer to feel good."

Client [Laughing]:
So do I. But it isn't always easy.

Communicating Equality and Respect for the Individuality of the Client.   The essence of interventions 5 through 10 is to communicate to the client that the therapist and client are on equal footing and that each is unique. The therapeutic partnership is based on this minor paradox of separate and unique but equal. By exploring the things the client finds interesting, the therapist communicates respect for the uniqueness of the other. By self-disclosing, the therapist takes away some of the role and contacts the client as another individual. Finally, the therapist teaches the client to change the idea that the worth of a person is judged by external standards. The uniqueness of individuals precludes this belief. The individual must come to evaluate performance against internal standards and to appreciate one's strengths and unique approach to life.

Pushing with Enthusiasm.   Interventions 11 through 14 demonstrate that encouragement is not merely support: it does not mean accepting the status quo. There is an element of confrontation and a sincere effort to produce movement in the client. Discouragement is seen as a defensive maneuver that has its effect by maintaining the status quo. Encouragement pushes the client by giving feedback, confronting the private logic of the client, asking for a commitment, and using humor to turn the client around (Mosak, 1987).

The Method of Encouragement

The following are general guidelines that can assist the therapist in dealing with discouragement. Again, although encouragement is typically employed at the beginning and the end of counseling sessions to recognize strengths and produce compliance and application of new learnings, the method is intertwined with other therapy techniques and serves to increase their effectiveness. Rather than provide a case example, in this section, a description of counselor activity or client/counselor dialogue demonstrating the technique will accompany each step.

Step 1: The Counselor Identifies Through Assessment an Area of Client Functioning Where Encouragement Would Increase Client Effort and Persistence. Herb was a furniture salesman out of a job. He was very pessimistic about getting hired. Although he had initially been rather active, recently he had spent more time driving around in his car than actually looking for a position. His wife accompanied him to the first counseling session but refused to return. She was angry and frustrated. According to Herb, he had lost all ambition, and he feared he would never be able to locate a new job. Initially, the therapist used reflective listening techniques to understand the client's problem. It appeared that the problem would be best handled by increasing the client's hope, expectations, and motivation.

Step 2: The Counselor Determines That the Client's Therapy Goals Will Be Enhanced by Encouragement Methods. Encouragement was considered to be the technique of choice because the client's demoralization seemed to be the major factor prohibiting a return to work. This was explained to Herb as follows:

Counselor: Herb, my feeling is that what you really need right now is a coach. You seem to have job-seeking skills, a good work history, and a positive attitude about your chosen profession. You've shown a lot of success in sales previously. Perhaps together we can help you find your enthusiasm again.

Step 3: The Therapist Notes Positive Aspects of the Client's Current Attempts, However Small, to Accomplish the Goal.

Client: I still get up at 6:30 A.M. like I did when I was working. I get dressed and start out all right. First, I read the paper and start to make a call or two. That's when I start getting down. I end up driving around town, killing time until dinner, making my wife think that I am out looking for a job. Why am I doing this?

Counselor: Well one of the things I notice is that the rhythm is still there. You are set to get back into a work routine, and you seem to like that. Even though you are not making the contacts, you are going through the motions, rehearsing for that day when you are back to work.

Step 4: The Therapist Recognizes the Individuality of the Client and Refuses to Accept Comparisons and Negative Evaluations.

Client: Let's face it, I am a loser. That's what my wife says. She would get so mad because I'd be salesman of the month in June, and then, in July, I'd be at the bottom.

Counselor: Apart from comparing yourself to other salesmen and even apart from your wife, did you feel effective in that job? Is this the job you enjoyed?

Client: Yes, I loved it. But sometimes it's hard living with all that criticism. It makes you think there's something wrong with you. To tell the truth, the money part was not that important; I enjoyed the people. Getting to know them, working with young couples, trying to help them and all.

Counselor: You enjoyed the contact with people. That's something special about you. But when you focus on the competition or other people's evaluations, you get down on yourself and become uncertain. Is that right?

Step 5: The Therapist Offers Feedback or Confrontation and Asks for Commitment.

Counselor: I've got some feedback for you if you want it.

Client: OK.

Counselor: You seem to want the approval of other people. And, yet, you seem to know that you must follow your own interests if you are to be happy. I have the feeling that you must choose a direction or stay in limbo.

Client: I need to get back to work.

Counselor: Yeah. You can do that. I'm sure of it. What do you think about setting some kind of goal in that direction for next week?

Step 6: The Therapist Shows Continued Enthusiasm for the Client's Goals and Interest in the Client's Feelings and Progress.

Client [one week later]: Since the last time we talked, I didn't do what we decided. I didn't make two calls a day looking for a job. I guess I averaged about one call per day. The first day I did three, then one, then one again, and I took the weekend off. I got no response.

Counselor: I am very glad to hear about this. That kind of progress is what we've been looking for. It seems that getting off dead center is the hardest part, and you've gotten through that. Besides, by being honest about it, you've now included me in what's going on. Now what is needed is keeping up your efforts. Right?

Client: I guess so. I'm afraid that this won't work, that it will be just like last time and fizzle out.

Counselor: Yes, it can be scary, but let's try to focus on the present if we can, rather than look back. I have been hoping that you'd make this beginning and then hang in there until something breaks. Let's continue with this plan. I'll call you about Wednesday to see how things are going. Again, I feel good about these first steps. Keep up the good work.

Problems and Precautions of Encouragement

Avoiding Rescue.   Karpman (1968) described the *drama triangle:* a trap in which helpers are very likely to entangle themselves. At each point of the triangle is one role in the life drama: victim, rescuer or persecutor. The client/protagonist begins in one of these three positions (typically victim). The other person in the drama (antagonist) is in one of the other positions (typically persecutor). When a crisis occurs, the players switch positions. Such patterns recur and have a game-like quality to them.

Berne (1972) describes a typical situation in which one partner in a marriage is the victim and the other is the persecutor. During the crisis, the victim sues the persecutor for divorce and, thus, becomes the persecutor while the other member of the couple takes on the role of the victim. Lawyers become the rescuers to finish out the triangle.

The drama triangle helps us understand secondary gains. *Secondary gains* are the rewards (usually social) a person receives for having a symptom. Many clients find themselves in the victim role and promote someone else as the persecutor, hoping the therapist will take on the job of rescuer. There is a certain seductive quality associated with these roles. The rescuer/helper/counselor must be aware of the tendency to accept the victim's bait to save him or her. Many helping professionals have rescue fantasies. We receive rewards by being seen as the one who pulls the client out of the fire. This kind of relationship is not consistent with the condition of equality demanded by encouragement.

Steiner (1974) has described rescuing as doing more than 50% of the work in a relationship. If the therapist emerges from the session exhausted, while the client remains in a "one-down" position, encouragement cannot have taken place. In the true sense, encouragement promotes individual responsibility for one's life circumstances. It accepts helping but rejects rescue.

Being Genuine.   Encouragement must be genuine. It means real involvement with a client, and for this, a commitment is needed. Many clients seem to test the therapist to determine if offers to help are real or just "what is said to all clients." Although the therapist should not fall prey to the gambit of trying to prove sincerity, neither should the therapist offer help then fail to deliver it. Showing a genuine interest includes exhibiting consistent presence, support, and follow-up; keeping track of the client's progress; reviewing case notes before each session; recalling the client's goals; showing enthusiasm for successes; and extending oneself through self-disclosure.

Cultural Differences.   Encouragement places emphasis on individuality. It is also designed to develop an internal locus of control in the client and to break down nondemocratic barriers between client and counselor (i.e., to put client and counselor on the same footing. Such concepts are distinctly Western and may not

---

Feedback Checklist #11

Encouragement

1. To what extent did the counselor assess and review areas of client functioning that might be enhanced by encouragement methods?

Not at All	*A Little*	*Somewhat*	*Moderately*	*A Great Deal*
1	2	3	4	5

2. To what extent did the counselor recognize and comment on the client's attempts to accomplish the goal?

Not at All	*A Little*	*Somewhat*	*Moderately*	*A Great Deal*
1	2	3	4	5

3. How well did the counselor convey respect for the individuality of the client and refuse to accept comparisons and negative evaluations?

Not at All	*A Little*	*Somewhat*	*Moderately*	*Very Well*
1	2	3	4	5

4. To what degree did the therapist offer feedback or confrontation and ask for commitment to agreed-upon goals?

Not at All	*A Little*	*Somewhat*	*Moderately*	*A Great Deal*
1	2	3	4	5

5. How much did the therapist show enthusiasm for the client's goals and interest in the client's progress?

Not at All	*A Little*	*Somewhat*	*Moderately*	*A Great Deal*
1	2	3	4	5

---

show appropriate respect for persons with differing cultural backgrounds. I am reminded of a story my teacher Harry DeWire used to tell about counseling a Chinese couple in Hong Kong and using a translator. The translation seemed to be excessively long. Finally, Dr. DeWire quizzed the translator about what he was adding to the conversation. Somewhat apologetically, the translator explained that the couple would not be satisfied if all they received was a reflection of their feelings. They were paying for his sage counsel. They would require advice, so he was adding it.

Paradoxical Interventions: Overview and Purpose of the Method

Definition and History of Paradox

Seltzer (1986) defines *paradox* as a "therapist directive that is perceived by the client, at least initially, as contrary to the therapeutic goals but which is yet rationally understandable and specifically devised by the therapist to achieve these goals" (p. 10). The definition, as we take it apart, first involves a directive or advice given to the client. Second, the advice is made to appear logical but is, in fact, antithetical to the goals previously established in the treatment plan. Third, it is designed and planned by the therapist to achieve the goals that it seems to be thwarting.

Seltzer's definition appears to be among the clearest and most eclectic available to us; however, some other conceptualizations enrich the one above. For example, Frankl's (1955) original description of a paradoxical intervention involved encouraging clients to seek what they are avoiding, to unite with what they have been fighting, and to replace a fear with a wish. L'Abate and Levis (1987) indicate that paradox always involves reframing (reconceptualizing) the symptom as a positive experience while asking the client *not* to change because change might be dangerous. Finally Egan (1990) calls paradoxical interventions a challenge, a way of moving a client to give up old ways and habits.

Egan's definition begins to link paradoxical techniques with the overall theme of this chapter. Paradox has been called a universal tool of encouragement (Mozdzierz, Lisiecki & Macchitelli, 1989) because it is used to produce motivation where other more direct methods have failed. Its illogical nature and novelty encourage the discouraged client who has already attempted to reinvigorate expectations and motivation through normal means.

Paradoxical interventions represent a class of therapeutic techniques rather than a single method. Paradox is truly eclectic in that it is not tied to any major theoretical approach. Family therapist tend to claim it as their own (Weeks & L'Abate, 1982), but Frankl, the existential therapist, was the first to describe its use in psychotherapy. Paradox is a technique also claimed by reality therapy (Wubbolding, 1988), transactional analysis (Massey, 1986), and individual psychology (Adler, 1972).

When Should Paradoxical Interventions Be Made?

Typically, paradox is implemented when clients fail to respond to directives (Ivey & Simek-Downing, 1980). L'Abate and Levis (1987), however, recommend the use of paradox in the early stages of therapy in order to combat resistance. They believe that the client is most vulnerable to these challenges in the beginning and that paradox tends to lose its effectiveness as time goes on.

Paradoxes seem to work best with clients who are involved in repetitive behavior patterns that seem out of control, involuntary, or automatic (L'Abate & Levis, 1987). Some client problems that have been treated in this manner are insomnia, impatience, blushing, enuresis, fainting spells (McKay, Davis & Fanning, 1981), eating disorders, obsessive/compulsive disorders, agoraphobia, and simple phobias (Seligman, 1990). It has also been utilized with oppositional and delinquent behavior (Brown, 1986; Kolko & Milan, 1983). In families, it is often implemented to help break up nonproductive relational sequences, including arguing, communication problems, and sexual disorders (Madanes, 1980; Weeks & L'Abate, 1982).

Why Does Paradox Work?

There is an embarrassment of riches in case studies supporting the effectiveness of paradox (L'Abate & Levis, 1987). In general, research seems to support its efficacy (DeBord, 1989). There is still some controversy, though, as to why paradox works (Riebel, 1984), probably because there are so many types and variations of paradox (Brown & Slee, 1989; Driscoll, 1985; Hunsley, 1988; Seltzer, 1986; Shoham-Salomon & Rosenthal, 1987). Nevertheless, there are numerous reasons for the effectiveness of paradox.

One set of explanations for the effectiveness of paradox comes from social psychology. The literature in that field in the area of persuasion has found, in general, that ordinary persuasive techniques are far less effective with people who are very certain about their beliefs than with people with weakly held beliefs. It seems that paradoxical interventions may actually be more effective in changing our strongly held beliefs than those about which we are mildly certain (Swann, Pelham & Chidester, 1988). McMullin (1986) claims that some client beliefs are so entrenched that clients are like fencers, able to parry even the most skillful attacks on their logic; however, paradoxical messages are unexpected and, therefore, have a greater chance at success of reaching defensive clients. Related to this is Beier and Young's idea (1984) that paradox is an asocial response; that is, it does not fit into the client's schema or representations of the problem. A paradoxical response creates a "beneficial uncertainty" in the client. In that moment of uncertainty, there is vulnerability to change.

According to reality therapy principles, paradox is effective since it gives clients a sense of control (Wubbolding, 1988). By exaggerating a symptom, the client realizes that the symptom can be manipulated (Rudestam, 1980) and that he or she has the power to manipulate it. In family therapy terms, paradoxical interventions place clients in a "double bind." If they follow the directive, they are complying with therapy. If they decrease the problem behavior, they are accomplishing therapy goals (Shoham-Salomon, Avner & Neeman, 1989; Lichtigman, 1990). Despite these explanations, it must be admitted that therapists are still far from a consensus about what is behind the effectiveness of paradox (Watson, 1985).

Types of Paradox

Symptom Prescription.   A paradox can be presented as a joke, as solemn truth, as an ironic twist, as a challenge, or as a provocation. The two most important types of paradox are symptom prescription and redirection. Of these two, the first to be developed was Frankl's (1955; 1975) *symptom prescription*. In symptom prescription, the client is urged to do the very thing he or she is avoiding. For example, the client who fears blushing during public talks is encouraged to blush as much as possible. Prochaska (1984) describes the successful treatment of a young college man who was afraid of vomiting when he went to the student union. He and the therapist jokingly discussed how he could explain this behavior to others if it occurred, and he was given instructions to go to the student union and vomit. Rather than vomit, he experienced a heightened sense of control over his anxiety.

A frequently used technique for couples who are having difficulty with sexual compatibility is to prescribe sexual abstinence for three weeks. Clients often return and sheepishly admit that they have not followed the therapist's instructions but have alleviated the symptom.

Redirecting.   A second major technique is called *redirecting*. It is a combination of symptom prescription and the behavioral method of stimulus narrowing. The symptom is prescribed to the client, but its scope is severely limited to a specific stimulus condition. For example, a client is asked to produce the symptom only at a particular time or place.

Redirecting is sometimes called *symptom scheduling* (Newton, 1968) or *massed practice of an unwanted behavior* (Rudestam, 1980), when the client is asked to produce certain amounts of the behavior at specific times. Nicassio, Liberman, Patterson, Ramirez, and Sanders (1972) reported a case of a chronic nervous tic (neck jerk) that was treated by this paradoxical method. The client determined first how often he usually jerked his neck (baseline). He then practiced the jerk for 10 minutes, six times per day. Following two weeks of this massed practice, the tic was almost gone. An 18-month follow-up showed no return of the symptom and no symptom substitution.

The Method of Paradoxical Intervention

The first two steps, assessment and goal setting, are two preliminary procedures recommended for all client problems; however, they are reiterated here to emphasize that a paradoxical intervention should be a planned method.

Step 1: Identify the Dimension to Be Changed.   Assessment of the client should include an understanding of the problem in the client's own words and data about the context of the problem. This means eliciting examples of the problem and attempted solutions as well as the exact steps in the behavioral sequence that has been identified. For example, a client who fears blushing is asked to describe the history and origins of blushing; to list all of the places where blushing incidents take place; and to describe the thoughts, feelings, and behaviors that precede and follow blushing, the frequency of the behavior, as well as its positive and negative consequences.

Step 2: Identify a Specific, Achievable Goal.   The goals that respond best to paradoxical interventions are specific recurring behavior sequences, such as insomnia, rather than vague complaints of loneliness or confusion about my job. The therapist should be reasonably satisfied from the assessment that the commonsense and usual methods for solving the problem have already been attempted. One reason for the assessment is to prevent the therapist from duplicating the client's failed efforts.

Step 3: Creatively Devise a Paradoxical Strategy.   A valuable starting point is for therapist to think of a clear directive that would help the client accomplish the goal (i.e., do _____ to solve the problem). Once an ordinary directive has been stated, its reverse is easier to create. The therapist simply concocts a directive that exaggerates or is opposite to the goal. This two-step process is illustrated in the dialogue that follows with both an opposite and an exaggeration.

> *Client:*   I need to get out of this relationship. There is nothing positive about it. I've been in it for seven years. She never shows any affection and has no time for me, and she actually hates my son. I

> guess I'm just loyal. And stupid. She won't get married, and she's been stringing me along all this time. She's been dating someone else. We fight constantly. We don't enjoy the same things. She becomes abusive when she is drunk, which is often. I just can't seem to break it off. I love her.

Directive: You must stay away from her completely to end the relationship.

Opposite: You must spend more time with her.

Exaggeration: Her power is so strong, you must move to somewhere in Europe to escape her influence.

Step 4: Choose a Delivery That *Involves*, *Motivates*, or *Enhances* the Client's Expectations and Present the Paradox.   Haley (1976) encourages seriously trying to sell the client on the paradoxical directive. In order to do this, matching the client's words, situation, and style to the directive will help to gain the client's acceptance. In some cases, this will simply involve giving a brief rationale for the use of the paradox. De Shazer (1989) adds that it is best to begin by complimenting the client to gain their cooperation and to increase the effect of the directive. L'Abate (1986) calls this compliment a *positive reframing of the symptom.* Using the example of the client who is in an intolerable seven-year-long relationship, the statement below reflects a use of (1) a compliment and (2) the client's words and understanding of the situation to bolster the effect of the intervention.

Counselor: I'm certain now that you are right, Barry. You are a loyal person. And part of loyalty means not giving up. Perhaps the situation seems hopeless to you. But I am certain that what is needed is another seven years in the relationship. Certainly that will be difficult. But as you say, it's love. I hope you will go home and really consider the fact that you have not tried hard enough and what is really needed is another seven-year commitment on your part.

Step 5: Include a Variation, If Possible.   Cases have been cited of paradoxical treatment of insomnia by asking the client to stay up all night. It has been recommended in these cases that the client engage in some repetitive, boring task, for example, scrubbing floors and windows (McKay et al., 1981). For some reason, adding a variation on the opposite seems to increase the effect. The variation may help break up the normal rituals associated with a deeply ingrained behavior. According to Jay Haley (1989), when a directive includes some ordeal (such as scrubbing the floor) as a variation, the therapist should choose tasks that are beneficial (such as exercise or the learning of a new skill).

Step 6: Track Client Responses to the Paradox.   At subsequent sessions, the counselor asks the client to describe progress toward the paradoxical goal. If the symptom fails to reappear, the counselor is not to complement the client initially but might enhance the paradox by expressing surprise, chagrin, and disappointment. If the counselor is not fully convinced that the problem has been eliminated, various types of "therapist pessimism" might be used (see "Variations on Paradoxical Interventions"). If the problem still exists in full force, the paradox might be enhanced by increasing the amount of paradoxical practice required or by asking the client to record attempts. The importance of tracking is that the therapist must be conscientious, making sure that the paradox is (1) being fully implemented by the client and (2) having the desired effect. Finally, tracking involves making follow-up contacts when therapy is complete to see if gains have been maintained and to determine if further work is needed.

Problems and Precautions of Paradoxical Interventions

It is important to recognize the limitations of paradox.

Compliance.   Often clients return to counseling after a paradoxical directive has been given saying that the intervention did not make sense and seemed to be antithetical to the aims of treatment. The counselor's response in most cases should be to build a more believable rationale and insist on client compliance. Giving a directive (even a paradoxical one) and not insisting on its use communicates a lack of confidence in the method.

Ethical Issues.   The major ethical issues with the use of paradox surround the question, How much does the therapist explain the method to the client? (Brown & Slee, 1986; Cavell, Frentz & Kelly, 1986). In other words, is the use of paradox a form of dishonesty?

DeBord (1989) recommends full disclosure since it makes the technique more attractive to the client. Others feel that unless the technique retains the elements of surprise and flim-flam, it will lose much of its power (Driscoll, 1985).

Connected to this is the argument against using techniques that are manipulative. *Manipulative* means that the client is being persuaded without conscious awareness. Deception in psychological experiments has been debated for many years. DeBord (1989) admits that all therapies rely on techniques that pressure clients to change and many of these involve implicit messages and manipulation. De Shazer (1985), for example, asks his clients, "Do you want to change quickly or slowly?" The message implies that clients want to change and that they will be a part of the process. I believe what many fear is producing change without the client's consent and according to goals that the client has not embraced. The major dangers with paradoxical and other manipulative methods is in their use in family settings. It is much more important that the therapist devise goals of therapy acceptable to all family members rather than promoting those of the therapist, the parents, or some other subsystem.

Effects on Client Perceptions.   McMillan and Johnson (1990) suggest that paradox may negatively affect the counselor's appearance as trustworthy, attractive, and caring. In other words, the paradoxical approach, especially if it is not successful, may hinder attempts to influence the client to follow other more straightforward or linear directives. Contrary to this, Haley (1989) suggests that the therapist should not accept credit for success of the technique, should appear puzzled at amelioration of the problem, and should predict a relapse. This apparently heightens the client's sense of control and efficacy.

Time Scheduling.   L'Abate (1986) and McKay, Davis, and Fanning (1981) all recommend prescribing symptoms that can be practiced at scheduled intervals and at definite prearranged times. The client is to keep a running account. This makes tracking much easier. For example, a client with fears and anxieties is told to set aside 10 minutes daily at a regular time for the next week in which to spend time worrying about the problem.

Exclusions from Treatment.   Wubbolding (1988) suggests that certain types of clients be excluded from treatments using paradox. This includes those who exhibit very little motivation for change, sociopathic (antisocial) individuals, and those with paranoid fears. Weeks and L'Abate (1982) and Wubbolding (1988) warn against its use with families where chaos and confusion are the rule. It is not recommended in dealing with crises and with acute grief reactions, nor is it helpful with extremely hostile families or where inconsistent or immature parents preside.

Therapist Preparation.   The paradox is a controversial method that most writers agree is an advanced therapy skill to be used with caution (Haley, 1976). West and Zarski (1983) describe paradox as an advanced technique that should be attempted only by therapists who have completed training and who have been well schooled in family systems training. This advice points out that therapists may be intrigued by the showiness of the method and may be tempted to use it before being fully prepared.

Initially, the therapist is tempted to present the paradox in a half-hearted way that may nullify its effect and produce a lack of confidence in the client. Alternately, a counselor may also attempt a very confrontive paradox. It is much more likely that the technique will be practiced successfully if it fits the counselor's own personality or style.

Like any skill, paradox must be practiced. Practice in real and in simulated settings will be effective if the counselor can get feedback on the delivery of the directive and track changes made by the client. Supervision and client self-monitoring is a must in the beginning.

Variations on Paradoxical Interventions

Therapist Pessimism.   A number of paradoxical interventions are designed to be implemented when some progress has been achieved. These messages seem to convey to the client that progress cannot be maintained. They include

1. *Predicting a relapse*—The counselor informs the client that therapy is proceeding too quickly and therefore it is very likely that the change will not last.
2. *Prescribing a relapse*—This method asks the client to fall back into old behavior patterns. The rationale usually is that this message prepares the client for a relapse when it occurs. The client is asked to relapse now rather than later.
3. *Restraining or forbidding change*—Here the counselor asks the client to slow down the change that is taking place or to stop it. Alternately, the client is told to seriously consider all of the negative consequences that changing could bring about.
4. *Declaring hopelessness*—Therapists have used this method to activate movement in recalcitrant families. The therapist predicts that nothing will change, although everyone is really trying (the family is aware they are not

trying), and the situation is described as chronic. Typically, someone in the family is angered by this, and this conflict leads to movement or motivation to prove the therapist wrong.

De-Reflection.   The technique involves actively encouraging the client to ignore the presenting problem and to focus attention on something more pleasant or neutral (Patterson, 1973). One treatment for insomnia is called the *tongue-in-cheek technique*. It requires the client to sleep on one side and to place the tongue between the teeth, just touching the cheek on the side of the mouth closest to the mattress. The client is not to attempt to fall asleep but is to concentrate on the tip of the tongue at the point of contact with the cheek and is not to allow the tongue to touch the roof of the mouth. Besides the relaxation induced by opening the jaw, these precise instructions distract the client from the frustration of trying to fall asleep.

Assigned Fights.   In marriage counseling where nonproductive fighting is a problem, clients may be ordered to fight at prescribed times in prescribed places for a particular amount of time.

Paradoxical Letters.   Sometimes it may be useful to put paradoxical instructions in the form of a letter to prolong and intensify the effect of the intervention. L'Abate, Ganahl, and Hansen (1986) describe a letter sent to an argumentative couple that encouraged them to keep on sending defeating messages to each other so as not to become too dangerously close.

Miscellaneous Paradoxes.   McMullin (1986) describes a paradoxical method from a cognitive therapy viewpoint that he calls *teach thyself*. It calls for clients to identify the irrational beliefs or misconceptions operating in their lives and then to develop an extensive curriculum as to how these beliefs could be taught to others.

Lazarus (1971) describes a technique, called the *blow up,* that involves exaggeration of the client's fears to ridiculous proportions. The client is encouraged to imagine the worst possible outcome. He documents a case of a severe fear of fires that was treated in this way. A milder example involves a colleague's treatment of a woman who was afraid that her unhappiness with family members would be a subject of gossip in the town where she lived. He responded to her fear by encouraging it. "Yes," he remarked, "No doubt it will be leaked to the press and tomorrow's headlines will read, 'LOCAL WOMAN RESENTS IN-LAWS'. Eventually this news will spread throughout the county. Soon every coffee shop and beauty parlor in the greater metropolitan area will be buzzing about the big fight. I don't know how you will manage all the phone calls, whispered innuendos, and the invitations from talk show hosts that will come flooding in." The client accepted this intervention, which was delivered in a humorous way, as a means of showing her that she was making mountains out of mole hills.

CASE EXAMPLE

Rob was a tall, 17-year-old high school senior and an only child. Rob had little time in his life for anything besides schoolwork. He was an honors student who had done very well on his college entrance exams. He was brought to therapy by his parents because of his compulsive bedtime rituals. He had been treated previously with anxiety medication and by a pastoral counselor with no success.

The rituals involved locking all the doors and windows, unplugging all the electrical appliances, and making sure all the medicine and shampoo bottles were tightly capped. His parents were extremely concerned by these symptoms and by his tendency to pull out his hair during exams. The client was very motivated to change his behavior. He was afraid that he was having a nervous breakdown and would "fly out of control." Although he was motivated, he had very low expectations of success since he had tried to control the rituals himself. At the time he was seen in therapy, the family was preparing to move to Argentina in connection with the father's employment. They would leave in three months and be gone for a year.

An assessment of Rob revealed that he had always been a very hardworking, rather unimaginative, compliant individual. Although he denied all negative feelings toward his parents, he was embarrassed to admit that he daydreamed frequently about being independent and moving away from home. There was no evidence of medical problems or indications of hallucinations or delusions.

The short-term goal of therapy was to decrease or eliminate the compulsive behaviors. The hair pulling was not put on the first part of the agenda because, although the client's parents were very upset by this, the client was less concerned about it and felt that that behavior had already decreased.

As a preamble to treating the rituals, the therapist indicated that such problems were quite common and that they could be treated very rapidly, but it was normally best to go slowly. The client insisted that rapid improvement was what he wanted, although he was warned that this treatment was rather demanding. Because of the client's previous lack of success in treatment and the failure of his attempts to directly control his rituals, the REPLAN system guided the therapist to choose a method from the activating expectations dimension. Paradoxical methods were selected since more direct methods had not had much effect.

The treatment began by recording Rob's nightly rituals in a step by step manner. These rituals were then prescribed to the client in the following way: "Your locking and checking behavior is a reflection of your concern for your parents' safety. Perhaps even more checking would help to reassure you that everything is all right and you would be able to rest more comfortably."

The therapist told the client to lock every door and window in the house, wait 15 minutes, unlock and relock every window and door, cap and uncap all the bottles in the bathroom, wait 15 minutes, and repeat. During the two 15-minute intervals, the client was to practice Japanese paper folding (origami), an activity that the client had expressed an interest in but had not pursued. The client was to record his activities as they were completed and was to return weekly for progress reports. Three days after the first session, the therapist telephoned the client to check on his progress. The client reported compliance but complained that the rituals were too time consuming and that he was not sleeping well. At the end of the first week, the client had forgotten to do any rituals on one evening but otherwise had been faithful to the instructions. Because of his lapse, the client was instructed to add one additional sequence of locking/unlocking to the ritual each evening. By the third therapy session, the client reported that the compulsion had ceased. Rob enthusiastically reported on his growing interest in origami. He was working on a paper nativity scene for his parents. The client requested that therapy be more directed toward "getting to know myself." The therapist agreed but predicted a relapse to occur right before the client moved to Argentina. Three additional sessions were held in which the client explored personal and career goals and college plans. Three months following the onset of treatment, the client went abroad and reported via mail that the symptoms had not returned. Also enclosed with his letter was a very elaborate and beautiful origami bird.

To summarize Rob's treatment, these six steps were followed:

1. *Assessment*—Background data was obtained on Rob. One resulting hypothesis was that Rob would be a compliant client who was very much concerned with the feelings and needs of his parents. Like most adolescents, he seemed to feel a strong need to establish a separate identity and to develop his own life goals, but he could not become openly rebellious. Still, the presenting problem was becoming quite costly to the client. It was robbing him of his self-esteem and sense of control.

2. *Goal setting*—The goal identified by client and therapist was to reduce compulsive rituals. Other issues identified by the counselor, such as the client's apparent need for autonomy and the parents' concern over Rob's hair pulling, were put on the back burner. The client's improvement on the compulsions did seem to lead to an interest in further self-exploration.

3. *Creatively Devise a Paradox*—The paradox was an opposite of the normal directive, stop or decrease locking and unlocking. It seemed from the assessment that both the client and his parents had already tried this directive several times. He had unsuccessfully tried to restrain himself from these behaviors for nearly six months.

4. *Deliver the paradox in a way that involves, motivates, or enhances expectations of the client*—In this case, the symptom of compulsive locking was normalized and described by the therapist as a reflection of the client's concern for his parents' safety. The counselor also enhanced expectations by implying that the symptoms could be rapidly eliminated and prescribed a rather rigorous ordeal for Rob.

5. *Include a Variation*—The therapist intuitively felt that the client should engage in some activity for its own sake rather than accomplish something with a well-defined payoff. The client's driven attitude about success and schoolwork might be better balanced by some artistic preoccupation. It is interesting that the client chose an art form that required specific steps and a great deal of precision.

6. *Track the paradoxical directive*—After two days the counselor called the client to try and increase compliance with treatment and to assure the client of the counselor's involvement. The counselor required written records of the client's activity and increased the paradox when the client seemed to be failing to follow the prescription. In this case, the client initiated the follow-up contact.

Feedback Checklist #12
Making a Paradoxical Intervention

1. To what extent did the counselor assess the relevant client background and the context of the problem situation to determine if the behavior was suitable for paradoxical intervention?

Not at All	*A Little*	*Somewhat*	*Moderately*	*A Great Deal*
1	2	3	4	5

2. How clearly was the counselor able to help the client define the problem situation and to set a specific achievable goal?

Very Unclear	*A Little*	*Somewhat*	*Moderately*	*Very Clear*
1	2	3	4	5

3. Did the counselor creatively devise a paradoxical directive that was the opposite of a goal-oriented directive?

Not at All	*A Little*	*Somewhat*	*Moderately*	*Very Well*
1	2	3	4	5

4. To what degree did the counselor present the paradox in a way that involved, motivated, or enhanced the client's expectations?

Not at All	*A Little*	*Somewhat*	*Moderately*	*A Great Deal*
1	2	3	4	5

5. How well did the counselor choose a variation that enhanced the paradox and that was beneficial to the client?

Not at All	*A Little*	*Somewhat*	*Moderately*	*Very Well*
1	2	3	4	5

6. How thoroughly did the counselor track and record the client's response to the paradoxical intervention, including follow-up contacts?

Not at All	*A Little*	*Somewhat*	*Moderately*	*Very Thoroughly*
1	2	3	4	5

Managing Resistance: Overview and Purpose of the Method

Traditional Definitions

Resistance is the psychoanalytic term used to describe client activities that are counter to therapeutic aims. Freud (1900/1952) first identified the concept as a defensive reaction against anxiety when unacceptable thoughts, feelings, and impulses were driven into conscious awareness through the uncovering process of therapy. Resistance is repression at work during the therapy process (Sundberg, Taplin & Tyler, 1983).

Resistance has become a topic of great interest especially because it is connected with the notion of the reluctant client (Dowd & Milne, 1986; Harris & Watkins, 1987). The *reluctant client* is one who does not wish to come to therapy in the first place but who has been forced or coerced to do so. It is estimated that 50–75% of clients could be described as reluctant (Dyer & Vriend, 1977; Haley, 1989; Ritchie, 1986). They are coerced by the courts or by the correction system, brought to therapy by a spouse or a family member, or are being disciplined by a school or college. Despite ethical problems involved in changing people who do not express the desire to change, there has been a great interest in techniques for engaging reluctant clients, probably because they represent such a large proportion of clients (Amatea, 1988; Larke, 1985; Larrabee, 1982).

Do Clients Want to Change?

Resistance has been described as present in every therapeutic situation (Brammer, Shostrom & Abrego, 1989) and as the cause of most therapeutic failures (Redl, 1966). Hart (1986) says, "Therapy is difficult because clients are resistant to change and defensive about revealing their urges" (p. 211). These definitions focus on the seeming unwillingness of clients to abandon symptoms. They ultimately point to oppositional behavior and blame the client.

Most therapies have recognized resistance more or less according to the definition above. Perls (1971) saw resistance as an attempt to decline responsibility for change. He felt that clients were full of avoidance (Brammer et al., 1989). Rational emotive therapy practitioners have thought of resistance as either laziness or fear (Mahoney, 1988a), and transactional analysts have accused clients of playing games.

Family therapists, in contrast, have traditionally seen resistance as attempts by the family to maintain a homeostatic balance. Jackson (1968) pointed out that most families come to therapy as a result of a change and are looking for security. They are seeking stability rather than disruption. Families who resist change have even been described as barracudas (Bergman, 1985), presumably because they can be aggressive when asked to change.

A different viewpoint suggests that resistance can be any behavior by client or therapist that moves the client away from therapeutic goals (Cormier & Cormier, 1991) or leads to anything less than full commitment to those goals (Cormier & Hackney, 1987). In this way of thinking, resistance is perhaps addressed more objectively as a problem affecting the therapy rather than an avoidance by the client. Also, therapist behaviors that detract from progress could also be considered resistance.

In addition, resistance can be perceived as communication. It gives clues to the client's common defenses and coping patterns. It signals the therapist that therapy is slowing down and may be headed for termination (Brammer et al., 1989). Blocks in the counseling relationship probably reflect similar difficulties in the client's other relationships.

A new view has been advanced by some cognitive therapists who point out that resistance is a natural reaction to changing one's schemata or mental constructs about the world (Dowd & Seibel, 1990; Mahoney, 1988b). It protects the core beliefs of an individual from sweeping changes that would bring chaos. The cognitive view is that change should be a gradual process of modifying constructs that limit the effects of resistant behavior.

Finally, a new viewpoint about resistance is developing in the strategic therapy school (de Shazer, 1985, 1988; Haley, 1976; Lawson, 1986; Otani, 1989). The extreme point of view in this school is that resistance does not exist. It is even said that a funeral for resistance was held at one training center. A client's failure to comply with directives is seen and interpreted as an attempt to improve on or to individualize assignments. It is the client's best possible response. These therapists believe that the notion of resistance implies that the client does not want to change. Expecting resistance becomes a self-fulfilling prophecy; if the therapist searches for resistance, he or she will surely find it (O'Hanlon & Weiner-Davis, 1989).

Manifestations of Resistance in the Client

Some common manifestations of resistant behavior have been reported by various writers (Blanck, 1976; Brammer et al., 1989; Lerner & Lerner, 1983; Sack, 1988; Wolberg, 1954):

1. The client criticizes the counselor or the counseling progress.
2. The client comes late to sessions, fails to keep appointments, or forgets to pay fees.
3. The client is silent.
4. The client intellectualizes and philosophizes.
5. The client terminates prematurely or "flies into health" or a sudden remission is reported and is used as a protection against further change.
6. The client uses excessive humor, silliness, or facetiousness.
7. The client persistently says "I don't know."
8. The client does not wish to terminate and wants to extend session length.
9. The client delves into the counselor's personal life.
10. The client presents irrelevant material designed to intrigue the therapist.
11. The client develops insights but does not apply them, dissociating therapy from everyday life.
12. The client fails to complete homework and directives or to follow advice.

Causes or Sources of Resistance

As discussed above, the reasons given for resistance vary according to theoretical persuasion; however, a number of common factors seem to surface (Bugental & Bugental, 1986; McMullin, 1986; Ritchie, 1986). They are sometimes divided into client, therapist, and environmental variables (Cormier & Cormier, 1991); however, I will consider client and environmental causes here and discuss therapist contributions in the section entitled "Problems and Precautions in Managing Resistance."

Client Sources of Resistance.   Failures to comply with therapy have been attributed to skill deficits. The client's lack of skill to perform assignments hampers learning the therapeutic task. For example, clients may not possess certain social skills needed to overcome a fear of public speaking. The client's inability to follow homework assignments may be due to lack of skill in self-expression rather than an oppositional attitude.

A second area of resistance involves client fears. Clients fear therapy because they find self-disclosure with a stranger unfamiliar. They fear the intensity of emotions that might be unleashed. They lack trust and fear exposure. They are afraid that therapy will cause disequilibrium. They may fear change most of all (Bugental & Bugental, 1986).

Another major source of resistance is involuntary status, the feeling of being coerced into therapy by some third party: employer, spouse, or court (Driscoll, 1984). Some people are rebels. Others resist the system and see the therapist as Big Brother.

Some clients resist therapy due to a conflict between their own values and those of the therapist or the community. Some religious groups feel that therapy attempts to shift their values toward those of an unhealthy society. Others feel that exposing problems to a professional is shameful to their families. Some reject therapy because of cultural injunctions against being dependent on strangers when one should rely on the family or on one's own resources.

Dislike of the counselor is another source of client resistance. The reasons for this include sex, religion, appearance, class, and culture. The therapist's personal style and even the school of therapy to which the therapist belongs can be aversive to the client (Stream, 1985).

Environmental Sources of Resistance. Lack of money and basic needs inhibit therapeutic progress. Clients who are dealing with interpersonal issues must (according to Maslow's hierarchy) put marital and family issues aside when the need for food and shelter are threatened. Many families who experience marital and family problems cannot spend leisure time together because of the pressing need to work or to recuperate from work.

Gains made by the client may not be supported by family and friends. The client attempting to lose weight may be tempted and encouraged to eat by family members. Clients also feel that some changes, such as increased assertiveness, may not be accepted by others and that they will be rejected.

Miscellaneous Sources of Resistance. McMullin (1986) reminds us that clients come to therapy for a variety of reasons and that acceptance of initial therapy goals may not be genuine. As mentioned previously, the real goal may be hidden behind a calling card or a pseudogoal advanced as a test in the early rounds. If a client does not seem committed to therapy goals, there may be some other reason for coming to therapy. Some of these are loneliness or wanting companionship or an intelligent and sensitive friend. They may enjoy unloading their feelings and frustrations or they may simply be sampling therapy as some people go for a massage.

Readiness as a Reason for Client Resistance and Lack of Motivation. Resistance is sometimes conceptualized as a lack of client motivation. One way in which counselors protect themselves from feelings of failure is to blame the client for lack of motivation. Again, this presumes that the client is either highly motivated (compliant) or unmotivated (noncompliant). A different view now appears to be developing that prescribes that differing levels of motivation call for different types of intervention. Two very similar ideas have been advanced. One is promoted by the transtheoretical eclectic therapists Prochaska and DiClemente (1983, 1986) and one in the brief strategic work of de Shazer (1988). All see the client's level of readiness for therapy as an important aspect of planning treatment.

The eclectic model of Prochaska and DiClemente proposes that clients move through four stages in the process of change. Each stage represents a period of time and a set of tasks needed for movement to the next stage. Clients who are unaware of a problem are in the stage of *precontemplation*. At this point they are not even considering a change and are more surprised at the confrontation than they are defensive. Such people are rarely in treatment although others may be affected by the actions of the client and may express concern.

When persons become aware that a problem exists they reach the stage of *contemplation*. Still, these clients are described as ambivalent. Although they admit that a problem may exist, they deny the seriousness of it and the need for help. For example, the first step in Alcoholics Anonymous's Twelve-Step Program begins with the admission of a problem, that one's life has become unmanageable because of alcohol. Some individuals, however, recognize the problem but fail to make substantial change. They may remain in the "I'll quit tomorrow" stage of contemplation for long periods.

Action, or *determination,* is the phase of treatment in which the individual initiates change or begins to seek outside help. The balance finally tips in favor of change. This may be experienced as a sudden event or the result of a gradual process. Ordinarily the person experiences significant discomfort and feels "something has got to change." These clients begin counseling or treatment programs.

Finally, the *maintenance* stage begins. Once the client problem has come under control, the client attempts to change his or her life-style to accommodate the changes made. This is a crucial period in the process of change and one that is often neglected. the maintenance stage may lead to stable change or relapse, depending on how well the therapist is able to extend treatment through follow-up and the degree to which the client can develop personal and environmental supports for new behaviors. This model is particularly applicable to the addictions field since it mirrors the process that individuals undergo in the decision to receive treatment and in their relapse or recovery (Marlatt, 1988). The model also indicates that the same interventions are not necessarily effective at each level of motivation (see Table 9.2).

Steve de Shazer's short-term strategic therapy model of stages of change divides clients into three categories: visitors, complainants, and customers. *Visitors* are individuals who seemingly have no complaints. They may be forced or coerced into therapy by some third party who does have a complaint. Without a complaint, therapy can not begin, according to de Shazer. If the therapist conceptualizes the client as a visitor, this may take some of the pressure off the therapist to bring about a change and may lead to more pleasant interaction. Rather than accept the complaint of the third party, the therapist looks for any client complaint as a basis for counseling. This may even be an agreement to "get the court system out of my life" or any problem that is salient to the client. Besides this approach, de Shazer recommends being as nice as possible and taking the side of the client. The aim is to change visitors into complainants, if possible.

TABLE 9.2
Stages of motivation and change.

Prochaska & Di Clemente	de Shazer	Possible Interventions
Precontemplation	Visitor	Awareness exercises Education Feedback Relationship enhancement Observations/confrontation
Contemplation	Complainant	Encouraging commitment Noting rewards and drawbacks Promoting ownership/responsibility
Action	Customer	Action strategies Rehearsal/practice Tasks, ordeals, and homework
Maintenance		Follow-up contacts Support groups Self-control strategies Relapse prevention

Complainants are those who seek solutions. They clearly wish to consider a change of some kind. The complainants may not be ready to do something about their complaints. If they want to take action, they are called, *customers*. Only customers should be given tasks. Individuals at lower levels of motivation fail tasks. Table 9.2 shows a comparison of de Shazer's and Prochaska and DiClemente's viewpoints and some possible interventions associated with each level of motivation.

Interventions for Managing Resistance

Before dealing directly with this subject, let us think about some ways to prevent resistance in the first place. Meichenbaum and Turk (1987) have addressed this issue especially as it relates to compliance with medical treatment. Nonadherence with physicians' advice is thought to be around 50%, but it is much lower with some special problems like diabetes (7%).

These writers suggest that when nonadherence with advice occurs, the practitioner should not overemphasize the event. The therapist should instead help the client see, in a scientific way, that he or she can learn as much from failure as from success. They have ten commandments for dealing with noncompliance that I paraphrase for counselors as follows:

1. Expect noncompliance and do not react negatively.
2. Consider homework and the therapeutic regimen from the client's point of view.
3. Develop a collaborative relationship and negotiate with the client.
4. Be client-oriented.

5. Customize treatment.
6. Enlist family support.
7. Provide the client with a system of continuity and accessibility to the counselor
8. Make use of community resources (such as support groups).
9. Repeat everything.
10. Don't give up.

In general there are three methods for managing resistance: combatting, tipping the balance, and accepting the client response. Combatting tends to be a standard way of thinking about confronting resistance. Let us examine that first.

Combatting.   The language of war has been used to characterize the therapist/client relationship when dealing with resistance. As Sifenos says, "Pounding patients with a truth produces good results" (Davanloo, 1978, p. 241). One popular method is to confront the client's actions directly and to help the client realize the underlying goal of oppositional behavior: to retain the status quo. This method is called interpretation of resistance (Brammer et al., 1989).

Two other avenues for combatting resistance worthy of mention are self-disclosure on the part of the therapist and threat of termination. Self-disclosure by the therapist can be a powerful tool, if it is used sparingly and when it is clearly directed toward helping the client, not simply a way for the counselor to vent frustration. It might be quite useful to the client to be told, "I feel rather bored. For the last few weeks, all we have talked about are your complaints about your mother. You describe one incident after another but nothing seems to happen. I wonder if this is a good way to spend our time."

Threat of termination as a method to control client resistance is an extreme measure. It has been used as a tool to disrupt self-destructive and suicidal behaviors of the client. I include it here only because it is frequently mentioned as a high-pressure technique for extreme circumstances. Threatening the client with referral or termination could devastatingly affect morale. Its use is founded on the presumption that the client will abandon the behavior rather than the therapeutic alliance. This kind of intervention would be ineffective early in a relationship, in a less intense therapeutic alliance, or if presented in a punitive manner.

Tipping the Balance.   Tipping the balance is my name for therapist activities designed to focus the client on the rewards of change and the negative aspects of the current situation. Tipping the balance rests on the assumption that the client's current behavior is a temporary result of supporting and restraining forces (Lewin, 1951). For example, being satisfied and remaining at a particular job is a condition of homeostasis that can be modified by reducing the things that hold one to the job or increasing the incentives to move on. One may stay at a job because of loyalty, high pay, fringe benefits, etc., but a person may change jobs when a better offer comes along or when something changes in the reasons for staying. Table 9.3 shows how a counselor might tip the balance for change using Lewin's concepts. By listing all of the forces restraining change on one side and all of the forces opposing it on the other, the client can identify which forces they might alter. A value can be attached to each of these forces on a 1 to 5 scale, based

TABLE 9.3
Restraining and propelling forces for change.

Factors Restraining Change		Factors Propelling Change	
1. _____	Weight _____	1. _____	Weight _____
1. _____	Weight _____	1. _____	Weight _____
1. _____	Weight _____	1. _____	Weight _____
1. _____	Weight _____	1. _____	Weight _____
1. _____	Weight _____	1. _____	Weight _____

on the weight that it plays in the decision. Remember, most problems, according to this definition, are a state of balance between forces. Rather than a comfortable homeostasis, the client feels pulled in both directions. Using this table or a similar one, the client might determine how to tip the balance in favor of change by adding to the valence of the propelling side or by subtracting from the side restraining change. For example, a client who wishes to lose weight could decrease the pleasure of eating (restraining force) by eating quickly. Conversely, the desire to feel more attractive (propelling force) can be increased by incentives, such as buying clothes in a smaller size or by obtaining positive feedback on attractiveness from supportive friends.

One way to persuade a client to move from a position of homeostasis is to create dissonance: to make the client confront the importance of competing attitudes, beliefs, or potential rewards. If the client is satisfied with his or her pay but then learns that a coworker is making more money, dissonance occurs. If a client is made aware of the importance of physical health, which is inconsistent with smoking, a motivational state will exist to propel change.

Therapeutic techniques for tipping the balance may involve persuasion and changing client beliefs, but it also means rewarding new behaviors and removing supports from old behaviors. For example, behaviorists recognize that it is important to ascertain which aspects of the client's environment maintain the behavior and they remove them. The family of a patient in chronic pain, for example, is asked to discontinue expressions of sympathy and to stop doing things for the client that he or she can do independently. Using methods of self-control (Kanfer, 1986), clients can also learn to increase the positive consequences associated with their own behavior and to build in rewards for change. Another way of saying all of this is that the client's resistance to change is due to the fact that the rewards for giving up the behavior are not as powerful as those for retaining it. Clients should try to use powerful rewards to tip the balance or up the ante. For example, losing 25 pounds might be better motivated by a trip to Europe than a new outfit.

Accepting the Client's Response. Adler, Rogers, Sullivan, and Maslow all assert that a hostile, competitive view of resistance with the rhetoric of warfare is counterproductive (Lauver, Holiman and Kazama, 1982). These therapists and a host of others have developed methods in response to client resistance that attempt to normalize and accept the opposition (cf., Brammer et al., 1990; Dyer & Vriend, 1977; Egan, 1990; Guidano, 1988; Walker & Aycock, 1986):

1. Remind the client that resistance is a normal part of therapy and that avoidance is an important coping mechanism.
2. Describe the client's resistant response to directives as a positive step forward rather than as a failure. The therapist may even ascribe noble intentions to the client's deviations from therapeutic goals. Palozzoli, Boscolo, Cecchin, and Parata (1978) call this process the method of positive conation.
3. Use group counseling procedures to provide needed encouragement and support for change.
4. Use self-examination by the therapist to remove any interventions that seem provocative or coercive.
5. Invite the cooperation and participation of the client in the setting of goals. Renegotiating goals may be a necessary result.
6. Tap social support systems of the client, including family, friends, and significant others, to help encourage or maintain change.
7. Get a foot in the door (Roloff & Miller, 1980), which involves asking for compliance with a very minor task and following it with a request for a larger one. Conversely, the door-in-the-face method asks the client to complete an impossible task and then follows this with a reasonable request.
8. Ask the client to change for one week only, as an experiment.
9. Decrease frequency and length of sessions when conflict arises. Slow down the pace of therapy.
10. "Travel with the resistance" by using a paradoxical intervention.
11. Ask the client to brainstorm all of the excuses he or she might give for not completing assignments or for accomplishing goals.

The Customer Is Always Right.   A slightly different viewpoint is stressed by strategic therapists (Haley, 1973, 1976; O'Hanlon & Weiner-Davis, 1989). Their approach might be called the "therapy of the weak" (Hoffman, 1981) or the "counselor as chicken" (Walker & Aycock, 1986). These counselors suggest translating client resistance as the therapist's error. Coyne (1983), for example, recommends apologizing to the client when there is noncompliance. Presumably, the therapist made a mistake in selecting that task. The assumption is that the client is trying to cooperate rather than compete. The client's response is an attempt to show the therapist what will be the most fitting kind of change. The therapist is to win through collaboration.

An important aspect of this way of thinking is that the therapist is to respond directly to the client's last activity and match it. If the client follows through and completes a straightforward assignment, the counselor gives another one just like it. If the client does not finish homework, homework is not assigned. If the client changes the assigned task, it may mean that the client likes to add a personal contribution to the assignment. The therapist constructs the next task so that it can be changed. If the client does the opposite of an assignment, perhaps a paradoxical task is called for (O'Hanlon & Weiner-Davis, 1989).

The Method of Managing Resistance

Step 1: Identify Behavior Not Consistent with Agreed-Upon Goals.   Although the therapist might identify resistant behaviors from the listing given earlier, the ones to be dealt with are those that directly impede the client's goal attainment. The client who is late for appointments may still be making steady progress.

Step 2: Determine Which Intervention Is Best Suited to the Client's Needs (Combatting, Accepting, or Tipping the Balance).   Here the therapist evaluates the client's behavior and attempts to determine which of the three major strategies or combination thereof would be the most effective method of increasing goal-directed activity. Although I know of no hard and fast rules, it seems that many clinicians adopt acceptance strategies initially, hoping to avoid a rupture in the client/therapist relationship. Later, tipping the balance strategies may be more effective. Combative approaches tend to be used with inpatients, groups, and reluctant clients since these clients cannot readily escape the confrontation. The combative methods are the stock in trade of many substance abuse paraprofessionals, but there does not seem to be any evidence that they are any more effective than gentler approaches.

Step 3: Devise and Implement a Strategy Based on the Client's Goal and the Individual Style of the Client.   Therapists should take the client's level of motivation into account and construct an appropriate intervention. It would be inappropriate to suggest education to the client ready to take action. It would be equally ineffective to promote action to the client who is just beginning to contemplate change and who needs additional awareness and consciousness-raising activities (Prochaska & DiClemente, 1986).

Second, the intervention should be tailored to the client's own style. The therapist should review assessment data and ways in which change has been successfully motivated in the past. Efforts used successfully before may, with some slight changes, be resurrected. The intervention should be consistent with client values and ideas about change, and goals should be reevaluated if there are any indications that the client is not committed to them.

Step 4: Track the Client's Response to the Intervention and Respond to Client's New Behavior.   The counseling record should reflect whether the client's reaction to the intervention was effective in moving therapy forward. Second, the therapist's next intervention should be a direct response to the client's individual reaction. Let us say that the client responds to the simple task of keeping a tally of nail-biting behavior by writing an elaborate narrative on the behavior and accompanying feelings. The therapist's reaction might be to set up a task where the client can expand or exceed expectations. The client's response to the assignment also suggests that the next task might also involve writing or self-expression since the client has strengths in those areas.

Problems and Precautions of Managing Resistance

The precaution most worthy of consideration here is to warn against therapist responses that are based on countertransference rather than on the goals of therapy. Counselor frustration is a common cause of attacks on the defenses of the client. Frustration is often seen by the client as punitive (Martin, 1983). The root of frustration may be that the therapist wants more for the client than the client wants (Cormier & Hackney, 1987). In essence, this means that goals have not really been negotiated properly. The client is being asked to operate on the therapist's plan. Some other common but ineffective responses to client resistance are

1. Doing nothing
2. Blaming the client
3. Inappropriate referrals
4. Taking it personally, feeling hurt, and feeling like a failure
5. Reacting in kind with aloofness, noncooperation, and revenge

Variations on Managing Resistance

Contingency Contracting: A Method for Tipping the Balance. Among the behavior therapists, contracting for change has become widespread in schools, counseling centers, and even in self-management (Kanfer, 1980). *Contingency contracts* are agreements between individuals who desire behavior change and those whose behavior needs changing, such as between parents and their children. Individuals can make formal contracts with themselves, their spouses, or others.

All contracts specify the positive consequences of adhering to the contract and the negative consequences of noncompliance. They also specify contingencies or if _____, then _____ statements, such as, "If you take out the trash without being told, then I will give you your allowance regularly." Such contracts have been effective with academic problems, social skills, bad habits, marital problems, and delinquent behaviors (Dowd & Olsen, 1985).

Based on Dowd and Olson's recommendations (1985), the following guidelines for effective contracts are suggested:

1. All aspects of the contract should be understood and agreed to by both partners.
2. The contract should be in written form with a solemn signing indicating commitment to the agreement.
3. The contract should stress rewarding accomplishments rather than reinforcing mere obedience.
4. The contract should be considered the first of a series of steps if the behavior is complex.
5. The contract is not a legal document and can be renegotiated at any time by any of the signers.
6. The behaviors to be achieved should be clearly and objectively defined. They should be relatively short-range goals.
7. If possible, behavioral goals should be quantified and specified (who, what, where, when, and how often) so that it is clear when the contract is being adhered to.
8. The contract should not set goals which either of the parties is incapable of achieving. Success should be simple to achieve.

9. The rewards and privileges for displaying each behavior should be specified.
10. The reward for each behavior should be commensurate with the behavior needed to earn it.
11. The reward should be timed to be delivered as soon after the behavior is displayed as possible.
12. The contract should specify small penalties for each person's failure to abide by the contract.
13. Bonuses should be given if goals are exceeded in amount or length of time.

Resistance in Groups.   Resistance shows up in group therapy as both an individual and a collective response. Following intense emotional work, *group flight,* which involves an unspoken agreement on the part of the group to keep things light, has been noted (Yalom, 1985). As in individual therapy, fear is a common source of resistance in group. Corey, Corey, Callanan, and Russell (1988) suggest the following tactics for therapists to help clients overcome resistance in groups (pp. 65–67):

1. Be sensitive to client fears. Pushing self-disclosure or introducing highly charged material too early can bring on resistance.
2. Model openness and self-disclosure by giving a personal reaction to the resistance that is being displayed.
3. Encourage clients to discuss their feelings of resistance and to be creative, exploring them with metaphor and fantasy.
4. Give information about the goals and organization of the group. Answer questions about areas that are unclear.

CASE EXAMPLE

A client returns to the second session, not having done the self-monitoring homework assigned by the therapist. The client is a professional writer with writer's block. The therapist asked the client to write down the number of minutes per day that she spends writing and sitting at her desk thinking about writing.

In the discussion that follows three different scenarios are constructed that demonstrate how the client's behavior might be approached and solved according to the three major intervention strategies.

Example 1: Combatting the Resistance

Client: I didn't do that assignment we talked about last week. To tell you the truth, I was so busy that I forgot about it. I also didn't do any writing.

Counselor [observation and confrontation]:
Interesting. On the one hand, you come to therapy to get over the writer's block and yet you don't do the things that might help you overcome it. Can you explain this to me?

Client: Well, I do want to get over it, but I just don't have the motivation.

Counselor [confronting]:
I think this idea of motivation is more of an excuse for not doing the assignment. How much motivation would it have taken to do the homework assignment?

Feedback Checklist #13
Managing Resistance

1. How well was the counselor able to establish that troublesome client behavior was not consistent with agreed-upon goals?

Not at All	*A Little*	*Somewhat*	*Moderately*	*Very Well*
1	2	3	4	5

2. Did the counselor take into account the client's unique situation in determining which method (combatting, accepting, or tipping the balance) would be most effective in increasing activity toward client goals?

Not at All	*A Little*	*Somewhat*	*Moderately*	*A Great Deal*
1	2	3	4	5

3. How well was the counselor able to devise and implement a strategy based on the client's goal and the individual style of the client?

Not at All	*A Little*	*Somewhat*	*Moderately*	*Very Well*
1	2	3	4	5

4. To what extent did the counselor track the client's response to the intervention and respond to the client's new behavior?

Not at All	*A Little*	*Somewhat*	*Moderately*	*A Great Deal*
1	2	3	4	5

Client: Not much, I guess.

Counselor [interpretation]:
I'm not so sure you really want to start writing again. I have a hunch that you are afraid that this book will never compare with your last effort.

Example 2: Therapist Questions to Tip the Balance

These questions might be used to identify areas where rewards and restraints may be instituted and modified:

- Can you talk to me about when writing was fun?
- How could it be fun again?
- What activities are more interesting to you now when compared to writing?
- What activities distract you from your writing?
- What rewards could you use to encourage your writing?
- What rewarding activities could you withhold until writing is completed?
- Make a list of all the things that (1) push you toward writing and (2) that keep you from writing. Which things on the first list could you increase or strengthen and which things on the second could you weaken?

Example 3: Accepting the Response

Client: I didn't do that assignment we talked about last week. To tell you the truth, I was so busy that I forgot about it. I also didn't do any writing.

Counselor: You sound sort of disappointed in yourself.

Client: I am. I am just avoiding it. Like that desk was deadly or something. Why can't I get started?

Counselor [positive conation]:

Well, I can understand your point of view, but it sounds like things are moving. You are busy accomplishing things. You are out of the doldrums. After hearing this, I realize that solitary homework isn't going to work. I think you instinctively knew this and that is why you you didn't follow through [ascribing noble intentions]. Instead, let us work on the writing here together. How does that sound?

CHAPTER SUMMARY AND CONCLUSIONS

Therapists encounter lack of motivation, discouragement, resistance, and reluctance in their encounters with most clients. The struggle for change against these homeostatic and regressive forces may be seen as a war or as a failure on the part of the therapist to fully understand the client. Clients who have difficulties reaching goals may benefit most from techniques that activate expectations and motivation. Three methods for generating enthusiasm and hope were described in this chapter: encouragement, paradoxical interventions, and methods for managing resistance. Encouragement is primarily an Adlerian notion, whereas paradox stems from existential and family systems approaches. Managing resistance, originally a psychoanalytic method, has been incorporated into most therapy approaches. In the next chapter, we take up the final curative factor in the REPLAN system: new learning experiences.

FURTHER READINGS

DeBord, J. B. (1989). Paradoxical interventions: A review of the recent literature. *Journal of Counseling and Development, 67,* 394–398. DeBord's article evaluates 25 research studies, conducted since 1980, that support and challenge the use of paradox. Although a variety of problems have been studied, including agoraphobia, stress, family arguing, and negative emotions, the bulk of the studies have shown paradox to be effective.

de Shazer, S. (1988). *Clues: Investigating solutions in brief therapy.* New York: W. W. Norton. Steve de Shazer's recent book about brief therapy expands the work of Weakland and others at the Mental Research Institute. As part of his theorizing, he has identified a number of ingenious methods, including the method of eliciting an exception. This method involves determining times and conditions when the presenting problem is completely absent and then trying to recreate those conditions to eliminate symptoms.

Tinsley, H. E., Bowman, S. L. & Ray, S. B. (1988). Manipulation of expectancies about counseling and psychotherapy: Review and analysis of expectancy manipulation strategies and results. *Journal of Counseling Psychology, 35,* 99–108. This is a review article of studies that manipulate client expectancies about therapy to observe the effects on therapy outcome. The article suggests that raising expectations of clients about therapy or the therapist does not consistently produce beneficial results.

REFERENCES

Adler, K. (1972). Techniques that shorten psychotherapy: Illustrated with five cases. *Journal of Individual Psychology, 28,* 155–168.

Amatea, E. S. (1988). Engaging the reluctant client: Some new strategies for the school counselor. *The School Counselor, 36,* 34–40.

Beier, E. G., & Young, D. M. (1984). *The silent language of psychotherapy: Social reinforcement of unconscious processes* (2nd ed.). New York: Aldine.

Bergman, J. S. (1985). *Fishing for barracudas.* New York: W. W. Norton.

Berne, E. (1972). *What do you say after you say hello?* New York: Bantam.

Blanck, G. (1976). Psychoanalytic technique. In B. B. Wolman (Ed.), *The therapist's handbook: Treatment methods of mental disorders* (pp. 61–86). New York: Van Nostrand Reinhold.

Brammer, L. M., Shostrom, E. L., & Abrego, P. J. (1989). *Therapeutic psychology: Fundamentals of counseling and psychotherapy.* Englewood Cliffs, NJ: Prentice-Hall.

Brown, J. E. (1986). The use of paradoxical intention with oppositional behavior in the classroom. *Psychology in the Schools, 23,* 77–81.

Brown, J. E., & Slee, P. T. (1986). Paradoxical strategies: The ethics of intervention. *Professional Psychology: Research and Practice, 17,* 487–491.

Bugental, J. F. T., & Bugental, E. K. (1986). A fate worse than death: The fear of changing. *Psychotherapy, 21,* 543–549.

Cavell, T. A., Frentz, C. E., & Kelly, M. L. (1986). Acceptability of paradoxical interventions: Some nonparadoxical findings. *Professional Psychology: Research and Practice, 17,* 519–523.

Corey, G., Corey, M. S., Callanan, P. J., & Russell, J. M. (1988). *Group techniques* (rev. ed.). Pacific Grove, CA: Brooks/Cole.

Cormier, L. S. & Hackney, H. (1987). *The professional counselor: A professional guide to helping.* Englewood Cliffs, NJ: Prentice-Hall.

Cormier, W. H., & Cormier, L. S. (1991). *Interviewing strategies for helpers: Fundamental skills and cognitive behavioral interventions* (3rd ed.). Pacific Grove, CA: Brooks/Cole.

Coyne, J. C. (1983, May). Brief marital therapy. Symposium presented at Ohio University, Athens, OH.

Davanloo, H. (Ed.). (1978). *Basic principles and techniques in short term dynamic psychotherapy.* New York: SP Medical and Scientific Books.

DeBord, J. B. (1989). Paradoxical interventions: A review of the recent literature. *Journal of Counseling and Development, 67,* 394–398.

de Shazer, S. (1985). *Keys to solution in brief therapy.* New York: W. W. Norton.

de Shazer, S. (1988). *Clues: Investigating solutions in brief therapy.* New York: W. W. Norton.

de Shazer, S. (1989, October). Brief therapy. Symposium presented at Stetson University, De Land, FL.

Dinkmeyer, D., & Losoncy, L. E. (1980). *The encouragement book.* Englewood Cliffs, NJ: Prentice-Hall.

Dowd, E. T., & Milne, C. R. (1986). Paradoxical interventions in counseling psychology. *Counseling Psychologist, 14,* 237–282.

Dowd, E. T., & Olson, D. H. (1985). Contingency contracting. In A. S. Bellack & M. Hersen (Eds.), *Dictonary of behavior therapy techniques* (pp. 70–73). New York: Pergamon.

Dowd, E. T., & Seibel, C. A. (1990). A cognitive theory of resistance and reactance: Implications for treatment. *Journal of Mental Health Counseling, 12,* 458–469.

Driscoll, R. (1984). *Pragmatic psychotherapy.* New York: Van Nostrand Reinhold.

Driscoll, R. (1985). Commonsense objectives in paradoxical interventions. *Psychotherapy, 22,* 774–778.

Dyer, W. W., & Vriend, J. (1977). *Counseling techniques that work.* New York: Funk & Wagnalls.

Egan, G. (1990). *The skilled helper: A systematic*

approach to effective helping. Pacific Grove, CA: Brooks/Cole.

Frank, J. D. (1985). Therapeutic components shared by all psychotherapies. In M. J. Mahoney & A. Freeman (Eds.), *Cognition and psychotherapy* (pp. 49–79). New York: Plenum.

Frank, J. D., Nash, E. H., Stone, A. R., & Imber, S. D. (1963). Immediate and long-term symptomatic course of psychiatric outpatients. *American Journal of Psychiatry, 120,* 429–439.

Frankl, V. E. (1955). *The doctor and the soul.* New York: Alfred A. Knopf.

Frankl, V. E. (1975). Paradoxical intention and dereflection. *Psychotherapy: Theory Research and Practice, 12,* 226–237.

Freud, S. (1900/1952). *A general introduction to psychoanalysis.* New York: Washington Square Press.

Guidano, V. F. (1988). A systems, process-oriented approach to cognitive therapy. In K. S. Dobson (Ed.), *Handbook of cognitive-behavioral therapies* (pp. 307–355). New York: Guilford.

Haley, J. (1973). *Uncommon therapy: The psychiatric techniques of Milton Erickson, M.D.* New York: W. W. Norton.

Haley, J. (1976). *Problem-solving therapy.* San Francisco, CA: Jossey-Bass.

Haley, J. (1989, May). Strategic family therapy. Symposium presented at Stetson University, De Land, FL.

Harris, G. A., & Watkins, D. (1987). *Counseling the involuntary and resistant client.* Alexandria, VA: American Association for Counseling and Development.

Hart, J. T. (1986). Functional eclectic therapy. In J. C. Norcross (Ed.), *Handbook of eclectic psychotherapy* (pp. 221–225). New York: Brunner/Mazel.

Hitz, R., & Driscoll, A. (1988). Praise or encouragement? New insights into praise: Implications for early childhood teachers. *Individual Psychology: Journal of Adlerian Theory, Research and Practice, 43,* 138–141.

Hoffman, L. (1981). *Foundations of family therapy.* New York: Basic Books.

Hunsley, J. (1988). Conceptions and misconceptions about the context of paradoxical therapy. *Professional Psychology: Research and Practice, 19,* 553–559.

Ivey, A. E., & Simek-Downing, L. (1980). *Counseling and psychotherapy: Skills, theories, and practice.* Englewood Cliffs, NJ: Prentice-Hall.

Jackson, D. (1968). *Therapy, communication and change.* Palo Alto, CA: Science and Behavior Books.

Kanfer, F. H. (1986). Implications of a self-regulation model of therapy for treatment of addictive behaviors. In W. R. Miller & N. Heather (Eds.), *Treating addictive behaviors: Processes of change* (pp. 29–47). New York: Plenum Press.

Kanfer, F. H. (1980). Self-management methods. In F. H. Kanfer & A. P. Goldstein (Eds.), *Helping people change.* New York: Pergamon.

Karpman, S. (1968). Fairy tales and script drama analysis. *Transactional Analysis Bulletin, 7,* 6–16.

Kolko, D. J., & Milan, M. A. (1983). Reframing and paradoxical instruction to overcome resistance in the treatment of delinquent youths: A multiple baseline analysis. *Journal of Consulting and Clinical Psychology, 51,* 655–660.

L'Abate, L. (1986). *Systematic family therapy.* New York: Brunner/Mazel.

L'Abate, L., Ganahl, G. L., & Hansen, J. C. (1986). *Methods of family therapy.* Englewood Cliffs, NJ: Prentice-Hall.

L'Abate, L., & Levis, M. M. (1987). Paradoxical therapeutic strategies: Current practices and evidence. In P. A. Kellar & S. R. Heyman (Eds.), *Innovations in clinical practice: A source book.* Sarasota, FL: Professional Resource Exchange.

Larke, J. (1985). Compulsory treatment: Some practical methods of treating the mandated client. *Psychotherapy, 22,* 262–268.

Larrabee, M. J. (1982). Working with reluctant clients through affirmation techniques. *Personnel and Guidance Journal, 6,* 105–109.

Lauver, P. J., Holiman, M. A., & Kazama, S. W. (1982). Counseling as battleground: Client as enemy. *Personnel and Guidance Journal, 61,* 105–109.

Lawson, D. M. (1986). Strategic directives with resistant clients. *American Mental Health Counselors Journal, 8,* 87–93.

Lazarus, A. A. (1971). *Behavior therapy and beyond.* New York: McGraw-Hill.

Lerner, S., & Lerner, H. (1983). A systematic approach to resistance: Theoretical and technical considerations. *American Journal of Psychotherapy, 37,* 387–399.

Lewin, K. (1951). *Field theory in social science.* New York: Harper & Row.

Lichtigman, A. (1990). Using paradoxical interventions in a school setting. Unpublished manuscript.

Losoncy, L. E. (1977). *Turning people on: How to be an encouraging person.* Englewood Cliffs, NJ: Prentice-Hall.

Madanes, C. (1980). Protection, paradox and pretending. *Family Process, 19,* 73–86.

Mahoney, M. J. (1988a). The cognitive sciences and psychotherapy: Patterns in a developing relationship. In K. S. Dobson (Ed.), *Handbook of cognitive-behavioral therapies* (pp. 358–386). New York: Guilford.

Mahoney, M. J. (1988b). Constructive metatheory II: Implications for psychotherapy. *International Journal of Personal Construct Psychology, 1,* 299–316.

Marlatt, G. A. (1988). Matching clients to treatment: Treatment models and stages of change. In D. M. Donovan & G. A. Marlatt (Eds.), *Assessment of addictive behaviors* (pp. 474–483). New York: Guilford Press.

Martin, D. G. (1983). *Counseling and therapy skills.* Prospect Heights, IL: Waveland Press.

Massey, R. F. (1986). Paradox, double binding and counterparadox: A transactional analysis perspective: A response to Price. *Transactional Analysis Journal, 16,* 24–46.

McKay, M., Davis, M., & Fanning, P. (1981). *Thoughts and feelings: The art of cognitive stress intervention.* Richmond, CA: New Harbinger.

McMillan, D. N., & Johnson, M. E. (1990). Paradoxical versus cognitive behavioral interventions: Effects on perceptions of counselor characteristics. *Journal of Mental Health Counseling, 12,* 67–75.

McMullin, R. E. (1986). *Handbook of cognitive therapy techniques.* New York: W. W. Norton.

Meichenbaum, D. & Turk, D. C. (1987). *Facilitating treatment adherence: A practitioner's guidebook.* New York: Plenum Press.

Mosak, H. H. (1987). *Ha ha and aha.* Muncie, IN: Accelerated Development.

Mozdzierz, G. J., Lisiecki, J., & Macchitelli, F. J. (1989). The mandala of psychotherapy: The universal use of paradox—new understand-

ing and more confusion. *Psychotherapy, 26,* 383–388.

Newton, J. (1968). Considerations for the psychotherapeutic technique of symptom scheduling. *Psychotherapy: Theory, Research and Practice, 5,* 95–103.

Nicassio, F. J., Liberman, R. P., Patterson, R. L., Ramirez, E., & Sanders, N. (1972). The treatment of tics by negative practice. *Journal of Behavior Therapy and Experimental Psychiatry, 3,* 281–287.

O'Hanlon, W. H., & Weiner-Davis, M. (1989). *In search of solutions: A new direction psychotherapy.* New York: W. W. Norton.

Otani, A. (1989). Resistance management techniques of Milton H. Erickson, M.D.: An application to nonhypnotic mental health counseling. *Journal of Mental Health Counseling, 11,* 325–333.

Palazzoli, M. S., Boscolo, L., Cecchin, G., & Prata, G. (1978). *Paradox and counterparadox: A new model in the therapy of the family in schizophrenic transaction.* New York: Jason Aronson.

Patterson, C. H. (1973). *Theories of counseling and psychotherapy* (2nd ed.). New York: Harper & Row.

Perls, F. S. (1971). *Gestalt therapy verbatim.* New York: Bantam.

Pitsounis, N. D., & Dixon, P. N. (1988). Encouragement versus praise: Improving productivity of the mentally retarded. *Individual Psychology: Journal of Adlerian Theory, Research and Practice, 44,* 507–512.

Prochaska, J. O. (1984). *Systems of psychotherapy: A transtheoretical approach.* Chicago, IL: Dorsey Press.

Prochaska, J. O., & DiClemente, C. C. (1983). Stages and processes of self-change in smoking: Toward an integrative model of change. *Journal of Consulting and Clinical Psychology, 51,* 390–395.

Prochaska, J. O., & DiClemente, C. C. (1986). The transtheoretical approach. In J. C. Norcross (Ed.), *Handbook of eclectic psychotherapy* (pp. 163–200). New York: Brunner/Mazel.

Redl, F. (1966). *When we deal with children.* New York: Free Press.

Reibel, L. (1984). Paradoxical intention strategies: A review of rationales. *Psychotherapy, 21,* 260–271.

Ritchie, M. H. (1986). Counseling involuntary clients. *Journal of Counseling and Development, 64*, 516–518.

Roloff, M. E., & Miller, G. R. (Eds.) (1980). *Persuasion: New directions in theory and research.* Beverly Hills, CA: Sage.

Rudestam, K. E. (1980). *Methods of self-change.* Monterey, CA: Brooks/Cole.

Sack, T. (1988). Counseling responses when the client says, "I don't know." *Journal of Mental Health Counseling, 10,* 179–187.

Seligman, L. (1990). *Selecting effective treatments.* San Francisco, CA: Jossey-Bass.

Seligman, M. E. P. (1975). Helplessness. San Francisco, CA: W. H. Freeman.

Seltzer, L. F. (1986). *Paradoxical strategies in psychotherapy: A comprehensive overview and guidebook.* New York: Wiley.

Shoham-Salomon, V., Avner, R. & Neeman, R. (1989). You're changed if you do and changed if you don't: Mechanisms underlying paradoxical interventions. *Journal of Consulting and Clinical Psychology, 57*, 590–598.

Shoham-Salomon, V., & Rosenthal, R. (1987). Paradoxical interventions: A meta-analysis. *Journal of Consulting and Clinical Psychology, 55*, 22–28.

Siegel, B. S. (1986). *Love, medicine and miracles.* New York: Harper & Row.

Simonton, O. C., & Mathews-Simonton, S. (1978). Getting well again. Los Angeles, CA: J. P. Tarcher.

Steiner, C. M. (1974). *Scripts people live.* New York: Grove Press.

Stream, H. S. (1985). *Resolving resistance in psychotherapy.* New York: Wiley.

Sundberg, N. D., Taplin, J. R., & Tyler, L. E. (1983). *Introduction to clinical psychology: Perspectives, issues, and contributions to human service.* Englewood Cliffs, NJ: Prentice-Hall.

Swann, W. B., Pelham, B. W., & Chidester, T. R. (1988). Change through paradox: Using self-verification to alter beliefs. *Journal of Personality and Social Psychology, 54*, 268–273.

Sweeney, T. J. (1989). *Adlerian counseling: A practical approach for a new decade.* Muncie, IN: Accelerated Development.

Tiger, L. (1979). *Optimism: The biology of hope.* New York: Simon & Schuster.

Walker, J. E., & Aycock, L. (1986). The counselor as "chicken." In W. P. Anderson (Ed.), *Innovative counseling: A handbook of readings* (pp. 22–23). Alexandria, VA: American Association for Counseling and Development.

Watson, C. (1985). A Delphi study of paradox in therapy. In G. R. Weeks (Ed.), *Promoting change through paradoxical therapy* (pp. 2–25). Homewood, IL: Dow Jones–Irwin.

Weeks, G. R., & L'Abate, L. (1982). *Paradoxical psychotherapy: Theory and practice with individuals, couples and families.* New York: Brunner/Mazel.

West, J., & Zarski, J. (1983). The counselor's use of the paradoxical procedure in family therapy. *Personnel and Guidance Journal, 62*, 34–37.

Witmer, J. M. (1985). *Pathways to personal growth.* Muncie, IN: Accelerated Development.

Witmer, J. M., Rich, C., & Barcikowski, R. S. (1991). Optimism as a mediating factor in coping with stress. Manuscript submitted for publication.

Wolberg, L. R. (1954). *The technique of psychotherapy.* New York: Grune & Stratton.

Wubbolding, R. E. (1988). *Using reality therapy.* Harper & Row, 1988.

Yalom, I. R. (1985). *Theory and practice of group psychotherapy* (3rd ed.). New York: Basic Books.

Young, M. E. & Feiler, F. (1989). Trends in counseling: A national survey. Manuscript submitted for publication.

CHAPTER TEN

New Learning Experiences

KEY CONCEPTS

▼ *Providing new learning experiences for clients includes helping them to develop new perspectives and new skills and to increase self-awareness.*

▼ *New Learning takes place in psychotherapy through direct instruction, modeling, reinforcement, reframing, use of metaphors, and many other techniques.*

▼ *Confrontation is a method that involves helping the client become aware of discrepancies between thoughts, feelings, and behaviors. Confrontation must be handled in a way that does not alienate the client.*

▼ *Reframing is the art of helping the client learn to view the problem differently. Reframing is more than just gaining a positive attitude. It involves thinking about the problem in a completely new way.*

▼ *Enhancing marital communicaiton is an example of direct instruction in counseling. Increasing communication is an important first step in many marriage counseling situations since clients can then begin to deal with their problem together.*

INTRODUCTION

The final curative factor in the six-part REPLAN acronym is new learning experiences (Figure 10.1). This factor refers to ways of teaching the client new skills, of developing new awareness, and of accepting alternate views of the problem. Learning these new ideas can take place directly through instruction, modeling, and reinforcement or indirectly through the use of metaphors and imagery. In this chapter, we will present two important new learning methods: confrontation, which leads to insight into one's behavior, and reframing, which helps clients learn a new way of looking at problems. In addition, we will present an educational format that focuses on a specific goal for couples: enhancing marital communication.

DEFINITIONS OF NEW LEARNING

Egan (1986, 1990) calls new learning experiences *awareness stimulation* and *new perspectives*. Besides these two terms, a number of related terms are descriptive of

FIGURE 10.1
Six curative factors in the REPLAN system.

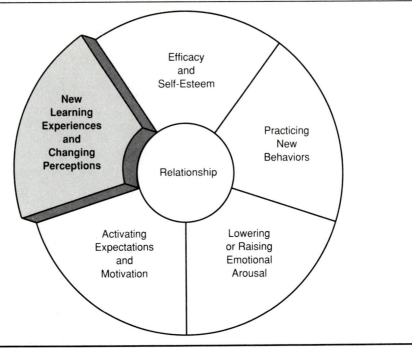

the process: changing the worldview, redefining personal mythology, developing insight, outlook skills, perception transformation, cognitive restructuring, reframing, meaning attribution, perception shifts, the "aha" experience, re-labeling, redicision, and so on. There is some overlap in the definitions of these terms, primarily because they all describe a part of the larger curative factor.

NEW LEARNING AS A CHANGE IN THINKING

We ordinarily think of learning as being associated with a classroom, to be mainly cognitive, devoid of emotion. Jerome Frank's (1985) idea of learning is that acceptance of new attitudes and values is most effective when cognitive and affective experience is involved. Combining new learning experiences with emotional arousal is quite common in psychotherapy. Most techniques include an amalgam of these two factors. For example, psychodynamic psychotherapy (Garske & Molteni, 1985) couples the more intellectual processes of "clarification, interpretation and working through" with the arousal of strong feelings evoked through confrontation (pp. 106–107).

CLIENT PROBLEMS AND GOALS THAT RESPOND TO NEW LEARNING

A number of client problems are the result of inadequate training or lack of knowledge about available resources. These include difficulties associated with stress management (Tubesing, 1979), improper understanding of one's interests and abilities, career indecision (Bolles, 1990), poor interpersonal communication, and feelings of helplessness. Other less obvious problems that may be overcome through new learning include (1) dealing with painful remembered events, (2) pathological grieving, (3) extreme anger and negative views of others and the self, and (4) avoidance and fear situations (Young, 1990).

Elliott (1985), in reviewing client perceptions of helpful and nonhelpful events in therapy, identified gaining a new perspective as one of the most frequently helpful experiences cited by therapy clients. Martin and Stelmaczonek (1988) found that insight and understanding were among the most significant factors noted by clients following therapy. These same clients were able to recall these learnings up to six months following therapy.

MAJOR METHODS OF PROVIDING NEW LEARNING

This section includes brief descriptions of some ways in which therapists provide new learning experiences. Following this discussion, three additional techniques are examined in detail: confrontation, reframing, and direct instruction (enhancing marital communication).

Teaching a Philosophy or a Comprehensive Model

Some psychotherapies, such as transactional analysis (TA), begin by teaching the client the language and premises of the therapy. The ability to understand ego states, Parent, Adult, and Child is a first step in identifying and changing one's orientation through TA. If the client wishes to converse with the therapist, it is almost essential to adopt the TA worldview and understand the jargon of scripts, games, and strokes. In the same way, Alcoholics Anonymous instructs members in the disease concept of alcoholism. Rational emotive therapy, too, may begin with explanations of the A-B-C model of emotional disturbance promoted by Albert Ellis. This changing of worldview has two effects: it involves and intellectually fascinates the client, and it begins immediately to change the client's beliefs about the self and about the problem by placing them in a new context.

Developing Client Values

A number of studies report that successful psychotherapy involves changes in client values in the direction of the therapist's beliefs (cf., Pande & Gart, 1968;

Parloff, Goldstein & Iflund, 1960). *Values* are attitudes and beliefs shaped by our thoughts and experiences and are subject to persuasion and influence. Cognitive therapy, for example, has, as its primary aim, the changing of dysfunctional beliefs.

Sometimes people seek help when their belief systems are inadequately organized to handle life's problems. They have not established a coherent life philosophy. Others have rigid belief system that hamper their ability to deal with new information and change. Still others experience moral dilemmas. Values development or moral development often occurs in a group-training setting in schools and in correctional institutions, especially with adolescents. Moral values, beliefs, and preferences are all examined in psychotherapy because they represent a significant part of our frame of reference and our highest aspirations.

Changing values can take place through a number of instructional methods, including covert messages (slogans, posters, and advertising), modeling, role playing, symbolic identification (heroes in history, fiction, films, etc.), religious or transpersonal events and peak experiences, values clarification methods, analysis of values, exposure to dilemmas and higher levels of moral development, and through taking moral and social action (Young & Witmer, 1985).

Modeling

Bandura (1971) is responsible for sensitizing therapists to the role of modeling in psychotherapy. Identification with the therapist or with other group members is considered a major curative factor in group therapy (Yalom, 1975). Modeling can take place in counseling either as an intentional process or as an unexpected byproduct. Intentional modeling may include exposing clients to symbolic, biographical, or fictional models in books, tapes, and films (Milan, 1985). These models exhibit successful performance, and the client learns by reproducing the skill along with feedback from trainers (cf., Mitchell & Milan, 1983).

Developing Insight

Insight is the term from the psychodynamic approach that refers to the client's degree of self-understanding. It is considered a prerequisite to change. It includes intellectual and emotional understanding of the causes and meaning of one's problems and the extent that one is free from perception-clouding defense mechanisms. For example, a client's reaction to his boss may be due to historical interactions with his father. Once this reaction is interpreted, confronted, and clarified in analysis, the client may start to see the unconscious motives behind his actions. Insight may occur suddenly (aha!) or may dawn gradually. Once it occurs, the learning may be applied to other situations. In this example, the client may become aware of similar tendencies in his relationships with other authority figures.

Metaphors

The use of metaphors, stories, parables, and tales are common means for creating new learning in clients (Barker, 1985; Gordon, 1978). Metaphors and stories engage the listener with imagery, suspense, and humor. These elements make metaphors effective in reframing, that is, in changing the client's viewpoint of the problem.

Exposure to Avoided Stimuli

Exposure is the *in vivo* practice of facing feared stimuli either gradually or through flooding (Emmelkamp, 1982; Foa & Goldstein, 1978). Exposure was discussed earlier but it deserves attention here. Clients learn important lessons from facing rather than avoiding. They learn that many of their fears are groundless and that their perception of other people and the world may be erroneous.

Humor

Gardner (1971) suggested that, in a light atmosphere, learning is facilitated. Humor also provides a way to shift a client's viewpoint (Ansbacher & Ansbacher, 1956; Mosak, 1987). Like a metaphor, a joke tells a story and sometimes contains a philosophical shift, interpretation, or message.

METHODS AND TECHNIQUES OF NEW LEARNING

Confrontation: Overview and Purpose of the Method

Confrontation is an advanced counseling technique that involves facing clients with inconsistencies between affect, cognition, and behaviors (Taylor, 1990). Paul (1978) considers confrontation as "essentially, a disgnostic formulation, a remark about the patient [that] points out a fact and doesn't explain it or integrate it with other facts—it 'holds up the mirror'" (p. 146). Egan (1990) prefers the term *challenge* rather than confrontation because it sounds less like a battle between counselor and client. Challenge is really a broader term that involves all therapist activities that encourage the client to follow through with plans and goals.

Confronting the client does not mean that the positive feelings associated with the therapeutic relationship end, but when confrontation is used, it represents a shift in emphasis from relationship building to a focus on the goals of therapy. During the initial phase of counseling, the counselor struggles to understand the client's world. The counselor eventually begins to recognize that many of the clients goals, feelings, values, thoughts, and behaviors are contradictory:

- A client says she wants an equal sharing relationship but dates domineering men.
- A man says that he loves his job but complains about it repeatedly.

- A client states that he wants to improve his marriage but forgets to come to marriage counseling sessions.

According to Hammond, Hepworth, and Smith (1977, pp. 287–318), discrepancies can exist in cognitive-perceptual, affective, or behavioral realms. Situations or problems for which a counselor might use a confrontation technique are illustrated in the examples of *cognitive-perceptual* inconsistencies that follow.

- Inadequate or erroneous information
- misconceptions about the self
- interpersonal misconceptions and perceptual distortions
- irrational fears (perception of danger versus perception of harmless stimulus)
- denial of problems
- denial of responsibility (seeing self as victim)
- failure to see alternatives
- failure to consider consequences

Examples of *affective* inconsistencies include

- differences between real and expressed feelings
- feelings expressed verbally versus nonverbally
- intensity of feelings expressed versus real feelings

In the *behavioral* realm, frequently mentioned discrepancies are

- dysfunctional life-styles or patterns of addiction
- differences between expressed goals and behavior
- manipulative behaviors
- dysfunctional communication patterns
- resistance

These writers go on to suggest a five level-scale that is similar to Carkhuff's levels of emphatic response. Higher scores on this scale reflect a better ability to confront effectively. At level 1.0, the counselor overlooks or accepts the discrepancies, inconsistencies, or dysfunctional expressions of the client or uses a hard or abrasive confrontation. At level 2.0, the counselor does not focus on discrepancies but responds with silence or reflects without noting the inconsistency. Since confrontation must be appropriately timed (timing is right when the relationship seems firmly established), this category also includes poorly timed confrontations. At level 3.0, the counselor focuses attention on the discrepancy or dysfunction by questioning or pointing out the inconsistency. At level 3.0, the timing is considered appropriate and the confrontation is not abusive. Level 4.0 is a direct confrontation, which includes a challenge to modify the behavior or resolve the inconsistency while protecting client self-esteem. Finally, level 5.0 contains all of the positive characteristics of the lower levels but is conveyed in a caring and helpful way with enthusiasm for growth.

As the preceding discussion suggests, the counselor's response to inconsistencies may simply involve basic listening skills. The counselor may also confront the incongruity to help the client become aware of the conflicts and to begin to work actively on modifying situations. When the counselor chooses to confront, the statement usually takes one of the following forms:

- You said _____ but acted _____.
- You said _____ but also said _____.
- You acted _____ but also acted _____.
- You said _____ but I see _____.

Five of the most common contradictions or incongruities expressed by clients are illustrated in the following dialogues:

Incongruities Between Verbal and Nonverbal Messages

Client: It's been hell. This whole thing. It's almost funny [laughs]. You know. Sometimes he loves me, sometimes he hates me.

Counselor [confrontation]:
Your laughing and smiling make me think the problem is not serious, and, yet, I can tell by what you've said that it has been very painful for you.

Incongruities Between the Client's View of the Self and the View of Others

Client: I do the best I can. But I'm not really good looking. I've been dating the same two guys for about four months now. They say I'm pretty, but I don't believe it.

Counselor [confrontation]:
You tell me you're not attractive and then you describe going on a lot of dates.

Incongruities Between What the Client Says and How the Client Behaves (Perceived Self and Ideal Self)

Client: I've been going to Cocaine Anonymous as I said I would. But it's not really helping. Every time I see one of my old friends, I'm back into it again.

Counselor [confrontation]:
I'm confused. You say you want to give up cocaine, and, yet, you continue to see your old drug friends.

Incongruities Between Client Objective and Environmental Factors or History

Client: Sure my girlfriend and I have been having a lot of problems lately. But if we moved in together, I think things would improve.

Counselor [confrontation]:
Isn't one of the problem that whenever you spend any length of time together, you fight violently for days? How will living together and spending even more time together help the relationship?

Incongruities Between Two Verbal Messages

Client: My wife makes twice as much money as I do. It doesn't bother me. But I always feel that she looks down on me because of it. I should be making a lot more than I do. I often think about getting another job.

Counselor [confrontation]:

> OK, on the one hand, you say it doesn't bother you, and, yet, you feel inadequate in her eyes and often consider a career change!

Why Should Inconsistencies Be Confronted?

Ivey and Simek-Downing (1980) say that "the resolution or synthesis of incongruities may be said to be a central goal of all theoretical orientations" (p. 177). Grinder and Bandler (1976) indicate that the major reason for using confrontation or incongruities is to establish a point of contact between polarities, or disparate parts of the self, that may be producing inconsistent behavior patterns. As a result of confrontation, client awareness of inconsistencies is stimulated, and the client moves to resolve this. In essence, it is an educational process that brings information to the client's attention that has been previously unknown, disregarded, or repressed.

Cohen (1981) adds that confrontation produces a critical investigating attitude and expectation about the therapy situation. This attitude may be a useful step beyond unconditional positive regard, once the client recognizes that he or she has gained the counselor's acceptance. Recent research confirms that highly trained (doctoral) counselors use confrontation more often than students (Tracey, Hays, Malone & Herman, 1988). The study also found that the doctoral counselors demonstrated less dominance and verbosity than did student counselors. It may be that experience and training teaches us that highly confrontive therapy does not need to be demeaning or domineering.

How Do Clients Respond to Confrontation?

Clients generally respond to a confrontation in three basic ways:

1. There may be a denial that a discrepancy even exists. Examples of denial include attempts to discredit the counselor, to change the topic, to seek support elsewhere, or falsely to accept the confrontation. The counselor must then make a decision whether to pound away continually until the confrontation is accepted or to bring the topic up at a later date. The combative approach can be detrimental to the relationship.

2. The client may choose to accept one part or portion of the confrontation as being true. In the earlier example where the man's wife out-earned him, the client might have responded to the confrontation by admitting that her salary bothered him. This partial acceptance could lead to further exploration of the meaning that the client attaches to the event. He may experience her higher salary as a failure to fulfill his role as a husband and father. He may feel unnecessary in her life or any of a number of other possibilities.

3. The client may be helped to develop a position that synthesizes the two sides of the inconsistency. With sufficient exploration and reflection by the therapist, the client may be able to develop a new position that connects the incongruent parts. For example, consider the client who poses the following inconsistency:

Side 1: I want to accept a new position and leave my old job.

Side 2: I've worked at this company since I was 20. I helped build it. I can't let everyone down by leaving. It would be disloyal.

The counselor's response to these statements might be to encourage the client to struggle with a way to both (1) accept the new challenge and (2) remain loyal to his old company.

The Method of Confrontation

Step 1: Use Clarification and Reflection of Feeling to Fully Understand the Client's Message When an Inconsistency Is Noted.   *Clarification* means asking the client to define a term in his or her own words. Reflection of feeling helps the client to become aware of the emotional aspects of the incongruency, as in the following dialogue:

Counselor [clarification]:
   Can you tell me what you mean by the word *independence?*

Client: Well, what I mean is that I am tired of having to report to my wife. I don't know what I'd do without her. But she is a pain in the neck most of the time.

Counselor [reflection]:
   You really resent her interference as if she were your boss at work.

Client: But she's a wonderful wife. I don't really mean it when I say those things, you know.

Counselor [confrontation]:
   You think she's wonderful, and, yet, you find yourself angry at her a great deal of the time.

Step 2: Gain the Client's Acceptance of the Confrontation.   Present the incongruity tentatively, as an observation, nonjudgementally, briefly using language that matches the client's formulation of the problem. Tentative and brief confrontations are less likely to be rejected by the client.

Step 3: Whenever Possible, Follow the Client's Response to the Confrontation with One That Maintains Pressure, Reinforces the Confrontation, or Forces the Client to Explore and Synthesize the Two Sides of the Incongruity.   Following the idea that clients respond to confrontation by denying, agreeing, or synthesizing, the counselor must be ready to follow up with increased exploration, another confrontation, or clarification. Because a confrontation can be uncomfortable, it is easier, but not productive, to allow the client to move away from the issue.

Counselor: I'm a little confused. You have been telling me for the past four weeks that all you want to do is reunite with your wife. Now a marriage counseling session has been scheduled and you don't want to attend.

Client: I do want to get back together, but I'm just not ready.

Counselor [reinforcing the confrontation]:
   When you say, you're not ready, I feel very surprised. You've been

ready for months now. Have you been saying that you want to get back together and feeling at the same time like you don't want to?

Client: Yes, I dread the idea of going back to that fighting. I have to admit, I've been enjoying the peace and freedom.

Step 4: Follow Up the Confrontation with Action. Finally, it is important to recognize that when a client develops an insight or responds positively to a confrontation, it does not necessarily mean that a goal has been reached. Although it brings the discrepancy to the client's awareness, behavior change may take longer. Once an incongruency is identified, a goal based on new awareness must then be negotiated.

Problems and Precautions of Confrontation

Confrontation, if mishandled, may arouse the defenses of the client rather than increase the awareness of discrepancies. Therefore, such interventions must be advanced carefully. Although the force of the confrontation must not be watered down with qualifiers, confrontation must be presented in a way that does not damage self-esteem and that is palatable to the client. Earlier, the notion of timing was mentioned. *Timing* means knowing when in the relationship and when in the course of therapy confrontation will do the most good. Obviously, confrontation should wait until the client/counselor relationship is well established. Knowing when confrontation will do the most good is a more tricky clinical judgement. In my experience, frequent and premature confrontations that are based on very little information tend to erode the credibility or expertness of the therapist. I would consider waiting to confront an issue until after it has been raised on several occasions and the chances of acceptance by the client are high.

Confrontation has several other drawbacks associated with the effect on the therapy relationship. Confrontations, if made too forcefully, may seem to blame or humiliate the client and, thereby, would be contradictory to the goal of raising self-esteem. They place the counselor in a judgmental and superior position, and they may arouse defenses rather than provide insight to the client.

Before confronting, the therapist must be clear that the reason for the intervention is to increase client awareness and is not just a sense of frustration that the counselor wishes to unload. Egan (1977) has always contended that one needs to earn the right to confront one's friends. The same is also true in the counseling relationship. Biting confrontation without the client's trust is not likely to be successful. Likewise, the counselor who gives only positive feedback will not help the client delve very deeply (Cormier & Cormier, 1985).

A general caveat has been made several times in this book that using a technique with a client that is in opposition to the client's social and cultural values may not only be disrespectful but also ineffective. Confrontation is an excellent example of a technique with these implications. For example, Lazarus (1982) discusses how this technique can backfire with certain native American children in a school counseling setting. The method should be analyzed before use and discarded or modified when employed with individuals from differing populations.

Variations on Confrontation

Shock Confrontation. Confrontation can also act as a shock treatment. Provocative therapy, Gestalt therapy, and some others use confrontive language to arouse emotions rather than to promote learning. Sometimes clinicians use loud voice tones or even curses to intensify confrontations. Some early group therapy methods (the Synanon approach) use individual and group degradation and abusive confrontation from the very beginning of therapy. Many alcohol and drug treatment facilities still favor these methods. Such confrontation is designed to provoke an emotional response, such as anger or sadness, in "hardened" clients. These confrontations compare the client to some external standard set by the counselor. Below is an example of this shock treatment type of confrontation:

> *Client:* I'm always, you know, the last one, the fifth wheel. My parents favor my sister. At work everyone ignores me. You only talk to me because I pay you. What's wrong with me? Why doesn't anybody like me?
>
> *Counselor:* Maybe it's because they don't want to be around a whiner!

Prochaska (1984) describes an experience in which his co-therapist confronted a husband about his domineering behavior toward his wife by saying, "You make me want to vomit!" The man returned to an individual session filled with consternation over this abuse. This emotion triggered a great deal of discussion, introspection, and therapeutic movement because the client was able to see how he brought out these responses not only with the therapist but with his wife.

The counselor responses in both these examples could be called feedback. They are verbalizations of the therapist's genuine reaction to the client (Prochaska, 1984). The client must either agree or become defensive, refuting the counselor's statement. But an important aspect of this type of confrontation is that it is unexpected and promotes emotional arousal. Confrontive therapists such as Fritz Perls are able to get away with this kind of behavior because of their charisma, reputation, and the piercing accuracy of their confrontations. Shock confrontation cannot be recommended, especially to the beginning therapist, because of its effects on the therapeutic alliance and on client self-esteem. The reason for including it in this text is that such methods are often portrayed in films, books, and dramatic demonstrations. They are appealing in their power and cleverness, but the implications for the counseling relationship should be the primary consideration.

CASE EXAMPLE

Previously an example was given in which a counselor confronted an individual (a) who stated that he wanted to give up cocaine and (b) who continued to associate with old, drug-using friends. This example is continued here to show how the counselor can promote exploration even when the client does not seem to accept the confrontation.

> *Client:* I've been going to Cocaine Anonymous as I said I would. But it's not really helping. Every time I see one of my old friends, I'm back into it again.

Feedback Checklist #14
Making Confrontations

1. How well did the counselor employ basic listening skills to explore an inconsistency when it was discovered?

Not at All	A Little	Somewhat	Moderately	Very Well
1	2	3	4	5

2. Check the following characteristics if they were demonstrated in the counselor's confrontation:
a. It was presented as an observation rather than an accusation. _____
b. It was done in a tentative manner. _____
c. It was done in a nonjudgmental way. _____
d. The confrontation matched the client's words and showed a recognition of the client's special understanding of the problem. _____

3. The counselor continued to reinforce the confrontation by continuing to explore the client's statements or by helping the client synthesize the two sides of the conflict.

Strongly Disagree	Disagree	Neutral	Agree	Strongly Agree
1	2	3	4	5

4. The counselor developed follow-up plans with the client, involving homework or plans for further discussion.

Strongly Disagree	Disagree	Neutral	Agree	Strongly Agree
1	2	3	4	5

Counselor [confrontation]:
I'm confused. You say you want to give up cocaine and yet you continue to see your old drug friends.

Client: I do want to stop using. But what am I supposed to do? Stay by myself all the time?

Counselor [follow up]:
So what you really need is to be around people, socialize, have friends. So how could you do this—stay away from cocaine and still have friends?

Client: You tell me.

Counselor: Hold it. I don't have all the answers to this. But you said you want to have friends and you want to stop using. Is this possible?

Client: It must be. People do it.

Counselor: Yes, but how do they do it?

Client: I don't know. I guess they have new friends that don't use. But it's hard to start all over again.

Counselor: I'm not an expert on this. But some people who have been off cocaine for a while must be familiar with this problem. It seems like it might be fairly common. Between now and when we next meet, would you be willing to think about this? Go to your next Anonymous meeting and ask one or two people about this, then let me know what they have to say.

Client: All right. And I'll talk to my friend, Michelle. She's been sober for a year now.

Reframing: Overview and Purpose of the Method

Some Popular Examples of Reframing

Many of us are familiar with an advertisement for the Peace Corps that ran on television during the 1960s. It challenged viewers to determine whether they saw a glass as half-empty or half-full. This commercial was constructed to show that there are two ways of looking at a situation: in terms of its assets or its deficits. *Reframing* is the therapeutic technique of persuading the client to view the positive or healthy viewpoint: to see the glass as half-full.

An even better example of reframing comes from Mark Twain's story of Tom Sawyer, who convinces his friends that painting a fence is fun and a privilege, not work. A final illustration of reframing comes from the motion picture *Moonstruck*. The hero of the story is rejected by his fiancée when his hand is severed by a bread slicer. The hero had always blamed his brother for distracting him at the crucial moment when the accident occurred. The reframing takes place when the hero's new girlfriend convinces him that the real reason for the accident was the hero's unconscious wish to stay single. She elegantly uses the metaphor of a lone wolf and accuses the hero of gnawing off his own leg to avoid the trap of marriage.

Psychological Definitions of Reframing

Most notable in developing the concept of reframing has been the Mental Research Institute in Palo Alto, California, and Milton Erickson, an innovator and pioneer in strategic therapy. Erickson defined reframing as positively defining a situation so that the client develops a different way of looking at the problem and therefore responds differently (Levy, 1987). These methods have become very popular in family therapy.

According to Watzlawick, Weakland, and Fisch (1974), reframing means coming up with a new definition of the problem that fits the facts just as well as the old notion. So, before reframing can take place, the therapist must understand the client's frame of reference with regard to the problem. *Patient position* is a term that describes the client's idiosyncratic way of looking at the world. It involves the person's values, beliefs, and inclinations. Through verbal peculiarities and through nonverbals as well, the individual communicates his or her special understanding and meaning associated with a problem (Fisch, Weakland & Segal, 1982). In our earlier discussion of assessment issues, this notion was addressed. Taking a client's verbatim understanding of a problem is a starting point in treatment planning. Analyzing a client's problem statement even further, gives us vital clues about how to select language and interventions that will be consistent with the client's frame of reference and that should, therefore, be more successful. For example, a client who continually refers to the burden of her many responsibilities as a reason for not being more assertive may be best be persuaded by a reframe that emphasizes that she has a responsibility to herself.

The Method of Reframing

Step 1: Make a Complete Assessment of the Problem.   Problem assessment is important since it must be determined if a reframing of the client's situation would be useful in the first place. If the client has clear goals and seems to have an appreciation for the positive dimension of the problem, the reframing process might not be of help.

If the client's complaint has been presented as unsolvable or grandiose and is seen only in a negative light, suggesting that the client does not have the resources to solve it, a reframe is needed. In addition, as a prerequisite to developing a good reframe, the therapist must have a firm grasp of the details of the problem, including individuals involved, their relationships, and the environment where the problem exists. Examples of problems needing to be reframed may be stated in the following manner:

- Everybody else has a direction for their lives by the time they're my age. What's wrong with me?
- My marriage is on the rocks. We're not in love anymore.
- I can't stand the anxiety anymore. I want it to go away.

Client goals following reframing may take the form of these client statements:

- Many people don't discover all of their talents right away. There is no time table that fits for everyone. The average person changes careers five to seven times. It's better to still be exploring and growing than stuck in something I hate. I need to take what I have learned from my experience and apply it to my future exploration.
- I need to improve communication with my partner.
- I am now very motivated to learn to decrease my anxiety, little by little.

Step 2: Understand the Patient Position.   Beyond the facts of the case, the therapist should be able to gain a qualitative sense about the client's problem. Beyond the facts, what is it about the problem that is unique to this client? How does the client present the problem? Use a metaphor or an image, if necessary, to describe the *feel* of the client's difficulty.

Step 3: Build a Bridge.   Develop a reframe that bridges the client's old view of the problem with a new viewpoint that stresses the positive aspects of the problem or presents it as solvable.

Step 4: Present the Reframe as a Directive or as an Invitation.   Examples of the way this step can be accomplished are given in the dialogue that follows.

Directive to Client A: I want you to start thinking a bit about how lucky you were to have a grandfather like that. I don't know how

New Learning Experiences   285

you could have had a better example of what happens to someone who fails to build intimate relationships. Because of that example, I don't think such a thing could ever happen to you.

Invitation to Client B: I wonder if you could start thinking about this in a different way? Although it is hard because you are so wrapped up in the pain right now, I am hoping you can get in touch with some of the new opportunities that may come from having to change jobs? What are the things you have always wanted to do? What might you now have a chance to try?"

Step 5: Reinforcing the Bridge.   A shift in perspective is often something that develops slowly. The therapist needs to gently correct the client in the sessions following a reframing. One way to do this is to accept the old point of view and then replace it with the new perspective. For example:

Therapist to Client A: I know you're feeling some of that old resentment toward your grandfather again. That's easy to do. At the same time, I see a greater tendency on your part to be thankful that you were saved from that fate. It seems to be more pity on your part now rather than anger.

Another way of accomplishing the same thing is to take the reframe for granted and build upon it, as in the following example:

Therapist to Client B: I know there are several things you're excited about exploring in terms of careers [taking the reframe for granted]. I also have some ideas I want to share with you about how we could conduct our search more systematically [building on the reframe].

In addition, guided imagery and role playing can be used to reinforce the bridge. The client can be guided through an imagined behavioral sequence in which the problem is viewed in the new perspective and the client imagines the positive outcomes associated with the new way of conceiving the problem. Role playing can be used to demonstrate through modeling (by therapist or group members) how one acts if they lived according to the new frame of reference.

Step 6: Homework.   Homework assignments for reframing simply ask or force the client to see the new perspective rather than the old frame of reference. For example, the client might be given an assignment to list all of the things he can do as a single person that he was not able or willing to do when he was married.

Problems and Precautions of Reframing

Reframing is most likely to be successful if the client is able to relate the significant aspects of the new frame of reference to corresponding features in the old frame of reference. For example, an algebra teacher used to try to reframe her examinations as sharing experiences. The analogy was not successful, though, probably because sharing is usually not a graded activity (an important feature).

It may be impossible to identify all aspects of a problem that might be important to the client; however, every effort should be made to imagine those that could be crucial. In a metaphor or story told by the therapist, the basic elements of the tale must conform to the client's situation or risk being rejected.

A corollary to the caution above is that very simplistic reframing can be worse than none at all. One example that comes to mind concerns the reframes sometimes extended to persons grieving over the death of a family member. Well-meaning friends are apt to say such things as, "It is God's will." Because strong emotions of sadness and loss are present, most people cannot accept a reframing that does not take into account the most salient feature of their experience—the grief itself. Reframing must be a well-considered move, based on firm knowledge of the client, not just pat answers.

Variations on Reframing

Cognitive Restructuring. *Cognitive restructuring* (McKay, Davis & Fanning, 1981; McMullin, 1986; Meichenbaum, 1977; Meichenbaum & Cameron, 1974) involves modifying what clients say to themselves about their own abilities and capacities and about problem situations as well. (One aspect of cognitive restructuring was discussed when the technique of countering was explained earlier in this book.) Changing one's imagery or appraisal of a problem is also part of cognitive restructuring. For example, if a person has an image of butterflies in the stomach before a speech, he or she might be asked to develop a more powerful image—horses or bulls. The resulting feeling is one of confidence rather than fluttering weakness. This reappraisal is conceived of as something that can be learned and so must be practiced.

The term cognitive restructuring could also be applied to rational emotive therapy. *Catastrophizing* is a type of irrational thinking identified by Albert Ellis. It means accentuating the negative aspects of a situation and imagining the worst things that might happen. Ellis frankly disputes catastrophizing or awfulizing by asking the client to see the real effect of the situation rather than the exaggerated view. For example, a client who imagines that he would be embarrassed to death if a woman refused him for a date would be challenged to see that he was catastrophizing. In reality, neither death nor serious injury would occur. A refusal would instead be a drag, disappointing, or a pain in the neck, not the end of the world. The approach has appeal because it is logical and reveals fears as mostly unrealistic. In subsequent sessions, a client's tendency to awfulize would be confronted and disputed, perhaps with humor until he or she became a partner in identifying the predilection to appraise events as catastrophes.

Alternate Interpretation.   McMullin (1986) uses a technique called *alternate interpretation* to help clients change the meaning of a situation. He points out that one's first interpretation of an event is often incorrect. For instance, many people continue into adulthood to misinterpret childhood events. An example that comes to mind occurred in a family therapy session, when an adult client was discussing an incident from his childhood. His siblings also attended the session to help improve relationships within the family. As evidence of his father's vicious nature, the client related a memory of his father striking him in the face at an amusement park for dropping his ice cream cone. The family members corrected the client and explained that to them the incident had been funny. Their mother had tickled the father, who, in turning around, accidentally slapped the client in the face at the same moment as he dropped the ice cream. For them, it had been a fond and rare memory of family togetherness.

The method of alternate interpretation does not attempt to reach into the past to find the correct interpretation or meaning of an event. Rather, its sole purpose is to convince the client that there are several possible alternatives to an initial nonproductive interpretation. The method tends to loosen the hold of outmoded ideas and convinces clients that there are many possible ways of looking at a problem, some of them helpful and some of them self-defeating.

The technique of alternate interpretation is first explained to the client. Some examples concerning how an event may have several meanings are given. Following practice in the office, the client is assigned the homework task of developing three or four alternative explanations to the first interpretation of some event that occurs between sessions. The only requirement for the alternatives is that they have as much likelihood of being true as the first impression. For example:

Event

On Monday my boss mentioned that I had not finished last week's reports.

First Interpretation

My boss is criticizing me. Things are starting all over again. I know I'll lose this job now.

Alternate Interpretations

1. I have received feedback that will help my performance. In reality, this feedback will help me keep the job.
2. In the past, I have not received this kind of criticism. It is unfamiliar. Perhaps she is trying to help me improve and become a better employee.
3. This is the first time that my work has been criticized. My boss probably doesn't place that much importance on a single instance like this. She's probably forgotten about it. I am just nervous because of my past history.

CASE EXAMPLE

Judie was a 35-year-old woman living in New York City who had grown up on a farm. She was quite attractive and considered marriage to several different men during her twenties. Each time she ended the relationship when marriage seemed to be the next step in the relationship. She was an only child and was quite close to her parents despite the fact that they had fought bitterly for years. She believed that they had stayed together for her sake. She admitted that she saw love as "chains." The reason Judie came to therapy was that she had finally met a man that she wanted to marry. She was filled with confusion and had changed the date of the wedding twice. In the first few counseling sessions, reflective listening uncovered her fears, thoughts, and feelings about marriage and relationships.

She felt better about her decision to get married after these sessions, but one night (a week before the wedding), the client telephoned the therapist in a crisis of doubt about whether to go through with the ceremony. On the telephone her therapist told the following story:

> When I was a boy, we lived on a farm, and we had a very healthy and strong mare. She was high spirited, but gentle. She also had one peculiarity. She hated it when we closed the gate of the corral. In fact, she would run around in circles, rearing up, sometimes even hurting herself on the wooden fence. One day we discovered by accident that if we left the gate open she calmed down. And she never ran away. She didn't mind being in the corral. She just wanted to make sure that she could leave at any time.

The therapist credited this story as the turning point in the client's therapy and in restoring her sense of control. Although no interpretation was made for the client, she apparently grasped that she did not have to feel imprisoned by marriage, that she could retain a sense of freedom. The therapist used the farm story because of his knowledge about the client. He used the corral because the client saw marriage as a form of bondage. By leaving the gate open, the metaphor provided a bridge between the notion of being restrained and being free.

Enhancing Marital Communication by Direct Instruction: Overview and Purpose of the Method

A psychoeducational viewpoint of counseling has been proposed that suggests that counseling should be seen as a progression of teachings appropriate to the developmental level of the client (cf., Authier, Gustafson, Guerney & Kasdorf, 1975; Gazda, Childers & Brooks, 1987; Goldstein, Sprafkin & Gershaw, 1976; Guerney, Stollack & Guerney, 1970, 1971). According to this psychoeducational model:

1. Participants need not be diagnosed as suffering from emotional or mental disorders.
2. Participants are treated as students, not as patients.
3. Program leaders function not as therapists but as teachers, demonstrating, describing, and discussing skills.
4. The goal of the program is not to provide specific skills but skills that are broad enough that they can be generalized to future problems. In other words, there is a preventive emphasis (Brown, 1975).

Gazda and colleagues (1987) have empirically identified *generic life skills*. The three large families of these skills are fitness and health maintenance, interpersonal communication/human relations, and problem solving and decision making. They advocate a less medical/therapeutic and more educational model that can be applied to all types of client problems. Gazda and his colleagues make the point that several therapeutic systems are already based on a skills-training model, including structured learning therapy (Goldstein et al., 1976), multimodal behavior therapy (Lazarus, 1976), developmental approaches to therapy (cf., Hayes &

Feedback Checklist #15
Reframing

1. Did the counselor make a thorough assessment of the client's problem?

| *Strongly Disagree* | *Disagree* | *Neutral* | *Agree* | *Strongly Agree* |
| 1 | 2 | 3 | 4 | 5 |

2. To what extent did the counselor's reframing take into account the client's special viewpoint and position concerning the problem?

| *Not at All* | *A Little* | *Somewhat* | *Moderately* | *A Great Deal* |
| 1 | 2 | 3 | 4 | 5 |

3. How well was the counselor able to create a reframing that took into account elements of the old situation?

| *Not at All* | *A Little* | *Somewhat* | *Moderately* | *A Great Deal* |
| 1 | 2 | 3 | 4 | 5 |

4. Was the reframe presented as either a directive or as an invitation?

Yes   No   N/A

How well was the reframing accepted by the client?

| *Not at All* | *A Little* | *Somewhat* | *Moderately* | *Very Well* |
| 1 | 2 | 3 | 4 | 5 |

5. How well was the counselor able to reinforce the new frame of reference later in the session?

| *Not at All* | *A Little* | *Somewhat* | *Moderately* | *Very Well* |
| 1 | 2 | 3 | 4 | 5 |

6. To what extent did homework assignments force the client to adopt the new frame of reference?

| *Not at All* | *A Little* | *Somewhat* | *Moderately* | *A Great Deal* |
| 1 | 2 | 3 | 4 | 5 |

Aubrey, 1988; Wood, 1975), relationship enhancement (Guerney, 1977), and many others.

Direct instruction of skills is currently practiced with a number of client problems: alcoholism and substance abuse, phobias, problems with assertiveness, parenting problems, and coping with medical problems or serious psychological disorders.

Teaching Marital Communication

For some time it has been known that good marital adjustment correlates with good communication in the marriage (Rappaport, 1976). Poor communication has been identified as the most common cause of marital discomfort (Lederer & Jackson, 1968). Refer to Figure 10.2, which compares the percentage of marriage counseling cases to specific problems.

FIGURE 10.2
Rankings of marital problems reported by family counseling agencies.

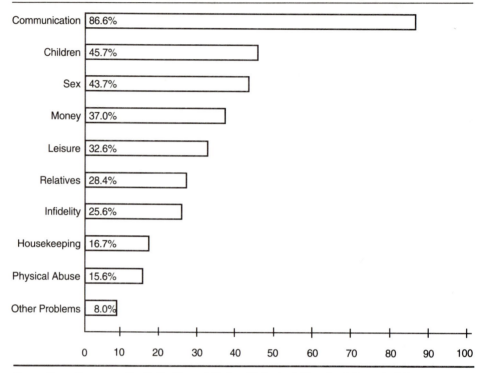

Source: From *Progress on Family Problems: A Nationwide Study of Clients' and Counselors' Views on Family Agency Services* by Dorothy Fahs Beck and Mary Ann Jones, 1973, New York: Family Service Association of America. Copyright 1973 by Family Service Association of America. Reprinted by permission.

Considerations for Using an Educational Model in Marital Counseling

One of the major hurdles clients have to overcome in improving their marriages is the strong conviction that their partners are mostly to blame. In an instructional model, both participants begin on an equal footing, and the question of blame is not germane. The problem need not be framed as sick marriage but as a learning task.

In this section of the chapter, a rather simple procedure is described. It involves teaching the couple to express themselves and listen to each other. Although better communication is an important advance in a stalemated marriage, it will not solve all of a couple's problems. In addition to learning, listening, and expressing skills, negotiation skills must also be acquired in order for progress to continue.

The early effect of communication training is to bind the couple together, to increase hope, and to provide a format and a beginning for the resolution of more complex problems. In addition, through better communication, the relationship begins to develop a positive valence. Avoidance behavior, characterized by silence and the leading of separate lives, diminishes. The relationship regains some of its attraction as a source of encouragement and safety.

Rules of Marital Communication

One way of presenting the skills of marital communication is as a set of rules. These rules are sometimes part and parcel of basic communication training or are learned as preparation for homework assignments. Using these rules, couples feel safe to begin solving problems with each other. The following list of rules has been compiled from a number of sources (Bach & Wyden, 1968; Baruth & Huber, 1984; Gottman, Notarius, Gonso & Markman, 1976; Guerney, Brock & Coufal, 1986):

Establish Beltlines. *Beltlines* are the couple's unique rules, based on their history, that make them feel safer when beginning to open communication. The name of the rule stems from the boxing analogy of not hitting below the belt. In this case, it means that the couple decides for themselves what kind of behavior should be ruled out. Rather than negotiate these rules, any rule proposed by either member must be accepted by the other. For example, one member of the couple might rule out bringing parents' or family members' names into the discussion. The other might rule out screaming, name calling, and threatening divorce.

No Kitchen Sinking. This term refers to the tendency for couples to start with one topic about which there is disagreement and to bring many other topics (everything but the kitchen sink) into the discussion rather than remaining on one topic until it is resolved (Gottman et al., 1978).

The "I" Rule. This is a suggestion that statements that start with *I* such as, "I am angry that the clothes are still lying on the floor," are preferable to, "You make me mad. You haven't even picked up the clothes." The first statement takes responsibility for the feelings involved and is not accusatory. It is more likely to lead to constructive communication rather than defensiveness.

Make Requests. Complaining is nonproductive unless it is followed by a request. Requests should be framed politely and timed appropriately. The time for making a request may not be when the emotional experience is at its peak.

Don't Try to Mind Read. *Mind reading* is a tendency for couples to imagine that they can anticipate the reaction of the other person simply because of their history and knowledge of the person. Consider the following statements:

- I didn't ask you because I knew you'd refuse.
- I could tell by the way you were driving that you didn't want to stop at my mother's.

These examples are quite simple. In reality, communication between couples can become quite confused and complex when assumptions are made about what the other person really means.

Be Polite.   It is interesting that we are often more polite to our guests than to our families. For instance, we would never think of reading a book at the breakfast table when company is present. Gottman et al. (1978) suggest nine rules of politeness for couples:

1. Say what you can do and what you want to do.
2. Give sincere and positive appreciation.
3. Be courteous and considerate.
4. Express interest in your spouse's activities, try to listen, and ask questions.
5. Say things that you honestly feel and you think your spouse would like to hear.
6. Criticize your ideas, not yourself.
7. Focus on the present rather than the past.
8. Give your spouse a chance to finish speaking before responding.
9. Think of your spouse's needs and desires; be empathic.

Marital Communication Skills

Marital communication training with couples or with groups of couples tends to identify a number of different skills. Guerney et al. (1986) have identified nine competencies or sets of skills that should be included in a comprehensive relationship enhancement program.

1. *Expressive skills*—Teaching the client to gain self-understanding and to give information to others about wants and needs in a positive, assertive way.
2. *Empathic skills*—Teaching listening, including reflecting feelings, increases the flow of communication.
3. *Mode-switching skills*—Teaching the technique of negotiating a change from listener to speaker. The empathic listening technique means responding to the other person as a listener. Sometimes, though, the listener has a personal reaction to the speaker's statement. In that case, the listening mode must be temporarily exchanged. Making this switch with the partner is something to be negotiated and is a special social skill.
4. *Problem-conflict resolution skills*—Teaching creative problem solving, compromise, and negotiation.
5. *Self-change skills*—Teaching the setting of realistic agreements to increase or decrease some behavior.
6. *Helping others change skills*—Teaching spouses to help the other accomplish goals of self-change embodied in agreements.
7. *Generalization-transfer skills*—Teaching the client to use learned skills in other daily settings besides couple interaction.
8. *Teaching supervisory skills*—Teaching techniques to train others around the learner (including those not in the formal training sessions) to use communication or other relationship enhancement skills. This increases the client's ability to practice and employ these techniques.
9. *Maintenance skills*—Teaching activities that can help the client practice problem solving and prevent problems from recurring. It also includes relationship enrichment activities.

Even this brief overview of skills shows that relationship enhancement can be a major undertaking. It is still possible, though, to achieve some goals even if the entire program is not implemented. The method described in this part of the chapter encompasses only the expressive and empathic skills, as described by Guerney (1977). Still, relationship enhancement can be a useful beginning to marital therapy whether proceeding along the psychoeducational format or not. Its advantages include a structure that diminishes anxiety and immediately involves discouraged clients in an active process.

The Method of Enhancing Marital Communication

Step 1. Establish a Rationale for the Educational and Communication Model. Begin with a recognition that the couple may have some problems with motivation. They may feel forced and fearful of being analyzed. By beginning with a didactic format, some of this kind of resistance can be overcome. At the minimum, basic communication theory should be described as well as goals that might reasonably be achieved.

Step 2. Learn the Roles of Sender and Receiver. Each member of the couple should learn to take on the distinct roles of sender and receiver. Tell the couple that good marital communication involves both good sending and good receiving. If the sender does not fully and openly express the message, it will be hard for the receiver to reflect back its content and feelings. Conversely, if the reflections are inadequate, the sender will not be able to be as open or to explore a topic fully. Sherman & Fredman (1986) recommend that the couple draw up a list of topics ahead of time with problem areas divided into three categories: easy to discuss, moderately difficult, and difficult. The therapist who will be suggesting topics and increasing the level of intensity as time goes on can refer to this list.

Tell the couple the sender will choose a topic and speak about it in simple I language. The sender cannot ask any questions and also may not employ attacking or blaming. The sender is to limit the message to six or eight statements.

The role of the receiver is now explained to the couple. The receiver is to listen carefully to the sender's message with appropriate nonverbals. Rather than respond to his or her own feelings, the receiver is to reflect content and feelings that seem to summarize the sender's message in short sentences. The receiver may not ask questions nor respond personally.

During the session each of the members alternately takes on the role of sender and receiver. The sender shows open, expressive communication. The receiver uses reflective listening, paraphrasing, and clarification (see chapter 2) and is encouraged to use the you feel _____ because _____ format (see chapter 2).

Step 3: Use Modeling and Demonstration to Teach the Skill. Therapist modeling of good receiving and sending is useful; however, using films or reading about the skills of basic communication techniques can be employed in addition to therapist modeling. Because the notion of identifying feelings is difficult for some to grasp, using lists of feelings words and workbook exercises can be quite helpful.

Step 4: Supervise In-Session Practice of the Skill. In-session practice is conducted much like a role-playing exercise, with the therapist/trainer directing the conversation. The therapist stops action to enforce agreed-upon rules regarding blaming, questions, etc. The therapist provides feedback on each member's performance after each round. Sherman & Fredman (1986) suggest that 90% of the counselor's feedback should be positive in the beginning.

Step 5: Assign Homework.   Homework assignments for couples wishing to improve communication should be given when they have mastered the sender/receiver exercise. At first they are to practice once or twice per week, using the same ground rules and strategies in session; however, they are to begin to give feedback to each other on their performance in the roles. The couple is to record any unusual problems and may even audiotape the practice for review by the therapist.

Problems and Precautions of Marital Communication

Firm control by the therapist tends to alleviate some of the anxiety clients may experience at the prospect of reawakening painful issues. The therapist must be certain to reinforce rules of communication, emphasizing the educational nature of the process and not allowing it to be seen as a ventilation session.

It is often useful to introduce the word *noise*, communication jargon for anything that keeps the receiver from fully attending. Noise can come from intrusions into the communication process, such as ringing phones, the needs of children, and other external demands from within the individual. External noise can and should be eliminated for the best communication to take place. The receiver should be asked to notice the existence of internal noise as well. This noise is most likely to be feelings of anger, sadness, and fear that may hamper the ability to hear the other person and respond as a good listener. Recognizing strong feelings is the first cue for learning to negotiate mode switching from receiver to sender.

Homework should not be assigned to the couple until the therapist is reasonably certain that the elements of good communication have been learned. The therapist may wish to build in the requirement that either member of the couple may call a halt to nonproductive arguing should it surface and terminate the practice session. Practice should resume the following day.

Couples must be screened before entering communication training. Of course communication must be identified as a central concern. Physical abuse must be eliminated before communication exercises may begin. Lack of motivation should not be a reason to exclude a couple from training. If one member or both members of the couple are reluctant, the therapist's efforts should be aimed at increasing motivation.

There is some evidence to suggest that couples have better success in marital enrichment programs if outcomes are identified as intimacy and marital satisfaction and if they participate in group interactions and discussions as a treatment rather than simply receiving information alone (Worthington, Buston & Hammonds, 1989). The implications of this research are that counselors working with groups of couples (especially those with well-functioning clients) should definitely include group discussion, role playing, and couple interaction along with didactic material.

Variations on Marital Communication

The major variation to the teaching of basic expressing and listening skills in marital situations is to employ the method as a major component of a marital enrichment or a relationship enhancement group. This approach has many advantages. The didactic portion of communication training is enhanced in the group setting where films and small lectures are appropriate. Learning may be enhanced by the modeling of other couples and through class discussion. In addition, some couples find relief in discovering that their problems are not unique. Guerney et al. (1986) indicate that even an individual whose significant other does not attend group counseling can benefit.

CASE EXAMPLE

Ron and Adele had been married for 18 months when they came for marriage counseling following an incident in which Adele had attempted to run Ron over with her car. The incident was the culmination of a series of fights in which both members had destroyed household objects. The police had been summoned on one occasion in response to raised voices.

Both partners agreed that they wished to eliminate fighting but had not been successful. In discussing their family backgrounds, it appeared that neither had been exposed to models who could successfully negotiate; instead they resorted to power plays. The couple's idea was that they could avoid areas of diasgreement. In fact, it was this "solution" that created a great deal of the problem in the first place. Rather than deal with problems when they arose, both parties admitted that they tended to withhold feelings and not to discuss them until the next fight occurred and everything came out.

The therapist attempted to reframe the couple's situation slightly by indicating that the trouble was not the fighting but allowing things to build up. The couple agreed to some basic ground rules for communication before beginning training. They agreed that no physical violence to persons or property would occur, that no name-calling would be used, and that shouting would be prohibited. This discussion took up the whole of the first session, but an agreement was reached to begin communication training the following week.

A week later, the second session was held. For four weeks the couple practiced the sender/receiver method. A list of feeling words was distributed to each of them, and they were asked to become quite specific in their use of feeling adjectives. The couple, in general, did little reading. They seemed to respond to in-therapy practice and modeling sessions rather than homework assignments. A breakthrough occurred after the second training session when Ron was able to respond with empathy to a problem Adele was having with her mother. He enthusiastically recounted to the therapist how the method had worked like magic in reducing Adele's anger and in helping her think about solutions. Adele responded that even though she knew that Ron was using a technique she still felt good about the incident.

Feedback Checklist #16
Teaching Marital Communication Skills

1. How well did the counselor establish a rationale for the use of an educational and communication model?

Not at All	A Little	Somewhat	Moderately	Very Well
1	2	3	4	5

2. How thoroughly did the therapist describe the technique and the roles of sender and receiver?

Not at All	A Little	Somewhat	Moderately	Very Thoroughly
1	2	3	4	5

3. How well did the counselor model and demonstrate the skill?

Not at All	A Little	Somewhat	Moderately	Very Well
1	2	3	4	5

4. The counselor actively supervised in-session practice of the skill and provided feedback to the participants.

Strongly Disagree	Disagree	Neutral	Agree	Strongly Agree
1	2	3	4	5

5. The homework assignment was adequately explained and was given when an appropriate degree of skill mastery had been attained.

Strongly Disagree	Disagree	Neutral	Agree	Strongly Agree
1	2	3	4	5

CHAPTER SUMMARY AND CONCLUSIONS

In this chapter we finish our description of the methods and techniques organized around the curative factors of the REPLAN system. This chapter dealt with the curative factor of providing new learning experience to clients within and outside of the therapy session. Confrontation is the method of making the client aware of discrepancies between two aspects of functioning, for example, between what one says and what one does. Confrontation is one of the first methods that beginning therapists use to bring insight or awareness.

Reframing is the art of seeing things in a different way. It is a strategy for changing a client's negative or mistaken views and for interpreting them in a more positive and constructive manner. A number of methods are used by therapists to change or shift a client's thinking. Among these are therapeutic stories and imagery.

Finally, this chapter looked at the direct instruction of skills as a therapeutic technique. We choose to illustrate enhancing marital communication through direct instruction since working with couples is an important skill for counselors to develop and is a foundation for many other therapeutic changes in the marital relationship. In the next chapter, we leave behind the discussion of curative factors and focus on the skills involved in charting client progress and in moving the client toward termination.

FURTHER READINGS

Coyne, J. C. (1985). Toward a theory of frames and reframing. *Journal of Marital and Family Therapy, 11,* 337–344. Coyne's professional interests involve the effect of social interaction on individuals and strategic family therapy. In this article, he combines these two areas and examines the effects of reframing on client relationships. In addition, Coyne examines several practical issues in selecting reframes.

Hedlund, P., Furst, T. C. & Foley, K. (1989). A dialogue with self: The journal as an educational tool. *Journal of Humanistic Education, 27,* 105–113. The article concerns the use of the therapeutic journal, diary, or log, originally designed for use in psychotherapy by Progoff. The journal as described here can be used in educational or psychoeducational settings as a means of making sense of one's personal history and as a tool for integrating new learnings about the self. The article also includes suggested reading assignments to stimulate journal writing.

Mosak, H. H. (1987). *Ha ha and aha.* Muncie, IN: Accelerated Development. Mosak's book outlines theories of humor and the role of humor in diagnosis and therapy, in termination, and as a skill for turning the client around. It contains more than 150 humorous jokes and anecdotes relating to therapy.

REFERENCES

Ansbacher, H. L., & Ansbacher, R. R. (Eds.). (1956). *The individual psychology of Alfred Adler.* New York: Basic Books.

Authier, J., Gustafson, K., Guerney, B. G., Jr., & Kasdorf, J. A. (1975). The psychological practitioner as a teacher: A theoretical-historical and practical view. *The Counseling Psychologist, 5,* 31–50.

Bach, G. R. & Wyden, P. (1968). *The intimate enemy.* New York: William Morrow.

Bandura, A. (1971). Psychotherapy based on modeling principles. In A. E. Bergin, & S. L. Garfield (Eds.), *Handbook of psychotherapy and behavior change: An empirical analysis.* (pp. 653–708). New York: Wiley.

Barker, P. (1985). *Using metaphors in psychotherapy.* New York: Brunner/Mazel.

Baruth, L. G. & Huber, C. H. (1984). *Introduction to marital theory and therapy.* Pacific Grove, CA: Brooks/Cole.

Bolles, R. N. (1989). *What color is your parachute?* Berkeley, CA: Ten Speed Press.

Brown, S. D. (1975). Self-control skills training. *Professional Psychology, 2,* 319–330.

Cohen, A. I. (1981). Confrontation analysis in groups: Goals of treatment. *Psychotherapy: Theory, Research and Practice, 18,* 441–456.

Cormier, W. H., & Cormier, L. S. (1985). *Interviewing strategies for helpers.* Monterey, CA: Brooks/Cole.

Egan, G. (1977). *You and me: The skills of communicating and relating to others.* Monterey, CA: Brooks/Cole.

Egan, G. (1986). *The skilled helper: A systematic approach to effective helping* (3rd ed.). Pacific Grove, CA: Brooks/Cole.

Egan, G. (1990). *The skilled helper: A systematic approach to effective helping* (4th ed.). Pacific Grove, CA: Brooks/Cole.

Elliott, R. (1985). Helpful and nonhelpful events in brief counseling interviews: An empirical taxonomy. *Journal of Counseling Psychology, 32,* 307–322.

Emmelkamp, P. M. G. (1982). Exposure in vivo

treatments. In A. Goldstein & D. Chambless (Eds.), *Agoraphobia: Multiple perspectives on theory and treatment.* New York: Wiley.

Fisch, R., Weakland, J., & Segal, L. (1982). *Tactics of change.* San Francisco, CA: Jossey-Bass.

Foa, E. B., & Goldstein, A. (1978). Continuous exposure and complete response prevention in the treatment of obsessive-compulsive neurosis. *Behavior Therapy, 9,* 821–829.

Frank, J. D. (1985). Therapeutic components shared by all psychotherapies. In M. J. Mahoney & A. Freeman (Eds.), *Cognition and psychotherapy* (pp. 49–79). New York: Plenum Press.

Gardner, R. A. (1971). *Therapeutic communication with children: Mutual story-telling technique.* New York: Science House.

Garske, J. P., & Molteni, A. L. (1985). Brief psychodynamic psychotherapy: An integrated approach. In S. J. Lynn & J. P. Garske (Eds.), *Contemporary psychotherapies: Models and methods* (pp. 69–115). Columbus, OH: Merrill.

Gazda, G. M., Childers, W. C. & Brooks, D. K., Jr. (1987). *Foundations of counseling and human services.* New York: McGraw-Hill.

Goldstein, A. P., Sprafkin, R. P., & Gershaw, N. J. (1976). *Skill training for community living: Applying structural learning therapy.* New York: Pergamon.

Gordon, D. (1978). *Therapeutic metaphors.* Cupertino, CA: Meta Publications.

Gottman, J., Notarius, C., Gonso, J., & Markman, H. (1976). *A couple's guide to communication.* Champaign, IL: Research Press.

Grinder, R., & Bandler, J. (1976). *The structure of magic II.* Palo Alto, CA: Science and Behavior Books.

Guerney, B. G., Jr. (1977). *Relationship enhancement.* San Francisco, CA: Jossey-Bass.

Guerney, B. G., Brock, G, & Coufal, J. (1986). Integrating marital therapy and enrichment: The relationship enhancement approach. In N. S. Jacobson & A. S. Gurman (Eds.), *Clinical handbook of marital therapy* (pp. 151–172). New York: Guilford Press.

Guerney, B. G., Jr., Stollack, G., & Guerney, L. (1970). A format for a new mode of psychological practice: Or how to escape a zombie. *The Counseling Psychologist, 2,* 97–104.

Guerney, B. G., Jr., Stollack, G., & Guerney, L. (1971). Practicing psychologist as educator: An alternative to the medical practitioner model. *Professional Psychology, 2,* 276–282.

Hammond, D. C., Hepworth, D. H., & Smith, V. G. (1977). *Improving therapeutic communication.* San Francisco, CA: Jossey-Bass.

Hayes, R., & Aubrey, R. (1988). *New Directions for counseling and human development.* Denver, CO: Love Publishing Company.

Ivey, A. E., & Simek-Downing, L. (1980). *Counseling and psychotherapy: Skills, theories and practice.* Englewood Cliffs, NJ: Prentice-Hall.

Lazarus, A. A. (1976). *Multimodal behavior therapy.* New York: Springer.

Lazarus, A. A. (1982). Counseling the native American child: Acquisition of values. *Elementary School Guidance and Counseling, 17,* 83–88.

Lederer, W., & Jackson, D. (1968). *Mirages of marriage.* New York: W. W. Norton.

Levy, T. M. (1987). Brief family therapy: Clinical assumptions and techniques. In P. A. Keller & S. R. Heyman (Eds.), *Innovations in clinical practice: A source book* (pp. 63–77). Sarasota, FL: Professional Resource Exchange.

Martin, J., & Stelmaczonek, K. (1988). Participants' identification and recall of important events in counseling. *Journal of Counseling Psychology, 35,* 385–390.

McKay, M., Davis, M., & Fanning, P. (1981). *Thoughts and feelings: The art of cognitive stress intervention.* Richmond, CA: New Harbinger.

McMullin, R. (1986). *Handbook of cognitive therapy techniques.* New York: W. W. Norton.

Meichenbaum, D. (1977). *Cognitive behavior modification.* New York: Plenum.

Meichenbaum, D. H., & Cameron, R. (1974). The clinical potential of modifying what clients say to themselves. *Psychotherapy: Theory, Research and Practice, 11,* 103–117.

Milan, M. (1985). Symbolic modeling. In M. Hersen & A. S. Bellack (Eds.), *Dictionary of behavior therapy techniques* (pp. 212–215). New York: Pergamon.

Mitchell, Z. P., & Milan, M. (1983). Imitation of high-interest comic strip models' appropriate classroom behavior: Acquisition and generalization. *Child and Family Behavior Therapy, 5,* 25–30.

Mosak, H. H. (1987). *Ha ha and aha.* Muncie, IN: Accelerated Development.

Pande, S. K. & Gart, J. J. (1968). A method to quantify reciprocal influence between therapist and patient in psychotherapy. In J. Shlien, H. F. Hunt, J. D. Matarazzo, & C. Savage (Eds.), *Research in psychotherapy.* Washington, DC: American Psychological Association.

Parloff, M. B., Goldstein, N., & Iflund, B. (1960). Communication of values and therapeutic change. *Archives of General Psychiatry, 2,* 300–304.

Paul, I. H. (1978). *The form and technique of psychotherapy.* Chicago, IL: University of Chicago Press.

Prochaska, J. O. (1984). *Systems of psychotherapy: A transtheoretical approach.* Chicago, IL: Dorsey Press.

Rappaport, A. F. (1976). Conjugal relationship enhancement program. In D. H. L. Olson (Ed.), *Treating relationships* (pp. 19–43). New York: Graphic.

Sherman, R. & Fredman, N. (1986). *Handbook of structured techniques in marriage and family therapy.* New York: Brunner/Mazel.

Taylor, P. (1990). Confrontation: A psychotherapeutic technique. Unpublished manuscript.

Tracey, T. J., Hays, K. A., Malone, J. & Herman, B. (1988). Changes in counselor response as a function of experience. *Journal of Counseling Psychology, 35,* 119–126.

Tubesing, D. (1979). *Kicking your stress habits.* Duluth, MN: Whole Person Press.

Watzlawick, P., Weakland, J., & Fisch, R. (1974). *Change: Principles of problem formation and problem resolution.* New York: W. W. Norton.

Wood, M. M. (1975). *Developmental therapy.* Baltimore, MD: University Park Press.

Worthington, E. L., Buston, B. G., & Hammonds, T. M. (1989). A component analysis of marriage enrichment: Information and treatment modality. *Journal of Counseling and Development, 67,* 555–560.

Yalom, I. R. (1975). *Theory and practice of group psychotherapy.* New York: Basic Books.

Young, M. E. (1990, March). New Visions: Changing client perceptions of the world. Address delivered at the American Association of Counseling and Development, Cincinnati, OH.

Young, M. E., & Witmer, J. M. (1985). Values through inculcation, identification and awareness. In J. M. Witmer, *Pathways to personal growth* (pp. 291–318). Muncie, IN: Accelerated Development.

CHAPTER ELEVEN

Documenting Progress and Termination

KEY CONCEPTS

▼ *Progress notes document progress and remind the counselor to focus on agreed-upon goals. The REPLAN system advocates reevaluating the treatment plan on a regular basis, and progress notes provide data to determine whether goals are still viable.*

▼ *Termination of counseling, according to the REPLAN system, is appropriate when mutually agreed-upon goals are met. New goals may be negotiated, if, in the counselor's estimation, they are genuine concerns rather than simply an attempt to maintain the relationship.*

▼ *Termination by the client after only a few sessions may be the result of client goals having been achieved. On the other hand, the client may be dissatisfied with some aspect of counseling that could be resolved by discussion, negotiation, or referral. Follow-up can help identify these problems.*

▼ *Therapists should prepare clients for termination by discussing the prospect of ending the relationship well in advance of actual termination and by reviewing the therapeutic gains. Feelings of loss can be lessened by preparation, spacing appointments, and reframing the termination.*

INTRODUCTION

Earlier we discussed a five-part model that described the progression of counseling from its initial *relationship-building* issues through *assessment, treatment planning, implementing counseling methods,* and finally concluding with *evaluation* (see Figure 11.1). Evaluation is the process of reviewing and replanning counseling goals. Termination may soon follow the evaluation stage, as a result of therapeutic gains, or a client may indicate that new issues have arisen. If new issues arise at the evaluation stage, they are addressed by following the diagram clockwise from evaluation to assessment. As the cycle begins again, these new areas of therapeutic interest must be looked at closely during the assessment process.

In this final chapter, we will examine two issues related to the evaluation phase. First, we will take a look at client progress notes, which are an integral part of helping clients achieve treatment goals. Second, we will examine termination from a practical point of view. In this discussion, methods for avoiding early

FIGURE 11.1
Stages of the counseling relationship.

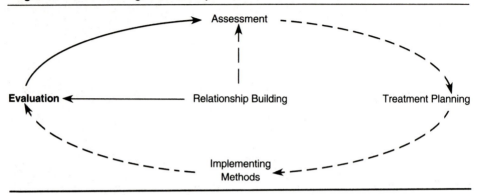

termination by the client are suggested along with recommendations about how to handle termination when goals have been reached or if they have not been achieved.

DOCUMENTING PROGRESS

Documenting progress via case notes or progress notes is an activity almost universally hated by clinicians. Still, most recognize it as an important legal necessity and as a useful record of the client's progress over time (Piazza & Baruth, 1990; Snider, 1987). Beyond this, it is possible that case notes can keep the counselor on track from session to session. Without some kind of guide, client progress can easily be sidetracked by incidental problems. A second and real temptation for some therapists is to spend time socially with the client, reviewing the mundane happenings since the last session. Keeping therapy on track by repeatedly referring to goals is another reminder to the client that therapy's major objective is the attainment of therapeutic objectives and is not to be wasted on less important issues.

A common problem with progress notes is that the clinician begins note taking on a blank sheet of paper. The sheet may contain only a place for a name and a date. There are several reasons for being a little more detailed with respect to progress notes. In many states, counselors and psychotherapists are required to keep records of client contacts. Out of loyalty to clients or because of outright laziness, many therapists simply note the date of the contact and little else. At a recent professional meeting, about half of the 30 private practitioners attending admitted that they keep no progress notes and only supply them from memory when legally required to do so.

Although there are legal and ethical reasons to keep records of client progress, there is also value in providing supervisors and other professionals with information about progress. Records are needed at the time of referral and during supervision of the therapist. An open-ended report does not allow the reader an easy way of telling what the goals and outcomes of therapy have been. Such reports also tend to be aimless and are sometimes filled with speculation about underlying problems and pathology. In most cases, progress notes will be much more useful to fellow professionals if they itemize what has been tried and what has worked.

Types of Progress Notes

The Problem-Oriented Record (POR)

In response to the considerations above, many clinicians have adopted a method known as the *problem-oriented record (POR)* (Weed, 1971). The POR system has four major parts: the data base, the problem list, plans, and follow-up. The *data base* contains information collected during the assessment process and generally follows a medical model, identifying the chief complaint and documenting a psychosocial history, mental status exam, and other test data.

The *problem list* numbers each of the problems *identified by the clinician.* For example, imagine that the following problems have been identified: (1) major depression (2) unemployment and (3) refusal of medications. Later in the record and in the progress notes, the same numbers are used to indicate what plans and follow-up strategies are to be used for each problem.

Plans are the strategies and techniques outlined for overcoming each of the client problems. The POR system advocates the use of behavioral objectives for every goal. These goals must be measurable. The method has the advantage of setting clear expectations of success for client and counselor. The case notes indicate changes and results of plans.

Finally, *follow-up* includes those activities the clinician feels should be monitored throughout treatment to gauge responsiveness to treatment. This might include making observations at each session, discussing client symptoms, or keeping other data, such as summaries of medication use. The POR system has been criticized for not taking into account the client's subjective notions about the problem (Sturm, 1987) and for focusing on the medical or pathological point of view, not incorporating developmental or learning viewpoints (Sundberg, Taplin & Tyler, 1983).

The SOAP System

Another system of recording comes from the medical community and is known as the *SOAP system.* In this system, the physician records subjective (S) reports of the client (symptoms) and then includes objective data or observations by the physician (O). Next, a diagnosis or assessment is made (A), and finally a plan (P) is developed based on the diagnosis. The POR system is often used for treatment planning, and the SOAP system is the method utilized to record client progress in the case notes.

After each session, the counselor records data from all four SOAP areas. This allows for the integration of new information into the diagnosis and treatment plan, as they are noticed by the client or by the counselor. New and continuing symptoms are recorded at each session along with new observations by the clinician. These are continually reviewed to determine if the assessment is accurate. If new information changes the assessment, a new treatment plan is formulated.

The REPLAN System

The REPLAN system includes elements of both the POR and the SOAP systems. It can be implemented using the treatment planning process, identifying the curative factor and selecting treatment strategies as described in chapter 4. It is also possible to use the eclectic REPLAN system for compiling case notes while using a more diagnostically oriented treatment planning method. The REPLAN system is considered easy to use because, rather than being confronted with a blank space, the therapist is asked to answer specific questions about the treatment goals:

1. What progress was made since the last session as a result of client homework or independent practice?
2. What important crises changes have occurred in the client's life or mental status since the last session?
3. What progress was made toward each client goal in today's session?
4. What plans, homework, or referrals were made today?
5. When should the client's goals be reviewed?

The REPLAN record (Table 11.1) begins by listing previously agreed-upon client goals. The notes do not allow for more than three goals to be considered at any one time. This may not be appropriate for every client, but it has been observed that working on a few major goals at a time is better than attempting to work on a wider range.

The first step for the clinician is to briefly note any changes or progress on goals reported by the client since the last session. This reminds the counselor to check on homework assignments and to gauge the current severity of the symptoms. Second, the counselor records any new information—a job change, a change in relationships, changes in other psychosocial stressors, or changes in client's mental status, for example, an increase in suicidal risk—or events of major importance. Third, the therapist documents the strategies employed to achieve counseling goals during this session. Fourth, the therapist indicates what plans were agreed upon for homework, practice, and outside referrals.

Notice that the therapist is not asked to plan for the next session at the end of the notes as is the case in some formats. The reason for this is that the treatment plan has already been arranged, and the plans are to continue to work on the treatment goals unless they are changed in some way.

The REPLAN system allows new goals to be be added or removed from consideration at each session, or a replanning session may be held every five or six sessions to evaluate the course of therapy. As a reminder, a date for this evaluation, or replanning session, can be scheduled and noted at the bottom of the record next to the therapist's signature. A follow-up card is a useful reminder. It is filed and pulled when the follow-up date arrives.

TABLE 11.1
REPLAN counseling record and case notes.

Client Name _____   Session No. ___   Date ____/____/____

Client/Counselor Negotiated Goal Statements

1.

2.

3.

Any Progress in Goals Since Last Session

1.

2.

3.

New Information (Changes in Client's Situation or Mental Status)

Counseling Activity During This Session

Goal 1.

Goal 2.

Goal 3.

Homework Assignments, Referrals, and Plans

Goal   Plan

1.

2.

3.

Counselor Signature _____   REPLAN date ____/____/____

The numbering system in the progress notes always refers to the same goal from the client/counselor negotiated goals at the top of the form. Consequently, there is no need to rewrite the description of the goal in later portions of the notes.

Table 11.1 shows a blank record form. Table 11.2 is identical to Table 11.1 but the record is shown horizontally. Some counselors like moving across the page as they record activity on each goal. Table 11.3 shows a completed record as it might appear in the client's file. Again, the form can be adapted for almost any theoretical orientation, assuming that achievement of goals is compatible with the model. The REPLAN system of case notes has been tested in a variety of settings, including a college counseling center, a mental health clinic, an inpatient alcohol treatment center, and an elementary school counseling program. Counselors have found it to be thorough, yet case notes can be completed in five minutes or less.

TABLE 11.2
REPLAN counseling record and case notes (horizontal form).

Client Name _____   Session No. ___   Date ____/____/____

Goal No.	Client/Counselor Negotiated Goals	Any Progress/Changes in Mental Status	Activity Directed Toward Goals During Session	Homework Assignments/Referrals/Plans
1				
2				
3				

Counselor Signature _____   REPLAN Date ____/____/____

TERMINATION

Table 11.4 shows the stages of a counseling relationship as described in this book. The final phase, according to this description, involves saying goodbye, resolving unfinished business, and follow-up contacts. The process of saying goodbye is crucial since it conveys a sense of confidence in the client's ability to solve problems independently (Ward, 1984). Some therapists see the counselor's role as that of a family physician whom one consults throughout life; however, this model goes against the notion that the counselor's job is mainly to help the client overcome demoralization and to fight it in the future. In the latter view, the counselor promotes independence and encourages the client to move on even when the client may not feel entirely ready to do so.

The notion of unfinished business is highlighted in Gestalt therapy and psychodrama where practitioners have found clients struggling with problems because closure on important issues was never reached. Sons and daughters who never thanked their parents or asserted themselves may end up dealing with unresolved feelings in therapy. Similarly, as therapy ends, the client and counselor should take some time to be certain that important issues have attained closure.

Finally, the counselor renews support for the client by making contacts that encourage the client's progress toward goals. These contacts may be made after three months, six months, or a year. Follow-up contacts provide openings for

TABLE 11.3
Sample REPLAN record and case notes.

Client Name *John Doe*   Session No. <u>3</u>   Date <u>4</u> / <u>18</u> / <u>94</u>

Client/Counselor Negotiated Goal Statements

1. Decrease depression and suicidal thoughts.

2. Resolve family problems. Increase brief contacts.

3.

Any Progress in Goals Since Last Session

1. Client indicates that depression decreased significantly but still having suicidal thoughts 1 time per day.

2. No effort or progress toward this goal.

3.

New Information (Changes in Client's Situation or Mental Status)

Denied that suicidal thoughts were intense or increasing.
Denied any planned method or available suicide means.

Counseling Activity During This Session

Goal 1. During session, client was confronted on self-downing and was taught to challenge negative self-statements.

Goal 2. We did not address this goal except for client to indicate that he is not quite ready to work on this issue. I suggested he consider attending Adult Children of Alcoholics as a preliminary step. He agreed.

Goal 3.

Homework Assignments, Referrals, and Plans

Goal	Plan
1.	Client to challenge negative self-statements as homework and call if suicidal thoughts increase.
2.	Will call friend to accompany him to first ACOA meeting.
3.	

Counselor Signature *B. B. Jones*   REPLAN date <u>6</u> / <u>9</u> / <u>94</u>

clients to return to therapy without feeling that they have failed. Frequent and repeated contacts by the therapist might convey a lack of confidence, but appropriately spaced communications can serve as a reminder of therapy goals.

An Overview of Termination

It must be recognized that up to this point in the history of psychotherapy, termination has referred to longer term, more intense, therapeutic relationships. Many earlier writers (cf., Wolberg, 1954) emphasized the sense of loss and disori-

TABLE 11.4
Phases of the counseling relationship.

Phase	Relationship (Description)	Therapeutic Goals
Phase I Initial contact	- Acquaintances - Testing	1. Saying hello 2. Encouraging self-disclosure 3. Initial transference and resistance issues
Phase II Commitment	- Teacher/student - Negotiating	1. Assessment 2. Treatment planning
Phase III Intimacy	- Conspirators	1. Identification of continuing transference issues 2. Therapist self-disclosure
Phase IV Untying	- Coworkers - Confronting	1. Encouraging client independence 2. Relating "here and now" relationship to treatment goals 3. Resolution of transference
Phase V Termination		1. Saying goodbye 2. Resolving unfinished business

entation that clients feel over ending relationships. Even more recent writers (Ward, 1984) have compared termination to death. Therapeutic relationships today are shorter, more goal focused, and less likely to require periods of weaning. Writers of the future will undoubtedly place more emphasis on paving the way for return to therapy, reinforcing the need for follow-up contacts and maintaining therapeutic gains.

In the beginning of this book, we identified a distinguishing feature of eclectic therapists—their practical inclination. In considering how to deal with the topic of termination, it seems best to consider the subject from a pragmatic point of view, that is, as a set of skills. These are competencies that most of us do not gain in the course of counseling training (Gladding, 1988). To help conceptualize termination in terms of skills, each section of this discussion begins with how to and is followed with a phrase describing a common problem connected with termination.

How to Prevent the Client from Terminating Early in Therapy

It is discouraging to a therapist when a promising client does not return after the first or second session. There is evidence, though, that even one-session counseling is viewed as helpful by many clients. In general, clients expect a shorter duration in therapy than the counselor (June & Smith, 1983). Yalom (1975) has suggested that early termination by the client may be a good thing since it acts as a safety valve when the client/counselor match is not correct (see also Epperson, 1983).

Still, an argument can be made that it is preferable to complete therapy with a bang not a whimper—to come to a formal ending or to refer the client after a few sessions rather than letting the relationship wind down. A positive ending may pave the way for the client to return to therapy (Kramer, 1986, 1990). A petering out may cast the therapist as ineffective or the client as a failure.

The suggestions listed here are a combination of observations and recommendations from the literature concerning ways of preventing clients from leaving therapy for reasons other than that therapy has been ineffective (Mennicke, Lent & Burgoyne, 1988; Pekarik, 1985):

1. Avoid delays in seeing clients. Although some clients seem to come only during emergencies and fail to follow through, clients who must wait two or three weeks for an appointment may not arrive at all or may be hostile and less motivated.
2. In cases and settings where clients might be expected to drop out early, make contracts with clients for completing a small goal or a small number of sessions (6–10).
3. Do not process clients through several channels. Clients who are interviewed by an intake counselor or secretary for screening and then referred to the real therapist may be lost because they have been treated impersonally. It is difficult enough for many people to reveal their need for therapy by making the phone call for an appointment. Asking them to reveal their problems to several people may be asking too much.
4. Provide orientation to clients about therapy and offer information about the qualifications of the therapist. Some counselors use a written handout that describes the therapy and the therapist. The client is either sent this material ahead of time or is asked to read it in the waiting room. Such a process can develop positive and realistic expectations and diminish client fears. Fees, billing procedures, expectations of client behavior, confidentiality, and other issues can be dealt with in this manner. Otherwise, it is a good idea to address these issues immediately in the first session.
5. Use reminders to motivate client attendance. Obtain the client's permission to call or to write a brief reminder just before the next session.
6. When a client terminates early, find out why. There may be several unexpected reasons for the client's termination other than a feeling that the therapy is unproductive. These reasons range from having seen an acquaintance in the waiting room or rudeness from support personnel.
7. In cases where the client decides to terminate before goal completion seems likely, the therapist should try to go the extra mile (Kaplan & Sadock, 1987) by making it easy for the client to return. This may mean agreeing with the client's idea to interrupt therapy and directly inviting the client to return later by setting a follow-up date.

How to Negotiate New Goals

The REPLAN system recommends renegotiating client goals when there is agreement that the original problems have been solved to mutual satisfaction. The therapist must carefully consider whether these new goals are really important or simply a way for the client to retain the therapeutic relationship. Claude Steiner (1976) recommended quizzing the client carefully to determine if the goal is a vital one by asking questions such as, "How does this hurt you?" The therapist's job then becomes determining which would be most productive, accepting a new goal or allowing the client to develop confidence in his or her own abilities to cope independently. If the therapist determines that the reasons for staying in therapy are not convincing, termination should be recommended.

How to Tell If Termination Is Needed

Most professional organizations, including the American Association for Counseling and Development (1989), the American Psychological Association (1981), and the American Association for Marriage and Family Therapy (1985), agree that a client should be terminated immediately if it appears that the client is not making progress. They also agree that referral to another source of help is a duty of the therapist. The decision about whether a client is making progress is not a cut and dried issue, though. It may take some time, discussion, and preparation to make this decision.

Besides the fact that the client is not benefiting from therapy, other signs that have traditionally been recognized as suggesting that the client is ready for termination include missing sessions, coming late for sessions, failing to do homework, and showing discouragement. These are all considered signals of resistance or problems of motivation as well. They should be explored with the client, and alternative treatment strategies or referral should be considered when they are identified.

Wolberg's (1954) discussion of termination gets at a fundamental idea concerning termination. How do we know when the therapy has been successful? Should we consider success from the standpoint of the client or from the standpoint of the therapist? Should we define success in terms of societal standards (dangerousness, employment) or from some ideal of mental health advanced by other theorists? Mathews (1989) suggests reviewing one's caseload and asking oneself, "If I had a waiting list right now, would I be seeing this client?" (p. 37). Based on Maholich and Turner (1979), Sciscoe (1990) identified five questions the therapist might ask himself or herself to assess the client's readiness for termination:

1. Is the presenting problem under control?
2. Has the client reduced the level of stress by developing better coping skills?
3. Has client achieved greater self-awareness and better relationships?
4. Is life and work more enjoyable for the client?
5. Does the client now feel capable of living without therapy?

The first four questions get at improvements in functioning that have occurred and the achievement of therapy goals. The last question is especially important since it asks the therapist whether or not the client is able to maintain the gains of therapy on an independent basis. The answers to these questions might help the therapist work through a knotty problem about which it is hard to be objective. Still, the client's viewpoint must also be taken into account. In this book, I have suggested that success in psychotherapy and termination should be determined as that point in time when therapist and client agree that mutually designated therapy goals have been reached. It has been argued here that such a viewpoint blends the professional expertise of the therapist and the personal experience of the consumer of therapeutic services.

How to Use Goal Attainment Scaling

One graphic method for evaluating progress is *goal attainment scaling* (Kiresuk & Sherman, 1968). Goal attainment scaling has been advocated for demonstrating accountability, but its best use may be that it can provide a useful way of providing information to the client and counselor about progress (see Table 11.5).

The goal attainment guide in Table 11.5 is used in the following way:

1. Each goal is briefly described in the goal statement section.
2. Specific indications of success are noted in the sections just beneath the goal statement. A simple example of a goal is to "maintain social support for sobriety." The specific success indicators might be "regular attendance at support meetings."
3. The least and best outcomes for each goal are then described on the goal attainment guide. These descriptions should be as specific as possible since they will be used as a means for judging client progress. In this case, the best outcome might be "three meetings per week"; and the least, "one meeting per month."
4. The client's current functioning is recorded on each on the goal attainment scales at the bottom of the guide. First, the client's initial or baseline functioning should be arrived at by the therapist and client. Let us say that the therapist and client agree that the client, at intake, is functioning at less-than-expected outcome concerning attendance at support groups. Using the letter *B* for beginning or *S* for start, the therapist records this information on the goal attainment scale on the goal no. 1 line at the *2* position.
5. At various points in therapy, additional notations can be made on the scale showing progress or relapse.
6. Besides the ability to monitor progress, the goal attainment guide provides a tool for review of therapy during the termination process. At times, the client may be discouraged because one of the goals was not achieved. The guide may be able to show that even if the best outcome was not achieved, progress was made. (Blocher, 1987). Once again the therapist should consider this scaling method as a tool for exploring goals and the issue of termination rather than an objective method for determining the need for ending the counseling relationship.

TABLE 11.5
Goal attainment guide.

Case of _____

	Goal Statement No. 1	Goal Statement No. 2	Goal Statement No. 3
	_____	_____	_____
	_____	_____	_____
	Specific success indicators	Specific success indicators	Specific success indicators
	_____	_____	_____
	_____	_____	_____
	_____	_____	_____
	Outcome Description	**Outcome Description**	**Outcome Description**
Least favorable likely outcome			
Less than expected level of attainment			
Expected goal attainment			
Better than expected outcome			
Best outcome			

Goal Attainment Scale

1	2	3	4	5
Least Favorable Outcome	**Less Than Expected Outcome**	**About Expected Outcome**	**Better Than Expected Outcome**	**Best Probable Outcome**

Goal scale _____
Goal no. 1 _____
Goal no. 2 _____
Goal no. 3 _____
Average goal attainment with this case _____

Source: Reprinted by permission of Macmillan Publishing Co. from *The Professional Counselor* by Donald A. Blocher. Copyright © 1987 by Macmillan Publishing Co.

How to Prepare the Client for Termination

In general, most writers agree that sudden termination is not advisable (Brammer, Shostrom & Abrego, 1989). Guidelines for preparing the client to terminate vary. Dixon and Glover (1984) recommend that at least three sessions in advance of termination be devoted to issues of termination; Lamb (1985) recommends at least seven sessions. As much time as was spent in relationship building in the beginning of the therapy should be devoted to termination, according to Cormier and Cormier (1985); and one-sixth of the time spent in therapy should be devoted to termination, according to Shulman (1979). In other words, there should be a period of preparation. How long this should take is a matter of judgement and should be determined by the length and quality of the counseling relationship.

The second step in preparing the client for termination is to review the counseling process and progress made. In general, it is important to emphasize the client's strengths and end on a positive note; however, areas left untreated or unresolved must also be discussed (Anderson & Stewart, 1983). One way to review is to use the goal attainment scaling method described in this chapter. Another is to simply compare before and after client functioning from both the therapist's and the client's viewpoint. Other suggestions include reviewing an early session in counseling, using case notes to show progress. Finally, any unfinished business between client and therapist should be addressed. The client should be encouraged to project how he or she will look at the counseling experience in the future.

How to Make a Referral

Referral is called for if the client presents a problem that is beyond the therapist's competency, if there are personality differences too fundamental to explore, if the client is a friend or relative of the counselor, and if the client is unable to discuss the problem with the therapist, despite repeated invitations (George & Cristiani, 1981).

Follow up is a crucial aspect of any referral. Contact should be made by phone or letter to insure that the referral succeeded. It is said that up to 70% of all referrals do not make it to the appointed destination. This is partially due to the fact that the client's needs were not taken into account including proximity to the client's home, cost, and the meaning attached to receiving the help. In addition, referral can be taken as either rejection or the client sees the referral as more evidence that he or she is a hopeless case. These attributions about the referral and the reasons for changing therapists should be examined and positively reframed.

Some other suggestions are to refer the client to a specific contact person in an agency or service rather than simply supplying the name of the service. Also have names and resources easily available and give accurate information. To expedite matters, obtain the client's written permission in advance to send a summary of the client's records (George & Cristiani, 1981).

How to Explore and Ease Feelings of Loss

Gladding (1992) points out that loss is a two-way street. Counselors sometimes hesitate to terminate clients because of their own attachments and feelings of sadness. Goodyear (1981, p. 348) lists several reasons why counselors may have this kind of reaction: the relationship is quite significant to the counselor; the counselor is uncertain that the client will be able to function independently; the counselor feels that he or she was not effective; the therapist feels that his or her professional identity is challenged by the client's premature termination; the termination represents a loss of continued learning for the therapist who was looking forward to gaining experience from the client's peculiar problem; the counselor misses the vicarious excitement of the client's exploits; the termination uncovers historical events associated with loss in the counselor's life.

To this list I would add that therapist feelings of loss may be due to a reliance on therapy relationships to meet needs for intimacy (friendship) as well as a conscious or unconscious sexual attraction. Kanfer and Schefft (1988) suggest that the counselor needs to learn to accept the fact that termination inevitably occurs at a point far short of perfection. The effect of these counselor reactions to loss is generally an extended period of therapy in which areas relating to the therapist's interests rather than those of the client are discussed. Krantz and Lund (1979) feel that counselor trainees may have special difficulty with termination. Trainees may keep clients in therapy beyond the need because of positive feelings or because of a hope that the client will accomplish even greater goals. They may also be unprepared for their own feelings or for the powerful loss experienced by the client, no matter how much they are intellectually informed. A supportive supervisory relationship (Sciscoe, 1990) can help trainees through difficult terminations.

The issues just discussed suggest that the therapist has become engaged in therapy, intentionally or unintentionally, to satisfy personal needs. Counselors may even feel guilty and embarrassed by the importance they place on the relationship (Mathews, 1989). Preventing these reactions may not always be possible, but supervision by another therapist is the most effective antidote for and means of becoming aware of these attachments (Beier, 1966).

Turning next to the viewpoint of the client, Ward (1984) suggests that clients may be upset by termination because the ending of therapy is associated with other historical losses. The general strategy for the counselor is to directly explore client feelings of loss associated with the ending of the relationship. Some suggestions to help prevent, explore, and resolve these feelings and to move the termination forward include the following (Cavanagh, 1982; Dixon & Glover, 1984; Hackney & Cormier, 1979; Munro & Bach, 1975):

1. Bring termination up early.
2. Reframe termination as an opportunity for the client to put new learning into practice.
3. Limit the number of counseling sessions in the beginning of therapy.
4. Use a fading procedure: spacing appointments over increasing lengths of time.

5. Avoid making the relationship the central feature of therapy. Although relationship building is crucial, it may be unwise to employ only this curative factor.
6. Play down the importance of termination; play up the sense of accomplishment and the value of independence.
7. Use reflective listening to allow the client to express feelings of loss.

Ernst Beier (1966) has made some valuable comments about the causes of client dependency that produce a sense of loss at termination. In general, he lays the blame at the therapist's door for creating a social (rather than an asocial) relationship. The antidote for dependency (or habituation to therapy) is, Beier believes, inherent to the relationship itself (p. 129):

> The resolution to the habituation problem lies in the pseudoreality of the hour. The patient may love or hate the therapist. He may emote or test various ways of involving the therapist, but he knows that these feelings are not really reciprocated. Both the setting of the therapeutic hour and the therapist's communications give the patient the information that the therapist is concerned: he wants to help him, he wants him to be free to explore new choices and he may even want him to experience life with greater pleasure. But through thousands of asocial responses the therapist also informs the patient that he is not really the person the patient wants him to be; he is not really a friend or a lover and he does not really want to spend his time outside the hour with him. In other words, while the patient experiences a sense of bondage to the therapist and an experience of being better understood and more readily accepted than in the outside world he also has the experience that this sanctuary is sterile. He begins to realize that there are no true reciprocated feelings of friendship and love (or at least not with their customary consequences) and there is no future. . . . It is this experience which works against dependency and habituation and encourages the patient to direct his newly found courage toward new objects and toward people with whom he can have a real relationship and a future.

How to Maintain Therapeutic Gains Following Termination

The term follow-up is sometimes used to identify therapist activities that are aimed at making a brief contact to determine how the client is progressing and to remind the client that the door is open if counseling is needed in the future (Wolberg, 1954). On the other hand, there are a number of activities that therapists employ that go beyond a brief reminder. They are designed to help maintain therapeutic gains and are actually means for extending therapy following termination. Here are some suggestions to that effect (Cavanagh, 1982; Perry & Paquin, 1987):

Fading

Use fading or follow-up sessions spaced over a one-year period. For example, a six-week, six-month, and one-year follow-up can be negotiated at termination. In direct instruction of skills, such as assertiveness training, stress management, and communication, these follow-ups can be called *booster sessions* or *refreshers* with the stated aim of reviewing learning. One benefit of planning for follow-up at termination is that the client need not later feel a sense of failure if a return to counseling is needed. If the client decides to cancel the later visits, this can be framed as a sign of success.

Home Visits or Observation

A possible follow-up to marriage or family counseling is to review therapy progress later with the family at home. Observing the family in this setting can convey a great deal about progress. The same can also be said for naturalistic observation of individuals. I recall the shy client of a colleague whose follow-up plan included hosting a party and inviting the therapist.

Contacts with Paraprofessionals

Many agencies provide follow-up services for clients on a free or inexpensive basis. Many mental health clinics, for example, provide home visiting to monitor and maintain progress of clients suffering from severe mental disorders.

Self-Help Groups

Self-help groups, if improperly conducted, can be a case of the blind leading the blind. The quality of such groups is quite variable, and so the therapist must be familiar with groups in the client's vicinity before making a recommendation. As an adjunct to individual, group, and family therapy, they can provide an important means of maintaining gains made in counseling by providing regular peer support and education.

Self-Monitoring Activities

Clients who are asked to return for a follow-up session can also be encouraged to engage in continued self-monitoring or practice of desired behaviors. A less formal assignment is teaching the client to use a personal journal to explore thoughts and feelings (Kalven, Rosen & Taylor, 1981).

Self-Management Skills

Clients can learn to use behavioral principles to reward positive behaviors and to punish negative ones (Kanfer, 1975; Kazdin, 1980; Rudestam, 1980). For example, students can learn to make watching a one-hour television show contingent on completing several hours of study.

Audio-Visual Material

Both printed and magnetically recorded materials can be sent by clients back to the therapist as evidence of practice on therapy goals following termination. Clients can send in monthly self-monitoring forms or tapes of communication practice. Likewise, therapists can send clients reminders of their goal statements. Young & Rosen (1985) describe a group activity in which clients write a letter to themselves during the last session before termination. The letter reminds the client of the therapy goals. It also contains a list that the client drafts that predicts some of the excuses the client may use to try to avoid achieving the goals. The therapist mails the letters to clients about a month after the completion of group therapy.

CHAPTER SUMMARY AND CONCLUSIONS

In this chapter, two issues have been examined: how to monitor client progress toward goals, and, second, how to end counseling once goals have been reached. The general criticism has been made that often counseling records simply take up space in a file. Greater effort should be made to keep progress notes goal oriented and, therefore, more useful in keeping the therapist on track. Such an approach avoids the trap of mulling over the client's personality failings and provides much more useful information to therapists and supervisors who later read the record.

Just as progress notes are based on goals, it is also recommended that termination be based on the achievement of therapeutic aims. The therapist should discuss termination with the client, reviewing changes and successes and building in plans for maintaining the gains of therapy. In lieu of success, the therapist should refer the client to another helping professional or close therapy in a way that minimizes the client's sense of failure and paves the way for the client to return to therapy at some later date.

FURTHER READINGS

Kramer, S. A. (1990). *Positive endings in psychotherapy: Bringing meaningful closure to therapeutic relationships*. San Francisco, CA: Jossey-Bass. Kramer identifies the steps for therapy termination when no time limit has been set. The book addresses both client and counselor concerns and recommends addressing termination at all stages of therapy.

Woody, R. H. (1991). *Quality mental health care*. San Francisco, CA: Jossey-Bass. This is primarily a legal and ethical guide to quality practice of psychotherapy; however, Woody identifies crucial issues related to systematic record keeping. The book contains sample forms and guidelines for record keeping.

REFERENCES

American Association for Counseling and Development (1989). *Ethical standards of the American Association for Counseling and Development* (rev. ed.). Alexandria, VA: AACD Press.

American Association for Marriage and Family Therapy (1985). *AAMFT code of principles for marriage and family therapists*. Washington, DC: Author.

American Psychological Association. (1981). *Ethical principles of psychologists* (rev. ed). Washington, DC: Author.

Anderson, C. M., & Stewart, S. (1983). *Mastering resistance: A practical guide to family therapy*. New York: Guilford.

Beier, E. G. (1966). *The silent language of psychotherapy: Social reinforcement of unconscious processes*. Chicago, IL: Aldine.

Blocher, D. (1987). *The professional counselor.* New York: Macmillan.

Brammer, L. M., Shostrom, E. L. & Abrego, P. J. (1989). *Therapeutic psychology: Fundamentals of counseling and psychotherapy* (5th ed.). Englewood Cliffs, NJ: Prentice-Hall.

Cavanagh, M. E. (1982). *The counseling experience.* Monterey, CA: Brooks/Cole.

Cormier, W. H., & Cormier, S. L. (1985). *Interviewing strategies for helpers: Fundamental skills and cognitive behavioral interventions* (2nd ed.). Pacific Grove, CA: Brooks/Cole.

Dixon, D. N., & Glover, J. A. (1984). *Counseling: A problem-solving approach.* New York: Wiley.

Epperson, D. L. (1983). Client self terminations after one counseling session: Effects of problem recognition, counselor gender, and counselor experience. *Journal of Counseling Psychology, 30,* 307–315.

George, R. L., & Cristiani, T. S. (1981). *Theory, methods and processes of counseling and psychotherapy.* Englewood Cliffs, NJ: Prentice-Hall.

Gladding, S. T. (1992). *Counseling: A comprehensive profession* (2nd ed.). Columbus, OH: Merrill.

Goodyear, R. (1981). Termination as a loss experience for the counselor. *Personnel and Guidance Journal, 59,* 349–350.

Hackney, H., & Cormier, L. S. (1979). *Counseling strategies and objectives.* Englewood Cliffs, NJ: Prentice-Hall.

June, L., & Smith, E. (1983). A comparison of client and counselor expectancies regarding the duration of counseling. *Journal of Counseling Psychology, 30,* 596–599.

Kalven, J., Rosen, L., & Taylor, B. (1981). *Value development: A practical guide.* Ramsey, NJ: Paulist Press.

Kanfer, F. H. (1975). Self-management methods. In F. H. Kanfer & A. P. Goldstein (Eds.), *Helping people change* (pp. 309–355). New York: Pergamon.

Kanfer, F. H., & Schefft, B. K. (1988). *Guiding therapeutic change.* Champaign, IL: Research Press.

Kaplan, H. I., & Sadock, B. J. (1987). *Synopsis of psychiatry: Behavioral sciences, clinical psychiatry* (5th ed.). Baltimore, MD: Williams & Wilkins.

Kazdin, A. E. (1980). *Behavior modification in applied settings.* Homewood, IL: Dorsey Press.

Kiresuk, R. J., & Sherman, R. E. (1968). Goal attainment scaling: A general method for evaluating community mental health programs. *Community Mental Health Journal, 4,* 443–453.

Kramer, S. A. (1986). The termination process in open-ended psychotherapy: Guidelines for clinical practice. *Psychotherapy, 23,* 526–531

Kramer, S. A. (1990). *Positive endings in psychotherapy.* San Francisco, CA: Jossey-Bass.

Krantz, P. L., & Lund, N. L. (1979). A dilemma of play therapy: Termination anxiety in the therapist. *Teaching of Psychology, 6,* 108–110.

Lamb, D. H. (1985). A time frame model of termination in psychotherapy. *Psychotherapy, 22,* 604–609.

Maholich, L. T., & Turner, D. W. (1979). Termination: That difficult farewell. *American Journal of Psychotherapy, 33,* 583–591.

Mathews, B. (1989). Terminating therapy: Implications for the private practitioner. *Psychotherapy in Private Practice, 7,* 29–39.

Mennicke, S. A., Lent, R. W., & Burgoyne, K. L. (1988). Premature termination from university counseling centers: A review. *Journal of Counseling and Development, 66,* 458–465.

Munro, J. N., & Bach, T. R. (1975). Effect of time-limited counseling on client change. *Journal of Counseling Psychology, 22,* 395–398.

Pekarik, G. (1985). Coping with dropouts. *Professional Psychology: Research and Practice, 16,* 114–124.

Perry, G. P., & Paquin, J. J. (1987). Practical strategies for maintaining and generalizing improvements from psychotherapy. In P. A. Keller & S. R. Heyman (Eds.), *Innovations in clinical practice: A source book* (vol. 6, pp. 151–164). Sarasota, FL: Professional Resource Exchange.

Piazza, N. J., & Baruth, N. E. (1990). Client record guidelines. *Journal of Counseling and Development, 68,* 313–316.

Rudestam, K. E. (1980). *Methods of self-change: An ABC primer.* Monterey, CA: Brooks/Cole.

Shulman, L. (1979). *The skills of helping individuals and groups.* Itasca, IL: Peacock Press.

Sciscoe, M. (1990). The termination of therapy. Unpublished manuscript.

Snider, P. D. (1987). Client records: Inexpensive liability protection for mental health counselors. *Mental Health Counseling, 9,* 134–141.

Steiner, C. (1976, March). Transactional analysis. Paper delivered at the University of Dayton, Dayton, Ohio.

Sturm, I. E. (1987). The psychologist in the problem-oriented record (POR). *Professional Psychology: Research and Practice, 18,* 155–158.

Sundberg, N. D., Taplin, J. R., & Tyler, L. E. (1983). *Introduction to clinical psychology: Perspectives, issues and contributions to human service.* Englewood Cliffs, NJ: Prentice-Hall.

Ward, D. E. (1984). Termination of individual counseling: Concepts and strategies. *Journal of Counseling and Development, 63,* 21–25.

Weed, L. L. (1971). *Medical records, medical education and patient care: The problem-oriented record as a basic tool.* Chicago, IL: Year Book.

Wolberg, L. R. (1954). *The technique of psychotherapy.* New York: Grune & Stratton.

Yalom, I. D. (1975). *Theory and practice of group psychotherapy.* New York: Basic Books.

Young, M. E., & Rosen, L. S. (1985). The retreat: An educational growth group. *Journal for Specialists in Group Work, 21,* 157–171.

INDEX